Russian Cognitive Neuroscience

Homo Technologicus, Social and Ethical Futures

Editors

James Giordano, Niko Kohls, and John Shook

VOLUME 1

The titles published in this series are listed at *brill.com/htse*

Russian Cognitive Neuroscience

Historical and Cultural Context

By

Chris Forsythe

In collaboration with

Mikhail V. Zotov
Gabriel A. Radvansky
Larisa Tsvetkova

BRILL

LEIDEN | BOSTON

Cover illustration: Cover image courtesy of V. I. Nekorkin and V. B. Kazantsev.

The Library of Congress Cataloging-in-Publication Data is available online at https://catalog.loc.gov
LC record available at https://lccn.loc.gov/2021056103

Typeface for the Latin, Greek, and Cyrillic scripts: "Brill". See and download: brill.com/brill-typeface.

ISSN 2666-8769
ISBN 978-90-04-50564-3 (hardback)
ISBN 978-90-04-50566-7 (e-book)

Copyright 2022 by Koninklijke Brill NV, Leiden, The Netherlands.
Koninklijke Brill NV incorporates the imprints Brill, Brill Nijhoff, Brill Hotei, Brill Schöningh, Brill Fink, Brill mentis, Vandenhoeck & Ruprecht, Böhlau Verlag and V&R Unipress.
All rights reserved. No part of this publication may be reproduced, translated, stored in a retrieval system, or transmitted in any form or by any means, electronic, mechanical, photocopying, recording or otherwise, without prior written permission from the publisher. Requests for re-use and/or translations must be addressed to Koninklijke Brill NV via brill.com or copyright.com.

This book is printed on acid-free paper and produced in a sustainable manner.

Contents

Notes on Contributors   IX
Acknowledgements   XI

SECTION 1
History and Tradition of Russian Neuroscience

1 Origins of Russian Cognitive Psychophysiology   3
   L. V. Sokolova

2 The Beginnings of Russian Cognitive Psychophysiology   26
   V. I. Shostak

3 Systemic Psychophysiology   56
   Yuri I. Alexandrov

4 Cognitive Activity from the Perspective of Functional Systems Theory   87
   K. V. Sudakov

   Section 1 Commentary: The Genesis and Development of Russian Experimental Neuroscience   118
   Gabriel A. Radvansky and Chris Forsythe

SECTION 2
Russian Research in Perceptual and Cognitive Processes

5 The Regulatory Role of an Unconscious Cognitive Set in the Perception of the Facial Expression of Emotion   125
   Eduard Arutunovich Kostandov

6 "Human–Neuron–Model": A Spherical Model of Signal Discrimination in the Visual System   154
   C. A. Izmailov, A. M. Chernorizov, and V. B. Polyansky

7   Individual Characteristics of Brain Activity and Thinking Strategies   178
    Olga M. Razumnikova and Nina V. Volf

    Section 2 Commentary: Neuroscience of Cognitive Skills
    and Abilities   215
    Gabriel A. Radvansky and Chris Forsythe

SECTION 3
Russian Electrophysiological Research

8   Brain Oscillations and Personality from an Evolutionary
    Perspective   221
    Gennady G. Knyazev

9   Oscillatory Dynamics of Spiking Neurons and the Modeling
    of Memory Functions   242
    V. I. Nekorkin and V. B. Kazantsev

10 Frequency-Selective Generators of Oscillatory Brain Activity
    as Mapping Structure and Dynamics of Cognitive Processes   275
    N. N. Danilova

11 Oscillatory Self-organization of Cyclic Synthesis of Sensory Information
    and Memory Content for Object Recognition   297
    Sergey A. Miroshnikov, Margarita G. Filippova, and Roman V. Chernov

    Section 3 Commentary: Models of Neural Dynamics Provide a
    Foundation for Neurocognitive Interventions   315
    Chris Forsythe and Gabriel A. Radvansky

SECTION 4
Russian Translational Neuroscience Research

12 Individual Alpha Activity Indices and Biofeedback   323
    Olga Mikhailovna Bazanova

13 The Psychophysiology of Combat Activity   343
    A. A. Bochenkov

14 The Use of Fuzzy Logic and Artificial Neural Networks to Predict the
    Professional Fitness of Operators of Technical Systems   371
      A. P. Bulka

    Section 4 Commentary: Neuroscience Applications Extending from the
    Clinical to the Professional to Everyday Domains   380
      Chris Forsythe and Gabriel A. Radvansky

    Index   385

Notes on Contributors

Yuri I. Alexandrov
Institute of Psychology, Russian Academy of Sciences

Olga Mikhailovna Bazanova
State Research Institute of Molecular Biology and Biophysics, Siberian Branch of the Russian Academy of Medical Sciences

A. A. Bochenkov
Russian Military Medical Academy

A. P. Bulka
Russian Military Medical Academy

Alexander M. Chernorizov
Department of Psychophysiology, Moscow State University

Roman V. Chernov
Psychology Department, Saint Petersburg State University

Nina N. Danilova
Department of Psychophysiology, Moscow State University

Margarita G. Filippova
Psychology Department, Saint Petersburg State University

Chris Forsythe
Sandia National Laboratories

Chingis A. Izmailov
Department of Psychophysiology, Moscow State University

Victor B. Kazantsev
Nizhny Novgorod State University, Novgorod Russia

Gennady G. Knyazev
Research Institute of Physiology and Fundamental Medicine, Siberian Branch of the Russian Academy of Medical Sciences

Eduard Arutunovich Kostandov
Institute of Higher Nervous Activity and Neurophysiology, Russian Academy of Sciences

Sergey A. Miroshnikov
Psychology Department, Saint Petersburg State University

Vladimir I. Nekorkin
Institute of Applied Physics, Russian Academy of Science

Vladimir B. Polyansky
Department of Psychophysiology, Moscow State University

Gabriel A. Radvansky
University of Notre Dame

Olga M. Razumnikova
Research Institute of Physiology and Fundamental Medicine, Siberian Branch of the Russian Academy of Medical Sciences

V. I. Shostak
Faculty of Psychology, Saint Petersburg State University

Ludmila Vladimirovna Sokolova
Department of Higher Nervous Activity and Psychophysiology, St. Petersburg State University

Konstantin Viktorovich Sudakov
P. K. Anokhin Institute of Normal Physiology, Russian Academy of Medical Sciences

Nina V. Volf
Research Institute of Physiology and Fundamental Medicine, Siberian Branch of the Russian Academy of Medical Sciences

Acknowledgements

This book consists of an unprecedented compilation of contributions from a variety of esteemed Russian scientists. For some, this was their first English-language publication. From some, it was their final publication. The editors would like to extend their gratitude to each of the contributors and thank them for their willingness to participate in this project and their patience as it came to fruition.

The editors also express their gratitude to Dr. James Giordano and Dr. John Shook, for their assistance with editorial matters as this book was prepared for publication.

SECTION 1

History and Tradition of Russian Neuroscience

CHAPTER 1

Origins of Russian Cognitive Psychophysiology

L. V. Sokolova

Among today's scientists, interest in history, specifically the history of science, is undeniable. It signifies not only a tribute of respect and attention to domestic and international culture, but also a desire to learn oftentimes contradictory trends in the advancement of science, bringing to light the true significance of many doctrines and their creators.

The life of science is a continuous advancement of new theories, hypotheses, models, and interpretations. Within the behavioral science of psychophysiology, the concept of *reflex* has remained a central topic through the centuries, regardless of differing definitions brought about by changing propositions concerning the driving forces of behavior (Sokolova 1995). The foundations of a *reflex theory* were laid by René Descartes (1596–1650) (Descartes 1662), the great French scholar and natural scientist of the 17th century. His reflex scheme of motor actions, mechanistic in essence, marked the beginning of a quest for the physiological mechanisms of behavior.

In the 18th century, specific features of a neuromuscular response were established (A. Haller), and a bond between *psychic phenomena* and properties of the neural substrate was recognized (La Mettrie 1748/1912; Cabanis 1981). Subsequent trends expanded upon the relation between the body and the environment. The principle of *biological conditioning of behavior* was introduced and elaborated in the biological theory of the Czech physiologist and anatomist G. Prochaska (1749–1820) (Prochaska 1957). Prochaska added an important intermediary link to the *"body-environment" scheme*, specifically mental processes (perception, memory, thinking, etc.) (Prochaska 1957). Mental processes enable the selective response of the body to environmental factors based on acquired experience and current needs. Given this approach, the *psyche*, as an outcome of the integrative activity of the nervous system, was encompassed within the behavioral activity of the body.

Notwithstanding theoretical proposals concerning the role of the psyche in the reflexive response of the body, researchers of the first half of the 19th century focused their efforts on studying mechanisms of involuntary neural processes with emphasis on the spinal cord as the structural basis of reflex activity (Bell 1811; Magendie 1822; Muller 1831). These ideas were crystallized in the **anatomical** *concept of the reflex*. It was believed that the mechanisms underlying the reflex arose from activity of lower brain regions. In contrast, discussions of the nature of voluntary (conscious) actions increasingly involved the terminology of subjective psychology. The role of the environment in the formation of specific behavior was basically nullified, resulting in the opinion that the body should be viewed as a self-contained, closed system.

Fundamental changes in the understanding of the biological nature of behavior are connected to the name of I. M. Sechenov (1829–1905), a distinguished Russian physiologist, and creator of the *psychophysiological concept of the reflex*. Sechenov truly ushered in a new era for investigation of brain functions. In his renowned "Reflexes of the Brain," Sechenov provided a deterministic explanation of active goal-directed behavior, in which goal-directed behavior is an integral and hierarchical process. He emphasized that the body "does not take a cue" from external stimuli, but behaves according to a program built in the course of its continuous contact with the environment. Furthermore, the reflex activity of the body is based on a principle of the coordination between motion and sensing. For Sechenov, the term "sensing" meant the manifestation of two determining factors: a motive (a behavior-driving factor) and an image (a product of the combined activity of sensory receptors). These two factors underlie the critical psychophysiological regulators of behavior that determine its goal-directed and active-selective nature.

Sechenov's investigations shaped the ideological and scientific focus of the Russian school of physiology that he established. Subsequently, the problem of investigating brain reflexes and their role in the behavior of humans and animals, as posited by I. M. Sechenov, was further developed in the school of I. P. Pavlov. In April 1903, Pavlov gave a presentation at the 14th International Medical Congress in Madrid titled "Experimental Psychology and Psychopathology in Animals" (Pavlov 1963, 2) that outlined the key points of a new behavioral science. Pavlov's proposal laid the groundwork for investigating the physiology of higher nervous activity, and justified the possibility of studying the psychic activity of animals using methods that focused on conditioned reflexes. Furthermore, Pavlov asserted that the temporary connections underlying the formation of conditioned reflexes serve as the physiological basis of the psyche, and the conditioned reflex itself is a psychic act.

Pavlov's main premise was based on recognition that inner-outer balance (adaptiveness) is a key biological principle of the activity of living systems. This inner-outer balance is responsible for the entire range of adaptive reactions of the body in response to the environment. At the same time, Pavlov believed that an equally important element in explaining the goal-directed nature of human behavior is subjective, and hence belongs to the realm of speculative psychology and nebulous dangerous "philosophizing" beyond the scope of precise physiological research methods. However, investigations of more complex forms of animal behavior require study of what Pavlov referred to as "the subjective state of the animal," which was believed to persistently manifest itself in reflex reactions. This corresponds to the intermediate link, or "middle term" in I. M. Sechenov's terminology, of the stimulus–response scheme. For psychophysiology, Pavlov's introduction of subjective states to the study of reflex reactions introduced the need for a set of entirely different systematic approaches for conducting experimental research, consequently furthering the science.

1   Theories of Ukhtomsky and Bertitashvili

A constructive review of Pavlov's experimental model and general biological theory was undertaken by two prominent Russian scientists, A. A. Ukhtomsky (1875–1942) and I. S. Beritashvili (1884–1974). Each created his own original trend in the science of psychophysiology.

Beritashvili. In 1916, Beritashvili began a series of experimental studies of animal behavior using the conditioned reflex method. But soon he realized that this approach, and its theoretical interpretations, did not explain the regularities of behavior under natural conditions. Beritashvili came to believe that it is necessary to study integrated behavior in freely moving animals. For the next twenty years, starting in 1926–27, he investigated the behavior of vertebrate animals using a free movement method that was dramatically different from the techniques used by the Pavlovian school. The Pavlovian school used experimental apparati that severely restricted animal locomotion. As a result of his investigations, Beritashvili came to the conclusion that reflexes and behavior are in essence two qualitatively different phenomena.

Beritashvili asserted that behavior relates to reflexes as the whole relates to a part (in line with theorizing of the Gestalt school, and neobehaviorists such as Tolman). Therefore, any direct generalization of the Pavlovian theory of conditioned reflexes from the domain where it was developed (the physiology of salivary glands) to a qualitatively new area of research (integrated behavior) must be inappropriate. In the course of Beritashvili's experiments, it was established that in dogs, as well as in other higher vertebrates, an *image*, or a specific idea, of the food and its location in the environment is created during the first experience of the food at a given location. This image is then retained, and upon later perceiving that environment, or any part thereof, the image is retrieved through an act of reproduction. As a result, the animal behaves similarly to the initial experience, i.e., "head movements oriented to the food, walks to the food location, sniffs it, and consumes it when the food is found" (Beritashvili 1975, 649). Unlike development of a conditioned reflex that requires training, the image is formed spontaneously and immediately via the activation of multiple cortical (sensory and pyramidal) neurons and their integration into a single functional system capable of maintaining arousal for some time after the stimulus is no longer present, which is required for an adaptive action. Beritashvili called such behavior regulated by images a "psychoneural" or *image-driven* behavior.

Beritashvili thought that due to the constant variability in the environment, sensory images must be dynamic, as well as the make-up of a given *psychoneural process*. These processes are continuously updated based on internal and external stimuli that are experienced over time. Beritashvili wrote "This particular variability and dynamics of the psychoneural process of representation determines the continuous variability of both subjective experiences and external motor reactions" (Beritashvili 1984, 337). He noted that activation of the functional system of sensory and pyramidal neurons that reproduces an image of a vital object is always accompanied by emotional arousal. Reproduction of the psychoneural process involves reproduction not only of a sensory image of the environment, but also of the emotional arousal and motor impulses that also occurred in the past. Hence, the cornerstone of psychoneural (image-driven) behavior is the ability of the brain to (a) spontaneously and immediately record an image of an important environmental component, convey it to memory, and (b) "extract" it from memory to satisfy current biological needs. Notably, activity of the psychoneural process and its dynamics (specifically, lability and plasticity) are contingent on the biological significance of a given object for the body. Thus, the image, according to Beritashvili, is a determinant for behavior in a probability-organized environment and a prognostic (predictive) function of the brain.

However, Beritashvili did not view the role of psychoneural processes in absolute terms. In addition to the image-driven psyche, he believed that conditioned and unconditioned reflexes also serve to shape behavioral actions. Behavior as an integrated reaction of the body is realized through the joint activity of multiple reflex coordinating mechanisms. Reflex reactions emerge following the "stimulus-response" principle, but their subsequent "activation and deactivation" across different circumstances is controlled by psychoneural activity.

Beritashvili further believed that psychoneural activity in higher vertebrates must play a dominant role in imparting purposefulness to behavior. In particular, this pertains to a human being endowed with consciousness.

Accordingly, daily behavior is guided by more abstract, conceptual images to a greater extent than by the specific concrete, natural stimuli that are underlying reactive behavior. Moreover, this higher type of psychoneural activity, corresponding to the conscious level of the psyche, is capable of transforming (or even eliminating) certain reflex responses that are "undesirable" for the body.

Ukhtomsky. The time period from 1923 to 1940 in Russian physiology was marked by the development of teachings on the *dominant* by Aleksey Alekseyevich Ukhtomsky (1875–1942). Like Beritashvili, Ukhtomsky was a disciple of N. E. Vvedensky, Sechenov's successor at the school of physiology established at Saint Petersburg University. Sechenov had defined a range of topics for study in the university school of physiology. The topics included nervous system functions in the context of body-environment relations. This laid the foundation for Ukhtomsky's transformative research having the goal of finding a systems approach to studying motivational determinants in human life.

In 1911, Ukhtomsky began a methodical investigation of integrative brain activity and the factors affecting the formation of goal-directed behavior. These studies culminated in 1923 with publication of his article "Dominant as a Working Principle of Neural Centers" in the *Russian Journal of Physiology* (Ukhtomsky 1923). In this paper, Ukhtomsky first introduced the *dominant*. This became one of the key principles of nervous system activity and a fundamental general biological law underlying the goal-directed behavior of humans and animals.

The main elements of the *dominant principle* are as follows. The dominant has characteristics of both schemas and an attentional filter. When the nervous system experiences some need, there is a sustained excitation within a group of neural centers, with simultaneous mitigation or blocking of other reactions. External stimuli will generally support and reinforce actions appropriate to the need of facilitating the formation of a constellation of neural centers. This group of neural centers temporarily dominates the nervous system and defines the character of the body's response to internal and external stimuli. It is through these mechanisms that the dominant gives rise to purposeful, goal-directed actions. So, in summary, through the dominant, functionally isolated neural centers are effectively tied together to produce a harmonious unified ensemble. These ensembles of neural centers then support coordinated actions of goal-directed behavior, appropriate given the relevant contingencies of a probabilistic environment.

In the life of a living organism, the dominant introduces casual formulations that are equally applicable to activity of individual reflex systems and functions of the whole body. Ukhtomsky wrote: "I consider it [the dominant – L. S.] to be the 'principle' of operation of the nervous system not because it somehow appears to be highly rational, but because it seems to be a rather persistent feature of neural system activity" (Ukhtomsky 1966). The dominant can have a subtle influence on our actions, and is not as passive as it may appear to be in the beginning. It is a dual-action tool, for it leads to a certain seemingly inevitable one-sidedness in the operation of the nervous system and to the self-reinforcement of a current reaction. This may lead to either good or bad outcomes. "It might be said that due to the persistent operation of the dominant in the activity of the nervous system, a certain 'subjectivity' is invoked with respect to the immediate environment. It plays a filtering role by preventing one from noticing environmental stimuli that a person would otherwise notice under different circumstances (such as would be expected by schema selection). But because of this, and a certain 'subjectivity' with respect to the immediate environment, one may be much more progressive and far-sighted with respect to a chosen path of action than one who is more 'objective' in their reactions to the immediate environment" (Ukhtomsky 1950–1954, 100).

Although Ukhtomsky demonstrated, in his numerous illustrative experiments, that the dominant principle could be applied to investigations of behavioral reactions in animals, the conceptual significance of his doctrine was underestimated by his contemporaries. His name was mostly connected to the discovery of the phenomenon that a stable focus of excitation in the nervous system was capable of affecting the reflex reaction process, thereby limiting his contributions to the area of purely physiological research. However, the true value of Ukhtomsky's work goes beyond the boundaries of investigations into fine physiological mechanisms of the brain. Ukhtomsky was a synthetic scientist: from the very beginning he declared that the phenomenon he discovered had a much broader significance. He tied the dominant principle to the fundamental issues of human life, cognition, and his own social identity (Batuev and Sokolova 1994a) (Batuev and Sokolova 1994b). However, the general public had very limited access to his writings and publications. As such, there was little awareness of the conceptual significance of the dominant doctrine for understanding brain activity mechanisms to serve as a basis for human social behavior. Only recently, through careful studies of the scientist's archives, were we able to recover what seems to be the most important part of his scientific genius. This is primarily related to an attempt to build the fundamentals of a complex human science (Ukhtomsky 1996) (Ukhtomsky 1997) (Ukhtomsky 2000) to fully explore the biological, psychophysiological, and socio-cultural foundations of human cognitive activity.

2   The Dialectic of Body and Environment

The problem of the dialectic unity of body and environment was at the center of Ukhtomsky's work. Ukhtomsky believed that the body does not respond to various transient environmental events by way of individual, isolated, and autonomous reactions, but instead as an integrated whole (similar to Tolman's molar behaviors). In Ukhtomsky's opinion, the integrity of the body as a system was a biological achievement that enabled its adaptation to the environment as well as the improvement of its adaptive reactions.

Unlike Pavlov, Ukhtomsky believed that the cardinal uniqueness of animate beings, combined with the goal-directed nature of their behavior, lies in the active drive to continuously explore the environment. According to Ukhtomsky, human reflection upon objective reality is inextricably intertwined with the continual transitions to new levels of activity. If the goal of conditioned reflexes in adaptation is to balance the body and the environment, the dominant will always introduce an element of imbalance. Any change to the normal level of homeostasis, or any other deviation, as a result of the dominant disturbs the balance in the body. Actualization of a newly created dominant sets a new level of equilibrium. Ukhtomsky had a profound understanding of the dialectic connection between adaptation and system activity in behavior. The conditioned reflex, while an essentially physiological reaction, could not be a vector for behavior. Desired results could not be achieved through conditioned reflexes alone, but required a system of conditioned reflexes to be interconnected via the influence of the present dominant. Ukhtomsky created a truly *dialectic concept of reflex* that reflects the systemic character of relations between the body and the environment.

Ukhtomsky always treated the scientific achievements of the Pavlovian school with great attention and respect. He viewed the relations between the schools not as a confrontation of scientific ideas but as an active constructive dialogue, directed at finding the leading determinants of human behavior and the psyche. He repeatedly emphasized that the dominant and the conditioned reflex must be treated uniformly in terms of their respective roles and interdependence within integrated behavior. It should be noted that I. P. Pavlov's (1923) book, "Twenty-Year Experience in Objective Studies of Higher Nervous Activity (Behavior) of Animals," summarized the multiyear investigations of the Pavlovian school in the area of conditioned reflexes. The same year, Ukhtomsky published his first article on the dominant, the product of many years of analyzing the mechanisms of behavior.

Ukhtomsky understood the deep-rooted dialectic unity of the dominant and conditioned reflexes. He believed that the dominant state of the body provided a general functional background, a "substratum for developing temporary connections, adopting new motives from the environment, and linking these new motives to reactions that occurred earlier" (Ukhtomsky 1950–1954, 301–302). Temporary connections are established against the background of the dominant, thereby prompting renewal of the dominant. The changing environment continuously triggers new temporary connections and expansion of the pool of reflex reactions, playing a key role in the body's adaptation to the environment and the development of adequate behavior. Therefore, as specific determinants of behavior, the dominants that are created do not belong to a stable and permanent resource. They represent an ever-expanding and transforming asset of the body.

A memory trace left by a previously established dominant represents an integrated subjective image, one that incorporates both the space-time structure of the past environment and the emotive state of the body. Ukhtomsky wrote: "Actual experience always occurs in finite and compressed integrals where inherited fortunes of the family, echoes of upbringing, current sensations, love, hatred, the general course of life and one's most intimate searchings play an equal role!" (Ukhtomsky 2000, 132). He pointed out that any human "concept" or "representation," (i.e., any individualized mental content) is a trace of a previously experienced dominant. At the same time, an integrated image serves as a kind of "matrix" for the reproduction of a dominant. Renewal of the dominant in new conditions involves its dynamic re-integration, the establishment of new temporary connections with the environment, and the development of new conditioned reflexes. These processes serve to improve the adaptive capacities of the body.

3   The Dominant within the Context of the Overall Biological System

To some extent, based on Ukhtomsky's concept of the dominant as a critical component in the organization of goal-directed behavior, we may reconstruct the scheme whereby the dominant functions within the overall context of the body (Figure 1.1).

At any moment, the body is affected by a huge number of environmental stimuli. As an integrated system, the body perceives this complex of polymodal *environmental stimuli* in an integrated fashion and forms an *integrated image*, a product of the *primary (afferent) synthesis*. According to Ukhtomsky, this type of synthesis is made possible by the brain's ability to immediately

ORIGINS OF RUSSIAN COGNITIVE PSYCHOPHYSIOLOGY

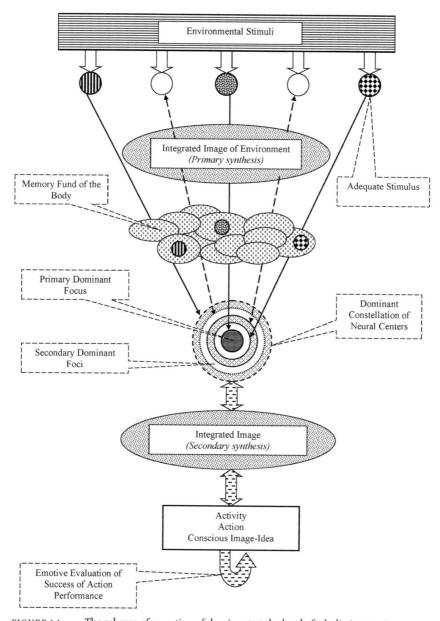

FIGURE 1.1   The scheme of an action of dominant at the level of a holistic organism

form and capture an integrated image, which he treated as a universal property of the reflective processes underlying the integrated character of perception.

The external environment is extremely variable (i.e., probabilistically organized). At the same time, environmental stimuli impinging on the body interact with the equally variable functional status of the body. This variability is attributable to a string of continuously alternating dominant states.

A dominant state arises as a product of bodily needs. These trigger the formation of a respective *primary dominant focus* in the nervous system. After a certain level of excitation arises, the primary dominant acquires the ability to "sum up" excitations, as though it attracts stimuli (see arrows on Figure 1.1) with the effect of supporting and reinforcing itself. Consequently, additional neural populations join in with the primary area of excitation leading to formation of *secondary dominant foci*. The latter merges into a single working ensemble, and form a *dominant constellation of neural centers*. This operates in accordance with principles of the spatial synchronization of nervous activity. This is where inhibition plays a role, by enabling behavioral vectors that may be at odds with biologically significant components of the environment. It is only through reciprocal inhibition (see dotted arrows in Figure 1.1) that there is a simultaneous canceling of the ability of other neural centers to respond to environmental stimuli, allowing a single degree of freedom and forming only one vector of action.

The formation of a dominant constellation of neural centers represents the initial phase in generating a program of actions to satisfy a current need. The corresponding dominant actualizes the *memory pool of the body* to elicit an aggregate of memory traces from previously experienced environments. These traces are structured to highlight components that signify important and relevant elements of past environments (see shaded circles in Figure 1.1). These *adequate stimuli* are reinforced through the formation of temporary neuronal connections, and provide the basis by which a given image-trace may be re-actualized. For this actualization to be adequate (i.e., to allow applying past experience to new environmental conditions), the aggregated memory traces must be compared to the integrated image of the current environment. Recall that this image is formed as a product of the integrated perception of the polymodal environmental stimuli that define the current situation. Inasmuch as this comparison takes place within the context of the active dominant state of the body, the memory traces preferentially recalled are the ones with a certain degree of probability of satisfying the current need. At the same time, the potential utility of these trace analogs to the current situation is relative: the traces extracted from memory will likely bear "only slight resemblance to the current situation" (i.e., similar only in key characteristic aspects).

Through the above mechanisms, there arises an *integrated image (secondary synthesis)*. Compared to the indifferent integrated primary synthesis, the secondary synthesis is qualitatively different and involves a subjectively-colored "integrated image" of the environment. The image produced through the secondary synthesis is not only a product of passive perceptual processes, but also a product of selective, active perception. From the total volume of environmental stimuli, the body selects a subset deemed meaningful based on similar stimuli having satisfied a comparable need during a past experience. By placing these two levels of synthesis against each other, and highlighting the dual nature of perceptual processes (its integrity and selectivity), Ukhtomsky believed that "there is a uniform environment that we break down and re-arrange following the history of our needs and their sequential interlinking over time" (Ukhtomsky 1966, 256).

Only through experience is it possible to assess whether an integrated image and the associated behavioral program corresponds to reality, and its various contingencies. According to Ukhtomsky, *activity* (as a process) and the resulting *action* (as its specific instantiation) are the unifying and integrating factors facilitating goal-directed behavior. Behavior is directed by rather flexible and changeable integrated sensory images which spontaneously emerge. This is distinct from the *conscious image-idea*, which is a result of imprinting (standardization) of the integrated image and its incorporation into the overall system of signs and concepts. The integrated image and conscious idea reflect the dialectic relation between conscious and subconscious in the human psyche and behavior.

The appropriateness (adequacy) of an integrated image is verified once a behavioral response has ended and there is an *emotive* evaluation of the success in satisfying a current need and resulting activation of a system of feedback (see arrows in Figure 1.1). If the degree of success is high, then the integrated image will be retained in memory. Otherwise, the analysis of the pool of memory traces, as well as of the informational component of the environment, will be re-initiated to try to extract new solutions to the problem. Where there is re-organization of the behavioral response, temporary connections are established with specific environmental stimuli that, once incorporated into the re-integrated image, become additional activators of the dominant. In Ukhtomsky's opinion, this process for "new growth of environmental reflexes" gives a considerable boost to the adaptive capacities of the body thereby supporting a broad spectrum of activities of the organism. In addition, by referring to the integrated image as "a probabilistic projection of anticipated reality" (Ukhtomsky 1966) Ukhtomsky emphasized that the primary synthesis retains in memory those environmental components that were not significant or relevant at the time. This, in return, provides for initial redundancy of information stored in memory which dramatically increases the potential influence of a past experience.

By postulating the fundamentally *image-based character of the psyche*, Ukhtomsky depicted the process of human cognition of the environment in a new light. Opposing the traditional representation of human cognitive activity as a discrete-linear relationship of "analysis – synthesis", Ukhtomsky put forward a truly revolutionary idea of cognition as a reflection of a dialectically continuous circle: "synthesis – analysis – synthesis" (Ukhtomsky 1966).

4   The Chronotrope

Having emphasized the importance of the dominant in the formation and organization of behavior, Ukhtomsky outlined a comprehensive, integrated plan of psychophysiological studies of it. These studies primarily pertained to human perception.

In 1925, Ukhtomsky proposed the idea of a chronotope (from the Greek "chrónos" – time, and "tópos" – place), or space-time continuum within the bounds of which human cognitive activity was believed to take place (Sokolova 2000). He wrote: "Time everywhere is fused into a spatial image for everywhere it is perceived in motion" (Ukhtomsky 2000, 433). "Space, individually independent of time, just like time, individually independent of space, are separated from a real *chronotope* only via abstraction and artificial preparations, whereas live and concrete perception always physiologically occurs in the indivisible 'space-time'" (Ukhtomsky 1950–1954, 191). We build our integrated space-time representation of reality by perceiving the basic space-time laws of the environment and matching them to the rhythms of internal processes and prior experiences. The integrity and indivisibility of the integrated image, according to Ukhtomsky, are largely related to the integrated nature of perception.

From this perspective, Uktomsky re-examined the established scientific definition of sensation as merely a product of the activity of a sensory system, and as a phase preceding perception. For Ukhtomsky, sensation, viewed as a basic "building block" of perception, is an artificial contrived abstraction. In reality, a sensation, even in its most primitive form, is an integrated image which is already a synthesis, a product of inter-sensory integration taking place against the background of the present dominant (i.e., conceptually-driven processing).

Ukhtomsky focused significant attention on defining the role of the dominant for the processes of attention and objective thought. He considered the dominant to be a systemic reaction of the nervous systems that is triggered by information on events or objects in time and space. Moreover, he believed the dominant itself expressed the relation of the body to the environment. This included perception directed to biologically important objects and events, as well as the suppression of other reactions incompatible with the current dominant. It is specifically by means of the dominant that the body forms an active position relative to the environment. The dominant participates not as a passive observer but as an active force of existence. The body does not passively follow environmental changes, but, in accordance with a given dominant, it actively selects from a multitude of environmental factors only those components that it considers to be of "biological interest." This constitutes the basis for human individualism that becomes apparent in the fact that out of the total content of incoming information, each individual selects that which has significance for that person at a given time.

5   Development of Human Cognition

Concerning the development of human cognitive activity, Ukhtomsky attached much importance to the role of object-related activity. Based on his belief that the dominant served as a physiological basis for the act of attention and objective thought, Ukhtomsky proposed three consecutive phases in the development of the cortical dominant, which also correspond to his phases of objective thought:

The first phase is a phase that largely involves a strengthening of the present dominant, when "a sufficiently stable dominant evolves within the body and under the influence of internal biological processes and the effects of reflexes, attracts a variety of sensations as motives for arousal" (Ukhtomsky 1950–1954, 169).

The second phase is when a stimulus associated with a given dominant is sensed, and this stimulus is internalized, thereby separating it from the environment. Out of a multitude of active stimuli, the dominant singles out a group of stimuli of particular biological interest (i.e., that has a biological significance at the current time period). In accordance with the dominant, multiple external stimuli are weeded out to find the ones that, by way of an earlier established connection, correspond to a given internal need. Here, the active role of coordinating inhibition becomes prominent. It is for this reason that Ukhtomsky used another name for this development phase of the dominant, calling this phase the *development of conditioned reflexes*. This phase is marked by the development of specific conditioned reflexes that become automated after multiple repetitions.

The third phase is a more or less exclusive linkage of the dominant with associated stimuli, when each of the counter-agents (internal and external) invokes and reinforces each other. This phase is associated with reproduction of the dominant (i.e., a process involving retrieval of traces from previous experiences). Thus, the objectively given and physically uniform external environment is completely broken down into "objects" each corresponding to a specific subjectively experienced dominant, the so-called "biological interest of the past." "I recognize again external objects," Ukhtomsky wrote, "so far as I reproduce the past dominants, and I reproduce my dominants so far as I recognize respective objects within the environment" (Ukhtomsky 1950–1954, 170).

With regard to the role of memory in human cognition, Ukhtomsky emphasized that the "integrated image" of an object includes not only products of inter-sensory integration, but the entire host of sensations related to a specific prior stimulus. Each integrated image is a trace, a remnant of the past dominant, by which one time point exerts a determining influence on the next. The ability to generate memory traces of the "environment" was considered by Ukhtomsky to be a powerful tool for spatial orientation. He wrote: "These are our concepts and reminders, integrated images we lean on in order to build our current projections of future behavior" (Ukhtomsky 1950–1954, 197).

The integrated image incorporates a "fused" space-time representation of the environment and serves as a unique "memory card" of the experienced dominant, a "matrix" and a "key" to its reproduction, to some degree of completeness. Moreover, when traces (of "integrated images") stored in memory are retrieved, the same dominant (current dominating need of the body) plays the role of a dynamic initiating factor supporting the process of recombination of memory traces relative to current challenges.

In this way, Ukhtomsky underscores the conventional and relative character of his *Integrated Image* concept (Ukhtomsky 1966). In his opinion it is not a static but "an essentially raw complex." When the dominant is actualized, the integrated image that was built within its context during prior experiences undergoes active re-integration in light of ongoing experiences. Given the extreme variability within the environment, its analysis is occurring continuously followed by selection of stimuli that are biologically interesting relative to current needs. The outcome of this process is a system of new temporary connections that enrich the content of the previous integrated image, which, in general, results in an expanded pool of reflexes and improved adaptability.

Ukhtomsky's thinking is deeply rooted in historicism: he believed that the integrated image as a dynamic construct combines three time domains: past, present, and future. The past that lies at the root of the image-trace is continuously corrected by the present, which ultimately makes sense for enhancing the adaptability of the body for its future activity. The integrated image has an active prognostic function that facilitates a temporally integrated determination of behavior.

At the same time, Ukhtomsky noted an important consideration: the integrated image as a trace product of the dominant is not just a record of experiential outcomes, but a representation of an object, characteristic, or relationship with regard to their necessity and possibility. It encompasses both prognostic and probabilistic reality. Probability, in Ukhtomsky's opinion, is embedded in the trace image. From his standpoint, evolution reinforced an ability to instantly form and memorize a comprehensive image of the environment that encompassed details of external stimuli not relevant or meaningful at the time. Each trace stored in memory is fundamentally redundant, but it is this redundancy which dramatically increases the determining potential of past experience. Through these mechanisms, past experience may be applied to an indeterminate future (Kruglikov 1988), because the integrated image represents a system of basic and most essential laws.

Memory traces of past experiences and actions entering the realm of consciousness seem "somewhat similar to the current" experience. Ukhtomsky wrote that the goal of the organism, "given the inflow of new environmental data, is to rapidly search through its stockpile of past experiences and by quickly comparing them to each other, select a more or less relevant dominant and apply it to a new challenge" (Ukhtomsky 1966, 258). This allows renewal of the dominant under slightly different, but fundamentally similar, conditions. The integrated image as a product of the dominant contains an imprint of the integrated activity of the body, directed at satisfying its current needs in a given environment. This presumes that the integrated image also incorporates both sensory and motor programs to reach a goal, which has vital importance for organizing goal-directed behavior. Accordingly, within a continuously changing environment, only a probabilistic approach can be used to select a behavioral program.

In addressing the organization of adaptive behavior, Ukhtomsky appreciated the important role of emotions as inherently involved in the formation of behavioral reactions. Emotions are an objective (not controlled by consciousness or will) indicator of the actual need and feasibility of meeting a need (i.e., probability of reaching the goal). Emotions therefore have a distinctive regulatory value in organizing goal-directed behavior. Their probabilistic component contributes to behavior modifications towards maximization (positive emotions) or minimization (negative emotions). Emotions resulting from activity, as a component of an ideal cortical "image-trace," can later serve as a distinct "initiator" for reproduction of the image-trace, and serve to help predict the probability of attaining a goal.

Ukhtomsky's appreciation of the importance attached to probabilistic prediction in organizing goal-directed behavior was also reflected in his understanding of the integrated image as the combined product of the dominant and the environmental stimuli prompting specific behavior. In his opinion, the integrated image is a "probabilistic projection of anticipated reality." The conformance of a selected behavioral program to the actual environment is tested in the course of daily activities. Ukhtomsky believed that the only "criterion of truth" reside in our evaluation of expectations through direct encounters with actual reality. We are fundamentally designed for continual testing, disappointments, and mistakes.

Stressing the important role of the integrated image as an integral part of psychic activity in determining current as well as future behavior, Ukhtomsky notes: "The physiology- and reflex-based concept of psychological activity, and in particular, thinking, leads one to conclude that any thought, including the most abstract, is a more or less real *projection of reality*. Through one's thoughts, they replicate reality. Furthermore, one would conclude that, in thinking and acting by way of reflexes, there is a concrete reality impinging upon one's sense, and one transforms it into an internal reality that is just as concrete. In one's thinking, including even the most abstract modes of thought, e.g. mathematics, one builds *projections* of reality. One forms projections of a concrete existence built in accordance with one's motivations!" (Ukhtomsky 1997, 125).

Ukhtomsky believed that the human experience of reality is always a predictive projection, an anticipation of the reality that lies ahead. "At all times in our searchings," he wrote, "each of us is a carrier of trials, projections, attempts and expectations that are more or less far-reaching into time-space, but we always remain in the position of an experimentalist testing whether the reality corresponds to what is projected. For the strongest of us, the depth of the chronotrope may be extensive, and the projection in time may be extremely long" (Ukhtomsky 1950–1954, 313).

Ukhtomsky saw an idealized process in the formation of the integrated image through object-related activity. He wrote, "construction of a probabilistic reality is a typical act of the brain as it expands and grows in its drive towards reality. Thus, *idealism*, faith in this ideal future reality as if it were a given fact, although the anticipated visual image would appear to be illusive and deceptive ..., all of this is a direct consequence of our physiological modus operandi" (Ukhtomsky 1997, 163–164).

The ideal image is an organic unity of two underlying principles: (a) the internalization of objective reality and (b) setting of practical goals by an individual. The objective world interacts with the individual and is reflected in his consciousness in the form of ideal constructs, integrated images, which in turn regulate actual behavior. Thus, in Ukhtomsky's doctrine, the "idealistic" and the "materialistic" branches of philosophical thought come together to describe two different aspects of human cognition, and to understand the representation of the external environment within the living brain substrate.

6   Uktomsky's Perspective on Consciousness

Another key issue addressed by Ukhtomsky was the problem of the relationship between the conscious and the unconscious in human activity. He wrote: "The unconscious perceives more accurate imprints of reality than the higher consciousness. This is because the latter is more active in carrying out higher tasks – it does not have time to deal with details and other particulars, and quickly interpolates filling in whatever it did not have time to examine!" (Ukhtomsky 1997, 127). And then: "It is from the complex deep layers of the subconscious that a man is fixed in his actions, experiences, and perceptions. If he desires to master his behavior, first he must master those deep layers of the subconscious (i.e., the flow of physiological events in his body), so that through them he may master and predetermine his behavior, his perceptions, and his expression of life in the environment" (Ukhtomsky 1997, 238). According to Ukhtomsky, the conscious and the unconscious should be considered to be inextricably connected entities; and continuous mutual transitions from one level of the psyche to the other represents a normal event of human psychic activity.

In the context of viewing the dominant as a unique "organ of behavior", Ukhtomsky believed that the phases of dominant formation occur at the unconscious level, whereas the phases of its realization or actualization require conscious involvement. In the event its underlying need is not satisfied, the dominant returns to the level of the unconscious while preserving its vital relevance for the body. Ukhtomsky wrote: "Dominants are able to continue their influence on the psyche even when they themselves have sunk below the threshold of consciousness" (Ukhtomsky 1997, 137). In short, while our consciousness is unaware of being bombarded by impulses from the internal environment, these stimuli not only affect perception, but proactively participate in activation of neural centers, and ultimately, in behavioral acts.

Ukhtomsky devoted much attention to the nature of human conscious activity. In his opinion, thinking constitutes the highest level of human cognition, and the evolution of thought was characterized as a path from prelogical thinking to the development of laws of logical thinking. According to Ukhtomsky, consciousness can be accomplished only when the object assumes its symbol-embodied form whereby the economizing role of thought becomes evident.

With respect to the existence of prelogical cognitive structures, Ukhtomsky identified intuition as one form of prelogical thinking. He believed that intuitive thinking is characterized by a moment of spontaneity in cognition, in contrast to the mediated discursive character of logical thinking (i.e. intuition does not have a comprehensive logical and proven *de facto* plan). Intuition is not immediately controlled by consciousness, but serves whatever need dominates the hierarchy of needs of a given individual, hence elevating intuition to a higher order process. Intuition is not random; it is a subconscious search process subject to the rules of recombination of previously accumulated experience. Intuition plays a profound role when it is necessary to step outside "the box" of existing cognitive methods to explore the unknown and perform the most important function of creativity.

Development of a logically structured idea, or idea image, at the level of consciousness, involves the standardization of a sign (semiotic) system. In a broad sense, a sign (or sign system), as a carrier of information, is an object of unspecified nature that under certain conditions acquires a meaning that can be a physical object (phenomenon, process, situation) or an abstract concept. Assuming the sensory-intuitive (unmediated) images characteristic of prelogical thinking are relatively flexible and mobile entities, then the final product of this process, a conscious idea-image, may be considered the result of reinforcement (standardization) of a sensory-intuitive image in a sign-concept system, such as speech or a system of exact mathematical signs.

With respect to the nature of consciousness, Ukhtomsky placed special emphasis on important human functions such as speech, pointing to a deep-rooted interconnection between the processes of thought formation and speech development. In his opinion, articulated speech comes from reflex-imitative reproduction of sounds, and through their comparative differentiation from the speech sounds of others, they acquire objective meaning with the pronunciation of words as symbols of objects.

According to Ukhtomsky, in addition to serving as a sign system, speech plays a defining role in the formation and realization of important human communicative functions such as interpersonal communication. Any social communication starts with the interaction of people via the use of a signal-sign-symbol form (speech, facial expressions, gestures, expression of emotions, etc.). This lower level of social communication has a solid psychophysiological foundation. In general, language, words, and symbols represent cortical "scars", integrated images of experienced dominants that were genetically or ontogenetically related to generalized objects and emotions. A word itself creates a dominant attitude and forms an integrated image in the cortex. This "top-to-bottom" example of the dominant formation is characteristic of a human being, and as it develops in the ontogenesis process, it becomes predominant in a socially advanced individual.

Ukhtomsky regarded the word as the most powerful stimulus. It is different from others not only in quantitative terms (i.e., the force of impact on the nervous system), but also in qualitative terms. Human words are able to change both the "natural" behavior of the body and its conditioned-reflex connections, and even hereditary unconditioned reflexes. (It is for this reason that I. P. Pavlov called the word "a signal of signals.") Uktomsky wrote, "Words break no bones. Yes, they do and will continue to 'break bones' more often than not. Just by using one word or expression, skillful individuals intentionally inflict harm. A word is used to create an attitude in one's self, and a word is used to pass it on to somebody else" (Ukhtomsky 1997, 209). Furthermore, "A word, if only it is able to appropriately resonate with an interlocutor, triggers a long inertial process that attracts current stimuli and defines in its own way current impressions and types of behavior! A word ties a lasting cortical-humoral knot that initiates activity of long duration" (Ukhtomsky 1997, 238–239). This happens not only when speech affects the individual directly and immediately. Thoughts, in the form of internal speech, may exert an equally powerful influence on all aspects of human activity.

7   Sociocultural Determinants

The review of Ukhtomsky's teachings on the dominant would not be complete without an attempt to briefly highlight aspects of his teachings pertaining to sociocultural determinants of the human psyche and behavior. Representing a new synthetic approach to human nature, Ukhtomsky's concept of the dominant sits at the intersection of several scientific disciplines: biology, physiology, psychology, philosophy, sociology, and ethics. This whole amalgam revealed a dialectic unity encompassing the biological and social roots of human nature. This enabled Ukhtomsky to organically tie natural-science concepts of human behavior and the psyche to the laws of human moral conduct, which took the content and meaning of human life beyond its purely physiological natural limits (Batuev and Sokolova 1994a) (Batuev and Sokolova 1994b).

For Ukhtomsky, a human being is a unity of four entities: *individual, individuality, personality,* and *society* manifested as the *I* and *We* relationship in each

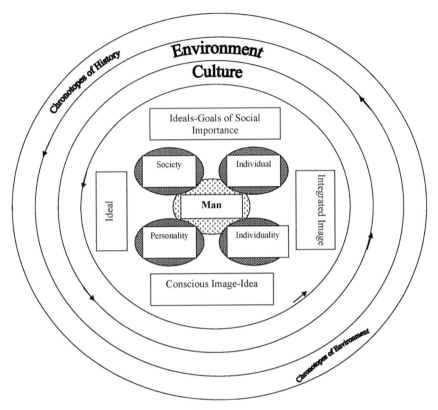

FIGURE 1.2   Biosociocultural space of a person

individual (see Figure 1.2). The *environment* for a human being is not just objective reality. It always appears before him in the context of *culture*. It unites the inner and spiritual worlds with cultural experiences of the previous generations, described by Ukhtomsky as "experience of fathers" and "experience of legends." In Ukhtomsky's opinion, the presence of cultural experience allows immense expansion of human creativity and, as a consequence, improvement of human adaptive resources.

Based on his understanding of the fundamentally image-based character of the human psyche and the systemic role of the *integrated image* in the formation of goal-directed behavior, Ukhtomsky introduced a novel approach to the conceptualization of the deep-rooted psychophysiological underpinnings of such concepts as *conscious image-idea*, *ideal*, and *ideals-goals of social importance*, and assigned to them the role of critically important determinants of the social behavior of people and society. Therefore, he viewed culture not as a static construct, but as a dynamically developing whole which is based on a quintessence of human ideals, and the results of actual human activity driven by these ideals. This in turn builds a biosociocultural space formed historically, and continuing to evolve in the course of activity undertaken by people and society. Accordingly, an individual in the process of their development learns both *chronotopes of environment* (i.e., constantly builds spatial-temporary images of reality), and *chronotopes of history* that help them to actively use the experience accumulated by people in general, which increases their adaptive resources.

Moreover, culture as an integral part of the human environment, provides a system of feedback. It is not only culture that predetermines the nature of a person, but the person forms and actively "creates" culture making his or her own individual contributions to the development of human society.

According to Ukhtomsky, everything in the world is interconnected and fundamentally interlocutory. Therefore, in addressing the issue of the biosocial nature of people, he gives special attention to the function of communication, and discusses it from the standpoint of the dominant principle. Considering the "dominant for the other" to be the most important human dominant, governing the development of biosocial and the personal status of people, Ukhtomsky formulated the laws of interpersonal communication. This consisted of the law of a *Double* and the law of a *Distinguished Interlocutor*, which are deeply rooted in psychophysiology and reflect the specifics and scope of human social dominants. Inasmuch as the communication process as a system of information exchange involves comprehension of the dominant attitudes of others, Ukhtomsky puts forward a concept of morals as one of the important constants of human behavior. According to Ukhtomsky, moral consciousness exists only in the context of human behavior, and any action thereof should be viewed in indivisible unity with subjective motives and consequences of social importance. Hence, morals are proclaimed by him to be perhaps the main "natural" law of human life facilitating creative development of an individual and progress in the development of mankind.

8 Conclusion

In summary, our reconstruction of Ukhtomsky's views on the relationship between internal and external dominants in human behavior and the psyche illustrates his influence as an originator of the systemic approach to studying basic human cognitive activity, as it develops in the course of human interaction with the environment. Using a multidisciplinary approach, Ukhtomsky created a forward-looking theory of the biosocial nature of people, the value of which for the current state-of-the-art of human sciences cannot be overestimated. It includes objective and subjective aspects of human existence, and the material and the ideal as primary and integral components of a single psychophysiological process by which a human being learns the outside world and forms their personality. Many of Ukhtomsky's ingenious scientific predictions were brilliantly confirmed in the experiments performed by his disciples and followers, and enabled all of them to make their own pioneering contribution to the development of psychophysiology (Ukhtomsky 1900) (Sokolova 1995). Today, it has become evident that Ukhtomsky's teachings form a view of the world based on an understanding of the key principles of human behavior and the psyche, and for new researchers, they suggest a broad path forward for experimental research into the mechanisms of cognitive and creative activity.

References

Batuev, A. S., and L. V. Sokolova. 1994a. "A. A. Ukhtomskii's ideas on the nature of man." *Neuroscience and Behavioral Physiology* 24, no. 2: 173–185.

Batuev, A. S., and L. V. Sokolova. 1994b. "A. A. Ukhtomskii on human nature." *Journal of Russian and East European Psychology* 32, no. 1: 13–45.

Bell, C. 1811. *An Idea of a New Anatomy of the Brain; Submitted for the observations of His Friends*. London: privately printed.

Beritashvili, I. S. 1975. *Selected Works: Neurophysiology and Neuropsychology*. Moscow: Nauka.

Beritashvili, I. S. 1984. *Works: Problems of Muscle Physiology, Neurophysiology and Neuropsychology*. Tbilisi, Georgia: Metsniereba.

Cabanis, P. G. 1981. *On the Relations between the Physical and Moral Aspects of Man*, ed. G. Mora, trans. M. D. Saidi. Baltimore, Md.: John Hopkins University Press.

Descartes, R. 1662. *De homine figuris et latinatate donatus a Florentio Schuyl*. Leiden, The Netherlands: P. Leffen & F. Moyardum.

Kruglikov, R. I. 1988. *Principle of Determinism and Brain Activity*. Moscow: Nauka.

Magendie, F. 1822. "Expériences sur les fonctions des racines des nerfs rachidiens." *Journal de Physiologie Expérimentale et de Pathologie* 2: 276–279.

de la Mettrie, J. 1748/1912. *L'homme Machine*. Trans. G. C. Bussey and M. W. Calkins. La Salle, Ill.: Open Court.

Muller, J. P. 1831. "Bestätigung des Bell'schen Lehrsatzes, dass die doppelten Wurzeln der Rückenmarksnerven verschiedene Functionen, durch neue und entscheidende Experimente." *Notizen aus dem Gebiete der Natur- und Heilkunde, Weimar* 30: 113–117, 129–134.

Pavlov, I. P. 1963. *Psychopathology and Psychiatry*. Moscow: Foreign Languages Publishing House.

Prochaska, G. 1957. *Traktat o funktsiiakh nervnoi sistemy*. Leningrad.

Sokolova, L. V. 1995. *History of Teachings on Brain and Behavior Paths of Psychophysiology Development*. Saint Petersburg: Saint Petersburg State University Publishing House.

Sokolova, L. V. 2000. "A. A. Ukhtomskiĭ's ideas of correlation between the temporal and the spatial factors in the nervous system activity." *Rossiĭskii Fiziologicheskiĭ Zhurnal Imeni I M Sechenova*, 86, no. 8: 946–952.

Ukhtomsky, A. A. 1900. *Teachings on the Dominant and Modern Neurophysiology: Collection of Scientific Papers*. Leningrad: Nauka.

Ukhtomsky, A. A. 1923. "The dominant as a working principle of nervous centers." *Russian Journal of Physiology* 6.

Ukhtomsky, A. A. 1950–1954. *Complete Works*. Leningrad: Leningrad State University.

Ukhtomsky, A. A. 1966. *The Dominant*. Moscow: Nauka.

Ukhtomsky, A. A. 1996. *Intuition of Conscience: Letters. Notebooks. Sidenotes*. Saint Petersburg: Peterburgsky Pisatel.

Ukhtomsky, A. A. 1997. *Distinguished Interlocutor: Ethics. Religion. Science*. Rybinsk: Rybinskoye Podvorye.

Ukhtomsky, A. A. 2000. *Dominant of the Soul: From Humanitarian Legacy*. Rybinsk: Rybinskoye Podvorye.

Ukhtomsky, A. A. 2002. *The Dominant*. Saint Petersburg: Piter.

CHAPTER 2

The Beginnings of Russian Cognitive Psychophysiology

V. I. Shostak

1   Introduction

Due to geopolitical and historical circumstances, Russia (within its present geographical boundaries) fell far behind Europe in science, education, and technology until the end of the 17th century. General reforms are usually connected with the name of Peter the Great, who was not only interested in solving military problems, but also in inquiring deeply into the state of things in developed European countries. He attracted qualified and talented specialists to Russia and sent young Russians abroad to study various sciences and technologies. The Saint Petersburg Academy of Sciences and several universities, along with some special educational institutions, were opened in Russia shortly thereafter. For more than two centuries this tradition has helped Russian science reach European levels. The most important aspect of these reforms is the integration of science and education. The creation of scientific schools and establishment of contacts with the leading scientific centers of Europe, as well as the appearance of Russian scientists' works in foreign press, indicate how Russia entered the world scientific and educational community.

The first physiological laboratories were established at the Academy of Sciences and corresponding university departments, primarily for medical education purposes (especially at the Imperial Medico-Surgical Academy in Saint Petersburg). The peculiar feature of early Russian physiology was the commitment to "nervism," an idea put forward by the outstanding French physiologist, C. Bernard (1813–1878) (Bernard 1865/1927), and then developed by S. P. Botkin (1832–1889) (Beliaeva 2007), I. M. Sechenov (1829–1905) (Sechenov et al. 1952), N. E. Vvedensky (1852–1922) (Vvedensky 1901), V. M. Bekhterev (1857–1927) (Bekhterev 1999), I. P. Pavlov (1849–1936) (Pavlov 1950), A. A. Ukhtomsky (1875–1942) (Ukhtomsky 1900), and others.

Pavlov wrote: "I understand by nervism a physiological theory that attempts to extend the influence of the nervous system to the greatest possible number of the organism's activities" (Pavlov 1950). The idea of nervism penetrated his brilliant works on the physiology of digestion, for which he was awarded the Nobel Prize in 1904, and provided the methodological background for his teachings on the physiology of higher nervous activity.

Physiology gradually accumulated data and formulated theoretical concepts. It reached its heyday in the 19th century with the cell theory, the law of conservation of matter and energy, the theory of evolution, and the concept of the internal environment. With these achievements, the physicochemical foundations of life had been discovered. At the same time, the soul or psyche had not yet become an object of physiological study. Psychology of that period was more closely linked to philosophy than to any other natural science. Even psychopathology (mental disorders, psychiatry) stood somewhat apart from medicine.

The development of a scientific approach to psychological studies in Russian physiology is associated with the names of I. M. Sechenov, V. M. Behterev, and I. P. Pavlov – the founders of prominent scientific schools which made a great contribution to the world science.

2   I. M. Sechenov (1829–1905)

Sechenov received both a technical and medical education. He studied at the leading European physiological laboratories (of J. Müller, E. du Bois-Reymond, F. Hoppe-Seylor, Magnus, O. Funke, C. Ludwig, and H. Helmholtz) (Mikhailovich and Sechenov 1973) and defended his dissertation, "Data for the future physiology of alcohol intoxication." At different times, he worked as Professor of Physiology at the Saint Petersburg Military Academy, the Novorossiysk University (Odessa), Saint Petersburg University, and Moscow University. He made a great contribution to physiology and was rightly called the "Father of Russian physiology." Nevertheless, again and again during his lifetime, Sechenov turned to psychology in an effort to link experimental physiological data to psychic processes. As a result, he published a few remarkable works on subjects related to psychology. These studies had a great impact on the development of psychophysiology, and they are still of considerable importance. One cannot fail to mention such works as "Reflexes of the Brain" (Sechenov 1863/1970), "Criticism on 'The Tasks of Psychology' by Mr. Kavelin" (1872) (Mikhailovich and Sechenov 1973), "Who must investigate the problems of Psychology, and How" (Sechenov 1873/1935a), and "The Elements of Thought" (Sechenov 1873/1935b).

His treatise, "Reflexes of the Brain" (its initial titles were "An Attempt to Establish Physiological Bases of Psychical Processes" and "An Attempt to Reduce the Mode of Genesis of Psychical Phenomena to Physiological

Bases") was intended as an article for the widely read literary, social, and political magazine "Sovremennik" ("The Contemporary"). The suggestion for the publication came from the editor-in-chief of the magazine, the outstanding Russian poet, N. A. Nekrasov (Mikhailovich and Sechenov 1973). By that time, basic principles of nervous system activity had already been formulated and established, appearing to dangerously invade the spiritual sphere of man. At first, the censorial department did not think fit to publish the treatise and even initiated a criminal investigation of its author, but they were eventually able to find a compromise. The article was published in the "Medizinsky Vestnik" ("Medical Bulletin") bearing the first of the above titles (Mikhailovich and Sechenov 1973).

Censors hoped that Sechenov's article would be lost among others in a small-circulation medical journal, but, on the contrary, the issues of "Vestnik" containing his work were passed from hand to hand, read to tatters, and soon became so rare that a new edition had to be prepared. The new terminology gradually entered the everyday language. This article was especially popular among the university youth. The main idea was given in the very first sentence of the work: "Dear reader, you have certainly been a witness to controversies about the nature of the spirit and its dependence on the body" (Sechenov 1863/1970). The question was not new, but, in the second half of the 19th century, it sounded topical. No one can say that this question is fully answered at the present time.

Sechenov started from idealism and turned to a revolutionary new view of psychic activity. Then he considered it necessary to "let some ideas concerning psychical activity of the brain go to the public, ideas which had never been expressed before in physiological literature."

One of these new ideas involved connecting the nervous system and motor activity. He wrote: "All the endless diversity of the external manifestations of brain activity can be finally reduced to just one phenomenon – that of muscular movement. Be it the child laughing at the sight of a toy, or Garibaldi smiling when he is persecuted for his excessive love for his fatherland, a girl trembling at the first thought of love, or Newton enunciating universal laws and writing them on paper, – everywhere the final manifestation is muscular movement" (Sechenov 1863/1970). And further: "Moreover, the reader will readily grasp that absolutely all the properties of the external manifestations of brain activity described as animation, passion, mockery, sorrow, joy, etc. are merely results of a greater or lesser contraction of definite groups of muscles, which, as everyone knows, is a purely mechanical act" (Sechenov 1863/1970).

"Reflexes of the Brain" consist of two chapters. The first chapter discusses involuntary movements. The author distinguishes three kinds of involuntary movements. (1) Reflexes, in a restricted sense of the word, of decapitated animals; movements of the body during sleep; and "when the brain, as the phrase goes, does not act." (2) Involuntary movements in which the end of the action is weakened relative to the more or less intense beginning – involuntary movements with an inhibited end. (3) Involuntary movements with an intensified end, such as fright and elementary pleasures; cases when the intervention of the psyche does not change the reflex, such as somnambulism, alcoholic intoxication, delirium, and so on. These speculations led him to the idea of the "brain machine." Further investigation of the problem, however, has shown that only under certain conditions (hence not in every case) the brain can act as a machine when its activity is manifested in so-called involuntary movements.

In this manner, the "brain machine" is based on the reflex mechanism. It is clear that this theory is directly related to the ideas expressed by René Descartes (1596–1650) in the 17th century, although they have developed in different ways in philosophy, physiology, and psychology.

Sechenov was familiar with the discovery of the inhibitory action of the vagus on the heart (peripheral inhibition) made by the Weber brothers in 1845, though by that time the concept of inhibition had been very ambiguous. Nevertheless, he claims in his "Theses" (1860) that "there are no nerves delaying movement." However, in 1862, while working at the laboratory of Bernard, he discovered neural centers of the brain that cause the delay of reflexes. Irritation of the optic thalami by rock-salt results in depression of spinal reflexes, which return to normal after saline washing. Consequently, purely reflexive, machine-like activity is influenced by the brain. During further experiments, he also found a facilitating influence on activity. These facts not only led to the discovery of central inhibition, but also laid the foundation for the development of the concept of the nonspecific activating system, which is indispensable for understanding mechanisms of psychic activity.

At the end of the first chapter Sechenov writes:

1. The origin of every involuntary movement is a greater or lesser excitation of the sensory nerve.
2. A sensory stimulation producing reflex movement may or may not call forth definite conscious sensations.
3. In "pure" reflex, free from the psychical element, the relationship between the strength of stimulation and the intensity of movement remains constant.

4. In case of psychical complication of a reflex process the strength of the relationship may vary.
5. Reflex movements are always quickly followed by sensory stimulation.
6. Stimulation and reflex movement are approximately equal in duration especially if the reflex is not complicated by a psychical element.
7. All reflex movements are rational from the point of view of preserving the integrity of the whole organism.
8. The kinds of involuntary movements considered are equally applicable to the simplest and the most complex reflexes, either to short movements lasting a few seconds or to various continued reflexes.
9. The possibility of frequent repetition of involuntary movement in one and the same direction presupposes the existence of a definite mechanism in the body, inborn (mechanism of sneezing, coughing, etc.) or acquired by learning (walking), that is the act, in which the ability to reason takes part.
10. In case, if the normal sensation is dulled in one, or several, or all senses (sight, hearing, smell, etc.), then all movements in the sphere of these particular senses – whether they are understood by origin or not, and whether psychical perception is related to them or not – will be reflexes, at least by the mechanism of their origin.
11. This mechanism consists of sensory and motor nerves with cells in the brain centers, serving as the beginnings of these nerves, and with projections of these cells in the brain. Along this path, the influence of the brain is transmitted to reflex movement either intensifying or inhibiting it.
12. The activity of this mechanism is therefore a "reflex."
13. The machine is started by an excitation of a sensitive nerve.
14. Thus, all involuntary movements are machine-like by origin.

The second part of the treatise, entitled "Voluntary movements," is described in the subtitle as "Solution to the problem of the nature of every psychical act – Inhibition of conscious movements – Emotions." Identifying concepts of voluntary movement and psychical activity, Sechenov argues that "voluntary activity in man is composed of reflexes which begin with sensory stimulation, continue by means of a definite psychical act, and end in muscular movement; that in definite external and internal conditions (i.e., given a definite environment and a definite physiological state of the man) a given sensory stimulus inevitably leads to the other two components of the whole phenomenon and always in the same sense."

Giving an explanation of the activity of a man with an ideally strong will, he points out that "the movements of such a man are not based on any obvious sensory stimulation … In his actions this man is guided only by the highest moral motives, the most abstract ideas, for example, of the good of mankind, love for his Fatherland, etc. ... The highly voluntary movements may run counter to the instinct of self-preservation. They are reasonable only from the point of view of the moral moment that caused them."

After examining a great number of common and scientific facts, Sechenov concludes: "All psychical acts without exception, if they are not complicated by elements of emotion, develop by way of reflex. Hence, all conscious movements resulting from these acts and usually described as voluntary, are reflex movements in the strict sense of the term."

It was noticed earlier that Sechenov allowed for the phenomenon of inhibition of either involuntary or voluntary reflexes. At the same time, mental reflexes with an intensified end (which he called emotions) were accepted as a general model. At the beginning of human life, all mental reflexes, without exception, can be described as emotions. The sphere of emotion, however, gradually gets narrower.

Sufficiently expressed, the intensity of inhibition of reflex movements results in the endless mental reflex – thought. That is why man separates thought from action in his consciousness.

The modern reader, not knowing the relevant historical context, may read this article, though composed for wide reading by plan, as well as by form and content, with some difficulty and surprise. It should be noted that Sechenov was familiar only with Beneke's psychology, and that was during his university years when the works of W. Wundt and other notable scientists had not yet appeared. So, by Pavlov's estimate, "Reflexes of the Brain" was an ingenious flight of thought.

Many works give a detailed account of the contribution of I. M. Sechenov to psychology and his role in its development. Unfortunately, their analysis is beyond the boundaries of this article. However, we cannot fail to mention Sechenov's remarkable article "Who must investigate the problems of Psychology, and How," which appeared in 1873. It should be noted that by that time, despite a great number of works on psychology, it had not yet become an independent science. Despite its acceptance in name, psychology was regarded mainly as a branch of philosophy.

Psychology, and especially scientific aspects of psychology, was discussed by academics with care, though typically within some polemical context. At that time, Sechenov was well known both in Russia and abroad only as an outstanding physiologist (i.e., a representative of the science), which had its methodological basis in physicochemical views on the nature of life. For Sechenov, psyche was a manifestation of life. In a brief conclusion to his article, he wrote, "Psychical life is subject to certain immutable laws; if it is true it is possible for psychology to become an exact science; but this will happen only after these laws have been established, not only in principle, but in detail. Among all the phenomena of the universe, only two groups are in any way comparable to the psychical life of man: the psychical life of animals and those nervous activities of the organisms of man and animals which are studied in physiology; these two groups of phenomena are more simple, and therefore, may help us to understand the psychical phenomena in man. The comparison of the concrete psychical phenomena of animals with those of man is the subject-matter of comparative psychology; the comparison of psychical phenomena with the nervous processes going on in the human body forms the basis of analytical psychology, since in the organism, the nervous processes are more or less differentiated. *It is thus manifest that only physiologists can conduct researches in the field of analytical psychology.*" (italics mine – V. S.)

Sechenov's scientific self-consciousness anticipated the future of psychology not only in a general view, but also in concrete detail. He accurately defined the most important achievements of physiology opening the door to scientific explanations of psyche. He pointed to the study of reaction time, perhaps having in mind the works of the outstanding Dutch physiologist F. C. Donders (1818–1889) (Newell, 1989), who had shown how more complex psychical acts are associated with longer durations for the action. Sechenov further states that the achievements of physiology prove "a close relationship between the character of perceptions and the structure of the respective organs of senses."

In Sechenov's opinion, human beings only have the ability to distinguish, select, or combine facts of spiritual life by means of words. However, verbal actions confront – due to the absence of verifying criteria – the danger of substitution of reality by fiction. How are we to distinguish the real from the nominal? The possibility of their separation is defined by physiology. Sechenov, committed to the physicochemical school, had to decide whether to stay within the bounds of molecular views or to study the mechanism (the manner of performing) of action without knowing what is going on in the brain centers and nerve conductors.

Sechenov had arrived at a strong conviction that the example of physiology indicates the right path for psychology, by advancing experimental, objective and concrete knowledge able to change human life. Under conditions where the only concrete basis for psyche – material processes in the nerves – is unknown, it is only to be expected that psychology will "follow the example of her sister science, physiology, and limit her research to the question of *how* a given psychical process (leading to a thought, etc.) takes place." It follows that the task of psychology (as that of physiology) is to study mechanisms of the process: the ways of the action. Hence, while physiological and psychical processes (image, feeling, thought, etc.) are different, their mechanisms are related.

It has been shown that the reflex is such a mechanism. With respect to this common principle, the psychological and the physiological are treated as related phenomena. Psychology, by Sechenov's word, is the "sister science" and not the "daughter" of physiology. By relying on physiology, he does not mean to reduce psychology to the "nervous" but instead to abstract the reflex organization from the whole picture of physiological activity.

Following Sechenov's arguments, psychical acts contain elements related to both physical and physiological categories, and so they can be considered as integral wholes. The integrity and indestructibility of the tripartite psychical act is treated as axiomatic. "The conception of psychical activity as a process of motion is merely a further development of the idea of the relationship between nervous and psychical act; we must accept it as an axiom."

We hope the reader will regard this account as historical background supplying the context for the impulse to undertake the scientific study of psyche, and not as a presentation of unchanged dogma. Scientific developments during the past 150 years display psychology's dynamic changes quite clearly.

3   V. M. Bekhterev (1857–1927)

Vladimir Mikhailovich Bekhterev played an extraordinary role in the development of Russian physiology and psychophysiology. He can rightly be regarded as the founder of modern Russian psychology.

Bekhterev came to psychology through psychiatry, at that time called "mental illnesses." After graduating from the Medico-Surgical Academy and defending his dissertation "The Experience of a Clinical Study of Body Temperature in Some Forms of Mental Illness," he left for a sojourn in Europe. He spent two years during 1884–85 training at famous psychiatric clinics and laboratories, including the Institute for Experimental Psychology at Leipzig, where W. Wundt, the founder of physiological psychology, impressed Bekhterev. Wundt had a great impact on his own work.

During his life, Bekhterev worked at the University of Kazan, the Military-Medical Academy, the Psychoneurological Institute (founded by him and now bearing his name), and other scientific and applied institutions established on his initiative. It should be recognized that he had to conduct his research during trying times for Russia due to the February Revolution, the October

Revolution, and the Russian Civil War. He never halted his intense clinical, scientific, and administrative work.

Bekhterev left his mark on several fields of science: anatomy and physiology of the nervous system; psychiatry; neuropathology; neurosurgery (on his initiative the world's first neurosurgical operating room was opened at the Military-Medical Academy); psychology; and psychophysiology. He authored nearly 650 scientific studies, including such fundamental works as "Conductive Tracts in the Spinal Cord and Brain" (Kukuev 1971), "Foundations of Knowledge about the Functions of the Brain" (Bekhterev 1903–1907), "Objective Psychology" (Bekhterev, 1909), "Collective Reflexology" (1921), and "General Foundations of Human Reflexology" (Bekhterev 1926).

His practical and scientific work as a clinician (especially as a psychiatrist and neuropathologist) could be the subject of a separate study. His treatises on various aspects of anatomy and physiology of the nervous system are of genuine interest. His works on psychology became classics in the field. However, within the boundaries of this chapter, our focus is on the development of psychophysiology. It should be noted that during his time the terms "physiological psychology," "psychophysiology," and "experimental psychology" had similar meanings, and, in essence, all of them were associated with the new term "psychophysics" coined by G. T. Fechner in 1860.

Bekhterev successfully combined morphology with physiology, neuropathology, psychology, psychophysiology, and empirical psychology, permitting him to describe scientific mechanisms of psychical activity. To this combination we should add the ideas expressed by Sechenov and almost simultaneous work carried out in Pavlov's laboratories. No unity of opinion prevailed among them, although this is not an unusual situation in any science, especially in psychology.

Bekhterev's contribution to the development of psychophysiology can be properly understood only from the perspective of his conception of psychology taken as a whole, and within the dynamics of its development. It is customary to distinguish five periods in his work:
– 1879–1888 – analysis of potential and limits of subjective psychology
– 1888–1904 – period of general psychobiology
– 1904–1910 – period of objective psychology
– 1910–1917 – period of psychoreflexology
– 1917–1927 – period of reflexology

Potential and limits of subjective psychology. Faced with practical medicine, Bekhterev, with his youthful interest in natural science (and particularly in biology), could not find sufficient answers to inevitable questions. This period culminated in his work "Consciousness and its Boundaries" (1888) where he indicated limitations to the widespread ideas about the psychical based on introspective approaches and metaphysics. The interaction between the field of consciousness and unconsciousness was not obvious. Taking "psyche" to be a unified whole of interacting consciousness and unconsciousness, having a "floating" boundary between them, was presented by Bekhterev from the position of an outside observer (i.e., who was outside the observed reality). During this early period of Bekhterev's search for a new psychology, the logic of his thought was called "cerebrocentrism" – answers to multiple questions about psychical activity are sought in the regularities of the brain's structure and functions. Consequently, behavioral (psychical) acts were primarily studied as the functions of the central nervous system. This led to a number of inconsistencies between the introspective and extraspective perspectives, stimulating further investigations.

General psychobiology. At this stage in the development of his ideas, Bekhterev's position can be characterized as a search for relationships between everything in the human organism, including anatomical and functional, as well as psychical, aspects. The starting point of this search is the same (the brain), while the psyche is increasingly referred to as the endpoint.

The development of these views is summarized in his monograph "Psyche and Life" (1st ed. 1902, 2nd ed. 1904). The title points to the problem of the relation between life and spirit, revealing the author's intention to bring psyche into the circle of the phenomena studied by natural science, and to relate the biological and the psychological within the framework of a new discipline: general psychobiology. The distinctive feature of this stage is a slow transformation of the psychophysiological problem into the psychophysical one. This may seem somewhat surprising because, as it was said before, the appearance of psychophysiology is usually associated with the principles of psychophysics. However, this apparent contradiction is not real. At the beginning of the 20th century, it became more and more obvious that the physiological can be reduced to the physical – the terms "physics" and "physiology" share the same root – and that, in essence, physiology can be considered as the physics of structures and processes of the living organism (this is biophysics in the modern sense of the word). Psychical and physiological (i.e. physical, material) processes are considered neither as parallel nor interacting processes, but as resulting from a single energy inherent in the world itself and inseparable from matter.

In general psychobiology, the entire internal world is presented as one of the manifestations of the general world energy. However, Bekhterev does not reduce subjective processes to passive internal reactions caused by external environmental influences. The nervous system is "the primary apparatus used (by animals) to relate to the environment," while psyche is the important and self-governing guiding factor, "the most important determinant of the relations between a living organism and its environment."

Thus, at the second stage in the development of Bekhterev's conception, the key problem is the study of relations in such complex system, as man. Bekhterev sees the future of psychology in its transformation to a new scientific discipline – general psychobiology.

Objective psychology. In 1904 Bekhterev came up with a plan to establish a Psychoneurological Institute, and in 1907 it was established. At the same time, he continued to develop his new psychology founded on criticism of the shortcomings of traditional, introspective psychology. He again exposed limitations to the method of self-observation, and returned to his earlier idea about two forms of the existence of psyche: subjective feelings and objective manifestations.

Bekhterev believed that the new objective psychology could be developed as an independent theoretical system free from traditional views about the psychical. This independence implies a prohibition against the use of psychological terms.

He sufficiently expanded the range of research beyond subjective psychology. This expansion encompassed not only psychical phenomena open to consciousness, but also unconscious ones; not only inner, subjective experiences, but also their external manifestations; not only the psychical itself, but also its biological bases. He still foresaw the future of the new psychology maintaining close relations to the natural sciences, considering it as their infant branch. The primary concept of objective psychology is that of neuropsychics (and for lower animals without a nervous system, biopsychics), which presupposed the solution for the physiological problem – the unity of psychical and physiological processes.

One cannot disregard how Bekhterev's description of neuropsychics is based on Sechenov's tripartite scheme: external stimulation (causing a centripetal impulse); central reaction; and a centrifugal impulse, together resulting in external action.

This system of objective psychology emphasizes the relation between external stimulus and external manifestation as mediated by past experience. Thus, the main difference between objective psychology and traditional subjective psychology is that the studied reality is seen from the point of view of an outside observer. This system covers all forms of interaction between the organism and the environment, and hence all kinds of activity of the living being from the simplest reflexes to the most complex psychological processes. Psychological study includes all sorts of relationships characterized by internal processing of external stimuli, which is mediated by past individual experience. From 1904 to 1910, Bekhterev's conception of objective psychology was set forth in a number of articles (including foreign publications) and most completely in the monograph "Objective psychology" (SPb, 1907).

Psychoreflexology. The fourth stage in Bekhterev's work lasted about eight years, and was not associated with any radical revision of his views. In one of the first articles written during this period, he almost identifies psychology with reflexology ("Osnovnye printsipy tak nazyvaemoi ob'ektivnoi psikhologii ili refleksologii" // Obozreniye Psikhiatrii, Neurologii i Experimentalnoi Psikhologii. 1910, No. 10–11 (*Basic principles of so called objective psychology or psychoreflexology // Review of Psychiatry, Neurology and Experimental Psychology*)).

A distinctive approach appears in a more explicit interpretation of neuro-psychic activity, defined during this stage "as a complex of reflexes of a higher order correlated to each other." Based on the reflex principle (mechanism) of psyche, he continued to describe the central part of the reflex in pure physiological terms, speaking of "intracentral nervous process" and "temporarily ceased" paths of associative reflexes.

Bekhterev, within the bounds of psychoreflexology, continued his work on the problem of personality (the "personal sphere") taking it to be "the main center of neuro-psychic activity, which underlies the active-independent relation of the living being to the environment."

Reflexology. The final period of Bekhterev's work was marked by the establishment, through his efforts, of the Institute for the Study of the Brain and Mental Activity. Its purpose was to make "a detailed study of human personality and the conditions of its normal development." Specifically, to undertake "(a) study of the brain and the whole nervous system, namely its structure in man and animals, its functions, nutrition, as well as biochemical processes, morbid neuro-psychic states, and the newest treatment methods, including serology and surgical neuropathology; (b) study of the various manifestations of human personality with reflexological methods, including infant, collective, pathological reflexology and bioreflexology; (c) study of the human personality with the methods of observation and experimental psychology, both general and individual; (d) study of different kinds of applied reflexology and psychology, such as pedagogical (including experimental psychology), professional (involving the study of neuropsychic organization of workers in connection with the choice of profession), legal, etc., as well as mental, school and nervous hygiene, and other allied fields of knowledge; (e) discussion of the results obtained in these fields at scientific conferences; and (f) carrying out collective research and preparing editions, when it was beyond the strength of one person."

Bekhterev emphasized that reflexology is the further development and extension of objective psychology. He defined its subject-matter as "the study of the organism's correlative activity in the wide sense of the word, and by correlative activity, we mean all the organism's inherited and individually acquired reactions, beginning from innate and complex-organic reflexes up to, and including, the most complex acquired reflexes, which in man go by the name of actions and comprise his characteristic behavior." Here Bekhterev's views are once again quite similar to those expressed by Sechenov in the article "Who must investigate the problems of Psychology, and How."

Bekhterev founded a large scientific school, so it is rather difficult to name all his pupils and followers. Research, medical, and educational institutions created by his efforts began following his intentions, but in time some of them took new directions which did not concur with Bekhterev's views. Among these are the departments of psychiatry at the University of Kazan, the Military-Medical Academy, and the Women's Medical Institute; psychophysiological laboratories in Kazan and Saint Petersburg; the Psychoneurological Institute; the Institute for the Study of the Brain and Mental Activity; the State Institute of Medical Knowledge; the State Reflexological Institute for the Study of Brain; the Institute of Moral Development; the Central Institute for the Study and Treatment of the Deaf-and-Dumb; the Oto-Phonetics Institute; and several more.

Currently, among independent scientific institutions, the Psychoneurological Institute n. a. Bekhterev and The Institute of The Human Brain n. a. Bekhtereva Russian Academy of Sciences, can be regarded as the direct successors in the development of Bekhterev's scientific ideas.

Bekhterev's views were quite different from those expressed within traditional psychology. To a certain degree, this forced the younger scientists close to him, such as A. F. Lazursky, M. Y. Basov, and V. N. Myasishchev, to discover and develop new approaches allowing them to explain principles needed for the objective study of psyche, as well as the wide variety of subjective states.

After Bekhterev's death, his work fell into oblivion for a long time. This neglect is often explained in the literature by political and ideological causes. In our opinion, this is highly unlikely. The story of his violent death enjoys no conclusive evidence. Pointing to personal conflicts among leading scientists makes matters more explicable. Sometimes these disputes are solved on a scientific basis, and occasionally, because of vanity or dishonesty, they get resolved with the aid of administrative and political mechanisms (similar to former times when the help of the church was recruited). Regardless of the actual causes for his eclipse, it is difficult to imagine Russian psychology, as well as psychology around the world, without the name of Bekhterev.

4 I. P. Pavlov (1849–1936)

Russian physiology of the 20th century is reasonably defined as "Pavlovian Physiology," due to the tremendous contributions made by him and his large scientific school to science, and owing to world recognition for his great services to physiology in particular. In 1935, at the Fifteenth International Physiological Congress, the British scientist G. Berger addressed Pavlov with these words: "I think there is no field in natural sciences where one person is so outstanding as you are in the field of physiology. You are undoubtedly princeps physiologorum mundi (the foremost physiologist in the world)."

A child of a Ryazan priest, Pavlov studied at the theological seminary. Breaking from the educational tradition of the Russian clergy, he entered Saint Petersburg University and took the course of the natural sciences in the Physics and Mathematics Department. Gradually he became more and more absorbed with physiology. In his third year of study he decided to devote himself entirely to this rapidly developing science. His favorite university teacher was an extremely unusual and contradictory person, professor I. F. Tsyon.

Having graduated from the University in a brilliant fashion, Pavlov obtained a position at the Department of Physiology (at that time headed by Tsyon) of the Medico-Surgical academy. At the same time he took his third year course at the Academy "not to become a physician, but to obtain the degree of doctor of medicine to have the right afterwards to a chair in physiology." After graduating from the Academy, he worked at the physiological laboratory of the eminent Russian physician S. P. Botkin for a long time. In 1883 he defended his dissertation on the centrifugal cardiac nerves and won a two-year sojourn abroad, during which he primarily worked at the laboratories of R. Heidenhain in Breslau and C. Ludwig in Leipzig.

A large part of Pavlov's work was devoted to the study of digestion, which was influenced by two circumstances. First, recognizing that the acute experimental approach suffers from limitations, Pavlov developed the chronic experimental method. The experimentalist, after a specially developed and carefully conducted operation, obtains an opportunity to study the operations of any section of the digestive tract on a healthy and active animal. Scientists from all over the world arrived at his laboratories to study this method. The second important circumstance was the idea of nervism, put forward by C. Bernard and assimilated by Pavlov in Botkin's laboratory, which considers the nervous system as the general mechanism of regulation of vital functions.

It was the study of digestion for which Pavlov – the first Russian scientist and the first physiologist in the world – was awarded the Nobel Prize in 1904, "in appreciation of his work on physiology of digestion, which has improved and enlarged our knowledge of important aspects of this field." Pavlov's successors continue studying this problem in many countries. At the same time, the methodology of nervism and the vast experimental data collected, along with his extraordinary power of observation and his inquiring mind, led Pavlov to the field of physiology, now well-known as the physiology of the higher nervous system. As data about the regulation of digestion accumulated, further observations were made, sufficiently explainable by the familiar theory of reflectory regulation. This led to a rapid but explicable change to the course of Pavlov's work as psychic activity became the subject of his research. He tackled the problem from the point of view of classical physiology, while avoiding terminology and methodology used by orthodox physiologists.

In the run-up to his next Nobel Prize Award, Pavlov was invited to deliver a speech at the International Medical Congress in Madrid in 1903. The audience expected to hear a summary report, or perhaps a speech devoted to his work on the physiology of digestion. Surprisingly, he presented a report on "Experimental psychology and psychopathology in animals." It should be noted that while not a professional psychologist, Pavlov aptly pointed out the strength of the experimental method for the study of psyche, including both normal and pathological states. It was very important for him as a physiologist to find an adequate biological model for solving the problems related to humanity. And he had found such a model in a dog, although not from the point of view of zoopsychology, but relating to the psychic activity of humans.

A new term, the "conditioned reflex," was used for the first time in this report. The conditioned reflex mechanism provided the basis for the study of the physiology of higher nervous activity. That is why the year 1903, to a certain extent, marks a beginning to the development of this field in physiology. Conditioned reflexes had been observed even earlier, in a sense, in Pavlov's laboratory. A previous section above notes how Bekhterev had discovered association reflexes. Previously, in 1898, this problem was studied by the American psychologist E. L. Thorndike. But it was Pavlov who used a purely physiological approach for the study of psychical activity. This dramatic alteration to his scientific aims aroused certain complications between him and his pupils, and some of them left his laboratory. At the same time, new collaborators appeared. For the rest of his life, Pavlov was primarily concerned with the problem of conditioning.

The legacy of his writings displays some peculiarities. Pavlov never published any fundamental monographs, and his views changed as new facts appeared, and even his terminology were modified as well. The evolution of his scientific views can be understood only through the consecutive study of his individual publications as they were composed. He obviously felt that this was important, so he published a two-volume collection of articles and placed them in chronological order. Thanks to fortunate circumstances, his famous work "Twenty Years Experience in Objective Study of Higher Nervous Activity (Behavior) of Animals" appeared in 1923, and went through six editions during his life. In the introduction to the last edition in 1936, he wrote: "Physiology, pathology with therapy of cortex of the brain and psychology with its practical applications start to join, to merge, so that they become the same field of scientific work, and, judging by the results, to their mutual benefit."

For the sake of objectivity, it should be noted that this merger was not easy; we will return later to this point. For twenty years after the death of the founder of the physiology of higher nervous activity, psychology was gradually replaced by physiology, even though Pavlov himself thought well of psychology. This situation resulted in a notable distance separating these fields of science, down to the present day.

The term "physiology of higher nervous activity" did not enter into usage all at once, and its formal semantics slightly changed through the course of time. Yet there remained an emphasis that it was centrally a matter of physiology, using its natural scientific methodology and objective experimental methods. The "psychic" was defined as higher nervous activity or behavior in this context. In 1906, Pavlov introduced the notion of "scientific study of the so-called psychical processes in the higher animals." Later he wrote: "this real activity of the cerebral hemispheres and of the nearest subcortex, which ensures normal complex relations between the organism as a whole and the external world, must be rightly considered and denoted as *higher nervous activity*, the external behavior of the animal, instead of 'psychical' as it was termed previously; it should be distinguished from the activity of other parts of the brain and of the spinal cord, which are mainly in charge of the correlations and integration of separate parts of the organism; this activity should be termed the lower nervous activity." This report was read at the Fourteenth International Congress in Rome on 2 September 1932. A more general definition is also used: "higher nervous (psychic) activity is the development of new behavior forms and the establishment of new relations between the organism and the environment." His "Lectures on the Work of the Cerebral Hemisphere" were devoted to the same subject, going through three editions. They represent his revised lectures, read before medical and scientific audiences in 1924.

It is unsurprising that his first step in the study of higher nervous activity was to make more precise investigations into its exact mechanisms and their laws. The term "conditioned reflex," coined by Pavlov in 1903, quickly came into use. Conditioned reflexes differ greatly from the well-known inborn reflexes; the latter, due to their constancy and genetic conditionality, were defined by Pavlov as unconditioned reflexes (similar to Sechenov's view). At the initial stage of study, the best-known works on the subject, apart from the above mentioned Madrid report, were "The Psychical Secretion of the Salivary Glands" (published in French in 1904), his Nobel lecture "The First Sure Steps along the Path of a New Investigation" (1904), "Scientific Study of the So-Called Psychical Processes in the Higher Animals" (1906), "Natural Science and the Brain" (1909), and a few others from the later period. In the last of these articles, the idea of the mechanisms of the physiology of higher nervous activity was formulated. To the end of his life, Pavlov commitment to this idea grew stronger, and it was further developed by his pupils and followers.

He wrote: "Every activity of the higher level of the nervous system which I have newly discovered, I have represented as two basic nervous mechanisms: first the mechanism of *temporary connection* (italics mine. – V. I.), the temporary closing of conducting circuits, as it were, between phenomena of the external world and the responses of the animal organism to them, and second, the mechanism of analyzers." The term "temporary connection," used here for the first time, has the same meaning as "conditioned reflex," because it is this connection that forms the basis of the mechanism of conditioned reflex. All aspects of psychical, adaptive activity, in all its manifestations, received treatment in light of these two mechanisms.

The *conditioned reflex* became defined as the nervous reflectory reaction of the whole organism to the factors of external and internal environment developed in the process of individual activity. The biological importance of the conditioned reflex appears primarily in its ability to provide a higher level of adaptation by the organism to various factors of its environment. Everyday observations show that environmental factors vary in their importance to vital activity, as well as in their intensity and temporal parameters. A stereotyped reaction alone cannot provide adequate behavior under such changing conditions. Even the most complex instincts are highly conservative, and do not always provide complete adequacy. Observations, under both natural and artificial experimental conditions, provide innumerable examples of the variability in reactions.

This feature reflects essential differences between the conditioned and unconditioned reflexes, namely:
– An unconditioned reflex is an inborn mechanism, so it is a specific feature, while a conditioned reflex is an individual feature, peculiar for a given individual.

- An unconditioned reflex is a mechanism which remains unchanged (at least in quality) for life or for a certain period of time, while a conditioned reflex exists until one or another environmental factor has an informative biological importance, so it can disappear temporarily or permanently.
- A conditioned reflex, being phenotypic by nature, is formed under certain conditions (hence it is 'conditioned') that will be specified in what follows.
- A conditioned reflex is formed with the participation of the higher levels of the central nervous system, while the simplest unconditioned reflex involves only the spinal cord. That is why Pavlov studied the regularities of the activity of the brain with the help of conditioned reflexes.

Taking into account these differences, it is rather clear that each representative of a certain species of animals has a strictly defined set of unconditioned reflexes, which is among distinguishing features of species. The set of conditioned reflexes has no restrictions, neither in quantity nor in quality, and reflects various forms of adaptive behavior.

It was established in Pavlov's laboratories that all reflexes, in spite of their variety, have a similar functional structure. It is customary to distinguish the following components of a conditioned reflex.

1. The base, on which a conditioned reflex is formed, is an unconditioned reflex, which is often defined as reinforcement in certain literature. Any unconditioned reflex can be such a base under certain conditions that will be discussed later. This characteristic is connected with the idea that, in highly organized animals, all unconditioned reflexes have morpho-functional representation in higher levels of the central nervous system, including the cortex (i.e., those brain structures, where association function is well represented). Factors within the external or internal environment, resulting in an unconditional response, are defined as the *unconditioned stimulus*. It follows that a conditioned reflex can be formed for any reaction. Given that nearly all functions of the organism have unconditional regulation, it can be stated that all functions – conscious and unconscious, voluntary and involuntary – have psychic regulation. This is evidenced within the extremely broad experience of practical medicine, as well as by many ceremonial rituals, yielding events denoted as special (altered) states of consciousness. These properties are inborn and constant in their basic biological essence.

2. The component defined as the unconditioned stimulus is ambiguous in its physical and biological essence. It can be almost any factor to the external or internal environment that, due to its natural modality (its type of energy) and under sufficient intensity, may be perceived by

one or another sensory system of the organism and cause a rapidly fading orientation response. Since such a factor lacks sufficient biological importance, it simply is a neutral stimulus at the initial stage of conditioning. However, under a set of certain conditions – primarily when an unconditioned stimulus is repeatedly combined with action – this factor becomes its signal, and a conditioned stimulus arises. Depending on how it is perceived by one or another sensory (afferent) system, the inborn morpho-functional structures (up to the level of cortex) are also utilized in this process (the *cortical representation of the afferent system of the conditioned stimulus*).

3. Another component that is newly formed during conditioning is the *temporary connection*. It should be considered as the principal element of the mechanism of the conditioned reflex, because there is no exaggeration in treating it as the key stage in the development of new forms of behavior and adaptation. The localization of the neurophysiological mechanisms of temporary connection plays a leading role in the problem of conditioned reflexes. A large number of works have been devoted to these mechanisms, both in our country and abroad, especially those from the laboratories developing Pavlov's ideas for the study of psychical (i.e. higher) nervous activity and accepting conditioned reflex as the basic mechanism.

As it has been said, this conditioning is possible under certain conditions. That is why the term "conditioned reflex" was coined, though other variants have also been suggested (for example, Bekhterev used the term "association reflex"). These conditions are as follows:

1. The animal should be in a state of passive wakefulness. Active wakefulness and sleep make it difficult or impossible to form the necessary temporary connection (i.e., the conditioned reflex).
2. The animal should be in a state of sensory isolation. Any stimuli from the external or internal environment (including conditions of organs and any diseases) should be excluded. To achieve such complete isolation, special "towers of silence" were built by Pavlov's project in the Institute of Experimental Medicine. Experimental animals were exposed to only two kinds of stimuli – the unconditioned stimuli and selected neutral stimuli – and during the later stages of conditioning the latter receives the label of the conditioned stimulus. These sharply limited conditions aroused the complaint that Pavlov's reflexes are only artificial and impossible under real conditions of life, where too many secondary stimuli are present. However, this objection has been rejected by further

experiments. Life itself provides evidence that conditioned reflexes are also formed under conditions of unrestricted behavior.

3. A neutral stimulus will achieve the significance of conditioned stimulus, if the beginning of its action precedes the unconditioned stimulus. This so-called "delaying" can last from tenths of seconds to dozens of seconds, depending on the biological character of the conditioned reflex.

4. Stimulus strength is also important. The physiological strength of a conditioned stimulus must be weaker than that of the unconditioned stimulus. Since we usually deal with polymodal stimulation, "strength" here means the intensity of the excitation process.

5. The neutral stimulus becomes a signal (i.e., the conditioned stimulus) after repeated combined stimulation (under the given temporal relation). The number of such combinations varies in a wide range – from one to many combinations – yet they all depend on a few factors. The first is the biological importance of reinforcement. Food and defense reflexes (as well as sexual reflexes during stages of life) are the quickest of all reflexes. The second factor, connected with the first, is the level of excitation of the centers of unconditioned reflexes. For example, the process of conditioning in a hungry animal requires far less time than in a fed animal. The third factor is the degree of "naturalness" of the connection between stimuli considered. In particular, a reflex to the smell of food (initially, at their initial combination, smell is a neutral stimulus) can be formed at the very first combination, while lights and sounds (and so forth) require a greater number of combinations.

6. The duration to preservation of a conditioned reflex depends on the regularity of reinforcement. If reinforcement is not provided for a long time, the result will be the disappearance (inhibition) of the reflex, although its restoration requires far fewer combinations than those first establishing it.

The temporary or permanent disappearance (i.e. inhibition) of conditioned reflexes is an important feature. Pavlov was concerned with this problem for nearly thirty years; ongoing investigations continue in laboratories in Russia and abroad. Nevertheless, in spite of this intense work, we cannot say that all problems are solved in this field at the present time. It is no mere chance that Pavlov once called inhibition the "accursed problem of physiology." It can be stated that its phenomenology, its regularities, and certain kinds of inhibition have been explained carefully and convincing. But scientists cannot always manage to describe them by neurophysiologic mechanisms understood at the present time. In truth, there is no unity of opinion, or even of terminology, between theoretical and methodical approaches.

We next describe Pavlov's basic views on inhibition, which was understood by him as the weakening or entire disappearance of conditioned reflexes, as well as the temporary delay of the response to a conditioned stimulus. Pavlov used two determinants as the criteria for classification of inhibition of conditioned reflexes. The first was the localization of the process that caused inhibition in relation to the components of a conditioned reflex, permitting him to distinguish external from internal inhibition. The second determinant was the necessity attached to forming an inhibitory effect. He distinguished unconditioned inhibition, which is formed after the first act inducing its development, and conditioned inhibition, which requires a number of combinations. Terms used here are consonant with the terms "unconditioned reflex" and "conditioned reflex," and this situation can cause semantic confusions and errors.

The external inhibition of conditioned reflexes, in Pavlov's opinion, occurs when another stimulus is introduced besides the unconditioned and conditioned stimuli. This additional stimulus (a 'distractor' in short) is responsible, depending on its physiological strength, for the constant or gradually fading inhibition. From the neurophysiological point of view, this kind of inhibition is based on simultaneous or successive negative induction, caused by formation of an excitation focus, which emerges from additional inhibition (in essence becoming an orienting reflex).

Conditioned (internal) inhibition is evidenced by the following phenomena:
– Extinction is observed when a conditioned stimulus is not followed by reinforcement. If reinforcement does not occur for a long time, then the initial conditioned response gradually weakens to the point of disappearance (acute extinction). If this situation is not repeated, the conditioned reflex resumes after a while. Chronic extinction is much more effective. It develops when a conditioned stimulus is repeatedly applied without reinforcement. The conditioned stimulus then becomes neutral again.
– Differential inhibition is manifested where the response, at the initial stage of the conditioned reflex, appears not only with the conditioned stimulus, but also in response to the stimuli closely allied to it. With the course of time the animal develops the ability to distinguish even slight differences.
– Delay is noted when, by increasing the duration between the conditioned stimulus and its reinforcement, the beginning of the conditioned-reflex response is delayed to an extent essentially impossible during the initial development of the reflex.
– Conditioned inhibition is characterized by the introduction of a new stimulus with negative signal meaning (the so-called "negative conditioned reflex").

Mechanisms of conditioned inhibition are connected with the regularities of the forming and functioning of temporary connections, which will be addressed below.

One phenomenon was considered separately – a so-called "transmarginal inhibition" – in which there is the weakening or absence of a conditional response to an overwhelming conditioned stimulus. Due to its biological importance, this kind of inhibition was regarded by Pavlov as protective, that is, as protecting the respective structures from the "overexcitation." This can be clearer if we look at the pessimum described by N. E. Vvedensky (1852–1922), a phenomenon that has received convincing neurophysiologic treatment. Transmarginal inhibition can be classified as unconditioned due to its development, and also as internal due to its localization.

Pavlov separately emphasized sleep inhibition, and he distinguished two kinds of sleep: passive sleep as a result of partial or complete depression of afferent signaling; and active sleep based on internal inhibition.

Pavlov and his successors have developed a detailed classification of conditioned reflexes according to their most significant criteria:

1. The biological importance of the response: food, defense, sexual reflexes, etc.
2. The degree of "naturalness" of the connection to real conditions of life, natural and artificial (see examples given above). There was even an opinion that a natural conditioned reflex was a transitional form to an inherent unconditioned reflex. What is the difference between salivation to the taste of food or to its smell? However, in general, Pavlov denied that conditioned reflexes could be inherited.
3. The character of response: secretory, motor, vascular, respiratory, and other effector reactions.
4. Positive and negative: the former appear during development or strengthening of any reaction, while the latter appear during its weakening or ceasing. At the time, the idea of the active nature of inhibition had already been in use.
5. The afferent structure receiving the conditioned stimulus: the exteroceptive, interoceptive, and proprioceptive reflexes and their variations. The word "reflex" as used here has been distinguished as applicable only to human beings.

Furthermore, a number of other criteria can be used for classification of conditioned reflexes, such as the complicity of the conditioned stimulus, the temporary relation between signal and reinforcement, the complicity of the temporary connection, etc.

Based on the works of the Polish physiologist J. Konorski, the notion has appeared that in instrumental conditioned reflexes (reflexes of type 2), a definite (usually motor) reaction to the conditioned stimulus is the requirement for reinforcement, as opposed to traditional conditioned reflexes (reflexes of type 1), in which reinforcement is given whether the conditional response is present or not.

For thirty years Pavlov studied the regularities of higher nervous activity nearly exclusively in dogs, a traditional experimental animal in physiology. In later years, to approach his initial aim to the study regularities of the higher nervous system in humans, he became absorbed by objective investigation of anthropoid (chimpanzee) behavior. He identified many interesting facts that could be interpreted from the point of view of psychic evolution.

The famous "Pavlov's Wednesdays" were popular among physicians, as well as physiologists. At these colloquiums, clinical analysis of patients was combined with the physiological analysis of symptomatology. It is notable that Pavlov once said that a patient is an experiment set up by life itself.

These and other materials allowed him to stress the following features of conditional activity in humans:

1. In most animals, only one stimulus can take a signal meaning (conditioned reflexes of the first kind); in "clever" dogs there may be a sequence of two stimuli (conditioned reflexes of the second kind); while in great apes three or four stimuli can be involved; while in humans the number of stimuli connected in one signal chain is almost unbounded, which makes his adaptive and cognitive abilities practically unlimited. This mechanism is one of the components for a fundamentally higher intellectual level in humanity.

2. Human conditioned reflexes are more flexible and variable, and they can disappear and be restored, again indicating a higher level of adaptive behavior in humans, since such reflexes take into account a wider variety of signal stimuli in combination with their subjective critical estimation.

3. The most essential feature of human conditional activity is the unique ability to perceive the signal meaning of a natural factor when it is modified by words. This is closely connected with Pavlov's theory of signal systems of reality as a physiological foundation for the higher mental functions peculiar to humans: those of thinking and speech.

In more detailed considerations, additional features of human conditional activity can be emphasized, closely connected with the peculiarity of perceptual and mnestic (memory) processes, neurophysiologic mechanisms, and with the influence of social factors.

The nature of the mechanisms of a temporary connection is a question of particular pertinence in the problem of the conditioned reflex. The temporary connection is a component that regulates conditioning; it is a phenotypic element of the organism. After various experiments, Pavlov concluded that a temporary connection was the function of the cortex exclusively. Experiments with the removal of the cortex showed how all previously developed conditioned reflexes disappeared, and new conditioned reflexes could not be developed. This paradigm survived for a long time after Pavlov's death. One of his successors, N. Y. Belenkov (1917–1985) used a refined neurosurgical technique to "switch off" (temporarily and reversibly) different structures of the brain, convincingly showing how a temporary connection is the result of integrative activity of many brain structures, having specific roles in the processing of information and structural-functional abilities for providing associative cooperation. A highly relevant idea here is the mechanism of dominance (A. A. Ukhtomsky, 1923), providing initial connections between the cortical projections of reinforcement and afferent systems of the conditioned stimulus. Currently, this material is supplemented by data concerning the cellular, molecular, and neurochemical components to analytical-synthetic brain activity.

As stated earlier, Pavlov thought that higher nervous activity was based on two mechanisms: conditioned reflexes and analyzers. In this context, the term "analyzer" was coined to designate the morpho-functional units responsible for reception of parameters of the external and internal environment, for encoding received information, and for conducting it to the structures that provide the analysis of the biological importance of these factors for an appropriate behavioral reaction. It is clear that this term is semantically similar to such notions as "organs of senses" (in the wide sense of the term), "afferent systems," and "sensory systems," and that its literal translation can lead to misunderstandings.

Pavlov developed a conception of the signal systems of life (1932) on the basis of his teachings on conditioned reflexes. The first signal system indicates the response through the direct reception of a signal stimulus. The second signal system refers to the response to the signal meaning, when the actual stimulus is replaced by a word designating it. He considered the second signal system as the foundation for speech and thinking, and demonstrated this idea using a large basis of clinical material. However, the use of this term leads to many common and theoretical complications. It was noted earlier, in Bekhterev's comments, that words can have different signal meanings, and a formal substitution of a fact by a word might result in rather conflicting theoretical conclusions. The outstanding Russian writer and Pavlov's contemporary, Leo Tolstoy, put it this way: "The only means of mental intercourse between men is by words, and for this intercourse to be possible words have to be used so as to evoke in everybody a corresponding and definite meaning."

Another traditional part of psychology concerns individualizing features of people. These features have been studied for thousands of years, so it must be difficult to mention many ideas on the topic. Pavlov's contribution to the development of this issue is widely known. He based his typology of mental (higher nervous) activity on the parameters of the main nervous processes – excitation and inhibition – yielding specific features of strength, balance, and mobility, estimated by the peculiarities of development and the course of conditioned reflexes. He distinguished the following types (using Hippocrates's terms):

1. Strong, balanced, mobile – vivacious (sanguine temperament)
2. Strong, balanced, inert – quiet, inert (phlegmatic temperament)
3. Strong, unbalanced, with predominance of the excitation process – unrestrained (choleric temperament)
4. Weak – (melancholic temperament)

Later two additional features were added by the Russian psychologists B. M. Teplov and V. D. Nebylitsyn: dynamism – the speed and the facility of formation of temporary connection, and lability – the speed of excitation and inhibition.

Pavlov was not fully satisfied with the basic classification, thinking that there are many intermediate types apart from the four main types. A new approach was developed by V. K. Krasusky (1955) which distinguishing four levels of strength, three levels of balance, and ten levels of mobility. This allowed him to construct an individual identifying "passport" for each animal.

Although the types of higher nervous activity are largely determined by genetics (a genotype), its manifestation is influenced by a great variety of factors (a phenotype). Pavlov stressed that this principle extends to humanity, and he wrote about types that were common for animals and humans. Yet at the same time he distinguished purely human types according to which signal system predominates for an individual. Individuals with greater expression of the second signal system, favoring abstract thinking, were referred to the thinking type. Those having a highly-developed first signal system, favoring visual thinking, were referred to as the artistic type. However, he noted that most people belong to a moderate middle type. This typology has been widely used in applied physiology, medicine, psychology, and agriculture.

The main concepts of Pavlov's teachings became the foundation for the study of other problems concerning analytical-synthetic activity of the brain, attention, emotions, learning, memory, consciousness, behavior, pathology of mental activity, etc. It would be difficult if not impossible to find a larger scientific school in the history of world science than Pavlov's school. The staff of his own laboratories was rather small, but he was connected with a vast number of non-staff personnel in Russia, as well as researchers in other countries. During the period from the 1880s until 1936, about two hundred and fifty specialists worked successfully in Pavlov's laboratories (for more details see (Kvasov and Fedorova-Grot 1967)).

Pavlov's school produced many outstanding physiologists who established their own scientific schools, and directed university departments, laboratories, and research institutes. Because it is rather difficult to compare their scientific services, their names can only be listed alphabetically here: P. K. Anokhin, G. V. Anrep, E. A. Asratyan, B. P. Babkin, D. A. Biryukov, V. N. Boldyrev, K. M. Bykov, V. N. Chernigovsky, G. V. Folbort, A. G. Ivanov-Smolensky, N. I. Krasnogorsky, E. M. Kreps, A. N. Krestovnikov, P. S. Kupalov, F. P. Maiorov, L. A. Orbeli, I. P. Razenkov, and others.

Some of Pavlov's close pupils headed research centers around the world. L. B. Popielski chaired a department at the old University of Krakow beginning in 1905; G. V. Anrep headed the physiology department of the largest Arab University in Egypt for nearly a quarter of a century beginning in 1931; B. P. Babkin worked as research professor of physiology at McGill University in Montreal, Canada, beginning in 1928; and J. Ten-Cate was connected with the University of Amsterdam in The Netherlands beginning in 1920. Some specialists from abroad who visited Pavlov's laboratories at various times should also be mentioned: J. Konorski and S. Miller (Poland), W. H. Gantt (USA), M. Mixa and Zd. Mysliveček (Czechoslovakia), H. Ishikawa and T. Hayashi (Japan), E. D. Cathcart (UK), R. Luman (China), B. Lönnquist (Sweden), and M. Minkowski (Switzerland). Pavlov's scientific school could rightly be viewed as international.

Many research institutions for the study of general physiology, as well as the physiology of the nervous system and higher nervous activity, were established under Pavlov's supervision and active participation. Their structure and names changed many times during the last hundred years, but the spirit of Pavlov's approach to physiology remained constant. Particularly, in 1890, the Institute of Experimental Medicine was created, and Pavlov was asked to chair it; having little interest in administrative work, he refused this offer. However, he worked intensively at this institution until his death in 1936. The Institute was his primary experimental and research base, where he studied the problems in physiology of digestion and questions of mental activity. In 1926 the biological station of this Institute was opened in Koltushi, near Leningrad. Pavlov called it "the capital of conditioned reflexes." The study of genetics of higher nervous activity was carried out there for some time despite later ideological conflicts, especially after World War II.

Pavlov chaired the Physiological Laboratory at the St. Petersburg Academy of Sciences beginning in 1907. After a series of transformations it became the I. P. Pavlov Physiological Institute of the Russian Academy of Sciences. Now it is the largest multidisciplinary research institution in Russia, located in Saint-Petersburg, with a main base in Koltushi. The Institute of Comparative Physiology of Higher Nervous Activity of the USSR Academy of Sciences was established in 1939. The Institute of Higher Nervous Activity and a number of other research institutions were founded in Moscow in 1950 (Bekhtereva 1988) (Langue 1997).

The relationship between Pavlov and political authorities became complicated after the October Revolution of 1917. Like the majority of Russian intellectuals, he did not accept the Revolution. He had several offers from abroad that promised to provide all the necessary conditions for his scientific work, so he applied to the authorities for permission to leave Russia. He was not permitted to go abroad for permanent residence, but V. I. Lenin, having understood the importance of Pavlov's work, signed the Decree of the Council of People's Commissars of 24 January 1921, "Concerning the conditions ensuring the research work of Academician I. P. Pavlov and his associates." It was decreed: "To authorize the State Publishers to print, in the best printing-house, a deluxe edition of the scientific work prepared by Academician Pavlov, summing up the results of his research over the past twenty years, leaving to Academician I. P. Pavlov the right of property in this work in Russia and abroad." Despite the serious economic and political situation in the country, all seized property and money, including a golden Nobel medal, were returned to him, excellent life conditions were created for his family, and his laboratories were provided with all necessary equipment. He was permitted to visit foreign countries without any limitation. For the last 15 years of his life, Pavlov lived in the most comfortable conditions possible, and sustained relationships with a wide scientific community. While acknowledging his special situation in public addresses, he often criticized the new communist government.

Pavlov has become a symbol of Soviet science. It is impossible to overestimate his contribution. He was an objective, self-critical, and honest researcher, and he had leadership characters combined with his choleric temperament. These circumstances, to a great degree, influenced the circle of his associates. This became especially evident after his death. As a famous scientist, Pavlov, in a sense, was canonized. Some of his concepts were regarded as dogmas, detracting from the scientific development of psychology.

The Scientific Session of the USSR Academy of Sciences and the USSR Academy of Medical Sciences in 1950 concerning on the physiological teachings of academician I. P. Pavlov had a dramatic impact. All leading representatives of Soviet physiology and allied sciences participated in this session. Those researchers who avoided a dogmatic conception of Pavlov's teachings and developed original approaches received severe criticism and censure, soon followed by serious staffing changes. After this, only a small number of researchers remained faithful to objective experimental physiology, and, to be honest, this fidelity would be impossible without the international integration of scientific knowledge.

As a general rule, this situation has been viewed from an ideological and political standpoint. Nevertheless, the author of this article holds a different opinion. It is correct that among the Soviet leadership there was no one able to give an objective and convincing appraisal of the current state of physiology, as well as of genetics, cybernetics, literature, and art. Some consultants and experts were selected who, through their corruption and dishonesty, constructed a so-called "scientific" indictment. The political situation in the USSR changed course somewhat thereafter, but the consultants and experts remained the same, though their views gradually began to alter.

Not long after this 1950 Session, a governmental order decreed that psychology (then a taboo term in Russia) should be taught only by physiologists. Departments of physiology of higher nervous activity were set up at universities across the country, while scientific demagogues actively participated in this process. Strangely, a resolution by J. V. Stalin later followed: "Physiology is physiology, and psychology is psychology." The academic situation began to improve slowly, but even now it cannot be considered resolved, because, along with the serious neurophysiologic investigations of psychic processes and significant works on psychological laws, the bridge between them, namely psychophysiology, has not been properly built.

References

Alexandrov, Y. I., ed. 1997. *Foundations of Psychophysiology. A Textbook.* Moscow: INFRA-M.

Asratyan, E. A., and I. V. Pavlov. 1981. *Life, Work, the Present State of the Doctrine.* Moscow: Nauka.

Bekhterev, V. M. 1903–1907. *Foundations of Knowledge About the Functions of the Brain.* 2 vols. St. Petersburg.

Bekhterev, V. M. 1909. *The Tasks and Method of Objective Psychology*. St. Petersburg.

Bekhterev, V. M. 1926. *General Foundations of the Reflexology of Man*, 3rd ed. Petrograd.

Bekhterev, V. M. 1999. *Selected Works on Psychology of Personality*. Saint Petersburg: Aletheia.

Bekhtereva, N. P., ed. 1988. *Physiological Sciences in the USSR: Establishment, Development, and Perspectives*. Moscow: Nauka.

Beliaeva, V. S. 2007. "Sergeĭ Petrovich Botkin – founder of physiological school in Russian medicine (to 175th anniversary of birthday)." *Eksperimental'naija i Klinicheskaija Gastroenerologiija* 5: 152–154.

Bernard, C. 1865/1927. *An Introduction to the Study of Experimental Medicine*. Trans. H. C. Greene. London: Macmillan & Co.

Danilova, N. N. 1998. *Psychophysiology: A Textbook for Students*. Moscow: Aspect Press.

Doty, R. W. 1963. "Higher Nervous Activity." *Joint Pavlov Conference of the New York Academy of Sciences and the Academy of Medical Sciences of the USSR*, 121. Moscow: Medgiz.

Graham, L. R. 1987. *Science, Philosophy, and Human Behavior in the Soviet Union*. New York: Columbia University Press.

Kukuev, L. A. 1971. "The classic work of V. M. Bekhterev: Conduction pathways of the brain and spinal cord on the 75th anniversary of its publication." *Zhurnal Nevrologii i Psikhiatrii Imeni S S Korsakova* 71, no. 9: 1397–1400.

Kvasov, D. G., and L. K. Fedorova-Grot. 1967. *Physiological School of I. P. Pavlov. Portraits and Characteristics of his Collaborators and Students*. Leningrad: Nauka.

Langue, K. A. 1997. *Physiological Sciences in Russia (19th–20th centuries): Studies on History*. Saint Petersburg: I. P. Pavlov Physiological Society.

Mikhailovich, I., and I. M. Sechenov. 1973. *Biographical Sketch and Essays*. New York: Arno Press.

Newell, F. W. 1989. "Franciscus Cornelis Donders (1818–1889)." *American Journal of Ophthalmology* 107, no. 6: 691–693.

Pavlov, I. P. 1950. *Scientific Session on the Physiological Teachings of Academician Ivan P. Pavlov: June 28–July 4, 1950*. Moscow: USSR Academy of Sciences Press.

Purpura, D. P. 1965. *Abstracts of Reports at the International Conference Devoted to the 100th Anniversary of the Publication of I. M. Sechenov's Work "Reflexes of the Brain"*. Moscow: Nauka.

Sechenov, I. M. 1863/1970. *Reflexes of the Brain*. Trans. S. Bell. Cambridge, Mass.: MIT Press.

Sechenov, I. M. 1873/1935a. "Elements of thought." In *Selected Works*, ed. I. M. Sechenov, 401–498. Moscow: State Publishing House for Biological and Medical Literature.

Sechenov, I. M. 1873/1935b. "Who must investigate the problems of psychology, and how." In *Selected Works*, ed. I. M. Sechenov, 337–391. Moscow: State Publishing House for Biological and Medical Literature.

Sechenov, I. M., I. P. Pavlov, and N. S. Vvedensky. 1952. *Physiology of Nervous System. Selected Works*. Moscow: Medizdat.

Sokolov, E. N. 1970. *Physiology of Higher Nervous Activity*. Moscow: Nauka.

Sokolov, E. N. 1995. "Vector psychophysiology." *Psychologicheskii Zhurnal* 16, no. 4–5.

Spondylitis, N. P. 1989. *Essays on the History of Psychophysiology of Higher Nervous Activity in the USSR*. Leningrad: Nauka.

Ukhtomsky, A. A. 1900. *Teachings on the Dominant and Modern Neurophysiology: Collection of Scientific Papers*. Leningrad: Nauka.

Vvedensky, N. E. 1901. *Excitation, Inhibition and Anesthesia*. St. Petersburg.

Yaroshevsky, M. G. 1968. *Ivan Mikhailovich Sechenov*. Leningrad: Nauka.

CHAPTER 3

Systemic Psychophysiology

Yuri I. Alexandrov

1 Summary

The objectives of this chapter are as follows: (1) provide a survey of systemic representations in psychophysiology rooted in the theory of functional systems (TFS); (2) compare dynamic representations at different stages of development of TFS with advancements in the world scientific community; (3) describe a systemic solution to the psychophysiological problem, and associated with it, of the consciousness and emotion problems; (4) compare systemic structures of subjective experience and culture; and (5) highlight features of Russian science and discuss their cultural specificity.

2 Theory of Functional Systems (TFS)

A considerable contribution to development of systemic representations in psychology and neuroscience has been made by the works of the V. B. Shvyrkov Laboratory of Neural Bases of Mind, Institute of Psychology of the Russian Academy of Sciences. This institute was created in 1972, with the active assistance of TFS founder, P. K. Anokhin, for research in fundamental problems of psychophysiology. TFS is the theoretical basis for laboratory research by specialists constituting the core of "Systemic Psychophysiology," which has been acknowledged to be one of the leading scientific schools in Russia.

Why did P. K. Anokhin's theory, which was originally formulated to solve problems in physiology, turn out to be such an effective theoretical basis (see in detail Alexandrov and Druzhinin 1998), and its founder P. K. Anokhin, a recognized leader in physiology, become considered among the giants in psychology (Cole and Cole 1971)? What is the difference between TFS and other variants of the systemic approach, and what determines the special value of TFS for psychology?

The idea of a system-forming factor was developed in TFS and confines the degrees of freedom of the elements of a system, thereby creating order in their interactions. This concept is generalizable across systems and enables analysis of quite different objects and situations. The system-forming factor is a product of systems and has a beneficial effect in the adaptation of an organism to its environment. Furthermore, it is *not past events – or stimuli related to them, but future events and their results* that determine behavior, from a TFS point of view.

How can a result that will occur in the future help determine current activity, and be its cause? P. K. Anokhin solved this "time paradox" using the future result model wherein an aim acts as the determinant, with a corresponding action result acceptor forming before the actual result and containing its predictable parameters. Anokhin thereby eliminates the contradiction between causal and teleological descriptions of behavior, making the latter acceptable even for "causalists" who believe that science deals only with causality and not explanation, and that no law is possible that does not address causality (Bunge 1962).

TFS assumes that to understand an individual's activity, the "functions" of separate organs or brain structures as traditionally understood (i.e., as immediate functions of this or that substrate, including the nervous system – the sensory, motor, and motivational functions, etc.) should not be the narrow objects of study, but instead the organization of holistic individual-and-environment interrelations involved in obtaining a particular result. Considering *function* in regard to the achievement of a result, P. K. Anokhin provided the following definition of a *functional* system: The idea of "system" is applicable only to complexes of selectively engaged components whose interaction and mutual interrelations enables the mutual cooperation of components aimed at obtaining a beneficial result. This "systemic" function cannot be localized. It is apparent only with the organism as a whole.

According to TFS, associations between elements of an organism are structurally embedded within mechanisms such as afferent synthesis, decision-making, action result acceptors (the apparatus for predicting parameters of future results), and action programs. These mechanisms provide the organization and realizations of the system (for more detail, see Anokhin 1973).

3 Systemic Psychophysiology

Long-term studies in the V. B. Shvyrkov Laboratory shaped a system-evolutionary approach (Shvyrkov 2006) and a new branch of learning: *systemic psychophysiology*. One of the most important landmark results was a systemic solution of the psychophysiological problem. Its essence is as follows. Mental processes characterizing an organism and its behavior act as a whole, and neurophysiological processes operating as separate elements are comparable only through information systems processes, that is, processes by which elementary mechanisms are organized within a functional system. In other words, mental phenomena cannot be compared directly with the localized elementary physiological phenomena (as in traditional psychophysiology), but only with those underlying their organization. Thus *psychological and physiological descriptions of behavior and activity are descriptions of the same system processes.*

The proposed solution of the psychophysiological problem avoids: (1) decoupling of mental and physiological, as the mental appears as a product of the organization of physiological processes in the system; (2) parallelism, as system processes concern the organization of elementary physiological processes; and (3) interaction, as the mental and physiological are both aspects of uniform system processes.

The systemic solution of the psychophysiological problem can be compared with neutral monism by Hegel (Priest 1987), according to which the spiritual and physical are two aspects of underlying reality, and comparable to a two-aspect theory (Chalmers 1995), according to which physical (brain processes) and mental are considered as two base aspects of "*some* information state." Priest (1987) claims that neutral monism and the two-aspects principle have one very important advantage: they are not subject to the disadvantages inherent to other solutions to the psychophysiological problem. However, they have one grave disadvantage in that the resulting conjectures tend to be vague. The systemic solution avoids this disadvantage. It is based upon definable information systems processes which may be studied through experimental studies (see, for example, Anokhin 1975; Shvyrkov 1990).

The proposed solution to the psychophysiological problem delivers psychology from the reduction of mental phenomena to the physiological that appears in traditional psychophysiology, which directly compares mental and physiological processes. The resulting emphasis within system psychophysiology is placed upon the study of patterns of systems formation and realization, their taxonomy, and the dynamics between system relations in behavior, as opposed to traditional psychophysiology which emphasizes study of the physiological correlates of mental processes and states.

Systemic psychophysiology rejects *the responsiveness paradigm* in favor of an *activity paradigm*, which focuses on future activity of not only single, but of multiple neuronal processes. This new paradigm considers psychological processes based upon activity and purposefulness, discarding eclectic representations, e.g. use of the concept of reflex mechanisms in explaining purposeful action (see in detail Alexandrov 1999a). Since opposing activity and responsiveness is of particular importance for systemic representations, the next sections provide a detailed account.

4 Responsiveness Paradigm

Based on analogies to physical *mechanisms*, Descartes regarded *reflected action* as a universal law manifested both in mechanisms and in living beings. With *reflected action*, the primary cause of behavior is the inner environment, and action is regarded as an objective reflection of components of the *inner* environment that influence the organism. Descartes also put forward a provision concerning the *constancy of the reflected action* in response to stimuli, which may be interpreted as a claim for the unambiguity of behavior determination by the inner environment.

Drawing upon the ideas expressed by Descartes, the *reflex theory* was developed (Pavlov 1949). We assert that the essence of the reflex theory may be expressed by the following formulation: *the individual in his action and state objectively reflects the precedent inner signal* (Krylov and Alexandrov 2006; Krylov and Alexandrov 2007). This statement can be represented by the following formula:

(1) $\quad Y(t + \tau) = f(\,S(t)\,), \tau > 0$

where:

$S\,(t)$ – an inner signal perceived by the individual;
$Y\,(t)$ – action of the individual at the moment t;
f – a function.

This formula indicates that there is *a functional dependency* between the perceived inner signal and subsequent behavior (Alekseev, Panin 1998). The formula (1) can be read as: a certain function f is applied to input signal $S\,(t)$, and, with the delay τ, the result is output. Descartes' *reflex objectivity* and its *constancy*, is consistent with the definition *of functional dependency*. Thus, the structure of the reflex arc and forward dynamics of the reflex follow from presence of the delay τ between the input signal S and the consequence Y caused by it, and from the condition $\tau > 0$, which means that the consequence comes later than the cause.

Despite wide acceptance of the reflex theory, it has been the subject of serious criticism (Lashley 1933; Anokhin 1978; Sudakov 1997; Alexandrov 1999; Shvyrkov 2006). This has prompted repeated modifications to the theory (see, for example, Batuev 1991; Petrovskiy and Yaroshevskiy 1996; Yaroshevskiy 1996; Sudakov 1997). For instance, the Cartesian reflex initially considered only a single determinant: the inner signal producing an effect. Then, additionally, *secondary* behavior determinants, or the state of the individual and their experience, were also considered. Claims regarding the importance of internal variables for behavior served to expand the set of determinants, recognizing these variables as inner determinants. However, the inner state and experience of the individual are both determined by an inner signal (Kruglikov 1982). It should be noted that in relying on this modification of the initial reflex theory, one may appeal to experience, to state of the individual, to their needs, etc., but they are not obligated to do so. Unlike the reflex theory, proper consideration for an individual's inner state as an essential behavior determinant occurred long ago with TFS.

If it is assumed that there are inner determinants, which are not conducive to reduction, Descartes's fundamentals are challenged: both the concept of the *reflected action* and his postulate concerning *constancy of the reflected action* in response to application of certain stimuli. The essence of modern concepts concerning the role of "inner states" can be formulated by the following equation:

$$(2) \quad Y(t + \tau) = f(\, S(t), Q(t)\,) = f^*(\, S(t), S(t\text{-}1), S(t\text{-}2), \ldots\,), \tau > 0$$

Here the inner state is designated as Q and f* represents a functional dependency. It follows that action reflects a functional dependency between the previous inner signal and the previous inner state. Consequently, since the inner state reflects previous inner signals and their history, action arises from the background of inner influences. In other words, both behavior and inner states are determined by a sequence of inner influences (Kruglikov 1982). Application of the "reflex" concept to phenomena means that causes may be found in *the past* and extend *beyond* the phenomenon. Thus, a phenomenon may be invoked by another inner phenomenon from the past. However, inclusion of the notion of inner states within the reflex theory does not provide a completely satisfactory solution.

5   The Activity Paradigm

Considering behavior and activity in reference to the future requires an understanding of *activity* as a basic property of a living entity; with the specific form of activity that is manifested depending on the nature of the entity (Anokhin 1978). The core ideas within this paradigm originated in attempts to overcome mechanistic response schemes (see Alexandrov and Jarvilehto 1993), providing broader homogeneity (Gibson 1979; Tolman 1932; Koffka 1935; Bernstein 1967; Dewey 1969; von Uexkull 1957, 5–80; and many others). The central point of the activity theory, as advanced in Russia, is the notion of the active subject (Petrovskiy and Yaroshevskiy 1996; Petrenko 1999).

The activity principle asserts that the action of any individual occurs in reference to the future, is purposeful, and is conditioned by the individual. Action determination relies on the inner nature of the individual and is connected with anticipation of future events. The concept of activity and purposefulness is connected with the concept of advance reflection (Anokhin 1978). *Advance reflection appeared with the nascence of life on the Earth* and is a distinct property of the latter. Non-living matter (or deceased organisms) reflect in a "delayed" manner. That is, it exhibits responses to past event-stimuli. The living reflect the world in an advanced manner: their activity at each given moment is preparation to ensure aspects of the future.

Advance reflection is inseparably connected with subjectivity because planning the future (aim formation) depends on the contents of individual memory and motivations. Furthermore, aims create an individual-specific division of the world, which was neutral beforehand, into "good" and "bad" objects and phenomena: those things contributing towards, or interfering against, achievement of individual aims.

The distinction between principles of determination on the basis of separating the living from the nonliving is surely an oversimplification. All reality cannot be reduced to a single-type categorical determination (Bunge 1962). Nonliving matter obeys not only stimulus causality, but also holistic determination (of parts to the whole) and self-determination (for example, the principle of inertia in mechanics). At the same time, *while considering the living organism not as a living individual, but as a physical body, determination by inner cause can be a convenient approximation*, appropriate within the structure of this limited domain. However, the teleological determination of aims applies only to descriptions of the living. Therefore, it is didactically justified to contrast teleological with stimulus determination.

Classical TFS included the notion of "trigger stimulus." It was supposed that all organization of processes in the system was determined by results attained by the given system. The stimulus initiates this integration and its significance goes no further. The seeming necessity for a central role to the "stimulus" falls away if the behavioral act is not regarded separately, but as a integral component of a behavioral continuum, within a sequence of coordinated acts performed by the individual throughout their life. The next act in this continuum is realized after the achievement and assessment of the results of the previous act. This cognitive assessment is an essential part of the organization processes (afferent synthesis and decision-making) which, in this way, can be considered as transitional processes from one act to another.

The activity principle not only addresses the functioning of an individual organism, but also the individual cells of a multicellular organism. From the position of the responsiveness paradigm, a response is based on the activation of a reflex arc. The neuron is an element within the reflex arc, and its function ensures the transmission of activation. Accordingly, it is logical to treat neuron impulses as follows: the response to a stimulus upon a part of the nerve cell surface can spread across the cell and act as a stimulus on other nerve cells.

The view that determinations of neuron activity conform with requirements of the system paradigm was reached by refusing to treat neuron activity merely as a response to synaptic inflow, and by accepting that a neuron, like any living cell, is genetically programmed to need metabolites coming from other cells (Shvyrkov 2006). Accordingly, the sequence of events in neuron activity is analogous to that characterizing an active aim-oriented organism, and neural activation is analogous to the action of the individual (Alexandrov 1999; Alexandrov 2008). Activity of the neuron, from this viewpoint, is a means of changing its relations with the environment, as the "action" references the future in eliminating imbalances between certain "requirements" of the cell and its local microenvironment. The neuron itself acts not as a "conductor" or a "summator," but as an organism meeting its "needs" at the expense of metabolites from other elements around it.

The difference between a neuron and a single cell organism lies in the fact that the neuron fulfills the "requirements" of its metabolism by directly joining with other nearby elements of the organism to form a functional system. Formation of such aggregations enables the metabolic cooperation of neurons. Satisfaction of the whole spectrum of metabolic cell "requirements" is ensured by diversity of the realized acts. There are arguments in favor of the neuron being active not only throughout its normal lifespan, but also during scheduled cell death in apoptosis.

Neuron activity is a component in the organism's achievement of desired results, which involves acts essential for obtaining required metabolites from the microenvironment. This new approach to understanding neuron functioning requires novel analysis methods, for example, plotting pre- (or peri-) result histograms (Figure 3.1), instead of post-stimulus depictions (Figure 3.2), and a new approach in research concerning the neural mechanisms of learning and memory (see below; more details in Alexandrov 2006).

SYSTEMIC PSYCHOPHYSIOLOGY

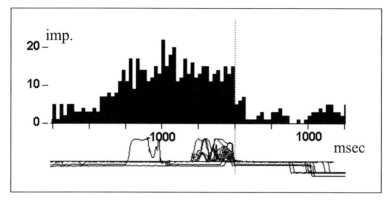

FIGURE 3.1   Post-stimulus histogram of neuron activity of the visual cortex in rabbits. The neuron is activated after presentation of a light flash. The moment of flash presentation is designated by the arrow.

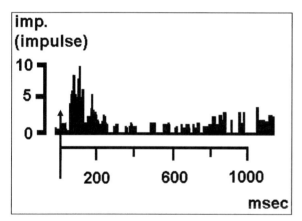

FIGURE 3.2   Pre-result histogram of neuron activity cingulate cortex in rabbits. The neuron is activated at the approach of the animal to the pedal or the ring, then pushing the pedal or pulling the ring trigger the feeder to dispense food. Activation persists till completion of pushing or pulling. Top: the histogram shows the moment of completion for pushing the pedal or pulling the ring. Bottom: Actograms of summarized realizations of behavior; deviations upwards – pressing a pedal or pulling the ring; downwards – muzzle dipping in the feeder.

6 History of Individual Experience Formation and Its Actualization

In addition to ideas of systemacity, at its core TFS advanced the idea of development as systemogenesis. Accordingly, it is claimed that heterochrony in laying the foundation and pace of development of separate morphological components of an organism at early stages of individual development are connected with the formation of "organism-wide" integrated functional systems, which require involvement of many elements from different organs and tissues (Anokhin 1975).

Within the TFS structure, it was shown (Shvyrkov 1978; Sudakov 1979; Shadrikov 1982) that systemogenesis also occurs in adults through acquisition of new behavioral acts and the accompanying formation of a new system, and also, that understanding the separate roles of neurons in ensuring behavior must take into account *the history of its systems formation* (Alexandrov 1989). That is, it must take into account the histories of consecutive systemogeneses, and the system-evolutionary theory and the system-selection conception of learning (Shvyrkov 1986; Shvyrkov 2006).

On this view, formation of a new system involves fixation upon a stage of individual development – the formation of a new *element of individual experience* in the process of learning. The basis for a new element is not a "re-specialization" of the prior specialized neurons, but an establishment of permanent specialization in a newly-formed system composed of "reserve" cells that were "silent" until then, and also of neurons emerging through the process of neoneurogenesis. Specialization of neurons within newly-formed systems – *system specialization* – is permanent, i.e. *the neuron is systemospecific*. Thus, in the process of individual experience, the newly-formed systems *do not replace the preceding systems, but "lay in layers"* on them, being "additive" with respect to the ones formed before.

It has been shown that realization of distinct behavior occurs through realization of new systems formed during activities associated with learning, as well as the *simultaneous* realization of a set of older systems formed at previous stages of individual development (Alexandrov 1989; Alexandrov et al., 2000; Shvyrkov 2006). Hence, *realization of behavior is*, so to say, *realization of one's behavior formation history* (*phylo-* as well as *ontogenetic*). In contrast to prevalent ideas within neuroscience whereby the neural mechanisms of learning and memory involve consolidation and increased efficacy of synaptic transfer to chains of connected neurons, systemic psychophysiology regards new systems of neuron specializations as not necessarily bound synaptically (see in detail Alexandrov 2006).

Neuron specialization occurring through individual experience does not directly reflect the outer world, but rather the individual's relations to it. Therefore, a description of system neuron specializations is simultaneously a description of the subjective world, and studying the activity of these neurons is the study of subjective reflection.

7 The Science of System Psychophysiology in World Science

Based on recent theoretical and experimental articles, the following assertions may be made. Neuroscience and psychophysiology are transitioning to a new phase away from Cartesian determinism towards ideas of antireductionism (Alexandrov and Järvilehto 1993; de Waal 1996; Ellis 1999; Freeman 1997; Jordan 1998; Wilson 1998; Mitina and Petrenko 1999; Engel et al. 2001; Schall 2001; Thompson and Varela 2001; Vandervert 1998; Webb 2004; Woese 2004; Fisher and Bidell 2006). This transition is not yet dominant in mainstream circles (though, for example, in neuroscience journals and molecular biology the number of articles in which the term "systemic" is used has increased by a hundred-fold), but it is gaining strength and support from authoritative authors.

The present stage, typical during a transition from one paradigm to another, is characterized by eclectic expression. The methodological basis of the overwhelming majority of papers reflects "activistic" and "responsive" determinism (see Alexandrov 1999).

Systemic psychophysiology, having become less eclectic, *has essentially outstripped neuroscience and traditional psychophysiology*. Empirical regularities that were discovered in systemic psychophysiology many years ago have become a subject of close attention of mainstream science only recently (see, for example, Alexandrov 2008). Conceptual transitions which have already been made or are being made by neuroscience and psychophysiology, largely repeat those undergone by systemic psychophysiology. One may attempt to predict developments within traditional science as this new paradigm progresses towards mainstream acceptance.

(1) Traditionally, behavior mechanisms have been thought of as sensorymotor. In the future, it will be understood that "functions" of these kind (as well as motivational, activational, etc.) are fictitious. Transition from the concept of strict "function" localization to the concept of "dynamic localization" and "distributed system" has already occurred. In the future there will be a transition to understanding that because function is systemic, and systems are not sensory or motor (nor sensory-motor), but organism-wide, function cannot be

localized in any structure of the brain (neither strictly nor dynamically), not even localized in the brain; it is organism-wide.

(2) In contrast to understanding the mechanism of behavior as reflex response, there will be a transition to regarding the individual as "reacting actively" or even "reacting purposefully." An understanding will follow that reflection is a primary characteristic of living organisms.

(3) There has been a transition from viewing the neuron as summarizing input on its surface membrane to the view of the neuron as a complex integrator of input that depends on the dynamics of intraneural metabolic processes, its history and presynaptic activity, and so forth. In the future, these views will be replaced by viewing the neuron not as a microcircuit transforming its inputs, but as a living "organism within the organism" which discharges not "*in response to*" but rather *to receive* the metabolites essential for its vital activity.

(4) In contrast to the view of learning as a top-down process of closing the circuit of local reflex arches, neuroscience has moved to an understanding of cerebral mechanisms of learning as complex, with memory modified through consolidation of the mosaic of neuromorphology, synaptic "conductiveness," and gene expression in many "associated" brain structures. There will be a transition to a view of learning as systemogenesis: the formation of a set of neurons not necessarily directly bound, but specialized in their relation to the newly-formed system by modification of cells pre-specialized in early ontogenesis and neurons formed in the process of neoneurogenesis.

(5) In contrast to a view of neurons specialized according to sensory, motor, etc. "functions" (see item 1), neuroscience and psychophysiology, without rejecting these views entirely, will shift to the perspective of "clever" neurons, specialized for various cognitive "functions" such as emotions, consciousness, imagination, etc. Furthermore, it will become clear that neurons may be similarly specialized in systems aimed at achieving different results.

(6) In contrast to the view of sensory stimuli coded as consecutive stages of processing information from receptors to cortical centers, there is a shift of attention to *top-down* regulation mechanisms. Within science, there will be increased incorporation of ideas of activity wherein anticipation is central, as well as an intensification of studies into efferent influences on peripheral elements. In the future it will turn out that the view of "aim" determination and system specialization is applicable both to the level of central elements as well as the level of peripheral elements.

(7) In contrast with the view consistent with the reflex theory concerning the consecutive inclusion of the "afferent" and "efferent," the central and peripheral structures in the evolution of behavior, there will be a transition

to theories emphasizing synchronization of brain structures operating as the mechanism for perception, memory, consciousness, etc. In the future, an understanding will arise that "afferent" and "efferent," central and peripheral structures work synchronously, not because it is merely a means of achieving greater efficiency between neural structures or binding together different parameters of the stimulus (binding theory), but because elements of these structures are simultaneously involved in ensuring evolving organism-wide system mechanisms of behavior. It will also become evident that perception, attention, consciousness, emotions, etc., are *not special processes* realized by special structures and mechanisms in cooperation with each other, but *special ways* of describing *various aspects of the uniform system*.

With respect to these issues, it may be asserted that contemporary modern psychophysiology and neuroscience is still behind the forward advances of systemic psychophysiology. How did its original ideas emerge? I believe that one of essential conditions was specifically the culture in which TFS and system psychophysiology were formed.

8 World Science and Its Culture-Specific Components

Science is a part of culture, and together with invariant characteristics reflecting its global character, it possesses certain national features (Gavin and Blakeley 1976; Lewontin and Levins 1980; de Waal 1996; Peng et al. 2001; Slobin 2004; Nosulenko et al. 2005; Graham and Kantor 2006; Alexandrov 2009). Distinctive national features characterize not only fundamental areas of research, but applied areas as well, such as medicine (e.g. radical differences between western and officially recognized Indian medicine see in Singh 2007).

With respect to cultural influences, we focus upon the specificity of sciences practiced within different cultures, without claiming any linear causal connection between culture and science, which may be impossible to establish (Graham and Kantor 2006). The confirming experiment revealing such a connection would be difficult. Borders separating science from other components of culture are vague especially because scientific knowledge includes significant amounts of everyday knowledge (Polanyi 1998).

The diffusion of western science, having its origin in ancient Greece, into western countries was connected with its merging with non-western mentalities, traditions, and language (Crombie 1995), which modified science. Thus it has been shown that in one culture, people can be more inclined to a convergent, and in others, to a divergent style of thinking (Peng et al. 2001); e.g.

in Asian and western countries the nature of "probabilistic thinking" differs (Wright and Phillips 1980; Whitcomb et al. 1995).

As to language, different languages, within cultures, do not reflect *different designations of the same phenomenon, but different visions* (Gumbolt 1985; Slobin 2004; Uorf 1960; and others). Recently cross-cultural features of thinking and perception have been demonstrated by a larger number of works. Thus, native speakers of different languages distinguish different (also in number) fragments during description of the same visual scenes (Stutterheim et al. 2002; Stutterheim and Nüse 2003). We will add that subjects speaking two languages reveal those features of scene subdivision and their description which are inherent to their native, to the first language(s) they learned (Carroll and Stutterheim 2003).

Cross-cultural covariance of differences has been demonstrated in the study of languages and in cognitive strategies concerning (1) spatial orientation (Haun et al. 2006); (2) discrimination of object characteristics, including colors (Baranski and Petrusic 1999; Winawer et al. 2007; Tan et al. 2008; Skotnikova 2008); (3) perception of mimicked emotion expressions (Barrett et al. 2007); (4) risk assessment (Hsee and Weber 1999); and (5) confidence in the correctness of choices (Yates et al. 1996). English and Chinese speakers supposedly think of time differently and use different regional metaphors to represent the flow of time: the former use horizontal metaphors (for example, "the best days are behind"), and the latter use vertical metaphors (for example, the "top" month in meaning "last") (Boroditsky 2001; see objections to Boroditsky 2001 in Chen 2007; Kako 2007; and also additional arguments made out by Boroditsky including data about opposite horizontal "time orientation" in Hebrew speakers in contrast to English speakers in Boroditsky 2008). It has been shown that native English or Chinese speakers solve arithmetic problems using different cognitive strategies enabled by different patterns of brain activation (Campbell and Xue 2001; Tang et al. 2006; Cantlon and Brannon 2007). Erroneous conclusions are connected with temporoparietal activity in English-speaking Americans and German-speaking Europeans, but not in other English-speaking children and English-speaking bilinguals (Kobayashi et al. 2006; Kobayashi et al. 2007). Perner and Aichorn (2008) consider these data as arguments in favor of culture or language influencing "brain functional localization" and they reject assertions attributing these functions to a maturation of congenitally-specified cerebral substrates.

Recently, arguments have been presented in favor of relating national features of thinking, culture, and politics with local features of different areas of science, including the natural sciences in general (Paló 2008), cosmology (Kragh 2006), statistics (Stamhuis 2008), neuroscience (Debru 2008), and geology and geography (Klemun 2008; Yusupova 2008). For the purposes of our discussion, it is important to emphasize that a number of authors similarly highlight features of Russian science (Gavin and Blakeley 1976; Graham and Kantor 2006; Nosulenko et al. 2005). I believe "systematicity" and "anti-reductionism" are key among them (Alexandrov 2005; Alexandrov 2009). Apparently, a detailed substantiation of systemology in "Tectology" by A. A. Bogdanov (1913–17) appeared at the time when the founder of the general theory of systems, Ludwig von Bertalanffy, was only 12 years of age. Similar advances can be noted for TFS. For good reason, the origins of TFS may be linked with formation of the systemic approach, which "released biological thinking from the deadlock of Cartesian mechanicism," and emphasized that "development of the concept of functional systems by Anokhin and his collaborators by 1935 anticipated development of both neurocybernetics by Norbert Wiener in 1948 and the general theory of systems by Bertalanffi in 1960" (Corson 1981).

At the same time, Cartesian mechanicism in the natural sciences and social sciences are considered especially characteristic of western science (Lewontin and Levins 1980; de Waal 1996; Graham and Kantor 2006; and others). Certainly, anti-reductionism can be found not only in Russia:

> Eager to study a living subject,
> and to receive a clear view of it, –
> The scientist first drives away the soul,
> Then divides the object into parts
> and observes them, but what a shame:
> > their spiritual bond
> In the meantime has vanished,
> > it was carried away!

One cannot attribute these lines to a Russian mentality – they belong to Goethe. More likely, they can be connected with ideas of German philosophy whose creators included Goethe's friends and correspondents who, as well as Spinoza long before ("nature of the part is determined by its role in the whole system" Edwards 1967), considered systematicity to be the primary characteristic of cognition and viewed knowledge as a system. These ideas surely influenced Russian science greatly.

The protest against mechanicism which exclusively captivated thought of the West, "the revolt against Cartesianism – the foundation and symbol of western thinking – took place namely in Russia" (Gavin and Blakeley 1976).

And in L. R. Graham's opinion, the "anti-reductionist approach roots deeply in the history of Russian and Soviet thought" (Graham 1991). S. Rose notes: "I have opposed ... reductionism of the Anglo-American school ... to much more perspective traditions ... especially to those originated ... in the Soviet Union, [and have caused development of views that] behavior cannot be reduced to a simple chain of combinations of various responses; it reflects aim-oriented activity, hypothesis formulation and many other things" (Rose 1995). To a high degree "in Soviet psychology and physiology, there exists a special Russian tradition of research interpretation" (Graham 1991). For example, a connection to the national style of thinking in Russia with features of mathematics development has been highlighted (e.g., progress in set theory; see Graham and Kantor 2006).

The above noted intercultural differences become more evident when taking into account the presence of a significant Eastern component in Russian culture and thinking (see in Alexandrov and Alexandrova 2009) and in research results. Nisbett et al. (2001), after comparing cognitive processes across peoples of Eastern (Asian) and Western cultures, arrived at this conclusion: in Eastern cultures *continuality* is regarded as the basic property of the world, while in Western cultures the world is represented as discrete, consisting of *isolated objects*. In the former, formal logic is scarcely applied, but *the holistic approach and "dialectic" argumentation are used*. In Western cultures *analytic* thinking is used, as *greater attention is drawn to objects separately rather than to integrity*. In Eastern cultures nothing in nature is wholly isolated because everything is taken to be interconnected, so any isolation of elements from the whole can result only in delusions. These differences appear in comparisons between ancient China and Greece (8th to 3rd centuries BCE) and still persist, characterizing distinctive features of modern China and other Asian countries in contrast with North America and Europe.

In this discussion of "Western" science, I do not mean to imply any homogeneity throughout the West. Consider, for example, contrasting features of German and American psychologies, which led (Watson 1934) and is now leading (Toomela 2007) authors to greater expressions of holism and systemacity in German psychology and reductionism in American psychology. It may be noted that A. Toomela (2007) credits Russia for taking a holistic direction.

M. Popovsky (1978) remarked that when one is in the USSR to hear talk of *Soviet* science, "foreigners ironically smile" because they presume the "maxim" that there is only one science. This ironic presumption is not a sign of acquaintance with the relevant scientific literature; on the contrary – it can only be proof of superficiality and preference for stock phrases. Differences between national origins of the sciences are themselves basic characteristics and values of world science, so that treating distinctions between global and local knowledge, or between national and world science, as mutually exclusive must be mistaken (Jackunas 2006). In other words, "theoreticians working in different traditions, in different countries, will arrive at theories which, although in agreement with all the known facts, are mutually inconsistent" (Feyerabend 1985, 60). Finally, I assert that differences of views emerging in the course of the development of world science has positive aspects. G. I. Abelev also remarks that diversity of national sciences is a major value of world science. N. A. Berdyayeva was right when she claimed that *truth is not national*, it is universal, but *different nationalities disclose its different aspects*.

World science can be described *as a system consisting of diverse components, in which local culturally-specific components are complementary and cooperate in producing useful results: development of global scientific knowledge.* This mutual assistance can be appropriately seen as a "division of labor" in world science, connected with national features of cultures (Alexandrov 2009): systemacity and holicism predetermine a greater affinity for working out new directions in science, to "chipping off blocks," while Cartesian reductionism prefers the approach of breaking "blocks" into pieces, the detailed elaboration of knowledge, and the search for practical applications. This approach conforms to the carefully justified position of E. S. Kulpina, who finds that Western (European) civilization connects knowledge with practical aims and market needs, while the Russian civilization regards momentary practical benefit as considerably less important; not applied knowledge, but fundamental knowledge, is much more significant.

It seems counterproductive to hope for a unification of culture-specific sciences, or for overcoming cultural specificity as an obstacle to creating "the world literature." A world literature "will arise mostly when distinctive features of one nation will be balanced via acquaintance with other [nations]" (Goethe 1827).

N. Bohr applied the complementarity principle, originally formulated in physics, in discussing relations between cultures. This is interesting because obvious parallels with the "cultural complementarity" view advanced above can be seen here. "We can truly say," N. Bohr writes, "that different human cultures are complementary to each other." However, unlike physics, he emphasizes, no mutual exclusion of features belonging to different cultures is observed (Bohr 2005).

Following this logic, and bearing in mind the afore-mentioned connection between features of language and styles of thinking, it is possible to conclude that confusion among languages of the Tower of Babel's builders yielded two results simultaneously: not just (if we credit authority to this story's source) abandoning its construction, but no less significant is an enrichment to the culture of the entire world. Confusion between languages is not a punishment upon humanity for its pride, but a gift awarded to humanity.

9 The Uniform Concept of Consciousness and Emotions

Regarding the systemic solution to the psychophysiological problem, we remarked that the physiological and psychological are two different descriptions of uniform system processes. Also these are descriptions "from below" – via the organization of brain activity. Let's consider the way system processes can be described "from above," using the examples of consciousness and emotions.

In the solution to this problem a disjunctive approach prevails, which includes the following provisions:

a) there exist heterogeneous cognitive and affective mental processes;
b) these processes are the product of different structures of the brain;
c) being separate mechanisms, cognitive and affective processes can "influence" each other, "conform" with each other, etc.

These provisions fit into Aristotelian logic, operating by oppositional pairs, such as "normal – pathological," "cognitive – affective," etc. K. Lewin (1935) insisted on giving greater consideration to the Galilean conceptual structure within which grouping into oppositional pairs is replaced by groupings using serial concepts, and S. L. Rubinstein (1973) proclaimed the possibility of discriminating intellectual and emotional processes without supposing a sharp disjunctive division.

In system psychophysiology, *a uniform conception of consciousness and emotions* has been formulated (Alexandrov 1999a; Alexandrov 1999b), which uses a non-disjunctive approach to understanding consciousness and emotions. It addresses the problem of the affective and cognitive in the context of phylo- and ontogenetic development. The central idea is that a non-disjunctive transition occurs in the development process, a transition from formation of systems having *characteristics of "emotions,"* to formation of systems *characterized by "consciousness."* Moreover, the former *do not substitute* for the latter. Behavior always possesses *both these characteristics*.

Analysis of writings by many authors (Edelman 1989; Gray 1995; John et al. 1997; Ivanitskiy 2001) suggest a connection between processes of consciousness and attention to ongoing environment changes, characteristics of the organism, and both anticipated and actual stimuli. An understanding of consciousness from the perspective presented here does not contradict this conclusion.

However, the majority of authors rely on provisions from a more modern approach using "stimulus-response" in the development of their views. This approach invariably leads them to an understanding of consciousness emphasizing an idea identified by D. C. Dennett (1993) as the "Cartesian theatre." Theorists relying on this idea "think of perceptual systems as providing 'input' to some central thinking arena, which in turn provides 'control' or 'direction' to some relatively peripheral systems governing bodily motion.... their models still presuppose that somewhere, conveniently hidden in the obscure 'center' of the mind/brain, there is a Cartesian Theater, a place where 'it all comes together' and consciousness happens." "... the Cartesian Theater will continue to haunt us until we have anchored our alternative firmly to the bedrock of empirical science." (Dennett 1993, 39, 227). From my point of view, the uniform concept of consciousness and emotions, rooted in the experimental foundations of TFS and system psychophysiology, can be considered as a soundly scientific alternative.

Given the above statements concerning the systemic structure of the behavioral continuum, one can suppose that processes of "monitoring expected and real parameters," considered in the literature as mechanisms of consciousness, occur *across the extent of the behavioral continuum*: both during realization of the behavioral act and at its conclusion. Accordingly, *not stimulus parameters, but the results parameters are expected and compared*, both final and intermediate. This analysis permits comparisons of development stages of the behavioral continuum with the stream of consciousness (James, 1890) and leads to the following *definition of consciousness*:

> Consciousness involves the assessment of intermediate and final behavior results obtained by the subject, accordingly, in the process of behavior realization (both "outer" and "inner") and at its end; this assessment is defined by the contents of subjective experience and leads to its reorganization.

Within the limits of such understanding, and considering the argued position of many authors about the necessity of levels of consciousness (Tulving 1985; Dennett 1993; Damasio 2000; and many others), the following *description of the "stream of consciousness"* can be cited:

> Comparison of real parameters of intermediate results with the expected ones (with the aim) during realization of the behavioral act corresponds to the First level of consciousness. Comparison of real parameters of the final result of the behavioral act with the ones expected (with the aim) during transient processes (from one act to another) corresponds to a Second (higher) level of consciousness.

A literature review (see Alexandrov 1999a) reveals the importance of the resemblance between consciousness and emotions for behavior organization. Emotions, as well as consciousness:
- take part in *activity regulation*;
- have a significant *communicative value*;
- are connected with *processes of comparison of expected and real results* during realization and completion of an action.

Taking into account these resemblances, one may see the similarity between consciousness and emotions, with respect to the assessment by the subject of his behavior results in the process of behavior realization (both "outer" and "inner") and at its completion.

Formation of new systems in the course of individual development causes progressive *differentiation* to the relationship of the organism with the environment (Werner and Kaplan 1956; Alexandrov 1989; Chuprikova 1997; Tononi and Edelman 1998; and others). Systems formed at *the earliest stages of ontogenesis* provide *a minimum level of differentiation*: good – bad, approach – withdrawal. Relationships with the environment at this level of differentiation can be described in terms *of "emotions"* (see also Schneirla 1959; Anokhin 1978; Zajonc 1980; Shvyrkov 1984; Davidson et al. 1990; Berntson et al. 1993; Alexandrov 1999a; Pankseepp 2000). These early systems are neither "positive" nor "negative." All systems are oriented to achievement of positive adaptive results.

Considering the system structure of behavior as a stable formation, it is possible to formulate the *key provision for the uniform concept of consciousness and emotions*: *consciousness and emotions are characteristics of different, simultaneously actualized levels of the system organization of behavior, represented as transformed stages of development and corresponding to various levels of system differentiation.* There is no critical moment at which consciousness emerges or emotions disappear during development. At each stage of development, at each level of systemic differentiation, behavior can be described using both characteristics. However, at each level, the ratio of these characteristics varies (see the right section of Figure 3.3).

Emotions characterize systems at the earliest stages of ontogenesis and provide *a minimum level of differentiation*. *Consciousness* characterizes systems at later stages of development where there is a progressive *increase of differentiation* in the correlation of the organism and the environment. It becomes obvious that the definition of emotions provided above and the linking of emotions with an assessment of results should be more accurate: *results provide the means for correlating the individual with the environment at a low level of differentiation.*

Distinctions between the uniform conception of consciousness and emotions, and conceptions of other authors are presented below. The most

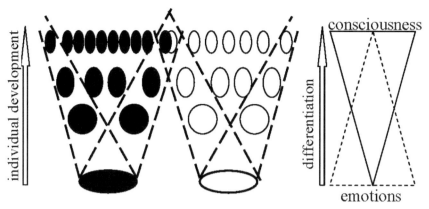

FIGURE 3.3   Consciousness and emotions at consecutive stages of behavior differentiation. Large ovals at the bottom designate systems of the least differentiation providing realization of behavioral acts of "approach" (positive emotions, white ovals) and "withdrawal" (negative emotions, black ovals) at the earliest stage of ontogenesis. In the process of development, differentiation increases and behavioral acts occur through actualization of an increasing number of systems. Dashed lines indicate systems of different age and differentiation, which are simultaneously actualized in achievement of behavioral results. The larger number of black ovals illustrates the empirically supported idea concerning greater differentiation of the withdrawal domain in comparison with the approach domain, and overlapping of black and white ovals – the idea that externally identical acts aimed at achievement of different aims (approach or withdrawal) are supplied with activity though partially overlapping, but essentially different sets of neurons (Sams, 2005; Alexandrov et al., 2007). Triangles illustrate the idea that consciousness (the triangle is turned with the apex downwards) and emotion (the triangle is turned with the apex upwards) are different characteristics of the same multilevel systemic organization.

important and original features are highlighted. We note that the uniform conception of consciousness and emotions, in contrast to conceptions of other authors whom I have supported, are not entirely different. This fact can be explained by the fact that they are not just separate proposals, but necessarily connected with each other as products of TFS and systemic psychophysiology.
– Currently, a perspective focused upon a systemic approach, as opposed to the Cartesian approach, has been applied in developing conceptualizations of consciousness and emotions (Freeman 1997; Jordan 1998; Vandervert 1998; Ellis 1999; Thompson and Varela 2001). In the proposed uniform concept, TFS and system psychophysiology are applied – in particular, that variant of the systemic approach in which the idea of activity is central, and seems to be *the least eclectic*. In interpreting experimental data, *it allows one to completely avoid descriptions in terms of the Cartesian paradigm.*

- Being based on a systemic solution of the psychophysiological problem, the proposed concept *allows one to avoid reductionism and eliminativism* in solving the consciousness and emotions problems.
- The proposed concept uses *system understanding of function* and consequently *excludes* the following fairly criticized approaches to understanding of consciousness and emotions: "boxology" (Thompson and Varela 2001); consciousness and emotions occurring as separate "localized entities" (Damasio 1994, Damasio 2000); or independent "modular" processes (Ellis and Newton 2000).
- *The contents of consciousness* are assessed, not with respect to stimuli or "sensory-motor binding" as is done in the overwhelming majority of concepts (see, however, Jordan 1998; Vandervert 1998), but *with construction of results models* (of both "outer" and "inner" behaviors) *and monitoring the parameters of actually reached results*. This is especially important in that *consciousness* is assessed with respect to *the behavior described, not as isolated behavioral acts, and as an uninterrupted continuum of intermediate and final results* of continually developing behavioral acts. This allows a depiction centering on the *dynamics of consciousness* corresponding to achievement and assessment of results, and also the elimination of the problem of "delayed consciousness."
- The proposed *concept of consciousness and emotions is based on Gallilean*, instead of the usual Aristotelian *logic*. In accordance with the latter, consciousness and emotions are treated non-disjunctively. Aristotelian logic leads to conclusions such as the *impossibility of "influence," "objectivity of action" and other effects of emotions on consciousness, or their "interaction"* that allow for behavior without an emotional "basis."
- In the proposed concept, *the similarity of consciousness and emotions as characteristics of systems having an identical architecture* is underlined. Though systems also differ at the level of differentiation, *all of them are oriented toward achievement of positive results*. The existence of special "systems" or "mechanisms" producing consciousness and emotions is denied.
- Consciousness and emotions are viewed as products of experience derived from memory acquired throughout a lifetime: from the oldest to the newest, and not as the characteristics of information associated with immediate stimulus action. Accordingly, *the proposed concept does not use "the metaphor of the light spot," inseparably connected with the fairly criticized ideology of the "Cartesian theatre."* This metaphor is based on the "false idea of spatial localization" characterizing most consciousness theories, even if it is not mentioned explicitly (Shanon 2001).

10   Systemic Perspective on Culture

Culture, from a systemic perspective, may be seen *as structure, represented as a set of elements (systems) and culture units which symbolize means of achieving collective results within a given society at a particular stage of its development* (see in more detail Alexandrov and Alexandrova 2007). Within the systemic structures of subjective experience and culture, analogies can be found. For example, after being formed, new and more differentiated elements of culture and subjective experience do not replace the previous ones, but stratify them (Figure 3.4). Actualization of units of culture and subjective experience

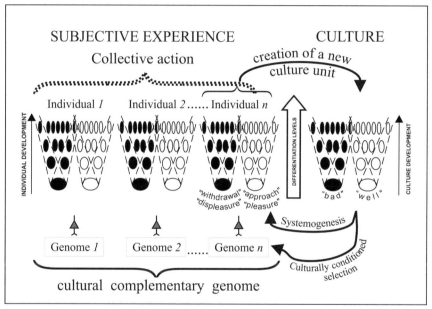

FIGURE 3.4   Structures of subjective experience (at the left) and culture (at the right). The arrow, "differentiation levels," designates the increase of differentiation of structures in their development. Large ovals at the bottom designate systems of subjective experience and culture of the least differentiation. As development progresses, the number of systems and level of their differentiation increase. "White systems" of subjective experience provide realization of behavioral acts of approach (positive emotions), black – of withdrawal (negative emotions). In the culture structure, white and black ovals symbolize culture elements. Dashed lines on the left show differentiated systems whose simultaneous actualization ensures achievement of behavioral results. Overlapping of black and white ovals designate identical acts of behavior oriented at achievement of different aims (approach, withdrawal). Arrows illustrate the idea gene-cultural coevolution, and "systemogenesis." Between the rectangle "genome" and the ovals symbolizing systems of subjective experience, a schematic image of the neuron specifies that genome realization in a given cultural environment is mediated by selection and specialization of neurons associated with newly formed systems.

occur at the expense of simultaneous activation of other elements formed at different stages of development of the society/individual. The formation of elements of subjective experience depends on cultural learning and the individual neural substrate arising from individual genomic features. To a certain degree, the genome also depends on culture. The culture not only defines the character of elements of subjective experience (even such basic skills as walking are culturally-dependent), but influences genome selection ("gene-cultural coevolution"), causing, in particular, "cultural genome complementarity" in society.

11   Conclusion

In this framework for systemic psychophysiology (Krylov and Alexandrov 2007), it may be asserted that psychology, molecular biology, physiology, psychophysiology, sociology, cultural science, and other disciplines address tendencies characterizing different links and aspects of a uniform cycle: from subjective experience to society; then through joint activity and achievement of joint results – to culture; from culture through genomes and individual genomes to neural specializations, and from neural specializations to subjective experience. Accordingly, an interdisciplinary methodology and interdisciplinary

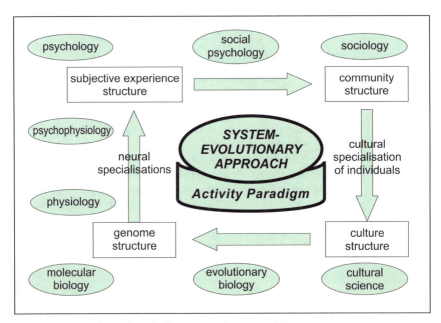

FIGURE 3.5   Relationship of subject areas of some disciplines

language for these interconnected and interdependent disciplines of systemic psychophysiology can be applied, and in particular, a system-evolutionary approach can be useful (See Figure 3.5).

Acknowledgment

This work has been supported by RFBR grant #08-04-00100 and by The Grants Council of the President of the Russian Federation of the Major Scientific Schools of Russia # NSh-602.2008.6.

References

Alexandrov, Y. I. 1989. *Psychophysiological Significance of the Activity of Central and Peripheral Neurons in Behavior*. Moscow: Science.

Alexandrov, Y. I. 1999a. "Psychophysiological regularities of the dynamics of individual experience and the 'stream of consciousness.'" In *Neuronal Bases and Psychological Aspects of Consciousness*, ed. C. Teddei-Ferretti and C. Musio, 201–219. New York: World Scientific.

Alexandrov, Y. I. 1999b. "Comparative description of consciousness and emotions in the framework of systemic understanding of behavioral continuum and individual development." In *Neuronal Bases and Psychological Aspects of Consciousness*, ed. C. Teddei-Ferretti and C. Musio, 220–235. New York: World Scientific.

Alexandrov, Y. I. 2006. "Learning and memory: traditional and systems approaches." *Neuroscience and Behavioral Physiology* 36, no. 9: 969–985.

Alexandrov, Y. I. 2007. "Effect of emotional context in auditory-cortex processing." *International Journal of Psychophysiology* 65, no. 3: 261–271.

Alexandrov, Y. I. 2008. "How we fragment the world: the view from inside versus the view from outside." *Social Science Information* 47, no. 3: 419–457.

Alexandrov, Y. I. 2009. "Global science and its culture-specific components." In *Liberalizing Research in Science and Technology: Studies in Science Policy*, ed. N. Asheulova, B. K. Pattnaik, E. Kolchinsky, and G. Sandstrom. Kanpur: Indian Institute of Technology.

Alexandrov, Y. I. and N. Alexandrova. 2007. "Subjective experience and culture: Structure and dynamics." *Russian Psychology* 1, no. 1: 3–46.

Aleksandrov, Y., and N. L. Aleksandrova. 2009. *Subjective Experience: Culture and Social Performance*. Moscow: Izdatel'stvo Instituta psikhologii.

Alexandrov, Y. I., T. N. Grechenko, V. V. Gavrilov, A. G. Gorkin, D. G. Shevchenko, Y. V. Grinchenko, et al. 2000. "Formation and realization of individual experience:

a psychophysiological approach." In *Complex Brain Functions: Conceptual Advances in Russian Neuroscience*, ed. R. Miller, A. M. Ivanitsky, and P. V. Balaban, 181–200. Amsterdam: Harwood Academic.

Alexandrov, Y. I. and T. Jarvilehto. 1993. "Activity versus reactivity in psychology and neurophysiology." *Ecological Psychology* 5, no. 1: 85–103.

Alexandrov, Y. I. and M. E. Sams. 2005. "Emotion and consciousness: Ends of a continuum." *Cognitive Brain Research* 25, no. 2: 387–405.

Anokhin, P. K. 1973. *Biology and Neurophysiology of Conditioned Reflex and its Role in Adaptive Behavior*. Oxford: Pergamon Press.

Anokhin, P. K. 1975. *Essays on the Physiology of Functional Systems*. Moscow: Medicine.

Anokhin, P. K. 1978. "Philosophical aspects of the theory of functional systems." *Russian Studies in Philosophy* 10, no. 3: 269–276.

Baranski, J. V. and W. M. Petrusic. 1999. "Realism of confidence in sensory discrimination." *Perception & Psychophysics* 61, no. 7: 1369–1383.

Barrett, L. F., K. A. Lindquist, and M. Gendron. 2007. "Language as context for the perception of emotion." *Trends in Cognitive Sciences* 11, no. 8: 327–332.

Batuev, A. S. 1991. "The hypothesis of the cortical mechanisms of operative memory." *Zhurnal Vysshei Nervnoi Deiatelnosti Imeni I P Pavlova* 41, no. 6: 1088–1093.

Bernstein, N. A. 1967. *The Co-ordination and Regulation of Movements*. Oxford: Pergamon Press.

Berntson, G. G., S. T. Boysen, and J. H. Cacioppo. 1993. "Neurobehavioral organisation and the cardinal principle of evaluative." *Annals of The New York Academy of Sciences* 702, no. 1: 75–102.

Bogdanov, A. A. 1913–1917. *Vseobschaya organizatsionnaya nauka (Tektologiya)* [The Universal Science of Organization (Tektology)]. 2 vols. St. Petersburg: Semenov.

Bohr, N. 2005. *Collected Works. The Political Arena (1934–1961)*. Amsterdam: Elsevier.

Boroditsky, L. 2001. "Does language shape thought? Mandarin and English speakers' conceptions of time." *Cognitive Psychology* 43, no. 1: 1–22.

Boroditsky, L. 2008. "How the languages we speak shape the ways we think." Paper presented at the 3rd International Conference on Cognitive Science, Moscow, June 20–25.

Bunge, M. 1962. "Causality: A rejoinder." *Philosophy of Science* 29, no. 3: 306–317.

Campbell, J. I. and Q. Xue. 2001. "Cognitive arithmetic across cultures." *Journal of Experimental Psychology* 130, no. 2: 299–315.

Cantlon, J. F. and E. M. Brannon. 2007. "Adding up the effects of cultural experience on the brain." *Trends in Cognitive Science* 11, no. 1: 1–4.

Carroll, M. and C. Von Stutterheim. 2003. "Typology and information organisation: perspective taking and language-specific effects." In *Typology and Second Language Acquisition*, ed. A. Ramat, 365–402. Berlin: de Gruyter.

Chalmers, D. J. 1995. "Facing up to the problem of consciousness." *Journal of Consciousness* 2, no. 3: 200–219.

Chen, J. Y. 2007. "Chinese and English speakers think about time differently? Failure of replicating Boroditsky." *Cognition* 104, no. 2: 427–436.

Cole, M. and S. Cole. 1971. "Three giants of soviet psychology: Conversations and sketches." *Psychology Today* 4, no. 10: 43–50, 78–90.

Corson, S. 1981. "Review of neurophysiologic investigation of systems mechanisms of behavior." *Pavlovian Journal of Biological Science* 16, no. 4: 222.

Crombie, A. C. 1995. "Commitments and styles of European scientific thinking." *History of Science* 33, no. 100: 225–238.

Damasio, A. 1994. *Descartes' Error: Emotion, Reason, and the Human Brain*. New York: G. P. Putnam's Sons.

Damasio, A. 2000. *The Feeling of What Happens*. London: Vintage.

Davidson, R. J., P. Ekman, W. V. Friesen, C. D. Saron, and J. A. Senulis. 1990. "Approach-withdrawal and cerebral asymmetry: emotional expression and brain physiology." *Journal of Personality and Social Psychology* 58, no. 2: 330–341.

De Waal, F. 1996. *Good Natured: The Origins of Right and Wrong in Humans and other Animals*. Cambridge, Mass.: Harvard University Press.

Debru, C. 2008. "Styles in neurophysiological research. The case of sleep and dreaming physiology in the nineteen-sixties in France and the U.S." Paper presented at the 3rd International Conference of the European Society for the History of Science, Vienna, September 10–12.

Dennett, D. C. 1993. *Consciousness Explained*. London: Penguin Books.

Dewey, J. 1969. "The reflex arc concept in psychology" (1895), in *The Early Works, 1882–1898*, vol. 5, ed. J. A. Boydston, 96–110. Carbondale: Southern Illinois University Press.

Edelman, G. M. 1989. *The Remembered Present: A Biological Theory of Consciousness*. New York: Basic Books.

Edwards, P. 1967. *The Encyclopedia of Philosophy*, 8 vols. New York: Macmillan.

Ellis, R. D. 1999. "Dynamical systems as an approach to consciousness: emotion, self-organization and the mind-body problem." *New Ideas in Psychology* 17, no. 3: 237–250.

Ellis, R. D. and N. Newton. 2000. "The interdependence of consciousness and emotion." *Consciousness and Emotion* 1, no. 1: 1–10.

Engel, K. A., P. Fries, and W. Singer. 2001. "Dynamic predictions: oscillations and synchrony in top-down processing." *Nature Reviews Neuroscience* 2, no. 10: 704–716.

Feyerabend, P. K. 1985. *Realism, Rationalism and Scientific Method, Volume 1: Philosophical Papers*. Cambridge, UK: Cambridge University Press.

Fisher, K. W. and T. R. Bidell. 2006. "Dynamic development of action, thought and emotion." In *Theoretical Models of Human Development: Handbook of Child Psychology*, 6th ed., eds. W. Damon and R. M. Lerner, 313–399. New York: Wiley.

Freeman, W. J. 1997. "Three centuries of category errors in studies of the neural basis of consciousness and intentionality." *Neural Networks* 10, no. 7: 1175–1183.

Gavin, W. J. and T. J. Blakeley. 1976. *Russia and America, A Philosophical Comparison: Development and Change of Outlook from the 19th to the 20th century.* Boston: D. Reidel Publishing.

Gibson, J. J. 1979. *The Ecological Approach to Visual Perception.* Boston: Houghton Mifflin.

von Goethe, J. W., and J. P. Eckermann. 1827. *Conversations of Goethe with Johann Peter Eckermann.* Trans. John Oxenford. London: Smith, Elder & Co.

Graham, L. and J. M. Kantor. 2009. "A comparison of two cultural approaches to mathematics. France and Russia, 1890–1930." *Isis* 97, no. 1: 56–74.

Gray, J. A. 1995. "The content of consciousness: A neuropsychological conjecture." *Behavioral and Brain Sciences* 18, no. 4: 659–722.

Haun, D. B. M., C. J. Rapold, J. Call, G. Janzen, and S. C. Levinson. 2006. "Cognitive cladistics and cultural override in Hominid spatial cognition." *Proceedings of the National Academy of Sciences* 103, no. 46: 17568–17573.

Hsee, C. K. and E. U. Weber. 1999. "Cross-national differences in risk preference and lay predictions." *Journal of Behavioral Decision Making* 12, no. 2: 165–179.

Ivanitsky, A. M., A. R. Nikolaev, and G. A. Ivanitskiy. 2001. "Cortical connectivity during word association search." *International Journal of Psychophysiology* 42, no. 1: 35–53.

Jackunas, Z. J. 2006. "Is it a meaningful dichotomy? Local vs global knowledge." Paper presented at The History of Science and the Cultural Integration of Europe, Krakow, September 6–9.

James, W. 1989. *The Principles of Psychology.* New York: Henry Holt.

January, D. and E. Kako. 2007. "Re-evaluating evidence for linguistic relativity: Replay to Boroditsky." *Cognition* 104, no. 2: 417–426.

John, E. R., P. Easton, and R. Isenhart. 1997. "Consciousness and cognition may be mediated by multiple independent coherent ensembles." *Conscious and Cognition* 6, no. 1: 3–39.

Jordan, J. S. 1998. "Recasting Dewey's critique of the reflex-arc concept via a theory of anticipatory consciousness: implications for theories of perception." *New Ideas in Psychology* 16, no. 3: 165–187.

Klemun, M. 2008. "Geological state surveys: Geological maps as acts of synthesis and as evidence of differing 'styles of thinking'." Paper presented at the 3rd International Conference of the European Society for the History of Science, Vienna, September 10–12.

Kobayashi, C., G. H. Glover, and E. Temple. 2006. "Cultural and linguistic influence on neuronal bases of 'Theory of Mind'." *Brain and Language* 98, no. 2: 210–222.

Kobayashi, C., G. H. Glover, and E. Temple. 2007. "Cultural and linguistic effects on neural bases of 'Theory of Mind' in American and Japanese children." *Brain Research* 1164: 95–107.

Koffka, K. 1935. *Principles of Gestalt Psychology*. New York: Harcourt, Brace, and Company.

Kragh, H. 2006. "The internationalization of physical cosmology." Paper presented at The History of Science and the Cultural Integration of Europe, Krakow, September 6–9.

Kruglikov, R. I. 1982. *On the Interaction of Neurotransmitter Systems in Processes of Learning and Memory*. New York: Raven Press.

Krylov, A. K., and Y. Alexandrov. 2006. "Modeling of a reflex-based agent situated in an environment reveals the limits of the stimuli presentation paradigm." *International Journal of Psychophysiology* 61, no. 3: 327.

Krylov, A. K., and Y. Alexandrov. 2007. "'Situatedness in an environment' as alternative to stimuli presentation: Model study." *Psikhologicheskii Zhurnal* 28, no. 2: 106–113.

Lashley, K. S. 1933. "Integrative functions of the cerebral cortex." *Physiological Reviews* 13, no. 1: 1–42.

Levins, R. and R. Lewontin. 1980. "Dialectics and reductionism in ecology." *Conceptual Issues in Ecology* 43, no. 1: 47–78.

Lewin, K. 1935. "The conflict between Aristotelian and Galilean modes of thought in contemporary psychology." In *A Dynamic Theory of Personality*, ed. K. Lewin. New York: McGraw-Hill.

Mitina, O., and Petrenko, V. 1999. "Attitudes toward political parties." In *The Russian Transformation*, ed. B. Glad, and E. Shiraev, 179–198. New York: St. Martin's Press.

Nisbett, R. E., K. Peng, I. Choi, and A. Norenzayan. 2001. "Culture and systems of thought: Holistic versus analytic cognition." *Psychological Review* 108, no. 2: 291–310.

Nosulenko, V. N., V. A. Barabanshikov, A. V. Brushlinsky, and P. Rabardel. 2005. "Man-technology interaction: some of Russian approaches." *Theoretical Issues in Ergonomics Sciences* 6, no. 5: 359–383.

NSF Task Force. 1996. "Introduction." *Newsletter of the Animal Behavior Society* 36, no. 4.

Paló, G. 2008. "Scientific nationalism: Historical approach to nature in the late 19th century." Paper presented at the 3rd International Conference of the European Society for the History of Science, Vienna, September 10–12.

Panksepp, J. 2000. "The neuro-evolutionary cusp between emotions and cognitions: Implications for understanding consciousness and the emergence of a unified mind science." *Consciousness & Emotion* 1, no. 1: 15–54.

Peng, K., D. A. Ames, and E. D. Knowles. 2001. "Culture and human inference: perspectives from three traditions." In *Handbook of Cross-Cultural Psychology*, ed. D. Matsumoto, 245–264. Oxford: Oxford University Press.

Perner, J. and M. Aichorn. 2008. "Theory of mind, language and temporoparietal junction mystery." *Trends in Cognitive Sciences* 12, no. 4: 123–126.

Petrovsky, A. V., and M. G. Yaroshevsky. 1996. *The History and Theory of Psychology.* Rostov on Don: Feniks.

Polanyi, M. 1997. *Society, Economics and Philosophy: Selected Papers of Michael Polanyi.* Ed. R. T. Allen. New Brunswick, N.J.: Transaction Publishers.

Popovsky, M. A. 1978. *Science in Chains: The Crisis of Science and Scientists in the Soviet Union Today.* New York: Collins.

Priest, S., ed. 1987. *Hegel's Critique of Kant.* Oxford: Oxford University Press.

Rose, S. 1995. "The rise of neurogenetic determinism." *Nature* 373, no. 6513: 380–382.

Rubinstein, S. L. 1973. "Man and the world." In *The Problems of General Psychology.* Moscow: Pedagogika.

Schall, J. D. 2001. "Neural basis of deciding, choosing and acting." *Nature Reviews Neuroscience* 2, no. 1: 33–42.

Schneirla, T. C. 1959. "An evolutionary and developmental theory of biphasic processes underlying approach and withdrawal." In *Nebraska Symposium on Motivation*, ed. M. Jones, 1–42. Lincoln: University of Nebraska Press.

Shadrikov, V. D. 1982. "The problems of occupational abilities." *Psikologicheskiĭ Zhurnal* 3, no. 5: 13–26.

Shanon, B. 2001. "Against the spotlight model of consciousness." *New Ideas in Psychology* 19, no. 1: 77–84.

Shvyrkov, V. B. 1978. *A Neuropsychological Study of Systemic Mechanism of Behavior.* Moskow: Nauka.

Shvyrkov, V. B. 1984. "Toward a psychophysiological theory of behavior." In *Psychophysiological Approaches to Human Information Processing*, ed. F. Klix, 47–72. Amsterdam: Elsevier.

Shvyrkov, V. B. 1986. "Behavioral specialization of neurons and the system-selection hypothesis of learning." In *Human Memory and Cognitive Capabilities*, ed. F. Klix and H. Hagendorf, 599–611. Amsterdam: Elsevier.

Shvyrkov, V. B. 1990. *Neurophysiological Study of Systemic Mechanisms of Behavior.* New Delhi: Oxonian Press.

Shvyrkov, V. B. 2006. *Introduction to Objective Psychology: Neuronal Basics of the Psyche, Selected Works.* Moscow: IP RAN.

Singh, A. 2007. "Action and reason in the theory of Ayurveda." *AI and Society* 21, no. 1–2: 27–46.

Skotnikova, I. G. 2008. *Problemy Subektnoi Psikhofiziki.* Moscow: Institut Psikhologii.

Slobin, D. I. 2004. "The many ways to search for a frog: Linguistic typology and the expression of motion events." In *Relating Events in Narrative*, eds S. Strömqvist and L. Verhoeven, 219–257. Mahwah, N.J.: Lawrence Erlbaum Associates.

Stamhuis, I. H. 2008. "A national style of statistical thinking." Paper presented at the 3rd International Conference of the European Society for the History of Science, Vienna, September 10–12.

Sudakov, K. V. 1997. "The theory of functional systems: general postulates and principles of dynamic organization." *Integrative Physiological and Behavioral Science* 32, no. 4: 392–414.

Tan, L. H., A. H. Chan, P. Kay, P. Khong, L. K. Yip, and KK. Luke. "Language affects patterns of brain activation associated with perceptual decision." *Proceedings of the National Academy of Sciences* 105, no. 10: 4004–4009.

Tang, Y., W. Zhang, K. Chen, S. Feng, J. Shen, and E. M. Reiman. 2006. "Arithmetic processing in the brain shaped by cultures." *Proceedings of the National Academy of Sciences* 103, no. 28: 10775–10780.

Thompson, E. and F. J. Varela. 2001. "Radical embodiment: neural dynamics and consciousness." *Trends in Cognitive Sciences* 5, no. 10: 418–425.

Tolman, E. C. 1932. *Purposive Behavior in Animals and Men*. New York: Appleton-Century-Crofts.

Tononi, G. and G. M. Edelman. 1998. "Consciousness and complexity." *Science* 282, no. 5395: 1846–1851.

Toomela, A. 2007. "Culture of science: strange history of the methodological thinking in psychology." *Integrative Psychological and Behavioral Science* 41, no. 1: 6–20.

Tulving, E. 1986. "Memory and consciousness." *Canadian Psychology* 26, no. 1: 1–12.

Uexküll, J. 1957. "A stroll through the worlds of animals and men." In *Instinctive Behavior: The Development of a Modern Concept*, ed. C. H. Schiller, 5–80. New York: International Universities Press.

Vandervert, L. R. 1998. "Consciousness: a preliminary multidisciplinary mapping of concepts." *New Ideas in Psychology* 16, no. 3: 159–164.

Von Stutterheim, C. and R. Nüse. 2003. "Processes of conceptualization in language production: language-specific perspectives and event construal." *Linguistics* 41, no. 5: 851–881.

Von Stutterheim, C., R. Nüse, and J. M. Serra. 2002. "Cross-linguistic differences in the conceptualisation of events." *Language and Computers* 39, no. 1: 179–198.

Watson, G. 1934. "Psychology in Germany and Austria." *Psychological Bulletin* 31, no. 10: 755–776.

Webb, B. 2004. "Neural mechanisms for prediction: do insects have forward models?" *Trends in Neuroscience* 27, no. 5: 278–282.

Werner, H. and B. Kaplan. 1956. "The developmental approach to cognition: its relevance to the psychological interpretation of anthropological and ethno linguistic data." *American Anthropologist* 58, no. 5: 866–880.

Whitcomb, K. M., D. Önkal, S. P. Curley, and P. G. Benson. 1995. "Probability judgment accuracy for general knowledge. Cross-national differences and assessment methods." *Journal of Behavioral Decision Making* 8, no. 1: 51–67.

Wilson, E. O. 1998. *Consilience: The Unity of Knowledge*. New York: Alfred A. Knopf.

Winawer, J., N. Witthoft, M. C. Frank, L. Wu, A. R. Wade, and L. Boroditsky. 2007. "Russian blues reveal effects of language on color discrimination." *Proceedings of the National Academy of Sciences* 104, no. 19: 7780–7785.

Woese, C. R. 2004. "A new biology for a new century." *Microbiology and Molecular Biology Reviews* 68, no. 2: 173–186.

Wright, G. N. and L. D. Phillips. 1980. "Cultural variation in probabilistic thinking: alternative ways of dealing with uncertainty." *International Journal of Psychology* 15, no. 4: 239–257.

Yaroshevsky, M. G. 1996. *Marxism in Soviet Psychology: The Social Role of Russian Science*. Westport, Conn.: Greenwood Press.

Yates, J. F., J. W. Lee, and H. Shinotsuka. 1996. "Beliefs about overconfidence, including its cross-national variation." *Organizational Behavior and Human Decision Processes* 65, no. 2: 138–147.

Yusupova, T. I. 2008. "National and nationalistic reasons in motivation for Russian expeditions in Central Asia." Paper presented at the 3rd International Conference of the European Society for the History of Science, Vienna, September 10–12.

Zajonc, R. B. 1980. "Feeling and thinking. Preferences need no inferences." *American Psychologist* 35, no. 2: 151–175.

CHAPTER 4

Cognitive Activity from the Perspective of Functional Systems Theory

K. V. Sudakov

1   Introduction

Cognition remains an enigmatic feature of psychicalal activity (i.e. activity of the mind) despite the current broad usage of this term. The term "cognitive" is often used as a substitute for the psychicalal activity of humans and animals. However, we believe that psychicalal activity is a much broader concept that includes cognitive activity as a separate component. In general, cognitive activity encompasses the processes of cognition, learning, memory, and sometimes thinking. Nonetheless, in addition to those, psychicalal activity also includes the processes of perception, sensing, emotions, motivations, creativity or imagination, thinking, remembering, forgetting, etc.

Cognitive activity has been viewed by the majority of Russian authors through the prism of the wide-spread reflex theory, where a leading role is assigned to external stimuli, and investigation focuses on the consequent reactions of living beings. According to the classical reflex theory, a reflex is formed based on a reflex arc and culminates in action.

Thus, modern research of human and animal cognition is a tribute to reductionism. Furthermore, in general, various manifestations of cognitive activity are typically artificially separated from the integrative activity of the brain and body.

In essence, psychicalal activity, being closely connected to the external environment, including the social environment in humans, is to a large extent an internal product of brain activity. Human psychicalal activity may manifest itself in behavior, but also may be information-based and occur in the form of thought without any external behavioral manifestation.

The theory of functional systems, formulated by P. K. Anokhin (Anokhin 1974), shed new light on the organization of psychicalal activity of humans and animals. Cognitive activity, and its association with the processes of thinking, learning, and memory and the underlying brain structures, is viewed by this theory as part of a general systems organization of psychicalal activity. The overall integrative organization of psychicalal activity and the place of cognitive processes in this organization were elucidated from a functional systems theoretical perspective.

A detailed description of the theory of functional systems was provided in a number of scientific publications (Sudakov 1997; Sudakov 1998). Here, the main emphasis will be on reviewing the basic principles of formation of the bodily functional systems and how these principles may be applied to develop an understanding of the organization of psychicalal and cognitive activity.

2 Body Functional Systems

With respect to its predecessors, the theory of functional systems has three scientific sources: I. P. Pavlov's ideas on analytical-synthetic brain activity and the human being as a "highly self-regulating, self-sustaining, self-restoring, self-correcting, and self-improving" (Pavlov 1955) system, A. A. Ukhtomsky's theory of the dominant (Ukhtomsky 1950), and, finally, the general systems theory formulated by L. von Bertalanffy (Bertalanffy 1967). However, the theory of functional systems is substantially more than just the sum of its predecessors.

The systems approach proclaimed by L. Von Bertalanffy and his numerous followers asserts the need to examine various phenomena and processes as a unity of their constituent elements through which the elements acquire a new quality, much like the Gestalt theory. However, this popular approach does not address the questions of what unites these separate elements into systems and how these systems function.

In contrast to the above, the theory of functional systems, proposed by P. K. Anokhin, clearly defines an organizing factor underlying formation of various functional systems. This produces adaptive results useful both for the functional systems, and for living organisms in general. *Functional systems are dynamic self-organizing and self-regulating constructs whose constituent elements are concomitantly united to achieve adaptive results useful for the system and for the whole body.* Useful adaptive results include metabolic results of reaction in tissues, various parameters of the internal environment that affect metabolic processes in tissues, and the results of behavioral and psychicalal activity that satisfy the numerous needs of living beings.

In general, the body has many interrelated, harmoniously interacting functional systems at metabolic, homeostatic, behavioral, and psychicalal levels of organization (Figure 4.1). Populations of living beings, including humans, also organize to form functional systems: at a "zoosocial" level for animals, and at a social level for humans (Sudakov 1997).

COGNITIVE ACTIVITY: FUNCTIONAL SYSTEMS THEORY

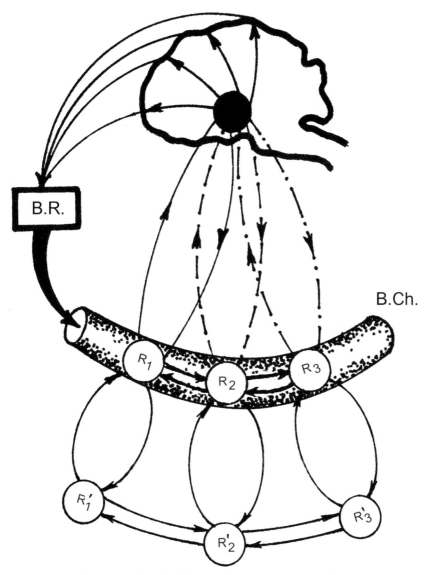

FIGURE 4.1   Interaction of multiple functional systems of the body $R_1^* R_2^* R_3^*$ – results of functional systems activity at the metabolic level; $R_1 R_2 R_3$ – at the homeostatic level; B.R. – result of behavior; B.Ch. – blood channel.

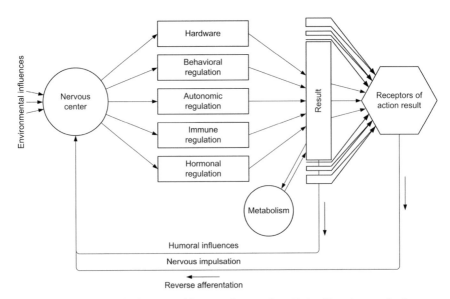

FIGURE 4.2   General schematic of functional system by P. K. Anokhin. As a result of functional system activity, given deviation from optimal levels, there is mobilization of numerous executive mechanisms (behavioral, vegetative, hormonal, and immune regulation) through engagement of the mechanisms of self-regulation, reverse afferentation, and excitation of relevant processes to return the system to an optimal level.

The main distinction of multi-level functional systems, that sets them apart from systems merely consisting of collections of constituent elements, is the dynamics of their operation. The adaptive utility of the results produced through the activity of functional systems is continuously evaluated. Evaluative functions are accomplished by special centers within the functional systems through reverse afferentation coming to *acceptors of action results*, which are units responsive to the parameters of these results (Figure 4.2). According to the self-regulation principle, any deviation of a result from the level providing optimal life activity is a reason for mobilizing all of the components of each functional system to bring that system back to its optimal point.

Functional systems arise in response to the current internal needs of living beings, or under the influence of external environmental factors. In addition, memory mechanisms can also lead to the formation of functional systems in living organisms. From the standpoint of the whole body, functional systems that are organized at various levels interact in accordance with certain principles: namely, hierarchic dominance, multi-parametric interaction, and sequential interaction.

The principle of hierarchic interaction presumes that at any moment, body activity is governed by a biologically dominant functional system. The other functional systems either support the activity of the dominant one, or are suppressed. Once the dominant need is satisfied, another dominant need takes over the body's activity, and forms a dominant functional system, and so on. Furthermore, at any time, the dominance of functional systems is determined by the vital significance of the underlying needs for survival in, or adaptation to, the environment. In relation to each dominant functional system, subdominant functional systems assume a position within a hierarchy that reflects their significance for a human being, from the molecular level to that of a person and society. Hierarchical relations between the functional systems of the body are formed based on the results of their activity.

The principle of multi-parametric interaction establishes the relationships between the results of the functional systems activity. The multiparametric principle assumes that the results of the activity of different functional systems are closely interrelated. A change in the result of one functional system's activity triggers dynamic reorganization of related results from other functional systems' activities. In general, multi-parametric interaction of the various functional systems provides a foundation for establishing homeostasis. In addition, multi-parametric interactions connect functional systems underlying behavior prompted by biological and social needs, and functional systems that support homeostatic parameters of the internal body environment.

Sequential interaction describes the relationship between the functional systems in time, and specifically, when the result of one functional system determines the activity of another functional system.

The interaction of functional systems reflects the harmonious inter-systemic relations within the body. From the point of view of functional systems theory, the normal human condition may be defined as a harmonious interaction of various functional systems operating at various levels to ensure a homeostasis that is optimal for human life and its adaptation to the environment. From the same point of view, social adaptation of a human being is defined as the ability of the functional systems to achieve socially significant results.

Contrary to classical physiology, in which the relationships between the organs of the body are dictated by principles of anatomy, the theory of functional systems postulates the systems organization of human functions from the molecular to the social levels, including psychicalal activity as a leading principle. Thus, the whole body represents a harmonious integration of multiple functional systems organized at various levels. Some functional systems are genetically determined; others are formed in life as the person interacts with various aspects of internal and external environments.

Due to the associated activity of multiple functional systems, any given vital parameter of the body reflects not only the activity of individual organs, but an aggregate result of their systemic interaction. Unlike reflex activity, a functional system is never limited by actions, but is always geared towards achieving some adaptive result. A reflex arc, which combines various reflexes, evolves from previous or newly organized dominant functional systems that are formed in meeting a certain need of the body. Driven by dominant needs, the functional systems facilitate the active transformation of the external environment and goal-directed activity of living beings.

Reflex mechanisms evident in the responses to a stimulus are only a component of a functional system (Anokhin 1974). Homeostatic and behavioral mechanisms of the functional systems' self-regulation are dynamically combined through the activity of the whole body (Figure 4.3). Self-regulating functional systems at the homeostatic and metabolic levels are involved in brain activity and act as a driver in the formation of psychicalal activity. Therefore, it is clear that human psychicalal activity is determined not only by brain functions but also by functions, of the whole body.

3 Cerebral Architectonics of Psychicalal Activity

In accordance with functional systems theory, cerebral architectonics of psychicalal activity includes the following key mechanisms arranged in sequence: (1) afferent synthesis, (2) decision making, (3) anticipation of a result satisfying the initial dominant psychicalal or metabolic need, (4) efferent synthesis, and (5) continuous evaluation of achieved results. Evaluation of achieved results involves comparing parameters of results observed through reverse afferentation and the expectations of the acceptor of action results.

At the afferent synthesis phase, the dominant motivation formed by a psychicalal or metabolic need, and accompanied by negative emotions, continuously interacts with afferent signals elicited by environmental stimuli, and also with various memory mechanisms. In accordance with the dominant principle (Ukhtomskiy 1950), interaction of external and internal factors during afferent synthesis sets the stage for the most important mechanism of psychicalal activity, namely, decision making. Decision making limits the degrees of freedom of neuronal activity of the brain and directs activity toward satisfaction of the dominant motivation formed at this time. Decision making through functional systems associated with psychicalal activity is affected by components of afferent synthesis, and in turn, exerts a continuous influence upon the processes of afferent synthesis.

COGNITIVE ACTIVITY: FUNCTIONAL SYSTEMS THEORY 93

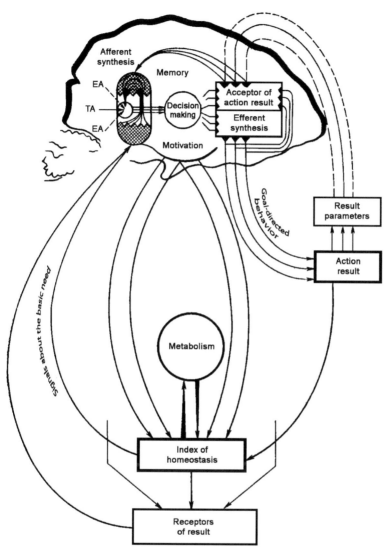

FIGURE 4.3 Functional system combining internal (homeostatic) and external (behavioral) self-regulation links. The internal link helps to maintain the homeostasis parameter at an optimal level. The external link through the system-organized central architectonics directs the subject to achieve a behavioral result satisfying the internal need. EA – environmental afferentation, TA – trigger afferentation.

Once a decision is made, cognitive activity may be limited by neurodynamic information, which includes related executive mechanisms of the brain, such as thinking, autonomic functions, or behavioral processes, including speech and other activity directed at meeting the initial need. But before these excitations are relayed to executive somatic, vegetative, hormonal, and immune mechanisms, the acceptor of action results is already formed in the central architectonics of the functional systems of psychicalal activity. The acceptor of action results provides a means for anticipating parameters of the initial need and the required result, while contributing to achieving this result.

The external environment affects the body, beginning with its receptors, and either satisfies or fails to satisfy the body's psychicalal needs. These environmental factors generate information-based afferent excitation fluxes (reverse afferentation) that spread through the CNS and become physically imprinted in the neural substrates underlying the action result acceptor. These representations then provide the basis for anticipatory assessment of key parameters of a result, as to whether current actions are likely to satisfy ongoing needs.

In addition to the physical and chemical processes of the brain, the central architectonics of human psychicalal activity also encompasses informational processes. Information is an essential aspect of life. It is manifested in the relations of objects to objects, subjects to objects, subjects to subjects, subjects to reality, etc.

In 1969, in his article "Psychicalal Form of Reality Reflection," P. K. Anokhin introduced the idea of "informational equivalent of reality" (Anokhin 1969). He was the first to formulate the idea that the human brain forms an internal representation of external reality (e.g., a mental model). It was believed that this representation arose when the receptors of the body are affected by the various parameters of useful adaptive results, in the context of having satisfied the needs of a living being, with the representation composed of informational equivalents.

To advance Anokhin's ideas about informational equivalence, we formulated the concepts of "informational equivalent of a need" and "informational equivalent of reinforcement" (Sudakov 1997). Information is generated through relationships among physiological processes that occur both within functional systems and between them. In these functional systems, the needs of the body, involving deviations of various parameters of the internal environment from an optimal level for life, are the primary cause for information generation. Through reverse afferent inputs and humoral molecules, needs generate information that goes into the central nervous system, and facilitates formation of a dominant motivation. In turn, by way of specific neurophysiological mechanisms, dominant motivations elicit appropriate behavior for meeting a need. Furthermore, regardless of the specific mechanisms, information associated with a need is retained at each phase within the formation of a related functional system.

Within the functional systems, information about a need is evaluated by the acceptor of action results. Moreover, the acceptor of action results, through reverse afferentation, continuously evaluates information related to need satisfaction. When the need has been satisfied on multiple occasions, the parameters of related reinforcing factors are imprinted in the structures of a respective action result acceptor, and it becomes possible to anticipate proper satisfaction of the need.

In the process of satisfying a dominant need, within the functional systems, information is generated concerning the *relation* between the significance of reinforcing factors and the magnitude of the need. Thus, the central architectonics of functional systems are responsible for psychicalal activity involving representations of the dynamics of information processes that are related to needs and their satisfaction. These representations include information processes concerning: (1) transformation of the dominant need into motivational excitation, (2) transformation of motivation into thought and behavioral activity, and finally, (3) transformation of reinforcing factors into operation of the action result acceptor, that in turn exerts an inverse informational influence on afferent synthesis. These processes occur at each phase of system-organized psychicalal activity with no loss of informational content regarding the initial need and its satisfaction.

Along with the spiking activity of neurons, a significant role in these processes belongs to the information molecules of DNA-RNA and other biologically active substances, specifically, oligopeptides. A group of oligopeptides transfers information about metabolic needs to the neurons of the brain, inducing an appropriate motivation. A second group establishes dominant motivations at the phase of afferent synthesis. A third group facilitates transformation of the dominant motivation into behavior. Finally, a fourth group supports assessment of actual results when reverse afferentation reaches the brain structures. Thus, the structural elements of the brain, neurons, synaptic connections, glial cells, and cerebral fluid, serve as carriers of information.

The information-based anticipations of the action result acceptors are continuously compared to actual results of behavior and evaluated in the process of thought or behavioral activity. Therefore, the acceptors of action provide a foundation on which functional systems are built at an informational level.

4 Informative Role of Emotions as Components of System-Organized Psychicalal Activity

Cerebral architectures formed by functional systems are built upon an emotional foundation. Prompted by self-sentiment and the essential sense of one's "Self," there is a continuous interaction with information coming from the internal body environment and from the outside world (MacLean 1989). The information aspect of a need, and its satisfaction, are primarily manifested in specific emotional sensations: the need generates a negative emotion, and its satisfaction generates a positive emotion, as a subjective *attitude* concerning the need and its satisfaction.

P. V. Simonov noted the information aspect of emotions in the need- and information-based theory of emotions that he formulated. According to Simonov, within the brains of humans and higher vertebrates, an emotion is "a reflection of a relevant need (its quality and magnitude) and probability (possibility) of its satisfaction, which the subject involuntarily evaluates based on his genetic and acquired individual experience" (Simonov 2004). Simonov emphasized that there is a dependency between the intensity of an emotion, the strength of the related need, and the probability of its satisfaction.

For P. K. Anokhin, emotions act as a special kind orienting mechanism, through which the needs of living beings and their achievement, as well as the impact of various external factors on the body, provide the basis for distinguishing the useful from the harmful. As a rule, psychicalal needs, as with biological needs, are accompanied by negative emotional sensations, whereas the satisfaction of needs is accompanied by a variety of positive emotions. Based on the repeated satisfaction of the same type of psychicalal needs, the subject learns to anticipate the positive emotions of need satisfaction, and incorporates this into the action result acceptor. In other situations, negative emotions can also be anticipated, which, in the long run, enables probabilistic prediction of emotional states.

5 Systemic Quantization of Psychicalal Activity

In 1983, we formulated the principle of systemic quantization of life processes, and subsequently, extended this principle to the realm of psychicalal activity (Sudakov 2005). The principle of systemic quantization of psychicalal activity implies that, at the psychicalal level, there is a continuum of activity of

COGNITIVE ACTIVITY: FUNCTIONAL SYSTEMS THEORY

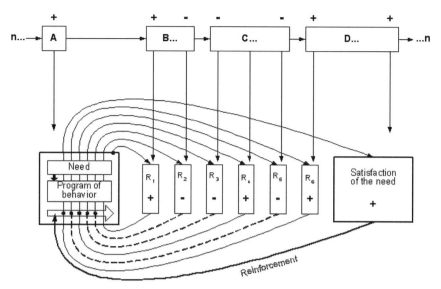

FIGURE 4.4 Phased restructuring of systemic quanta of behavior R_1–R_6 – intermediate results of behavior

various functional systems that may be broken down into separate discrete segments (i.e., systemic quanta): from a need to its satisfaction. Each systemic quantum of human behavioral and psychicalal activity arises from its respective functional system and incorporates: (1) the initial metabolic or psychicalal need, (2) dominant motivation based on this need, (3) behavior directed at satisfaction of the need, and (4) intermediate and final results of this activity, including evaluation, via reverse afferentation, as to whether the need was satisfied (Figure 4.4).

Dominant motivation and reinforcement are on the extreme points of the continuum and play a leading role in the formation of systemic quanta of human behavior and psychicalal activity. In each functional system, the acceptor of action results continuously evaluates the adaptive significance of the achieved results. This elicits continuous re-structuring of the entire central architectonics of the functional systems, which ultimately leads to an enhanced capacity for satisfaction of the subject's need.

Based upon the psychicalal needs of the body, psychicalal activity is broken into effective systemic quanta and psychicalal activity directed to satisfaction of needs and the assessment of the achieved results. Psychicalal systemic quanta are based on the information processes of afferent synthesis reflecting various internal and external effects on brain structures, and information processes of reinforcement, including the evaluations of the achieved results.

Systemic quantization of psychical activity obeys the principle of autoregulation. Accordingly, via reverse afferentation, there is continuous evaluation based upon intermediate (phased) results, relative to the subject's dominant psychical needs. Each phase of psychical activity is evaluated in regard to satisfaction of the body's dominant need. If the achieved results, and specifically, associated parameters causing reverse afferentation through the body's receptors, correspond to the properties of the action result acceptor indicating satisfaction of the need, the systemic quantization of psychical activity is terminated. Then, a new need forms with another systemic psychical quantum, and so forth. In the event that parameters of achieved results do not correspond to the properties of the dominant action result acceptor, searching-investigative activity takes place accompanied by a strengthened negative emotion. This triggers re-structuring of afferent synthesis, adoption of a new decision, and attempted correction of the action result acceptor, after which thought and behavioral activity is geared towards achieving a more satisfactory result.

Systemic quanta of human psychical activity can be formed during various stages of training and instruction, including self-instruction. Furthermore, the quantization of human psychical activity occurs in different forms: sequential, hierarchic, and mixed (Sudakov 2005, 12–29).

6   Systems Organization of Thought

From the point of view of functional systems theory, thought is an executive mechanism of the cerebral architectonics of system-organized psychical activity. We believe that human thought defines the operations of the brain that underlie information processing enabling "unique" behavior at the informational level. Thought culminates in an information result (i.e., formation of a thought).

The general functional systems theory presumes that thought processes include the following key universal components: (1) results serve as a leading factor in forming systems of human thought activity; (2) evaluation of the results of thought via reverse afferentation; (3) biological and social needs, and associated motivations and corresponding external stimuli, influence the system-formation of thought activity; (4) the organization of thought activity involves the mechanisms of afferent synthesis and decision-making, and the acceptor of action results; (5) there is effector manifestation of thought processes through behavior, somatic-autonomic components, and especially, vocalization. Furthermore, all of these processes are continuously evaluated by the action result acceptor via reverse afferentation.

The operational architectures of thought is built up from emotional and verbal equivalents of reality: the informational equivalents of needs, motivations, behaviors, and evaluations of achieved results. Thought processes are always accompanied by an individual's subjective appraisal of the extent to which external factors have led to satisfaction of dominant needs. Emotions prompt recollection of past experiences from memory. Emotions are further utilized in assessing needs, the related impact of external factors including the individual's interactions with objects and other individuals, and, finally, the satisfaction of those needs.

The role of emotion in the organization of thought is genetically determined. It is manifested in newborns, blind deaf-mutes, and also in people surrounded by others who speak a foreign language. As demonstrated by experiments with autostimulation, the influence of emotions upon thought is even evidenced in animals. Furthermore, morbid attraction to alcohol and narcotic drugs has its roots in strong emotional sensations.

During evolution, human beings acquired a capacity for the verbal evaluation of thought. The evaluation of needs and their satisfaction, the associated effects upon the body of various external factors, and corresponding emotional sensations is performed using language symbols, phrases, and both oral and written verbal constructs. This level of thought is only possible following acquisition of linguistic capabilities. Linguistic symbols are used to build language-based functional systems at the informational level of an action result acceptor. Thoughts in turn are realized in discrete phrases that can be part of internal speech or transformed into external speech and actions.

Human thoughts may be externally manifested in: (1) emotional reactions and behavior; (2) oral and written phrases, or (3) remain in the ideal form of brain information processes. A thought may be formed on the basis of afferent synthesis in response to signals coming from the internal environment, from various metabolic needs. On the other hand, thoughts may be formed in response to a certain situation. The processes of genetic and individually acquired memory play a significant role in the formation of thought. Finally, emergence of a thought may be stimulated by certain conditioned stimuli.

At the decision-making phase, a dominant thought of immediate significance to the subject is selected from a multitude of simultaneously accessible thoughts arising from afferent synthesis. The decision-making phase terminates with the formation of a system of thought activity and corresponding action result acceptor. At this point, the process of forming a thought as an anticipated action result comes to completion.

It should be noted that a thought always contains a goal that is formulated based on the information processes of afferent synthesis and decision making. Thought is contingent on the subject's upbringing and level of knowledge, with respect to his acquired ability to reach a goal. All of the above constitutes the process of goal planning.

Each phase involved in translating a thought into an action is evaluated using reverse afferentation through acoustic, visual, and kinesthetic channels. Thus, the systems formed through thought include its subjective and objective manifestations. Thoughts may be characterized as a subjective representation in the human brain of real needs, anticipation of objects, and means of satisfying needs through actions, and learned behavior, taken in response to external stimuli.

Therefore, thoughts, while products of reality, also represent a form of abstraction. The thought activity of an individual unfolds in the continuum of the people around him, and, ultimately, the entire human society in the context of its dynamic historical development.

In terms of individual human development, it is possible to talk about the systemogenesis of thought based on an individual's upbringing. Thought activity of a child begins when he becomes aware of a need and its satisfaction. First, the child perceives these states through specific emotions, just like animals do. Then, through the process of learning, he begins to associate these states with special words.

As a rule, the child first learns a word denoting the satisfaction of a need, and then establishes a link between his own satisfaction of that need and the people that surround him, especially with parents. At first, the needs themselves, as well as desires based on them, are manifested mostly through gestures, screaming, and crying. Finally, through multiple repeated satisfaction of the same-type need and its association with a specific word, the child begins to verbalize the need and later on, adds to it words that reflect desire. All of these processes are based on imprinting mechanisms. In the end, the emotional basis of systemic quanta of the child's behavior is enriched with verbal symbols.

The process of imitation plays an important role in the mechanisms of imprinting. Imitation of actions, also present in animals, leads to imitation of speech in humans. Consequently, imitation strengthens acquired knowledge.

The most critical point in the learning process is the "lessons learned," i.e. the process of acquiring new knowledge through experience with the world.

This process sets the stage for a qualitative transition from passive imprinting of reality by a child to active influence, exploration, and transformation of reality. It also involves anticipatory formation of an acceptor of action results. Furthermore, special role in the formation of thought activity belongs to preliminary instruction, whether in the course of learning languages, music, or various other skills.

A thought can become re-organized in the course of a goal-directed behavioral act. From the point of view of functional systems theory, any re-organization of thought activity occurs through reverse afferentation, and revision of achieved results by the action result acceptor. Systemic quanta of thought consist of links formed through internal and external auto-regulation. Auto-regulatory internal links direct the processes underlying internal speech. This largely involves memory mechanisms and operation of an information-based basic entity, the inner "Self." The product of internal speech may include meaningful concepts that reflect real objects existing outside the body and their relations, for example, reference words, results of mathematical operations, etc. Internal speech may be manifested in the activity of vocal muscles, ligaments of oral muscles, breathing, and other somatic-vegetative reactions. Reverse afferentation entering the CNS from the vocal cords and muscles and from special brain structures that facilitate emotional and semantic evaluation of thought plays a significant role in the organization of internal speech.

Auto-regulatory external links underlie the formation of an oral or written verbal phrase. Corresponding manifestations include general motor reactions, postures, gestures, facial expressions, eye movement, vocal reactions, as well as changes in breathing, heart rate, and electric skin reaction. Various technical devices, machines, computers, technologies, etc. have been incorporated by man into the external expression of thought activity, whereas evaluation of the results of their operation has been left in the human domain. Achieved results are assessed by means of reverse afferentation coming from the auditory and visual apparatus, muscles of the vocal cords, tongue and mouth cavity, breathing receptors, proprioceptors of facial muscles, eyes and body muscles, skin receptors, etc.

A spoken phrase is preceded by an anticipatory construction. Afferentation propagating from the peripheral apparatus to the action result acceptor allows dynamic evaluation of a thought expressed in a verbal phase and a mental replay of the thought during internal speech. The thought process in turn strongly depends on the state of peripheral organs. Following the principle of multiparametric interaction, they are connected to other vital body functions, with a range of interactions. The interaction between internal and external self-regulation of thought is based on equivalent information processes.

The highest form of thought activity is the creative process, when someone hindered by obstacles to need satisfaction and driven by imagination makes unusual decisions and achieves unusual results. Notably, the principle of systemic quantization is also manifest in human creative activity.

Thought activity may be organized in a rigid manner. Examples include: inherited forms of instinctive genetically determined activity related to satisfaction of biological needs; activity subject to special instructions; and automated activity taking place under consistent conditions. Rigidly organized thought activity encompasses intermediate and final results, and each successive step is completed only when the subject receives full information from the previously achieved result. In this case, the thought process often occurs at a subconscious level.

In contrast to the rigid organization, dynamic organization of thought activity occurs in response to variable conditions of life. This organization involves only the most meaningful external factors for the satisfaction of dominant human psychical needs. Dynamic programs of thought activity often ignore previously achieved intermediate results of activity that have little significance for the satisfaction of the dominant needs of the subject. The environmental cues used by the subjects to anticipate reinforcement are the conditioned stimuli studied by I. P. Pavlov.

Dynamic organizations of thought activity are generated in the process of learning and interactions with the external environment. Enrichment of action result acceptors occurs concurrently with improvement of the associated peripheral apparatuses, i.e. the mechanisms enabling an individual to achieve key results in satisfying individual or social needs. Consequently, the apparatus of efferent synthesis is further refined.

Individual consciousness arises through comparison of reverse afferentation from achieved results to action result acceptors of various functional systems and imprinting of these processes upon the acceptor structures. The more enriched is the action result acceptor, the richer is the intellect of an individual.

7 Dominant Motivation as the Basis of Psychical Cognitive Activity

Dominant motivation plays the key role in the formation of psychical and cognitive activity. Motivations are formed by internal needs and in humans, subdivided into biological (metabolic), and social needs. From the point of view of functional systems theory, motivations have a system-organizing role. This occurs through mobilizing brain neurons that initially interact in a random way into an organized constellation that underlies the preparedness to address one's needs.

As demonstrated by our experiments, biological motivations in animals in response to various metabolic needs are formed through specific ascending excitatory influences exerted by hypothalamic centers on other brain structures, specifically limbic formations, thalamus, reticular formation of the brain stem, and the cerebral cortex, especially its frontal regions. Regions within the hypothalamus associated with motivational processes act as a pacemaker influencing the complex cortical-subcortical structures of biological motivations. Destruction of these structures completely removes their excitatory influence on brain structures that produce biological motivations and goal-directed activity (Sudakov 2004).

At any time, the brain is affected by a dominant social or biological motivation formed in response to a need for survival or the adaptation of the subject to the environment. Other subdominant motivations support the dominant one, or are suppressed. Once the primary need is satisfied, other motivations become dominant in a hierarchical order.

Special experiments that we conducted attest to the fact that dominant motivations expressly alter the general properties of the brain. Convergent and discriminant properties of certain brain neurons become more enhanced in relation to various sensory effects: their sensitivity to neuromediators, neuropeptides, and other biologically active substances, undergo changes. Sensitivity of brain neurons to the effects of reinforcing and need-satisfying factors is dramatically increased. During motivation, expression of the early c-fos and c-jun genes is increased in numerous brain structures (Sudakov 1991; Sudakov 2004). It is also known (MacDonnell 1966) that the dominant motivation increases sensitivity of appropriate peripheral receptors. Thus, dominant motivations alter the properties of brain structures responsive to external stimuli and respective peripheral receptors in a controlled manner, selectively priming them to perceive and interact with stimuli that satisfy the needs underlying these motivations.

As shown by our research, the dominant motivation is clearly manifested in motivation-specific patterns of interspike intervals in the trains of neuron activity in various parts of the brain. The hunger motivation in rabbits is dominated by a distribution of neurons with interspike intervals of 10 and 150 ms; thirst motivation by intervals of 20 and 150 ms; and defensive motivation by intervals of 40 and 150 ms. The percentage of neurons with a dominant distribution of interspike intervals is different in different brain structures. It decreases as one moves from the brain stem to the cerebral cortex (Zhuravlev et al. 1991). In addition, motivation establishes reverberant relations between the cortical and subcortical structures of the brain, which, in our opinion, contributes to a more prolonged and intense activity of subjects in response to a need.

Within human psychical activity, biological motivations during afferent synthesis involve much more frequent interactions with environmental, oftentimes socially determined, perceptual, and memory mechanisms, than are involved for animals. In humans, mechanisms of socially determined memory are sometimes engaged in the formation of motivations of higher social significance. Human social motivations significantly alter the nature of human biological motivations.

With regard to the formation of goal-directed activity, motivation is closely tied to the operations of the action result acceptor. The dominant motivation interacts with the acceptor of psychical activity results and extracts from it, in an anticipatory manner, previously established parameters of required results.

A. V. Masterov (1975) performed a number of experiments in our laboratory to investigate how the dominant motivation, after preliminary training of the animals, evokes traces of excitation prior to presentation of a reinforcing stimulus. To get a food reward, hungry rats had to leave the starting chamber and go through three consecutive compartments of a maze (Figure 4.5). Visual stimuli in the form of a circle, a cross, or a triangle were placed in front of each compartment on shutters that had to be pushed by the animals. The compartment marked with the triangle was the closest one to the food reward; the compartment with the circle was the furthest. After eating another portion of food, the rats would find themselves in a "distribution chamber" that had three exits with respective signals (circle, cross, and triangle) that would take the animals to the above-mentioned compartments. The fourth exit would lead them back to the starting chamber. The experiments demonstrated that after 10–15 passes through the compartments marked with the visual images, the animals in the "distribution chamber" exhibited a preference for the stimulus that was the closest to the food reward, i.e. the triangle. By the 30th pass through the maze, they would choose only this particular stimulus in the distribution chamber. As the animals became satiated, the situation began to change: again, they would begin to choose different intermediate stimuli.

Experiments conducted by a Georgian physiologist, T. N. Oniani (1980), demonstrated the role of motivation in eliciting memory traces. Hungry cats were placed into a special cage with two compartments. In the first compartment, the animals did not get any food, but had to note the location of a light cue indicating the location of food bowls in the second compartment. Light cues signified that food was to either the right or left. During the

COGNITIVE ACTIVITY: FUNCTIONAL SYSTEMS THEORY 105

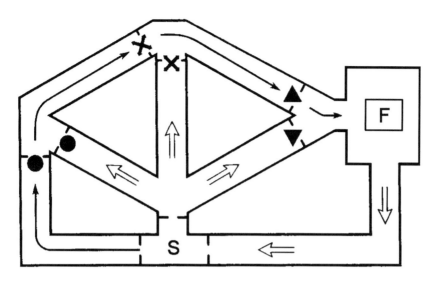

FIGURE 4.5 Maze diagram with intermediate results of behavior. *Arrows* – Possible lines animals' travel from the starting chamber (S). F – Food bowl. *Table A* demonstrates behavior of the rat in the maze as it is being trained. After 4 training sessions, the rat began to prefer the maze section with a triangle which was the shortest possible way to the food. *Table B* shows that as the animals become full they begin to select the maze section which is the longest way to the food.

experiment, the right or the left light cue was presented and after a delay interval, the door to the second compartment was opened, and the animal received food at the location previously indicated by the light cue. The animals were trained to produce a clear line of behavior. When the light on the right was flashed, the cats would run to the bowl on the right side once the door to the second compartment was opened; when the light on the left was flashed, they would run to the bowl on the left side of the door. Then, the level of difficulty in the experiment was raised: the time intervals between the light cue and the door opening were varied. The researchers measured the maximum duration which the animals would retain the signal trace and made no mistakes selecting the correct direction on entering the second compartment. It turned out that in a hungry state and in the presence of expressed food motivation the delayed reaction time could be significant. But it was substantially reduced as the animals became full, and as their dominant need was satisfied and the dominant motivation subsided. Thus, dominant motivation enables animals to anticipate and retain in memory the earlier developed means of satisfying the dominant need.

According to functional systems theory, memory is a system process closely linked with the systems architectonics of behavioral and psychical acts: afferent synthesis, decision-making, anticipation of required results, i.e. acceptor of action results, and efferent synthesis. Dominant motivation is involved in the formation of all phases of the systems architectonics of behavioral acts. However, the role of dominant motivation becomes even more prominent in the anticipation of required results, i.e. acceptor of action results. In the systems organization of human and animal behavioral and psychical acts, the acceptor of action results serves as a key behavioral vector.

8   Acceptors of Action Results in Functional Systems

The acceptor of action results in each functional system represents a mosaic of architectonics branching out into various structures of the cortex and subcortical formations. According to P. K. Anokhin's view, in terms of their structure, brain interneurons constitute a structural basis of acceptors of action results for the spreading, via the collaterals of the pyramidal tract, of copies of effector brain pyramidal neurons (Figure 4.6).

Due to the cyclic relations between the interneurons that make up the action result acceptor, excitations in these neurons based on reverberation mechanisms may last for a long time. This, in turn, enables them to remain in the excited state for extended durations. By doing so in response to the dominant

COGNITIVE ACTIVITY: FUNCTIONAL SYSTEMS THEORY

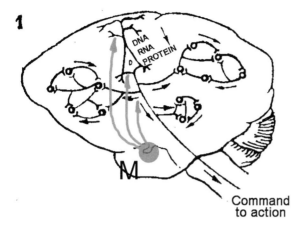

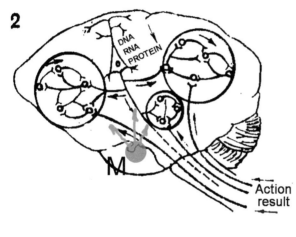

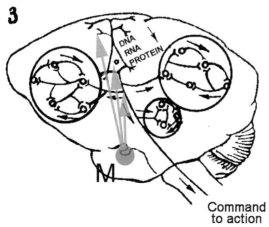

FIGURE 4.6
Schematic of formation of multi-level action result acceptor in brain structures and its extraction by dominant motivation: 1 – under the influence of the dominant motivation (M) and through the pyramidal tract, excitations are relayed to the system of interneurons located at various brain levels, i.e. action result acceptor; 2 – in the center: reinforcement engram is formed on interneurons under the influence of various parameters of achieved results; 3 – reinforcement engram is activated by the dominant motivation in an anticipatory manner.

motivation, they may continuously evaluate reverse afferentation from various parameters of results achieved by the subject.

The fact of pyramidal tract activation spreading via collaterals into interneurons was confirmed in special experiments, in which a microelectrode method was used to study responses of interneurons in various parts of the brain to antidromal stimulation of the central end of the pyramidal tract sectioned at the level of the olivary body. During the antidromal stimulation of the pyramidal tract, the interneuron responses were recorded in the somatosensory and visual cortex, and in the dorsal hippocampus. The same neurons displayed a clear response to stimuli of various sensory and biological modality, and also to stimulation of the motivation-producing centers of the hypothalamus, which suggests excitations of the pyramidal tract propagate via its projections through various brain structures.

9   Reinforcement as System Process

From the point of view of functional systems theory, reinforcement is a multicomponent process that includes: (a) parameters of the results achieved; (b) multi-channel reverse afferentation from receptors to neurons that make up the action result acceptor; and, finally, (c) evaluation of the incoming reverse afferentation by the action result acceptor.

Reinforcement acts as a system-forming factor. Once a subject attains the required results, a functional system with the mechanisms for advance anticipation of these results is established. In this regard, it seems appropriate to mention observations by our colleagues Bogomolova and Kurochkin. A newborn moose calf was lying down and trying to get on its feet. At first, it took a long time for it to do so. However, after its first successful attempt to stand (i.e. the achievement of an adaptive result), the next time the calf was able to stand at once and assume a vertical position.

Reinforcement, as demonstrated by our experiments, alters the properties of neurons involved in the dominant motivation. The spike train activity of these neurons reverts back to regular activity (Figure 4.7). Expression of the early c-fos and c-jun genes is decreased, and there is a change in the sensitivity of these neurons to the microiontophoretic behavior of neurotransmitters and neuropeptides.

The activity of individual neurons involved in various dominant functional systems and their spike train activity provide an anticipatory reflection of the properties of adaptive results required for need satisfaction (i.e. they are incorporated into the operations of the action result acceptor of relevant functional

COGNITIVE ACTIVITY: FUNCTIONAL SYSTEMS THEORY 109

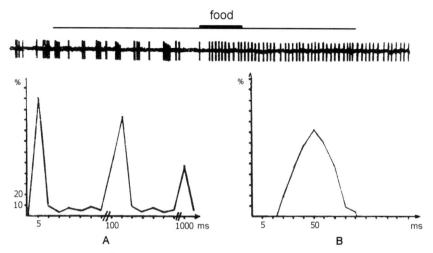

FIGURE 4.7   Typical response of rabbit's sensorimotor cortex neurons to feeding. Initial trains of spike activity of neurons involved in the dominant motivation of hunger are replaced by regular neuron activity during feeding. The graphs under the neurogram show distribution of the neuron interspike intervals: A – for the hungry state; B – after feeding; the ordinate shows percentage of the dominant interspike intervals; the abscissa shows duration of the interspike intervals.

systems). Hungry rabbits, whose spike train activity should normalize after the intake of food, were given an inedible item (i.e. foam) following the conditioned stimulus. Then, upon subsequent presentations of the foam, the animals displayed a higher level of initial spike train activity. Also, the interspike interval distribution was characteristic of the defensive state of the animals.

Our research has demonstrated that in hungry rabbits, neurons from various parts of the brain appear to be "primed" to respond to specific parameters of food reinforcement. In particular, within the visual cortex, the spike train activity typical of a state of hunger reverts to baseline activity when the hungry animal sees food. Similarly, the same effect has been observed in the thalamus when the food is put in the mouth, in the hypothalamus when the food enters the stomach, and in brain stem areas when glucose enters the blood stream.

Reverse multichannel afferentation from behavioral results is relayed to relevant brain structures receiving projections from the pyramidal tract, with visual, olfactory, gustatory, tactile, etc., activations going to the corresponding brain structures. Thus, reinforcing effects leave specific informational traces on corresponding areas of the brain. This occurs for both cerebral hemispheres and provides the architectonics of the action result acceptor arising from the dominant motivation, and is generalized over numerous brain structures.

Consequently, acceptors of action results serve as a foundation on which a structural and functional neural ensemble is built that reflects parameters of reinforcing events.

Multiple aspects of reality are imprinted on the structures of action result acceptors, including the location and sequence of events and their connection in time and space. Repeated achievement of desired results enriches the structure of the action result acceptor. This enrichment includes the sequential course of events, involving both positive and negative results, leading to satisfaction of the needs of the subject. Furthermore, during an individual's lifetime, the architectonics of the action result acceptor changes in a dynamic manner in accordance with variability of reinforcing parameters.

In accordance with the dominant motivation, learned experiences are retrieved in the same time sequence in which the real event happened during learning. In A. V. Kotov's experiments, rabbits were trained to make ritualistic movements, a 360-degree turn, before they were given food. During training, each 360-degree turn made by the animal was reinforced by a portion of food. Once the desired behavior was acquired, bipolar electrodes were implanted into the lateral hypothalamus. The tip of the electrode was positioned at a point in the lateral hypothalamus that, if stimulated, the sensation of being presented another portion of food was induced. The experiments were performed to find out whether artificial stimulation of a motivational "hunger center" in the lateral hypothalamus would evoke not only the feeding response but also the ritualistic 360-degree movement that each test animal was trained to make during the initial trials.

Experimental trials were carried out in the same location (the cage) where preliminary training in ritualistic food-procuring movements occurred. Test animals were fed before the experiment and demonstrated a state of complete calm in the experimental cage. However, following electrical stimulation of the lateral hypothalamus, they would jump up and make the ritualistic movement of the 360-degree turn, and then run to the feeding tray and exhibit eating behaviors. It is obvious that the dominant food motivation, evoked in the fed animals through artificial stimulation of the lateral hypothalamus, led to mobilization of the entire sequence of experiences that had preceded the food reinforcement during training.

These experiments confirm observations made earlier by Wirwicka (Wirwicka 1978) who demonstrated that stimulation of the lateral hypothalamus in a fed cat could cause not only feeding behaviors, but also an instrumental feeding response acquired prior to the lateral hypothalamus stimulation. Similarly, D. J. Foster and M. A. Wilson (Foster and Wilson 2006) demonstrated that anticipatory step-by-step replay of the entire sequence of previously presented stimuli is evoked in certain neurons of the dorsal hippocampus in rats.

It is well known that K. Lorenz (Lorenz 1965) was the first to report the phenomenon of imprinting in newborn chicks. He demonstrated that objects present in the environment are imprinted in memory and may evoke a following response. But neither Lorenz nor his followers, N. Tingbergen in particular, answered the question: what are the inner mechanisms of imprinting, and how long is imprinting manifested in the ontogenesis of living beings?

In 1978, we formulated a hypothesis of imprinting with respect to the formation of acceptors of action results. According to this hypothesis, the imprinted experiences are preserved throughout the life of an individual and are expressly manifested in the formation of dynamic brain stereotypes during learning. According to the imprinting hypothesis of the formation of action result acceptors, when behavioral results affect the body, their parameters become imprinted through reverse afferentation on appropriate structures of the action result acceptor.

Our experiments demonstrated that traces of reinforcing excitations are formed based on molecular informational processes of action result acceptors, and, primarily, protein molecules. Reinforcement forms molecular engrams on the structures of the action result acceptor. The next time the relevant needs arise, these engrams are activated. As shown by our experiments, protein synthesis inhibitors block the informational component of the animals' behavior (i.e. their attitude to the required result). Within the context of protein synthesis inhibition, oligopeptides with informational properties injected into the lateral ventricles of cerebrum restored the disabled motivational reactions of the animals (Sudakov 1987; Sudakov 1989).

Imprints of parameters of the behavior result may be graphically depicted using special geometric images (Figure 4.8). We believe that the action result acceptors of functional systems operate as screens exposed to continuous interference between motivational and reinforcing excitations. Close interactions between the dominant motivation and reinforcement in neurons that make up action result acceptors were clearly demonstrated in the experiments conducted by our colleague V. A. Pravdivtsev (1982).

The spike activity of interneurons of the visual cortex in cats was recorded as they developed a conditioned reflex reaction to combined electrical stimulation of the cut pyramidal tract and electro-skin stimulation. As the experiments demonstrated, after 8–10 combinations of conditioned antidromal stimulation of the pyramidal tract and electro-skin stimulation, neurons began to respond to the conditioned stimulation with a reaction characteristic of electrocutaneous stimulation (Figure 4.9). This shows that the subsequent nonciceptive

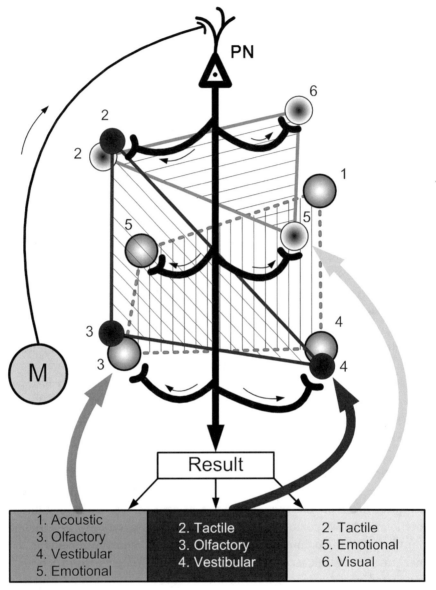

FIGURE 4.8 Geometric images of action result acceptor in various functional systems. Each figure is defined by parameters of reinforcement; M – motivation; PN – pyramidal neuron; 1–6 – parameters of reinforcement result.

COGNITIVE ACTIVITY: FUNCTIONAL SYSTEMS THEORY 113

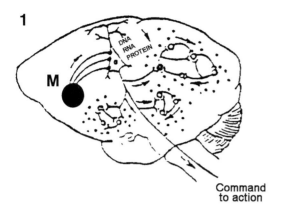

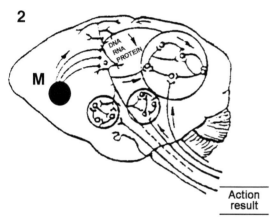

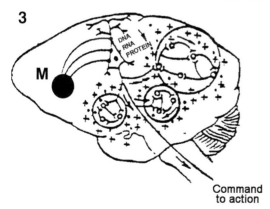

FIGURE 4.9
Formation of molecular engram of action result acceptor under the influence of action result, i.e. reinforcement. Through its influence, reinforcement (2) alters initial properties of effector protein molecules expressed by the genome of neurons involved in the dominant motivation (shown as *circles* in Fragment 1). After reinforcement, neurons begin to synthesize effector oligopeptides (shown as *crosses* in Fragment 3) participating in the organization of appropriate behavior. Synthesis of these oligopeptides is inhibited by cycloheximide and actinomycin D at various phases. M – motivation-producing center of hypothalamus.

effect is imprinted in the activity of these neurons and reproduced in advance by the conditioned antidromal excitation of the pyramidal tract.

Our experiments highlighted the significant role played by reinforcing oligopeptides, such as substance P, delta-sleep inducing peptide, prolactine, beta-endorphins, etc. (Sudakov 1989), in acquisition of "reality imprints" (after I. P. Pavlov) in the structures of action result acceptors. Later, these oligopeptides create integrated molecular processes that reinforce acquired skills.

In addition to oligopeptides, the interaction of motivation and reinforcement on neurons that make up the action result acceptor involves immunological mechanisms. It was once assumed by K. Pribram that brain responses are based on a holographic principle. He thought that memory is not localized in certain areas but spread across the entire brain (Pribram 1981).

Generalized brain interaction of motivational and reinforcing excitations on neurons that make up the action result acceptor is confirmed by the holographic principle of brain activity. Based on the analogy of physical holography, motivational excitations are regarded as a reference wave, and excitations from reinforcing factors affecting various body receptors as an object wave. Interaction of these two waves stemming from motivation and reinforcement forms interference holograms on the structures of the action result acceptor.

According to the holographic principle, each separate fragment of a hologram carries full information on the whole hologram. Similar properties are present in the functional systems of the body, inasmuch as dominant motivations and reinforcement, as noted earlier, are manifested in animals motivated by a dominant need, specifically in the patterns of interspike activity of neurons that make up acceptors of action results.

Through the information signals associated with needs and their satisfaction, the brain continuously generates information models of the body's internal environment and outside reality. Most functional systems converge in the same brain structures; consequently, through multiparametric interactions, action result acceptors of individual functional systems are integrated into a single generic informational holographic representation.

This generic informational holographic representation is based on the dominant principle. At any time, the brain structures are dominated by the action result acceptor of a functional system that is of particular a social or biological significance. At each point in time, anticipatory reactions of the dominant functional system are expressed in the generic acceptor of action results.

In the formation and enrichment of action result acceptors of various functional systems, the outer and inner world of a living being, based on emotional sensations, are transformed into a specific internal image. This image encompasses the subjective experience of the individual's internal state and the outside environment. The ongoing subjective image of internal state reflects the body's internal and external environments in their tight informational relationship. Thus, individuals formulate an image-based perception of themselves and the outside world.

The representation of reality on the morphofunctional structures of action result acceptors forms the intellect of an individual starting from the early postnatal period, and updates it throughout life. In turn, action result acceptors allow each individual to adequately assess one's own "self," one's needs, accumulated knowledge, and the outside world.

Emotional stereotypes determine the individual's relation to other individuals, family members, colleagues at work, political leaders, religious cults, etc. Using emotions, both man and animals evaluate needs and the behavior of other individuals. The above processes, in our opinion, constitute the basis of the so-called "emotional consciousness" that emerges during activation of emotive elements of action result acceptors during the evaluation of needs and their satisfaction.

A particularly important role in the formation of human acceptor of action results acceptors is played by verbal symbols. Any type of training and instruction leads to formation of verbal stereotypes in the trainees.

Action result acceptors accumulated over the course of a lifetime are continuously exposed to fluxes of reverse afferentation from various parameters of reality. These are processes that underlie consciousness: the evaluation of reality by an individual and their comparison with genetically and individually acquired knowledge. Unlike animals who construct "reality imprints," primarily through emotions and discriminative properties of conditioned stimuli, through the process of evolution, human beings have acquired a qualitatively new language for constructing the "reality imprint."

Verbal or written instructions also enrich the action result acceptor in humans. This is where the acquisition of sequences of informational parameters associated with desired results takes place, including actions that lead to these results (i.e. programming of an informational holographic engram) that under the influence of motivation or triggering stimuli, is organized into functional systems of psychical activity. At the informational level, these functional systems are outwardly realized through an individual's goal-directed actions and achievement of material results having personal and social significance.

10 Conclusion

The theoretical and experimental data presented in this paper provide evidence that the theory of functional systems brings forth a new perspective on the place of cognitive processes in the systems organization of psychical activity. It clearly outlines the role of cognitive processes in the formation of the main phases of systems architectures of psychical activity in humans and animals: phases of afferent synthesis, decision making, anticipation of required result (i.e. generation of the action result acceptor), and evaluation of the role of reverse afferentation reaching the action result acceptor from parameters of achieved results. Furthermore, the theory of functional systems helps to uncover new aspects in the construction of thought and the processes of consciousness.

Acknowledgement

This work was made possible by a grant from the Russian Federation President in support of the leading scientific schools of the Russian Federation (Grant # NSH-3232 2008.4) with thanks to K. A. Volkova, E. I. Pevtsova and O. P. Suslova.

References

Anokhin, P. K. 1969. "The psychical form of reflection of reality." In *Lenin's Theory of Reflection and Modernity*, ed. T. Pavlov. Sofia, Bulgaria: Nauka i iskusstvo.

Anokhin, P. K. 1974. *Biology and Neurophysiology of the Conditioned Reflex and its Role in Adaptive Behavior*. New York: Pergamon Press.

Bertalanffy, L. 1967. "General theory of systems: application to physiology." *Social Science Information* 6, no. 6: 126–129.

Foster, D. J. and M. A. Wilson. 2006. "Reverse replay of behavioral sequences in hippocampal place cells during the awake state." *Nature* 440, no. 7084: 680–683.

Lorenz, K. 1965. *Evolution and Modification of Behavior*. Chicago: University of Chicago Press.

MacDonnell, M. F. and J. F. Flynn. 1966. "Control of sensory fields by stimulation of hypothalamus." *Science* 3727, no. 151: 1406–1408.

MacLean, P. D. 1989. *The Triune Brain Evolution: Role in Paleocerebral Functions*. New York: Plenum Press.

Masterov, A. V. 1975. "Features of the selection by rats of the stage-related results of an action." *Zhurnal Vysshei Nervnoi Deyatelnosti Imeni I P Pavlova* 20, no. 5: 1091.

Oniani, T. N. 1980. *The Integrative Function of the Limbic System*. Tbilisi, Georgia: Metsniereba.

Pavlov, I. P. 1955. *Selected Works*. London: General Books.

Pravdivtsev, V. A. 1982. "Efferent-Afferent Convergence in the Systems Organization of Motor Acts." Author's abstract of doctoral thesis in medical sciences. Moscow.

Pribram, K. 1981. "The brain, the telephone, the thermostat, the computer and the Hologram Cognition and brain theory." *Cognition and Brain Theory* 4, no. 2: 105–122.

Simonov, P. V. 2004. *Selected Works*. Moscow: Nauka.

Sudakov, K. V. 1989. "Brain neuron gene expression in the organization of innate and acquired behavior." *Pavlovian Journal of Biological Science* 24, no. 4: 127–132.

Sudakov, K. V. 1989. "Oligopeptides in organization of hypothalamically induced behavior." *Acta Physiologica Scandinavica* 136, no. 583: 35–39.

Sudakov, K. V. 1991. "Dominant motivation – reinforcement interaction in the systems organization of behavioral act." In *Reinforcement in Functional Systems*, ed. K. V. Sudakov, 1–14. New York: Gordon and Breach Scientific Publishers.

Sudakov, K. V. 1997. "The theory of functional systems: general postulates and principles of dynamic organization." *Integrative Physiological and Behavioral Science* 32, no. 4: 392–414.

Sudakov, K. V. 2004. *Dominant Motivation*. Moscow: RAMN.

Sudakov, K. V., B. Lazetic and N. Grujic. 1998. "Bases of theory of functional systems-perspectives." In *Basic and clinical aspects of theory of functional systems*, ed. B. Lazetic and K. V. Sudakov. Novi Sad, Serbia: Medical Faculty University.

Sudakov, K. V. and E. A. Oumrioukhin. 2005. "System quanta of universe." *Frontier Perspectives* 14, no. 2: 12–29.

Sudakov, S. K. 1987. "Feeding and defense motivation mechanisms of genetic memory." In *Motivation in Functional Systems*, ed. K. V. Sudakov, 313–324. New York: Gordon and Breach Scientific Publishers.

Ukhtomsky, A. A. 1950. *Selected Works*. Leningrad: Nuaka.

Wirwicka, W. 1978. "Effects of electrical stimulation within the hypothalamus on gastric acid secretion and food intake in cats." *Experimental Neurology* 60, no. 2: 286–303.

Zhuravlev, B. V., L. V. Timofeeva and N. N. Shamaev. 1991. "Firing pattern of rabbits deprived of water and food." In *Reinforcement in Functional Systems*, ed. K. V. Sudakov, 121–134. New York: Gordon and Breach Scientific Publishers.

SECTION 1 COMMENTARY

The Genesis and Development of Russian Experimental Neuroscience

Gabriel A. Radvansky and Chris Forsythe

In this section, the authors provide accounts of the development of Russian experimental neuroscience, and how this developmental path has influenced the nature of the field today. Shostak discussed the impact of early influential researchers, including Sechenov, Bekhterev, and Pavlov. Alexandrov, Sokolova, and Sudakov primarily focus on the theoretical perspective of system psychophysiology as it is captured by the theory of functional systems, and the concept of the dominant that is part of this perspective. All of these chapters focus on the development of neuroscience through the earlier work in physiology and related biological subfields. Much of that work ultimately had its origin, one way or another, in the writings of the French rationalist philosopher René Descartes and his attempts to explain thought and action from the perspective that the body, and the nervous system that runs it, can essentially be understood as a complex mechanism. This intellectual debt, along with attributions to Aristotle, Plato, the Empiricists, and other schools of thought in the philosophy of mind, has driven a great deal of psychological thinking more generally. What is noteworthy here is the strong emphasis on understanding how the psychological system functions as a whole as compared to more strictly reductionist perspectives that are typically found in the West. As such, the development of neuroscience has much more affinity with the German Gestalt school of thought compared to other neurologically-oriented approaches to human thought and cognition. Much of this perspective is captured by the strong emphasis on and exploration of the concept of the reflex.

The emphasis on the reflex and the reflex arc can be traced back to Sechenov, whom Shostak describes as the Father of Russian psychology. This emphasizes how deep the foundational basis of the reflex concept goes. This approach of giving the reflex a more central influence served as a foundational basis for many of the efforts that followed. From this view, again, elaborating on the ideas put forth by Descartes, neural activity could be strongly associated with physical, muscular activity in some form. From such simple reflex elements, more complex mental activity, including both thoughts and emotions, could be accounted for. This bears a resemblance to current views of embodied cognition (e.g., Barsalou 2008) that are currently in fashion that attempt to explain mental activity, in whole or in part, by reference to how cognition captures and is driven by principles describing how people interact with the world through their perceptions and their motor activity.

The one person at the center of the development of modern Russian thought and practice is Pavlov, whose contributions, acknowledgement, and influence are worldwide. He is one of the few figures found in most undergraduate introductory psychology courses in nearly every college and university. Pavlov served as a nexus to bring together and channel many of the ideas about the importance of the reflex, and how it could be altered by experience through the principles of classical conditioning, or Pavlovian conditioning. The important elements of Pavlov's approach that continue to mark the Russian approach is not only the emphasis on physiological mechanisms and learned reflexes, but the core conception of behavior as predictive and goal oriented. After all, classical conditioning, whether an organism is consciously aware of it or not, is a means for deriving and using causal relationships in the world, and then exploiting them to become better adapted to the environment and increase the probability of survival.

One of the other major figures in this history, in addition to Pavlov, is Anokhin, who is discussed in terms of his development of the theory of functional systems, which, as Alexandrov notes, was further developed by V. B. Shvyrkov, and as Sudakov notes, by Simonov. This theoretical approach shares a great deal in common with the general thrust of Pavlov's work on classical conditioning and its emphasis on the organism's ability to predict future outcomes and adequately prepare for them. Moreover, because this is a systems approach to the topics at hand, it is more holistic in is scope. There are a number of attractive aspects of this approach that gives Russian psychology the credibility to provide a valuable contribution to international studies. As outlined by Sudakov, the fact that this view takes into account and tries to reconcile the operation of processing at many different levels, as well as the connections across levels, has a great deal of value in the context of so many other modern views that are much more reductionistic. Furthermore, this view suggests that these various levels have a strict hierarchical relationship governing the flow of information and control across a wide range of types of experience.

In addition to Pavolv and Anokhin, two other major figures that have influenced the current direction of thought in Russian psychophysiology are Ukhtomsky and Beritashvili. As Sokolova notes, more complex ideas about the relationship between the reflex and the mind emerged out of work that soon followed Pavlov. For example, as with the Gestalt psychologists' maxim that the whole is different from the sum of its parts, Beritashvili noted that the behaviors that emerge from collections of reflexes had qualities that are not derivable from understanding the reflexes by themselves. Instead, behavior possesses emergent qualities that are governed by complexes of reflexes in much the same way that memories, consciousness, and emotions are emergent properties out of the neural elements that compose them. Also, akin to the Gestalt psychologists, these researchers held the firm belief that thought and behavior also critically depended on the elements themselves – collections of reflexes in this case – in addition to the emergent properties.

The complexes of reflexes that emerged out of the various neural processes could be grouped together. Some of these complexes serve as the basis for directing goal related behavior, and such a complex was described by Ukhtomsky as the *dominant*. This goal-directedness is important because it permits formulating methodical studies of the mind and brain as investigations of a purposeful and internally directed system having a degree of disconnection from the external environment. This allows the organism to respond more as a single unit. Ukhtomsky worked the concept of the dominant into nearly every aspect of human experience, including context-based processing, development, and larger societal issues.

A key aspect to the historical origins of Russian psychology and psychophysiology is the central and important role that emotions play in these schools of thought. Rather than having the status of a side project, emotion forms an important basis for understanding goal oriented behaviors, and how these interact with the dominant or the execution of various complexes of reflexes. By comparison, emotion in much of the development of psychology and neuroscience in the West has been given either a smaller role or, more often, gets no attention at all. It is only relatively recently that the value of emotion in understanding cognition has been given a much more privileged status (e.g., Kensinger 2009). The Russian schools of thought have been able to avoid neglecting emotion, allowing them to develop a more mature understanding of the driving role of emotion in thinking and behavior.

Overall, while some aspects of the historical influences of Russian schools of thought have achieved international recognition, such as the massively influential work by Pavlov, other aspects have not enjoyed similar recognition. As noted at various points in this volume, some of this lack of worthy influence is not due to problems with the ideas, concepts, and theories themselves, but with the political climate that prevailed between the Soviet Union and many of the Western countries for much of the twentieth century. Although this climate has changed, dramatically in some ways, there are still some vestiges of this separation of thought that are still present and that prevent the beneficial exchange of ideas in both directions. Our hope is that the unique and valuable perspective provided by the Russian approach to various issues of psychology and neuroscience will become more broadly understood and appreciated for what it has to offer.

Acknowledgement

Sandia National Laboratories is a multiprogram laboratory operated by Sandia Corporation, a Lockheed Martin Company, for the United States Department of Energy's National Nuclear Security Administration under contract DEAC04-94AL85000.

References

Barsalou, L. W. 2008. "Grounded cognition." *Annual Review of Psychology* 59, no. 1: 617–645.

Kensinger, E. A. 2009. *Emotional Memory across the Adult Lifespan*. New York: Psychology Press.

SECTION 2

Russian Research in Perceptual and Cognitive Processes

∴

CHAPTER 5

The Regulatory Role of an Unconscious Cognitive Set in the Perception of the Facial Expression of Emotion

Eduard Arutunovich Kostandov

1 Russian Origin of the Psychophysiology of Set – The Forerunner of Cognitive Neuroscience

The science of behavior, originated in Russia by I. M. Sechenov and I. P. Pavlov, was faced, at the very beginning of its development, with the need to recognize the integrated organism as a being who is active in the environment. Analysis of the evolution of I. M. Sechenov's ideas, which he continued to develop after the publication of his book "Reflexes of the Brain" (1863), provide good reason for considering him the author of ideas about mental causality as a special mode of behavioral regulation, as well as of ideas about a reflex ring in which "sensory factors" (the sensory image) function as determinants of purposeful behavior. According to I. M. Sechenov (1947), the role of sensory factors (representations, images, emotions) in the regulation of behavior is beholding to the same objective, and precise research as any other issues dealt with by the natural scientist.

Physiologists studying conditional reflexes have long noted that behavior does not always correspond to the signal that generated it, and that the experimental condition itself has substantial significance for the conditioned reaction. It creates a predisposition, a propensity for certain actions, and plays the role of "an instruction manual, in the physiological sense" (Beritashvili 1965). I. S. Beritashvili, following other psychologists (Uznadze 1958), called such an "instructional" effect of the external environment a *set*. For a physiological explanation of this phenomenon, he used his early observations of changes in the muscle tone of the extremities that occur with a change in an animal's head position. It was found that by turning the animal's head slowly and carefully, without causing significant irritation, the muscle tone of the limbs does not change. But if any irritation is inflicted after that – pinching the tail, squeezing the ear – then there will be a tonic reflex, corresponding to the specific position of the head. I. S. Beritashvili believed that this predisposition of the organism to a specific tonic reaction is due to increased excitability of the relevant tonic centers, because of "subminimal" impulses from proprioceptors of the cervical muscles, or the labyrinth receptors that are activated when the head turns.

By analogy with this mechanism, the entire prior and present external situation, with its "subminimal" effect, creates a state of heightened excitation in certain nerve centers, resulting in a predisposition or readiness for one behavioral act or another. Acting on the organism "subminimally," these regulating environmental stimuli, through a mechanism of a temporary connection, can not only create readiness for a specific behavior, but can also determine the direction of the behavior itself. The conditioned stimulus that produces a reaction plays the role of a starting signal.

Asratyan (1970a; 1970b) demonstrated, in a series of experiments, that the very same stimulus, applied to the same animal or human, may become a signal for different behavioral responses, that are even antagonistic to one another, if it is combined with each of these activities in different situations or under different conditions. For example, if an auditory stimulus is accompanied by the feeding of an animal in one experimental compartment, and, electro-stimulation in another compartment, it takes on two different meanings: in the first compartment the auditory stimulus evokes eating behavior, and in the second, defensive behavior. An analogous phenomenon is observed whenever a variable component of a situation, whether by its presence or absence, creates two different situations – that is, it plays the role of a kind of "switch" for conditioned reflex activity (Asratyan 1970a; 1970b). There may be cases when the eating response and the defensive response are produced by the same stimulus in the same compartment, but by different experimenters; or by the same experimenter at different times of day; or when the experimental animal is placed in the apparatus first with its head to one side, and then to the other side, etc.

These observations showed that the observed phenomenon is not an artifact of the laboratory, but reflects a common pattern in the higher brain centers, namely the formation of a certain functional state which determines and regulates the behavior of animals and humans to a significant degree. E. A. Asratyan (1970a) stressed the fundamental importance of the phenomenon he had identified, as confirming the possibility of a radical difference in reflexes conditioned to a given stimulus as a result of tonic changes in the functional state of the relevant cortical structures, "predisposing them to work in a specific way, adjusting them in a specific manner, forming in them a specific set – in other words, by unique programming of activity yet to occur."

Any experimenter studying behavior has to consider the influence of the experimental set-up, in general, or any of its elements, on the conditioned reflexes of the animal being studied. So, it is no surprise that the phenomenon of conditioned reflex switching has attracted the attention of many physiologists. The explanations they have given for the physiological mechanisms differ in details and terminology, but they all basically recognized how this phenomenon is based upon the formation of some more or less permanent internal states of heightened excitability in the higher brain.

As mentioned above, E. A. Asratyan (1970a; 1970b) used the term "tonic conditioned reflex." P. K. Anokhin (1974) wrote of an "anticipatory dominant state" which largely determines the response to a conditioned stimulus, playing the role, in these cases, of an eliciting signal. The universal role of the anticipatory dominant state, according to P. K. Anokhin (1974), is to organize specific, integrated, adaptive behavior by animals and humans. We see that this refers to the formation of an initial, dominant, stable state, i.e., a tonic state of increased excitability of higher brain structures, which determines, to a large extent, the nature of the organism's integrated activity in a particular situation.

According to I. S. Beritashvili (1965), the external environment as a whole, or by one of its components, during training, begins to exert regulating effects on the animals' behavior, by increasing the excitability of certain parts of the cerebral cortex. This not only creates readiness for a corresponding behavioral act, but also determines the direction of the integrated behavior.

In each of these interpretations, the central point is the formation of an internal state that predetermines the response of the organism in a particular situation. Although in one case this internal state is called a tonic conditioned reflex, and in another it is called an anticipatory or concealed dominant state, and in a third it is called a set, the essential explanation does not change. Namely, that the entire prior and present external situation or some component of it, by means of "subminimal" effects (the term by Beritashvili 1965), creates a state of heightened excitability in certain nerve centers, resulting in a predisposition, or readiness, for one behavior or another. Acting "subminimally" on the organism, these regulatory stimuli from the environment, by a temporary connective mechanism, can create not only the readiness for a particular behavior, but also determine its direction. The conditioned stimulus that produces a reaction plays the role of an eliciting signal. As P. K. Anokhin wrote (Anokhin, *The biology and neurophysiology of the conditioned reflex*), there is a "devaluation of the qualitative side" of the conditioned stimulus.

This was demonstrated by A. S. Batuev and L. V. Sokolova (1993), in a series of experiments on animals (cats, dogs, and rats), in which the same conditioned stimulus, depending on the level of motivation to drink, prompted the animal to quite different reactions (ingestive or aversive). In these experiments, it was the level of motivation of the animal, not an external stimulus, which served as the "switch." This gave A. S. Batuev (Batuev and Sokolov 1993) reason to consider that the key factors in the system of purposeful behavior are preliminary constructs formed on the basis of the dominant motivation – the equivalent of, in our terminology, internal states or sets.

We have observed discrepancies in physiological responses to a signal stimulus, in recordings of human cortical evoked potentials (EP) to auditory stimuli in the "Oddball" experimental situation (Kostandov and Zakharova 1992). In these experiments, a person was told that if he hears a low tone (400 Hz) in the right (or left) "relevant" ear, s/he should press a button (target stimulus), but if s/he hears a high tone (1,000 Hz), s/he should not (differentiating stimulus). The person was also told to ignore sounds in the other ("non-relevant") ear (stimuli to be ignored). After repeated presentation of stimuli, the ratio of the amplitudes of evoked potential for non-meaningful sounds presented to the non-relevant ear, to which the person was not supposed to respond to at all, were the same as those for the meaningful stimuli that were supposed to be recognized and which required responds accordingly (Figure 5.1). Interestingly, a comparison of results with younger and older adults showed that amplitude differences for the irrelevant sound appear in that component of the evoked response for which the differences in amplitude are observed for target and differentiating stimuli in the relevant ear. We believe that this reveals the effect of a so-called context-dependent physiological response. The cortical evoked potential is determined not only by the relevance of the signal and the need for a certain action (created in the person by the experimenter's verbal instructions), but also by a set, that is formed unconsciously from the repeated actions of all the stimuli perceived in a given situation, and by the cognitive tasks to be performed.

A kind of functional state, which affects the processes of perception, is created at an unconscious level in the higher regions of the brain. In a stable situation, such a set substantially facilitates perceptual processes, the evaluation of incoming information, and decision making based upon it; but if the circumstances or the signals change, this can cause difficulty or distortion in the perception of new stimuli.

V. S. Gurfinkel and Levik (1991; 1995) demonstrated a regulatory and coordinating role of the "system of internal representations" in the organization of voluntary movements at an unconscious level. Just as in studies of cognitive set, these experiments with humans created conditions for discrepancy between the internal representation (the set) and the actual situation. For example,

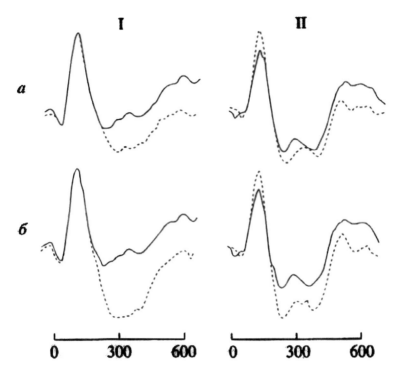

FIGURE 5.1 Grand mean of Acoustic Event Related in old (I) and young (II) subjects. Solid line – target stimulus; dashed line – differentiated (a) or ignorable (б) stimulus. Abscissa – time (ms); о – moment of stimulation.

vibration of certain cervical muscles led to the proprioceptive illusion of the head turning in the opposite direction. In another case, the so-called "return effect" was studied, assessing the position of the head: a man with his eyes closed and head turned to the side after a period of time begins to feel that the head has returned to the central position. In this case, the afferent impulses reaching the brain from the muscles of the cervical region do not change significantly. According to Gurfinkel and Levik, everything is determined by internal representation – a mental "drift" to the most familiar "reference" position. In both cases – at the time of the illusion of head rotation and during the illusory "return" of the head to the central position – the tonic activity of the leg muscles is modified. In the first case, this activity is asymmetrical, while in the second, in contrast, the asymmetry of the tonic response of the leg muscle due to the head turn, is eliminated. It is not hard to see that Gurfinkel's "system of internal representations" is very close to the idea of set, but transferred to the domain of motor activity.

The coordination of a behavioral act, and also integrated cognitive activity, are carried out by means of some kind of central brain organization (set, in our terminology), which determines the nature of the reaction and controls the individual reactions according to one central internal representation of the entire system of stimuli, and of their context. The set (in Ukhtomskii's expression, the "integral of experience") that forms inside a person (Ukhtomskii 1996), at any given moment during an activity, determines the internal cohesion and consistency of behavioral acts. Without such a coordinating mechanism, without the predisposition to some form of response, without the direction of a set, it is impossible to explain the individual's purposeful and coherent behavior in a constantly changing environment. It should be recognized that it is impossible, while remaining within the framework of conditioned reflex theory, to explain the variability of human behavior in the same situation and subject to the same stimuli, or conversely, the inertia of behavioral acts under obviously changing environmental conditions, when, in the words of Ukhtomskii, a "the blindness of bias" is present.

Thus, the above-mentioned works on the psychophysiology of set facilitate, to a large extent, the transition from the ideology of a "reactive model" of explaining brain mechanisms in animal and human behavior, to a model of an active organism, in which mental causality plays an important role in the organization of integrated behavior.

2 Set and Identifying Emotional Facial Expression

Human facial expression has great meaning in interpersonal relations. It serves as one of the major sources of visual information about the emotional state and intentions of another person; this is necessary for appropriate behavior in a particular situation. People's behavior during communication is largely determined by the subject's assessment of the other person's emotional facial expression (such as friendly or unfriendly). In recent years, psychophysiology has placed an emphasis on studies identifying the factors that affect this assessment, and defining both the brain structures involved and the mechanisms of their interaction. An enormous number of publications have been devoted to this problem (see Haxby et al. 2000; Mikhailova 2005). This is connected with the development of neuroimaging, primarily functional nuclear magnetic resonance (fMRI), but also magnetoencephalography (MEG) and the recording of evoked electrical potentials of the brain. By these means, we were able to show that emotional facial expressions are perceived through a hierarchically organized ramified network of brain structures (the visual and temporal cortices, the fusiform gyrus, the amygdala, the anterior cingulate gyrus, and the prefrontal cortex). Individual nodes of this structural-functional system are activated in a specific time sequence (Kreiman et al. 2000; Streit et al. 2000; Vuilleumier et al. 2002; Paller et al. 2003; Streit et al. 2003; Mikhailova et al. 2004; Williams et al. 2004; Fisher et al. 2005; Werheid et al. 2005; Balconi and Lucchiari 2006), which probably reflects their consistent participation in the individual stages of visual information processing and of evaluating signal significance.

Almost all these works describe the participation of the frontal (prefrontal) cortex of the left and right hemispheres, which is activated when perceiving and evaluating emotional facial expressions. An important point is that an analysis of latent periods of evoked magnetic potentials of the cortex showed that there are two phases of activation of the orbitofrontal cortex (Streit et al. 2003; Werheid et al. 2005), namely: a quite early phase (100–180 ms) and then a later, repeated one (240–360 ms, and even 500–600 ms), which also involves the anterior cingulate gyrus and inferior prefrontal cortex. It has been suggested that the first stage is associated with the rapid evaluation of facial expression and its general emotional significance, whereas the later stage involves the evaluation of the social meaning for a given person, by "social cognitive processes."

In addition to the general conjectures mentioned above, we have found no experimental studies designed to identify and study specific cognitive activity associated with activation of the prefrontal cortex, which may be regarded as one of the "nodes" of a structural-functional network that brings about the perception and evaluation of facial expression. It is difficult to understand what kind of contribution the prefrontal cortex makes to the organization of this integrated function that has such great meaning in human social life. Meanwhile, psychologists note the importance of past life experience in how this function is realized. They believe that during a person's life experience, "stereotyped expectations" or "standards of comparison" are formed, based on a special form of memory – "priming" – with the repeated perception of specific faces (Hess et al. 2004; Werheid et al. 2005; Stapel and Koomen 2006). In particular, the presence of "stereotyped expectations" explains the manifest gender differences in evaluation of facial expression by women and men (Hess et al. 2004). For example, an angry facial expression on a woman's face is usually evaluated as angrier than the same expression on a man, and a man's smile seems happier and friendlier than a similar smile on a woman.

Numerous studies by D. N. Uznadze (Uznadze 1958) and then by us (Kostandov et al. 2004; Kostandov et al. 2005a; Kostandov 2006) showed the regulatory role of unconscious sets in visual perception, in particular, in the phenomena of perceptual "bias" and its distortions (illusions). The frontal cortical regions were found to play a key role in the formation of sets and in the process of changing them into new ones, more appropriate to a changing situation (Konishi et al. 1999; Kostandov et al. 2004; Kostandov et al. 2005a).

Comparison of works on visual set with data on the perception of facial expression provided the basis to hypothesize that in evaluating emotional facial expressions, a substantial role is played by an unconscious set for the face of another person, which is formed with repeated perception. Experimental studies of this hypothesis will make clear the functional significance of the prefrontal cortex in processes of perception and evaluation of emotional facial expressions. This determined the main goal of one of our studies: to test experimentally the hypothesis that repeated perceptions of faces with a specific emotional expression evoke in the participant an unconscious mental set, which then substantially affects subsequent evaluations of facial expression. This set can be a source of "bias," of distorted evaluations. We used the classical set model of D. N. Uznadze (1958), which provides a comparative evaluation of a particular trait (in our study, the facial expression of emotion) in two simultaneous visual stimuli, followed by a sudden change of this trait in one of them. This allows us to determine the influence of prior experience of the perception of an emotionally negative face, on the evaluation of facial expression in subsequent trials.

3 Methods

3.1 *Participants*

We studied 35 people (20 women and 15 men) aged 25.1 ± 1.3 years. They were undergraduates, graduate students, and scientific colleagues. They had not previously participated in experiments on set. They were given a brief description of the task. They were convinced that the research procedure would not harm them. All participants gave their voluntary written consent to participate in the experiment.

3.2 *Stimuli*

In the center of a monitor, at a distance of 70 cm, two facial images taken from an atlas were shown simultaneously, on a dark gray background [10]. The size of each image was 60 × 45 mm. At the set formation stage, the face on the left had an angry expression, while on the right, the same face had a neutral, "calm" expression (Figure 5.2). The exposure time was 350 ms. After a pause of 1 sec, the test stimulus appeared in the center of the same screen: a green spot of

THE REGULATORY ROLE OF AN UNCONSCIOUS COGNITIVE SET 133

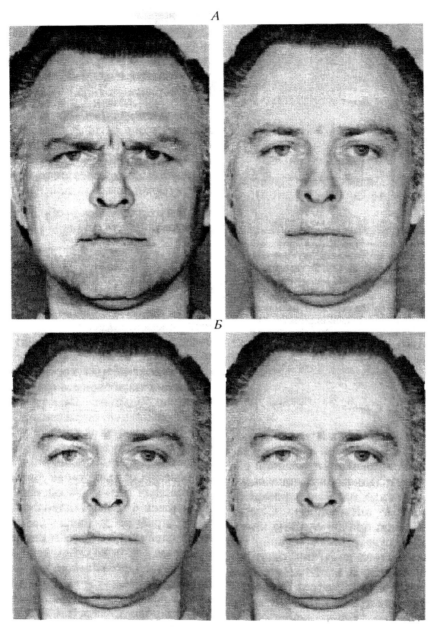

FIGURE 5.2   Stimuli presented when studying a set to emotional facial expression. A – set forming stage, Б – set testing stage.

light with a diameter of 3 mm, for a duration of 2 s. The pauses between sets of stimuli were 3–7 sec in length, changing in random order. At the set testing stage, which began immediately after the formation stage, two images were shown simultaneously of the same face with a neutral expression, and with the same stimulus parameters as in the previous stage of the experiment.

3.3 *Procedure*

The participant was seated in an armchair before a computer monitor, in a darkened, sound-proofed, shielded booth which had a microphone/speaker connection to the area where the experimenter was situated. The participant was told: "Sit quietly. Place a finger of your right hand on the button. Look at the screen; be attentive. You will see images of two faces, one beside the other. The images disappear. Then a spot of light will appear on the screen. In response, you must press the button as quickly as possible and then state whether the expressions on both faces are identical, or if one of them, in your opinion, seems more unpleasant. Use the word 'identical' if the expressions are the same, 'left' if the more unpleasant face is on the left, and 'right' if the more unpleasant face is on the right."

During the stage of set formation, the facial images with different emotional expressions appeared 15 times in sequence: an angry face on the left, a neutral one on the right. During the stage of set testing, all 30 trials showed the same face on both left and right, with a neutral expression.

3.4 *Equipment and Data Analysis*

Experimental control and recording of reaction time (RT) was done by computer. Verbal responses were relayed by microphone to the experimenter's room and recorded. ANOVA and Student's t-test were used for statistical analysis of the results.

4 Results

During set formation, upon presentation of a facial image with different expressions, all participants in all trials evaluated the emotional expression correctly, noting that the face on the left had an unpleasant expression. Recall that the exposure time of the facial stimuli, 350 ms, was long enough to allow correct evaluation of the facial expression. At the set testing stage, for 12 subjects there was no observed effect of the presentation of stimuli in the preceding stage of the experiment; that is, they correctly evaluated the facial expressions in the left and right visual fields as being the same. For the remaining 23 people,

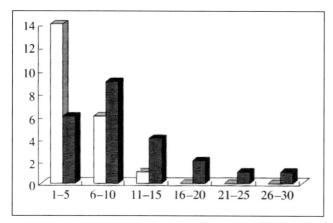

FIGURE 5.3 Distribution of subjects by the number of trials with illusionary recognition of emotional facial expression. Ordinate – number of subjects, abscissa – number of trials with illusions (a bin corresponds to 5). Light bars – contrast illusions, dark bars – assimilative illusions.

incorrect evaluations were observed during the testing stage in a certain number of trials: either the face on the left or the one on the right was seen as "unpleasant," although in fact it was the same face, with a neutral expression.

Figure 5.3 shows the distribution of participants by number of tests yielding an incorrect evaluation: the dark bars show the right visual field, opposite to where the images of angry faces were placed in the previous stage of the experiment (*contrasting illusion*); the light bars show the same, left visual field (*assimilative illusion*). Contrasting illusions (stimulus in the opposite visual field) were more common than so-called assimilative illusions. The latter were usually observed in later trials of the experiment's testing stage, while the number of contrasting illusions in evaluation of the emotional facial expression was clearly higher in the first trials, but after 6–10 trials, their number became substantially smaller. Figure 5.4 shows the change in the mean values of both illusions in one experiment testing the effect of the set (results were averaged over successive time intervals corresponding to 5 trials).

The RT to a test stimulus depended on two factors: the stage of the experiment and the presence or absence of illusory distortions. In those participants exhibiting no illusions, RTs decreased during the testing stage ($F(1, 22) = 31.03$; $p<0.0001$) with reduced scatter ($F(1, 22) = 10.17$; $p<0.004$). Such a RT reduction does not occur in the group in which illusions were observed during the testing stage (Figure 5.5). Moreover, with this group, the standard deviation increased

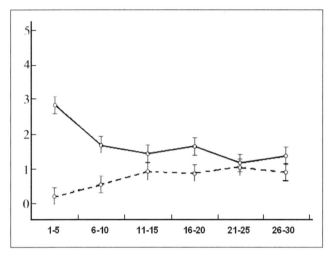

FIGURE 5.4   Dynamics of emotional facial expression recognition at the set-testing stage. Ordinate – averaged number of trials with illusions, abscissa – number of a current trial. Solid line – contrast illusions, dashed line – assimilative illusions. Standard deviation is shown.

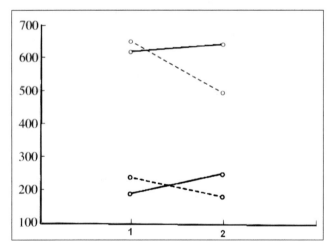

FIGURE 5.5   Reaction time to a probe stimulus (top) and its standard deviation (bottom) in subjects with and without illusionary perception of emotional facial expression. Ordinate – time, mc; abscissa – stages of the experiment: 1 – set formation, 2 set testing. Solid line – subjects who formed a set, dashed line – subjects who did not form a set.

significantly ($F_{(1, 22)} = 6.19$; $p<0.02$), indicating considerable scattering of RT during this stage. It should be noted that no differences are observed between the two groups in the length of RT to a test stimulus, at the stage of set formation (Figure 5.4). The differences become significant only at the testing stage, when the effect of the set is actualized ($F_{(1, 21)} = 26.81$; $p<0.0001$).

5 Discussion of the Results

The results of our experiments show that the set model, proposed by D. N. Uznadze (1958), can be used to study the perception and evaluation of emotional facial expression. Specifically, this is related to the question of the influence of past life experience on this function, as well as to understanding the neural mechanisms of "bias" and the erroneous perception and evaluation of facial expression. Furthermore, we believe that using models of cognitive set makes it possible to begin to elucidate the functional role of the prefrontal cortex.

Psychologists explain clear-cut gender differences in the interpretation of emotional facial expression in women and men by the formation, during a person's lifetime, of certain "standards of comparison," the "stereotypical expectations" (Hess et al. 2004; Werheid et al. 2005; Hess et al. 2004; Werheid et al. 2005; Stapel and Koomen 2006). According to these authors, people are more likely to associate the facial expression of a woman with a smile, a positive emotion, because her main role in life has long been to raise children, to preserve peace in the family, to subordinate herself to a man who is stronger in biological and social terms – a role that indeed demands from her expressions of positive emotions.

What is important for us in such discussions, is the idea that a person, throughout a lifetime, forms social norms, "stereotypical expectations," of the emotional facial expressions that are most characteristic of a certain group of people. This hypothesis was tested experimentally. The test revealed the effect of priming on emotional facial expression (Werheid et al. 2005). It was shown that people evaluated the same angry expression in a face with pronounced masculine features as less angry than the same emotional expression in a face with an obviously female appearance (Hess et al. 2004). Using a priming procedure, other researchers have shown that repeated display (15 times) on the monitor of an image of an angry or happy face, has a substantial effect on the evaluation of a neutral expression of a face that is presented on subsequent trials (Stapel and Koomen 2006). This effect is largely determined by the identification of the stimulus – the image of a sad or happy face – that is, at the stage of forming a memory trace (priming): when these stimuli were presented over a very short period of time, an assimilative effect was observed – that is, the evaluation of the expression of a neutral face corresponded to the same emotional expression that was presented in the first half of the experiment. For example, if it was sad, then a neutral face was evaluated as sadder. In experiments where the exposure time to faces was relatively greater – i.e., the faces could be identified to a certain degree – the priming effect had a contrasting influence; for example, the display of a happy expression resulted in a less positive assessment of a neutral face, whereas display of a sad face produced a more positive emotional evaluation. It is stressed that in both cases, the priming effect occurs automatically, without conscious involvement.

Analysis of the priming experiments mentioned above shows that, as a result of repeated exposure to a face with a particular emotional expression, some kind of internal state is formed in the human brain, at the unconscious level, which substantially affects the subsequent evaluation of facial expression. This effect cannot be explained only by the formation of a special kind of implicit memory, because the priming mechanism cannot provide the physiological basis for the observed contrasting effect. It can be understood within the concept of a cognitive set and, associated experimental findings obtained using the classical model of visual set (Uznadze 1958; Kostandov et al. 2005a; Kostandov et al. 2005b; Kostandov 2006).

The key point here is the need for comparative evaluation by the participants of two stimuli presented at the same time, differing by one attribute at the state of set formation, and identical at the stage of testing. In our experiments, emotional expression was that attribute: the face displayed in the left visual field had an angry expression, and was unambiguously evaluated by all participants as unpleasant.

The majority of the participants, in the testing phase, for some trials gave an incorrect evaluation of the emotional expression of one of two completely identical faces with exactly the same emotional expression. In the first trials, the faces were more frequently rated as more unpleasant in the field of view opposite to that where images of an angry face had previously been displayed. By analogy to visual illusions in experiments on a set of geometric shapes, we call these *contrasting illusions*. As trials were repeated in the testing stage, so-called *assimilative illusions* also began to appear, when a neutral face is evaluated as more unpleasant in the same field of view where an emotionally negative stimulus had previously appeared. We can assume that the assimilative illusions occur when the effect of the set weakens, and is extinguished. Let us recall that the assimilative effect in experiments with priming is seen on trials where images of emotional faces were shown for a very short time, whereas with relatively longer exposure, a contrasting effect was observed (Stapel and

Koomen 2006). These differences, in our view, can be explained by a cognitive set formed during the process of priming, whose stability depends substantially on the exposure time of the stimulus, i.e., to the degree to which the latter can be perceived.

We believe that the results support our hypothesis about the role of cognitive set in identifying emotional facial expression. This supports findings concerning the activation of the prefrontal cortex which have been reported in many studies (Mikhailova et al. 2004; Fisher et al. 2005; Sergerie et al. 2005; Werheid et al. 2005; Balconi and Lucchiari 2006). On the other hand, the formation of cognitive sets and the shifts to new ones has long been associated with activation of this cortical structure (Posner and Raichle 1997; Konishi et al. 1999; Monchi et al. 2001; Kostandov et al. 2004; Kostandov 2006). Therefore, there is every reason to think that the role of the prefrontal cortex, in a ramified brain structure system that identifies emotional facial expressions, involves higher cognitive functions, namely, unconscious internal representations, or sets.

As we know, the RT to a test stimulus is a good indicator of switching selective attention from one cognitive activity to another. The clear-cut differences in the length of RT in the testing stage between the group of subjects who had contrasting and assimilative illusions and the subjects who did not have them can be explained by the fact that in the former, the set formed for the face was more rigid, resulting in a mismatch between it and the new stimuli. In these cases, the solution of the cognitive problem is more difficult, requiring greater concentration, so the shift of attention to a test stimulus is more difficult, leading to a longer RT and greater scattering. Conversely, for people who evaluate new stimuli correctly, the length of the RT in the test phase decreases, which is obviously a result of practice, and is also an indicator for greater ease in switching attention from one activity to another. It should be noted that at the stage of set formation, the RT to the test stimulus is no different in the two groups. All these facts confirm our hypothesis about the formation of a visual set for emotional facial expression, and its substantial impact on cognitive activity.

6 Spatial Synchronization of Theta and Alpha Rhythms in the Prestimulus EEG for a Set of Emotionally Negative Facial Expressions

The issue of the spatial integration of cortical activity in the process of identifying emotional facial expressions is particularly relevant, because this mental function, as already mentioned, is achieved via a highly ramified system of brain structures. What neural mechanisms account for spatial integration and temporal coordination of the individual "nodes" of this functional system, resulting in an integrated function for identification of facial expression?

In recent years, there has been growing recognition in the field of psychophysiology of M. N. Livanov (1989) and his theory that cooperation of a spatially ramified network of brain structures, performing a specific function, occurs by means of the synchronization of the rhythmic oscillations of electrical activity among them. It was found that, in humans, the oscillations of electrical activity recorded from the scalp, in the theta rhythm band, are no less informative for understanding integration mechanisms within a given functional system, than the alpha rhythm that has traditionally been analyzed in human subjects (Guevara and Corsi-Carbera 1996; Bastiansen et al. 2003; Bastiansen and Hagoort 2003; Kirk and Mackay 2003; Masselmo and Eichenbaum 2005).

The substantial role of the theta rhythm in the cooperation of the individual parts of a functional system becomes understandable if we recall that its generation is associated with hippocampal structures, which has extensive afferent and efferent connections to many brain structures, as well as a direct relationship to the encoding of new information and to episodic memory. Ideas that the sources of the theta rhythm in humans are analogous to those discovered previously in animals are presently receiving confirmation, as is the view that there are two independent neural systems for the regulation and integration of cortical activity: the thalamo-cortical and cortico-hippocampal feedback systems (Guevara and Corsi-Carbera 1996; Bastiansen et al. 2003; Kirk and Mackay 2003; Masselmo and Eichenbaum 2005). In humans, the strengthening of cortical theta potentials is an indicator of synchronization between the hippocampus, along with other limbic system structures, and cortical areas, or between two cortical regions; this synchronization apparently facilitates the transfer of information between these brain structures.

The idea of recording theta rhythms from the human scalp to assess activity of the cortico-hippocampal system prompted us to use the analysis of coherence function for electrical activity, in an attempt to understand the physiological mechanism of interaction and coordination of individual nodes in the brain system that are relevant to evaluation of emotional facial expression. Moreover, this brain integration system includes the limbic structures, which are directly related to emotions in humans and animals. We proceeded from the standpoint that synchronization of theta rhythm oscillations of cortical electrical activity is realized through hippocampal-cortical connections, in widely separated formations of the cerebral cortex. This synchronization facilitates their interaction and binding, thereby forming the basis for processing information coming into the brain (Kirk and Mackay 2003). We can assume that human cognitive activity is closely connected with two types of spatial synchronization of the electrical activity of cortical elements: the alpha rhythm (fronto-thalamic system) and the theta rhythm (cortico-hippocampal system).

The purpose of this work is to identify the role of the cortico-hippocampal and fronto-thalamic feedback systems in spatial cortical integration, in the formation and change of a set for an emotionally negative facial expression. As such, our objective was to compare the results of the analysis of coherence function for electric potentials in the theta and alpha bands, recorded from different cortical regions during the pre-stimulus period, at different stages of the facial expression set. Behavioral data from these experiments have been discussed in previous sections of the chapter.

7 Methods

Electrical brain activity was recorded from 20 points on the skull (F3, F4, F7, F8, Fz, FT7, FT8, FC3, FC4, C3, C4, [sic] T3, T4, P3, P4, T5, T6, O1, O2), following the international 10–20 schema. The EEG lead was monopolar. After listening to instructions, EEG was recorded from participants in a state of quiet vigilance and operational rest, i.e., with their eyes open during set formation and testing.

In the condition of operational rest, six 8-second intervals of EEG were analyzed, and in the remaining stages of the experiment, 2-second intervals of EEG before the presentation of each stimulus.

For each EEG interval, we calculated the coherence function (COH) for all pairs of leads, based on the Fourier transform. To approximate the distribution of COH values to the normal, we used Fisher's Z-transform. For each subject, we averaged COH measurements of these EEG intervals for stages of the experiment. We singled out the maximum average COH in the frequency ranges of theta (4–7 Hz) and alpha (8–13 Hz). If the function had several peaks in a given range, we chose the largest. For further analysis, we used the values of the maximum COH measurements in excess of 0.35; this restriction was necessary for our statistical evaluation procedures (Bendatt and Peirsol 1958, 540).

For the maximum COH values along all pairs of leads in all experimental situations, we calculated 5% confidence intervals. The dynamic spatial organization of cortical activity was determined by subtracting the coherence measures of the electrical potentials in the background state, with the eyes open, from the data recorded at a certain stage of the experiment (the figures illustrate this difference). If the confidence intervals for the respective pairs of leads did not overlap, we concluded that there had been a significant change in the COH parameter. If the height of the peak at a given stage of the experiment was greater than in the starting state (with eyes open), then the schematic diagram shows a thick line between the corresponding pair of leads, and if it is less, there is a dotted line.

8   Results

For behavioral indicators, the participants were divided into groups characterized by plastic and rigid sets. In the first group (n = 12), no "actualization" was observed during the testing stage; that is, there was no consistent effect from the stimuli presented during the previous stage of the experiment, which showed an angry facial expression: the participants correctly evaluated the facial expressions in both fields of vision as being identical. In the second, "rigid" group (n = 23), erroneous evaluations were observed, such that the face on the right or left was perceived as "unpleasant," whereas actually it was the same face, with a "neutral" expression (actualization of the set).

People with a plastic set, after receiving verbal instructions about the cognitive tasks to be performed (identification of facial expression), showed increased coherence of theta potentials, mainly in the right hemisphere between adjacent parts of the frontal cortex, as well as between the frontal and posterior cortical zones, especially the dorso-lateral portion of the frontal cortex (lead F8) and the temporal region (T4). In people with a plastic set at the formation stage (two facial stimuli presented simultaneously, with angry and neutral expressions), the coherent connections of theta potentials in the anterior frontal areas were clearly weakened; in particular, the coherent connection disappeared in the right hemisphere between the dorso-lateral zone of the frontal cortex (F8) and the temporal region (T4). At this stage of the experiment, the primary observation was increased interhemispheric connections between the anterior frontal areas (F3 and F4). However, Figure 5.6 shows that the coherent relationships increased substantially between the posterior frontal areas and the central, parietal and temporal regions of the right hemisphere. Interhemispheric coherent ties increased, in particular, between the posterior-frontal zone of the left hemisphere (FC3) and the parietal region of the right hemisphere, as well as between symmetrical parts of the central and parietal regions.

At the stage of testing the set, when subjects correctly assessed the emotional facial expression, a clear-cut weakening of the coherent connections of the theta potential was observed, especially in the right hemisphere, compared with the previous stage of the experiment. It should be noted that at this stage,

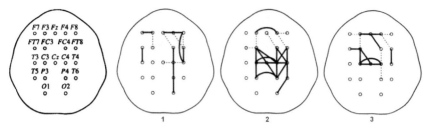

FIGURE 5.6   Topography of changes in the EEG coherence function in the theta band (4–7 Hz) at individual stages of the experiment in subjects who did not demonstrate set actualization to emotional facial expression. 1 – "operative rest" (the state immediately after listening to the instruction); 2 – set formation stage; 3 – set testing. A thick line corresponds to an increase in coherence whereas a dotted line corresponds to a decrease in coherence.

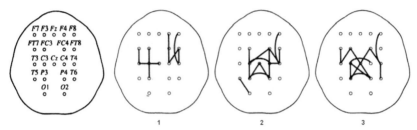

FIGURE 5.7   Topography of changes in the EEG coherence function in the theta band (4–7 Hz) at individual stages of the experiment in subjects who demonstrated set actualization to emotional facial expression (contrast and assimilative illusions). Designations as in Figure 5.6.

there was no coherent connection between the dorso-lateral zone of the frontal cortex and the temporal region.

After the participants with a rigid set had received instructions, the coherent connections were strengthened between the individual parts of the cortex in both hemispheres. In this group there was a significant increase of the coherence of theta potentials between the frontal (F8) and temporal (T4) regions of the right hemisphere, like the group with a plastic set. However, during the stages of the experiment when facial stimuli were presented, the changes in the coherence function of theta potentials in the frontal region were less pronounced than in the "plastic" group (Figure 5.7). These differences were most pronounced at the testing stage, during which people with a rigid set made erroneous evaluations of facial expression, in the form of contrasting and assimilative illusions. Figure 5.7 shows that, as in the stage of set formation, no changes in the coherence of theta potentials in the anterior parts of the frontal cortex are observed in this group. However, as in the previous two

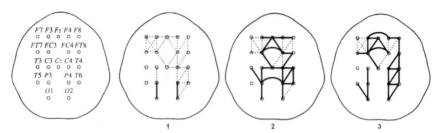

FIGURE 5.8   Topography of changes in the EEG coherence function in the alpha band (8–13 Hz) at individual stages of the experiment in subjects who did not demonstrate set actualization to emotional facial expression. Designations as in Figure 5.6.

stages (following the instructions and set formation), coherent connections were strengthened in the right hemisphere between the frontal and temporal cortex, particularly between the dorso-lateral part of the frontal cortex (lead F8) and the anterior temporal region (T4), as well as between the latter and the posterior-frontal zone of the cortex (FC4). It should be noted that in the stages of formation and testing of the set, as well as in the "plastic" group, there is an increase of interhemispheric coherent connections between the more caudally located cortical areas.

To compare the coherence indicators of the theta potentials and the alpha potentials, the coherence function of the latter was calculated at individual stages of the experiment, in relation to the initial "open eyes" condition. Data from this analysis are presented in Figures 5.8 and 5.9. These figures show a substantial difference in the indicators of spatial synchronization of alpha potentials between the groups with plastic and rigid sets. Unlike the data on theta potentials, the data for the alpha range displayed substantially decreased coherence potentials in the plastic set group, after they had received instructions about the cognitive task to be performed. This was particularly pronounced in the frontal region, and also in the more caudal zones of the right hemisphere (Figure 5.8). During the formation stage, and especially during testing of this group, the coherence of alpha activity increased substantially between adjacent parts of the frontal region, as well as in posterior cortical zones of the right hemisphere. A comparison of Figures 5.6 and 5.8 shows that the coherence of the alpha-range potentials in the frontal region changes substantially more than that of the theta potentials in the "plastic" group.

In the "rigid" group, the differences in the coherence values of the theta and alpha potentials were more pronounced. This is clearly seen by comparing Figures 5.7 and 5.9. Unlike the coherence data for theta activity, the coherent connections significantly increased among the alpha potentials in the frontal

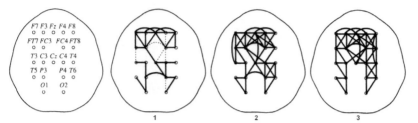

FIGURE 5.9   Topography of changes in the EEG coherence function in the alpha band (8–13 Hz) at individual stages of the experiment in subjects who demonstrated set actualization to emotional facial expression (contrast and assimilative illusions). Designations as in Figure 5.6.

region after subjects received verbal instruction. They increased even more at later stages of the experiment, and became more diffuse. Furthermore, at the stage of testing the set, when its actualization occurs in the form of erroneous evaluations of facial expression, this increased coherence of the alpha potentials is particularly strongly expressed in the frontal region of both hemispheres and in the more caudally located zones of the right hemisphere. At this stage, the coherent connection between the dorso-lateral cortex (F8) and the temporal region (T4) of the right hemisphere significantly increases.

9   Discussion

Analysis of the coherence function of cortical electrical potentials recorded in the pre-stimulus period at different stages of the experiment revealed substantial differences in the dynamics of spatial synchronization of alpha and theta oscillations. These results were particularly pronounced in the group with a rigid set formation. They appear primarily in the topography of the coherent connections: increased synchronization of alpha potentials is clearly more pronounced in the frontal region, and especially at the testing stage, when actualization of the set is observed in the form of visual illusions. In connection with forming and actualizing the set, coherence changes in theta activity do not occur in the frontal region; they are mainly observed in the more caudally located sections of the cerebral cortex. However, one very substantial exception should be noted: in the "rigid" group, at all stages of the set, there is a substantial increase in the coherent connections of theta potentials between the dorso-lateral part of the frontal region and the temporal region in the right hemisphere. The same connection is observed, also in the right hemisphere, and in the alpha potentials, but only at the testing stage; however, it is not as isolated as that for the theta potentials, and is accompanied by increases in the number of many other coherent connections.

That coherent links develop between the frontal and temporal regions (mainly in the "rigid" group, in which erroneous evaluations of facial expression are observed) is of clear relevance in the context of contemporary ideas about the role of identification of visual stimuli in the organization of descending influences from the prefrontal cortex to the higher visual centers in the temporal cortex (Kveraga et al. 2007). An important fact should be noted: the MEG data show that the activity evoked by the identifiable visual stimuli develops 50 ms earlier in the human orbitofrontal cortex than in the inferior temporal cortex (Bar et al. 2006; Kveraga et al. 2007). We realize that strengthening the coherence of the theta potentials between these regions cannot be a direct indicator of descending influences from the prefrontal cortex, whose source is the old set that leads to a distortion of the visual identification of facial stimuli, in the form of contrasting and assimilative illusions. However, M. N. Livanov's (1989) idea that the coherence level of the electric potentials from different parts of the cerebral cortex is an indicator of a functional relationship between them, and their degree of affiliation at the stage of predisposition to one cognitive activity or another, and during its implementation has been confirmed in recent years by many studies (Rappelsberger et al. 1993; Andrew and Pfurtscheller 1996; Farber et al. 2000; Paller et al. 2003; Fisher et al. 2005).

The strengthening of coherent relations between the frontal and temporal regions – which occurs only in people who have illusory distortions in the perception of emotional facial expressions during set testing – provides the basis to advance a hypothesis about the neural mechanism for the development of visual illusions. These illusions are the result of a descending, modulatory influence of the prefrontal cortex upon higher visual centers in the inferior temporal cortex. Their source lies in a previously formed internal representation (in this case, a visual set). At a certain stage, the descending influences of previously formed representations (the set) take precedence over the ascending visual impulses that arise in response to a new stimulus; this leads to a distortion in how it is perceived. With repeated presentations of a new stimulus during a learning process that occurs by comparing the ascending (bottom-up) visual impulse from the new stimulus with the descending impulses (top-down) from the old set, a new, "corrected" set is formed. This leads to the "harmonization," the "coincidence" of ascending and descending nerve impulses, resulting in the disappearance of visual illusions, so that the process of identifying the visual stimulus is facilitated.

Our conjecture is confirmed by data obtained with children of preschool and primary school age. At the stage in which the visual set is extinguished, after the participant has solved a cognitive task (i.e., a change of set has occurred), the synchronization of theta potentials between the frontal and temporal regions almost completely disappears, and the reaction time to a test stimulus is greatly reduced (Kostandov et al. 2007). This last point indicates that the cognitive task has become easier.

Recently, a similar but more daring hypothesis was made regarding the origin of hallucinations (i.e., pathological false perceptions), generally occurring in the absence of sensory stimulation (Kveraga et al. 2007). These authors believe that descending influences from internal representations can be not only modulatory, but can also evoke neuronal activity in the lower regions of the brain, particularly in the inferior temporal cortex, which would be indistinguishable from the response to an external stimulus.

It is interesting that strengthening functional connections between the dorso-lateral frontal cortex and the temporal region – two parts of a ramified system involved in identification of emotional facial expression – was found in coherence function analysis, especially of theta potentials, the generation of which is related to the cortico-hippocampal feedback system, which in turn is directly related to episodic memory (Guevara and Corsi-Carbera 1996; Bastiansen et al. 2003; Kirk and Mackay 2003). The manifest predominance of synchronized theta potentials in the right hemisphere at all stages of the experiment suggests that the cognitive task of evaluating emotional facial expression is based primarily on visual (episodic) memory, with less participation of semantic memory. Right-hemispheric asymmetry in spatial synchronization of alpha potentials is considerably smaller and, curiously, appears mostly in the group with a plastic set form.

These results and published findings allow us to assert that by analyzing the coherence function of alpha and theta potentials, we have two "windows" through which to "see" the activities of two functional systems that generate brain activity in the process of perception and evaluation of emotional facial expression: the cortico-hippocampal and the fronto-thalamic. Analysis of theta activity allows us to identify synchronization of cortical activity between the frontal and temporal regions in the right hemisphere when inert forms of set for the face are formed, and illusory distortions in the perception of facial expression are present. A key part of the cortico-hippocampal system in this case becomes fully comprehensible, since it includes not only the hippocampus, but also other structures of the limbic system that are directly related to emotion (Bastiansen et al. 2003; Kirk and Mackay 2003). The fronto-thalamic system in the cognitive activities we studied, judging from the spatial synchronization of alpha potentials, causes a more diffuse activation of the cerebral cortex, which is especially significant in the frontal regions and in the right hemisphere in cases where rigid sets for the face are formed and facial expression is misevaluated. It is suggested that the activation and integration of structures in the frontal regions, as well as between those regions and other parts of the cortex, are performed with direct involvement of the fronto-thalamic system.

We are aware that much remains unclear about the role of these two brain systems for the integration of cortical activity in the process of identifying the emotional facial expression, especially their relationships and interactions at the various stages of set formation and actualization. However, it should be emphasized that the set paradigm we are using, proposed by D. N. Uznadze (1958), has definite advantages in the experimental study of perception and evaluation of emotional facial expression. It provides an opportunity to study experimentally the meaning of past experience through the so-called bias in the perception of emotional facial expression; it makes it possible to compare cortical electrical activity in trials of appropriate perception of facial expression and in trials with illusory perceptual distortions; and finally, this model allows us to study the dynamics of cortical activity immediately after people have received verbal instructions (the stage of operational rest), as well as later in the process of formation of a cognitive set, at the stage of its actualization, manifested in contrasting and assimilative visual illusions, and at the stage at which, in a new situation, a change of set occurs. All of this creates the conditions for experimental study of the role of descending influences from the frontal cortex of the cerebral hemispheres in the perception of emotional facial expression, as well as of two systems of cortical activity integration.

10   Conclusion

In the process of perceiving a face with a specific emotional expression (in our experiments, an angry face), a cognitive set is formed, which may subsequently have a significant impact on the identification of facial expression. With D. N. Uznadze's model of set, we were able to show that this effect may lead to distortion in the evaluation of emotional expression, which takes the form of contrasting and/or assimilative illusions, where a face with a neutral expression is evaluated as emotionally negative.

These results allow us to assert that the model of cognitive visual set can be effectively used in experimental studies of human perception of emotional facial expression. The literature and our own data suggest the role of the prefrontal cortex in the organization of this function, which plays an important social role in human behavior. Our view is that in the ramified structural-functional organization of the brain's system of identifying emotional facial expression, the role of the prefrontal cortex is associated with the formation and change of cognitive sets for emotional facial expression, and with those unconscious internal representations, or "schemas," that people acquire during interpersonal communication.

By studying the coherence function of cortical electrical potentials in the theta and alpha bands, we found the involvement of two functional systems for the integration of brain activity during perception and evaluation of emotional facial expression: the cortico-hippocampal and fronto-thalamic feedback systems. Using coherence analysis of the theta potentials, we found increased synchronization of cortical activity between the frontal and temporal regions in the right hemisphere when inert sets are formed as well as when assimilative and contrasting illusions in the perception of emotional facial expressions are present. We propose a hypothesis concerning the neural mechanism for the development of visual illusions. The latter are due to the predominance of descending modulatory influences from the prefrontal cortex to the higher visual centers in the temporal cortex. Their sources are the previously formed internal representations (sets). The dynamics of spatial synchronization of alpha potentials, at different stages of the experiment, suggest that the fronto-thalamic system is associated with a more diffuse form of cortical activation than the theta rhythm, and is expressed especially in its frontal sections and in the right hemisphere when there are distortions in the perception of the emotional facial expression, in the form of contrasting and assimilative illusions. It is interesting that this does not change the coherence of the theta potentials between the individual parts of the frontal region. Finally, using coherence analysis of cortical potentials in the theta and alpha range, we found two "windows" allowing us to explore the work of two functional systems for the integration of brain activity: the cortico-hippocampal and the fronto-thalamic.

References

Andrew, C., and G. Pfurtscheller. 1996. "Event-related coherence as a tool for studying dynamic interaction of brain regions." *Electroencephalography and Clinical Neurophysiology* 98, no. 2: 144–148.

Anokhin, P. K. 1974. *Biology and Neurophysiology of the Conditioned Reflex and its Role in Adaptive Behavior*. New York: Pergamon Press.

Balconi, M., and C. Lucchiari. 2006. "EEG correlates (event-related desynchronization) of emotional face elaboration: a temporal analysis." *Neuroscience Letters* 392, no. 1–2: 118–123.

Bar, M., M. Neta, and H. Linz. 2006. "Very First Impressions." *Emotion* 6, no. 2: 269–278.

Bastiansen, M., Hagoort P. 2003. "Event-induced theta responses as a window on the dynamics of memory." *Cortex* 39, no. 4–5: 967–992.

Bastiansen, M., J. von Berkum, and P. Hagoort. 2002. "Syntactic processing modulates the theta rhythm of the human EEG." *Neuroimage* 17, no. 3: 1479–1492.

Batuev, A. S., and L. V. Sokolov. 1993. "I. P. Pavlov's Madrid speech and the psychophysiology of behavior." *Fiziol Zh Im I M Sechenova* 79, no. 5: 3–13.

Bendatt, J., and A. Peirsol. 1958. *Measurement and Analysis of Random Data*. New York: Wiley.

Beritashvili, J. S. 1965. *Neural Mechanisms of Higher Vertebrate Behavior*. Trans. W. T. Liberson. Boston: Little, Brown Company.

Farber, D. A., T. G. Beteleva, A. S. Gorev, N. V. Dubrovinskaya, and R. I. Machinskaya. 2000. "Functional organization of the developing brain in the formation of cognitive activity. The physiology of child development." In *Obrazovaniye ot A do Ya (Education from A to Z.)*, eds. M. M. Bezrukikh and D. A. Farber, 82–103. Moscow: NGO.

Fisher, H., J. Sandblom, J. Gavazzeni, P. Franson, C. I. Wright, and Y. Bǎckman. 2005. "Age-differential patterns of brain activation during perception of angry faces." *Neuroscience Letters* 386, no. 2: 99–104.

Guevara, M. A., and M. Corsi-Carbera. 1996. "EEG coherence or EEG correlation?" *International Journal of Psychophysiology* 23, no. 3: 145–153.

Gurfinkel, V. S., and Y. S. Levik. 1991. "The concept of body schema and motor control." In *Intellektualnye protsessy i ikh modelirovaniye. Organizatsiya dvizheniya (Intellectual processes and their modeling. The organization of movement)*, ed. A. V. Chernavskii, 59–105. Moscow: Nauka.

Gurfinkel, V. S., and Y. S. Levik. 1995. "A system of internal representation and control of movement." *Vestn. RAN (Bulletin of the Russian Academy of Sciences)* 65, no. 1: 29–37.

Hasratyan, E. A. 1970a. "Conditional reflex changes in the functional state of the brain." In *Ocherki po fiziologii uslovnykh refleksov (Essays on the physiology of conditional reflexes)*, ed. E. A. Hasratyan, 181–191. Moscow: Nauka.

Hasratyan, E. A. 1970b. "Tonic conditional reflexes as a form of the integrated brain activity," In *Ocherki po fiziologii uslovnykh refleksov (Essays on the Physiology of Conditional Reflexes)*, ed. E. A. Hasratyan, 164–173. Moscow: Nauka.

Haxby, J. V., E. A. Hoffman, and M. I. Gobbini. 2000. "The distributed human neural system for face perception." *Trends in Cognitive Sciences* 4, no. 6: 223–233.

Hess, U., R. B. Adams, and R. E. Kleck. 2004. "Facial appearance, gender, and emotion expression." *Emotion* 4, no. 4: 378–388.

Kirk, I. G., and J. C. Mackay. 2003. "The role of theta-range oscillations in synchronizing and integrating activity in distributed mnemonic networks." *Cortex* 39, no. 4–5: 993–1008.

Konishi, S., K. Nakajima, L. Uchida, M. Kameyama, K. Nakahara, K. Sekihara, and Y. Miyashit. 1999. "Transient activation of inferior prefrontal cortex during cognitive set shifting." *Nature Neuroscience* 1, no. 1: 80–84.

Kostandov, E. A. 2006. "The significance of context for cognitive activity in the formation of unconscious visual sets." *Rossiiskii Fiziologicheskii Zhurnal Imeni I. M. Sechenova* 92, no. 2: 164–177.

Kostandov, E. A., E. A. Cheremushkin, and M. L. Ashkenazi 2004. "Change in cortical electric activity during set formation under conditions of increased load on the working memory." *Zhurnal Vysshei Nervnoi Deyatelnosti Imeni I P Pavlova* 54, no. 4: 448–454.

Kostandov, E. A., E. A. Cheremushkin, and M. L. Ashkenazi. 2005a. "Features of nonverbal visual set in children of preschool and early school age." *Zhurnal Vysshei Nervnoi Deyatelnosti Imeni I P Pavlova* 55, no. 3: 347–352.

Kostandov, E. A., E. A. Cheremushkin, M. L. Ashkenazi, and N. E. Petrenko. 2007. "Dynamics of the spatial organization of cortical electrical activity during the formation and actualization of a cognitive set for facial expression." *Zhurnal Vysshei Nervnoi Deyatelnosti Imeni I P Pavlova* 57, no. 1: 33–42.

Kostandov, E. A., N. S. Kurova, E. A. Cheremushkin, and I. A. Yakovenko. 2005b. "The dependence of set on the involvement of ventral and dorsal visual systems in cognitive activity." *Zhurnal Vysshei Nervnoi Deyatelnosti Imeni I P Pavlova* 55, no. 2: 170–177.

Kostandov, E. A., and N. N. Zakharova. 1992. "Dependence of late evoked cortical potentials arising from a complex of cognitive factors." *Zhurnal Vysshei Nervnoi Deyatelnosti Imeni I P Pavlova* 42, no. 3: 477–490.

Kreiman, G., C. Kosh, and L. Fried. 2000. "Category-specific visual responses of single neurons in the human medial temporal lobe." *Nature Neuroscience* 3, no. 9: 946–953.

Kveraga, K., A. S. Ghuman, and M. Bar. 2007. "Top-down predictions in the cognitive brain." *Brain and Cognition* 65, no. 2: 145–168.

Livanov, M. N., and V. N. Dumenko. 1989. "Neurophysiological aspects of research on systemic organization of the brain." In *Prostranstvenno-vremennaya organizatsiya potentsialov i sistemnaya deyatel'nost' golovnovo mozga (Spatial-temporal organization of potentials and the systemic activity of the brain)*, ed. P. V. Simonov, 229–248. Moscow: Nauka.

Masselmo, M. E., and H. Eichenbaum. 2005. "Hippocampal mechanisms for the context-depended retrieval of episodes." *Neural Networks* 18, no. 9: 1172–1190.

Mikhailova, E. S. 2005. "The neurobiological foundations of identification of man's identification of emotion from facial expression." *Zhurnal Vysshei Nervnoi Deyatelnosti Imeni I P Pavlova* 55, no. 1: 15–28.

Mikhailova, E. S., E. S. Rosenberg, A. A. Abramova, and N. N. Logunova. 2004. "Identification of emotion from the facial expression by subjects with different personality profiles." *Zhurnal Vysshei Nervnoi Deyatelnosti Imeni I P Pavlova* 54, no. 6: 750–758.

Monchi, O., M. Petrides, V. Petre, K. Worsle, and A. Dagher. 2001. "Wisconsin Card Sorting Revisited: Distinct neural circuits participating in different stages of the task identified by event-related functional magnetic resonance imaging." *Journal of Neuroscience* 21, no. 19: 7733–7741.

Paller, K. A., C. Ranganath, B. Gonsalves, K. S. Yabar, T. B. Parrash, D. R. Gitelman, M. Marsel-Mesulam, and P. J. Reber. 2003. "Neural correlates of person recognition." *Learning and Memory* 10, no. 4: 253–260.

Posner, M. L., and M. E. Raichle. 1997. *Images of Mind*. New York: Scientific American Library.

Rappelsberger, P., D. Lacroix, and H. Petsche. 1993. "Amplitude and coherence mapping: its application in psycho- and pathophysiological studies." In *Quantitative EEG Analysis – Clinical Utility and New Methods*, eds. M. Rother and U. Zwiener, 179–186. Jena, Germany: Universitätsverlag.

Sechenov, I. M. 1947. "Reflexes of the brain." In *Izbranniye filosovskiye i psikhologicheskiye proizvedeniya (Selected philosophical and psychological works)*, ed. I. M. Sechenov, 69–176. Moscow: OGIZ.

Sergerie, K., M. Yepage, and J. Y. Armony. 2005. "A face to remember: emotional expression modulates prefrontal activity during memory formation." *Neuroimage* 24, no. 2: 580–585.

Stapel, D. A., and W. Koomen. 2006. "The flexible conscious: investigating the judgmental impact of varieties of unaware perception." *Journal of Experimental Social Psychology* 42, no. 1: 112–119.

Streit, M., J. Dammers, S. Simsek-Kraues, J. Brinkmeyer, W. Wölwer, and A. Ioannides. 2003. "Time course of regional brain activation during facial emotion recognition in humans." *Neuroscience Letters* 342, no. 1–2: 101–104.

Streit, M., W. Wölwer, J. Brinkmeyer, R. Yhy, and W. Gaebel. 2000. "Electrophysiological correlates of emotional and structural face processing in humans." *Neuroscience Letters* 278, no. 1–2: 13–16.

Ukhtomskii, A. A. 1966. *Dominance*. Moscow: Nuaka.

Uznadze, D. N. 1958. *Experimental foundations of the psychology of set. Eksperimental'niye issledovaniya po psikhologii ustanovki (Experimental Studies of the Psychology of Set)*. Tbilisi, Georgia: Press of the Academy of Sciences of the Georgian Soviet Socialist Republic.

Vuilleumier, P., J. Y. Armory, K. Clarke, M. Husain, J. Driver, and R. J. Dolan. 2002. "Neural response to emotional faces with and without awareness: event-related fMRI in a parietal patient with visual extinction and spatial neglect." *Neuropsychologia* 40, no. 12: 2156–2166.

Werheid, K., G. Alpay, I. Jentzsch, and W. Sommer. 2005. "Priming emotional facial expressions as evidenced by event-related brain potentials." *International Journal of Psychophysiology* 55, no. 2: 209–219.

Williams, Y. M., K. J. Brown, P. Das, W. Boucsein, E. N. Sokolov, M. J. Brammer, G. Olivieri, A. Peduto, and E. Gordon. 2004. "The dynamics of cortico-amygdala and autonomic activity over the experimental time course of face perception." *Cognitive Brain Research* 21, no. 1: 114–123.

CHAPTER 6

"Human–Neuron–Model": A Spherical Model of Signal Discrimination in the Visual System

C. A. Izmailov, A. M. Chernorizov, and V. B. Polyansky

Dedicated to the blessed memory of our teacher E. N. Sokolov

∴

Modern psychophysiology of cognitive processes is based on the integration of the methodology of psychological research used in experiments with humans with the methodology of neurophysiological studies of animals. This integrative approach is being most actively and consistently developed in the school of Prof. E. N. Sokolov and is provisionally referred to as the "Human-Neuron-Model" (Sokolov 1980; Sokolov 1986). In this approach, psychophysiological study of cognitive processes begins with experiments with humans, continues with neurophysiological experiments with animals, and is completed by the construction of a mathematical model that integrates the psychological and neurophysiological data.

This model is not a simple ad hoc description of the experimental data. Strict requirements are imposed: the entire model as a whole (the "neural network") must reproduce the results of psychological experiments, and the "neuron-like elements" of the model should reproduce the responses of neurons involved in the process under study. To understand the mechanisms underlying a cognitive process from the "Human-Neuron-Model" standpoint requires understanding the structure and logic essential to implement the operation of these neural networks, and not merely noting a correlation between brain structures and the psyche. Thus, the "Human-Neuron-Model" approach aims to explore the nature of interactions between neurons as the basis of cause-effect relations between brain structures and function (the psyche).

Many years of psychophysiological research (since 1971) into mental processes (memory, attention, perception) and states (emotions) were devoted to the focused development of the "Human-Neuron-Model" approach, under the direction of Prof. E. N. Sokolov (1920–2008), at the Faculty of Psychology (Department of Psychophysiology) and the Biological Faculty (Department of High Nervous Activity) of Moscow State University. Based on the synthesis of a large array of experimental data obtained from experiments with humans, as well as behavioral and neurophysiological experiments with animals, E. N. Sokolov proposed a "model of a conceptual reflex arc," and developed a "theory of vector encoding of information" (Sokolov 2003). All this laid the basis for the formation of a new field of research in psychophysiology: "vector psychophysiology" (Sokolov 1986).

1 Construction of a Geometric Model of Cognitive Processes Using Multidimensional Scaling

Our work substantiates the proposition that the most appropriate methods of mathematical modeling in the "Human-Neuron-Model" approach are the construction, by multidimensional scaling methods, of a geometrical model of "subjective space," whose points represent stimuli detectable by the subject, and interpoint distances – the "subjective differentiation" between stimuli. (Henceforth, to facilitate comparative analysis, the terms "subject," "subjective distinction," and "subjective space" are used for both humans and experimental animals.)

What distinguishes our geometric models of subjective spaces is that they are spherical. The spherical coordinates of the stimulus points are interpreted in the model as integral "output" characteristics of the "subject," and the Cartesian coordinates as a reflection of the contributions to the cognitive process made by the neurophysiological mechanisms (channels) that realize these subjective characteristics. Thus, the geometric modeling in our work is not simply a mathematical method for the formal representation of cognitive processes, but a special approach, a formal language that includes both cognitive phenomenology and the neurophysiological mechanisms that realize it. The main condition for implementing such an approach is to use a specific methodology for experimental research. It includes the measurement of large (supraliminal) differences between all pairs of stimuli, analysis of the resulting matrix of pairwise differences by the method of multidimensional scaling, and construction of a spherical model for discrimination among stimuli.

2 Perception as the Baseline Cognitive Process

The authors of most post-behaviorist theories characterize the nature of cognitive processes by such concepts as "self-organization," "motivation," "goal" or "activity." These terms are used because cognitive process is considered as purposeful behavior with a feedback and formation of plans (cognitive maps, models, schemes). This view is quite consistent with actual experience as well as with intellectual interpretation of this experience, and is supported by data from many experiments in the field of perception, thought, attention, and memory. The key concept for these ideas about the nature of cognitive processes is the notion of "categoriality." Cognitive processes are categorical, that is, they include "meaning," "sense," "intention," etc. Therefore, without understanding the processes of categorization, it is impossible to understand the nature of cognitive processes. Perceptual processes are baseline cognitive processes, and we can assume that research into such perceptual mechanisms as categorization can be used as the basis for understanding the nature of other cognitive processes. The present work concentrates on applying the "Human-Neuron-Model" approach to the study of visual perception, with the goal of establishing a connection between data describing the mechanism of visual perception as psychophysical and neurophysiological functions, showing the categoriality of perception that does not fit into the framework of behaviorist methodology. But at the same time it is not connected with influence on perception of higher cognitive processes, such as learning or the decision making, the categorization of stimuli is carried out by the same neurophysiological mechanism as well as color distinctions of lights with different spectral distributions.

The categoriality of perception usually means that the changes in the environment perceived by the organism (stimuli, events, influences) are characterized not only by physical properties, such as the intensity of light and its configuration (pattern, distribution of intensity in time and space), but also by meaning. These changes present the subject with various options for action, indicate what has already happened or should happen, have their individual character, and are situated within a broader context, i.e., these influences contain something that goes beyond physical properties (Neisser 1976). The main problem, a stumbling block to constructing a theory of cognitive processes, is the following dilemma: is "meaning" a property of the stimulus (Gibson 1979) or is it introduced into the learning process by the perceiving organism? (Gregory 1970) At the beginning of its development, the cognitive approach to visual perception was represented primarily by "information theories," based on processes of converting the retinal image using different classification algorithms. It was assumed that certain mechanisms of the visual system – detectors – distinguish specific excitation patterns at the retina. This information is then transmitted to the next, higher level of the visual system, where it is checked, screened, and combined with previously accumulated information. That is how the internal, subjective conception (image) of the influence of the environment is formed. Attempts to include cyclicity, the repetition of each cycle over time, into the model, (Neisser 1976; Ivanitsky et al. 1984) with a phased development process involving memory, attention, and experience, change nothing, since the basic acts of perception are associated with the first stages of sensory analysis. But if perception is considered as an entire, multi-stage process, it means that perception as such does not exist. Instead, there is a single behavioral act in which all cognitive processes are interdependent (Shvirkov and Alexandrov 1973). We propose a different approach to understanding the nature of visual perception, which combines the detector principle of information coding in the visual system with the principle of categorization. This does not require an appeal to processes of memory, learning, attention, or intelligence – i.e., the higher cognitive processes – and perception is considered as a separate and independent cognitive process. In this approach, the basic content of the act of perception is not the specification of the stimulus, i.e., recognizing "what" and "where," but involves the differentiation of stimuli and the detection of significant changes in the environment (Fomin et al. 1979; Izmailov and Chernorizov 2005). Specification (identification) appears as a byproduct of the process of differentiation. In this way, significant changes in the environment are more important for the organism than are just noticeable (threshold) changes. Accordingly, it is the data for analysis of suprathreshold differences between stimuli that form the basic material for our research.

3 Measurement of Large Suprathreshold Interstimulus Differences

3.1 *Subjective Scaling*

Subjective evaluations of differences between stimuli represent the cumulative effect of the activity of all neural networks involved in encoding the physical characteristics of the stimulus and of decoding the electrophysiological pattern into a cognitive image. To understand the overall structure of the cognitive system, it is necessary to distinguish contributions of the separate links in this integral estimation of interstimulus differences. Because the most important characteristic of the spherical model for stimulus discrimination is the unified representation of both the psychological and neurophysiological characteristics of the cognitive process, the unification of methods for measuring interstimulus differences in psychological and neurophysiological experiments holds a special place in the description of our approach. Methods of measuring large suprathreshold differences between stimuli in experiments with humans have a long tradition and are fully detailed in handbooks on scaling (Torgerson 1958; Stevens 1961). Electrophysiological techniques for such measurements are less well developed. They provide information on stimulus differentiation by large neural networks, by recording evoked potentials in the cortex and in the subcortical brain structures of humans and animals; as well as information about local area networks by recording extracellular and intracellular neuronal activity. At the foundation of these measurements is a method developed by researchers in our country for instantaneous exchange of stimuli (Bongard 1955), which is called in English-language literature *"stimuli exchange"* or the *"silent substitution method."* (Estevez and Spekreijse 1982).

3.2   The Instant Substitution Method

For electrophysiological measurements of large interstimulus differences, we developed a modified method for abrupt stimulus exchange. An important feature of the method is the exchange of the stimulus for itself, when the reference stimulus and test stimulus are physically identical. In this case, a "null response" is considered an indicator of background activity, with respect to which the response of the cognitive system is evaluated as a non-null stimulus difference. Then, at the moment of stimuli exchange, a change in activity is also observed, and, as the data show, the increase of the difference between stimuli evokes the increase of the response to their abrupt exchange (Paulus et al. 1984; Zimachev et al. 1986; Izmailov et al. 1998a; Izmailov et al. 2001; Izmailov et al. 2004).

This fact served as the basis for using a series of test stimuli, which vary monotonically on both sides of the reference stimulus for the parameter selected by the researcher. The function that relates the magnitude of the electrophysiological response of the visual system to the magnitude of the differences between the reference and test stimuli forms a V shape, with its minimum in the areas of the minimum difference between the test and reference stimuli (Shapley 1990; Zimachev et al. 1991). Such V-shaped functions were obtained for data recorded by electroretinograms (ERG) of frogs and carp. The evoked visual cortical potentials, which we named evoked potentials of differences (EPD), were observed in animals and humans in response to instant substitution of several kinds of visual stimuli (lights stimuli varying of colors and luminance, lines of varying orientation, stimuli of various forms) (Paulus et al. 1984; Zimachev et al. 1986; Izmailov et al. 1998a; Izmailov et al. 2001; Izmailov et al. 2004). In the given set of stimuli each of them can be used as referential. The set of V-shaped functions for all the reference stimuli forms a matrix of pairwise differences. This matrix is analogous to the matrix of pairwise dissimilarities that is obtained in psychophysical experiments with human subjects. In this way, the subjective estimations of the differences and the electrophysiological measures of the differences are closely correlated (Izmailov et al. 2001). Thus, the transition from V-shaped differentiation functions, to the matrix of pairwise differences between stimuli in psychophysical and neurophysiological experiments ensures the unity of experimental methods for obtaining initial data – both from the standpoint of content, by studying different cognitive systems, and also from the standpoint of comparing the experimental data from studies of humans and animals.

4 Analysis of the Matrices of Differences by Multidimensional Scaling Technique

An additional feature of our approach is the use of the multidimensional scaling technique to construct a geometric model of stimulus differentiation (Torgerson 1958; Shepard 1962; Kruskal 1964). Here a key role is played by the idea, underlying the method of multidimensional scaling, for representing the differences between stimuli as geometric distances. The dimension m of this space is determined by the number of positive eigenvalues of the matrix of scalar products, calculated from the original matrix of interstimulus distances. The factorization of the matrix of scalar products gives the values of the coordinates of a point on each of the m axes. This solution is based on the validity of the initial data, comprising a matrix of pairwise differences. However, experimental data are always accompanied by measurement errors, both random and systematic. These errors occur in the solution obtained, in part, from the m axes, and so the challenge is to identify the minimum necessary dimension k of the stimulus differentiation space. Further, since the space of the stimulus points is derived only from the interpoint distances, it is random with respect to the starting position of the frame of reference and their orthogonal rotation. Various options have been developed for determining the minimal dimension and unique coordinate system. The best known are algorithms based on the ideas of Shepard and Kruskal (Shepard 1962; Kruskal 1964).

4.1 Determination of Dimensions of the Subjective Space

In our work, we use algorithms based on a spherical model of stimuli differentiation. A detailed description of these algorithms appears in the works cited above (Izmailov 1980; Sokolov and Izmailov 1984). Our solution is based not only on formal, but also substantive conditions:

1. The relation between the interpoint distances and the interstimulus differences must satisfy the requirement of global linearity (Shepard and Carroll 1986; Shepard 1987). This condition is associated with the uniformity of subjective space, and is estimated to be the value of the linear correlation coefficient or Kruskal stress (Izmailov and Sokolov 1978; Izmailov 1980). The resulting space is centered so that the variation of lengths of the radius vectors of the points would be minimal (Izmailov and Sokolov 1978; Izmailov 1980). The variability of the radii is estimated as the ratio of the standard deviation of the radius vectors to the mean radius (coefficient of variation), expressed as a percentage.
2. In accordance with the concept of dual-channel coding of each attribute in the visual system (Sokolov and Izmailov 1988), coordinates of the point-stimulus for each pair of axes in Euclidean space reflect the contributions of the activity of two opponent neurophysiological channels in the differentiation of stimuli. The spherical coordinates of the points-stimuli in the Euclidean plane should reflect the subjective component of the process of stimulus differentiation. Satisfying this condition involves the direct connection within the geometric model of subjective phenomenology with the characteristics of the neurophysiological mechanisms of the visual system of humans and animals.

5   The Spherical Model of Differentiation of Visual Stimuli

In a series of experiments using a variety of visual stimuli, we obtained estimates of large interstimulus differences, which were analyzed by different methods of multidimensional scaling. In all cases, when the stimuli were varied by one subjective variable, analysis of the matrix of pairwise differences led to a spherical model of discrimination, similar to the one that was designed to encode brightness of light stimulus (Fomin et al. 1979). In particular, this model was achieved through the study of human achromatic vision using disk-annulus stimuli (Izmailov 1980; Izmailov and Sokolov 1991; Zimachev et al. 1991). It was shown that to meet the condition of linearity between the initial estimates of differences and interpoint distances (Shepard and Carroll 1966), a two-dimensional Euclidean space was required. This result is consistent with the two-dimensional geometric model of achromatic colors constructed by P. Heggelund (1974) on the basis of experiments with similar stimuli. However, our solution has significant differences from Heggelund's two-dimensional model. The stimulus points in the spherical model do not fill the entire plane uniformly, but form a curved trajectory in the shape of an arc. At one end of this arc are "black" stimuli, with a minimally bright disk and a maximally bright annulus. At the other end are the brightest stimuli, in inverse proportion to the luminance of the disk and the annulus. All the intermediate points also correspond to the luminance ratio of the disk and the annulus. To test the sphericity of the obtained configuration of points-stimuli, a procedure was used that determines the deviation (coefficient of variation of radii) of the experimental data from the equation for a (two-dimensional) sphere:

[1] $\quad Y_{1i}^2 + Y_{2i}^2 = R_i^2.$

The size of the coefficient of variation varies from 7–12% for various subjects. This shows that the stimuli actually form a circular trajectory on the plane. But unlike in the model of Fomin et al. (1979) where a spherical metric is proposed to measure differences between the stimuli our data show (Izmailov and Sokolov 1978; Izmailov 1980; Izmailov 1981; Sokolov and Izmailov 1984; Izmailov and Sokolov 1991) that estimates of perceived differences are described by a Euclidean metric:

[2] $\quad d_{ij}^2 = \sum_{k=1}^{n}(X_{ki} - X_{kj})^2$

Thus, the spherical model of stimulus differentiation proposed in our work is described by equations [1] and [2].

The circular trajectory of point localization means that a spherical coordinate acts as a subjective variable here – the horizontal angle formed by the stimulus point on the plane. This conclusion is easily verified by plotting the spherical coordinates of the points against the luminance of the stimuli (Izmailov 1982; Izmailov 1995; Sokolov and Izmailov 2006). Such graphs show that the resulting function corresponds to the standard logarithmic function, derived by G. Fechner in the past, and later confirmed by a number of psychophysical experiments (Hartridge 1950; Stevens 1961). According to the generalized spherical model of sensory systems proposed in the work of Fomin et al., (1979) the two-axes Y1Y2 of the Cartesian coordinate system represent the neural network of two channels that are formed by the ON- and OFF-cells of the visual system (Chernorizov 1995; Latanov et al. 1997; Chernorizov 2008). The channels are linked in a reciprocal relationship, so that when one channel in the network (for coding of brightness) is activated more with greater light intensity (axis Y1), then the other channel (for coding of darkness; axis Y2) is activated less, and vice versa. Thus the total activity of the channels, represented by the size of the circle's radius, remains constant, as expressed by the equation for the sphere (cf. equation [1]). One example of such a reciprocal system of visual neurons is a system of ON- and OFF- cells in the visual cortex of the cat (Poggio et al. 1969; Izmailov and Sokolov 1991).

The results of modeling human achromatic vision fully correspond with the results of experiments with other vertebrates on luminance discrimination. In these experiments we recorded responses of the retina (by electroretinogram) (Izmailov et al. 2006) and the visual evoked potentials of differentiation (Polanskiy 2000; Polanskiy 2008) to instant change of stimuli with the subsequent construction of a V-shaped differentiation function. The matrix of pairwise differences based on the V-shaped functions was analyzed using multidimensional scaling, as it was in experiments with humans. It was found that the geometric model for luminance discrimination in lower vertebrates (Izmailov and Sokolov 1991; Latanov et al. 1997; Polanskiy 2000; Izmailov et al. 2006; Polanskiy 2008) takes the form of a two-dimensional sphere. This means that the very same dual-channel mechanism for differentiating light intensity occurs in the visual system of humans and animals, as described by the spherical model of stimuli discrimination (Sokolov and Izmailov 1988; Izmailov and Sokolov 1991; Chernorizov 2008). Analogous results are obtained from multidimensional scaling of estimates of suprathreshold differences in orientation between lines of fixed luminance (Izmailov and Sokolov 1990; Izmailov et al. 2004). Stimulus points (lines of different orientation) are located along a circle in two-dimensional Euclidean space. Thus the subjectively perceived orientation is represented by the spherical coordinate of the stimulus points, and the two Cartesian axes represent two opponent channels: "vertical-horizontal" and "right-left inclination" (Shelepin 1981). Experiments recording the retinal activity of the frog, (Izmailov and Zimachev 2008) and the evoked potentials of the visual cortex of the rabbit (Polanskiy 2008) and human (Izmailov et al. 2004) in response to abrupt changes of lines of differing orientation, corresponded to the spherical model of stimulus differentiation.

6   A Dual Channel Neural Network as a Basic Mechanism (Module) of the Visual System

These similar two-dimensional spherical models for light intensity and orientation of lines could be explained from the standpoint of the separation of stimuli into the subjectively simple and the subjectively complex, according to the traditional divisions of sensory and perceptual aspects of perception. However, researchers have already confronted the problem of a priori designation of simplicity or complexity of a stimulus. We also discovered that not only light intensity and the orientation of lines, but also more complex stimuli – such as surface color (Izmailov 1995) or a figure consisting of two lines, (Izmailov and Sokolov 1990) or three lines converging upon a single vertex (corners, forks, arrows, T-shaped figures) (Izmailov et al. 2008) can also be represented in geometric terms by a spherical model of signal discrimination and, accordingly, in terms of the dual-channel neural network.

Based on our data, we can conclude that there are two states of the visual environment which constitute the basis of visual stimulus perception. On the one hand, there is the intensity and spectral composition of light, i.e., the energy characteristics of the stimulus. On the other, there are the boundaries dividing the visual field into local parts. This dichotomy is quite consistent with the data from ERG recordings of the vertebrate retina with homogeneous light stimuli and patterns in the form of a one-dimensional or two-dimensional lattice with different spatial frequencies (Maffei et al. 1985; Maffei and Fiorentini 1990). In the latter case, the terminology used for electroretinogram changes is "PERG," which refers to the response of the retina to the formed stimulus (pattern). Retrograde degeneration of retinal ganglion cells caused by section of the optic nerve leaves the ERG intact, whereas the PERG is reduced to the level of noise. These data allow us to conclude that the retinal ganglion cells play an essential role in the generation of the PERG. The data from intracellular recording of cellular activity in the retina of a monkey in response to stimuli that are homogeneous in luminance and structured in configuration (Hess and Baker; 1984; Maffei and Fiorentini 1990) confirm the thesis that the PERG is generated primarily by neurons of the inner plexiform layer, whereas the ERG reflects the activity of receptors and cells of the outer plexiform layer. Analogous results were obtained in our own studies of the frog retina (Izmailov and Zimachev 2008). These findings allow us to consider the division of cells into ON and OFF types as a fundamental neurophysiological characteristic of the visual system, conditioned not only by energy opposition arising from the duality of visual stimulation (light/dark), but also by the configurational opposition (homogeneity/heterogeneity).

The synthesis we propose is made concrete by a visual mechanism demonstrating a spherical model of stimulus discrimination. The identification of a mechanism that similarly encodes the energy and configuration features of the light environment supports the hypothesis of the modular organization of visual perception, where the modules are not defined by lists of physical or subjective characteristics, but by their description of each one separately. Examples of this modular principle are systems analogous to Guzman's "keys" (Winston 1978) or to the elements of a written alphabet. This approach to the organization of visual perception (Julesz 1984) has not been pursued, not only because of the vagueness of the "module" as a subjective unit, but also due to the inability to link it with a specific neural network. A spherical model of stimulus discrimination can eliminate these difficulties, because its most characteristic feature is that it encompasses both a mechanism for neurophysiological coding of stimuli in the visual system (Cartesian coordinates), and a mechanism for decoding a neurophysiological code into the subjective features of the visual image (spherical coordinates).

This makes it possible to assert the dual-channel module as the basic mechanism by which the visual system can represent subjective variables (Sokolov and Izmailov 1983; Sokolov and Izmailov 1988; Izmailov et al. 1988b; Sokolov and Izmailov 2006; Izmailov et al.). The main distinguishing feature of this module is that it is not directly connected either with an encoded stimulus, or with a decoded sensory response. It is a kind of structure that can be used to convert any stimulus into an arbitrary "subjective" feature. For example, the vibration frequency of air or liquid can be decoded into color, and the frequency of electromagnetic oscillations into the orientation of a line. The specificity of the stimulus is determined by the structure of the dual-channel module's input unit and the content of its code; its "subjective" value is determined by the correlation of the activity of the two opponent channels of the "two-dimensional module" and the special structure of the output unit. One advantage of this module is that specification of a subjectively simple attribute and its associated stimulus is not provided a priori, but is produced a posteriori, by identifying the spherical structure of these distinctions. Only if the matrix of pairwise differences between the stimuli is consistent with a spherical model of discrimination, is it possible to conclude that these stimuli are being decoded by a dual-channel neural network of the visual system, in a simple (one-dimensional) subjective mode.

7 A Three-Stage Model of the Visual System

The universal nature of the dual-channel module makes it possible to combine the most varied input and output structures of the visual system, and the corresponding neural networks sufficient to obtain information about the external environment. Each network will contain three links: an input receptor link, a set of dual-channel modules, and an output detector link (Sokolov and Izmailov 1983; Sokolov and Izmailov 1988). Corresponding to the network structure, three phases are formulated, or three stages for processing sensory information in the visual system of humans and animals.

8 Receptors and "Quasi-Receptors" of the Visual System

Theoretically, the input of the three-stage neural network, which forms the neurophysiological basis of perception, could consist of any of the receptors. In particular, the visual system is based on photoreceptors, which are the input structures of the neural networks that convert the intensity and frequency of electromagnetic radiation into brightness and color. However, the detection of lines, edges, and boundaries by the vertebrate visual system is considered by many researchers to be one of the key characteristics in the neural network's pattern recognition (Lindsay and Norman 1972; Winston 1978; Shevelev et al. 1999; Izmailov et al. 2004) The works of D. Hubel and T. Wiesel played a particularly important role in the development of this idea; in the visual cortex of the cat, they found neurons to detect the orientation of lines, as well as neurons that are selective for stimulus figures that represent certain combinations of lines (Hubel and Wiesel 1962). The first type of neurons was called "detectors of simple attributes of a visual stimulus", and the second, "detectors of complex attributes." Subsequent studies have shown that these properties of the visual cortex occur in the most species of higher vertebrates (Supin 1981). Our approach considers the cortical detectors of line orientation as an input structure which forms the basis for all the key elements of the next level of the visual system: the whole "configurational alphabet," including a line as a segment. The purpose of these structures is to gather information about the area of extended changes of light intensities, in the form of boundaries that separate one part of the visual field from another. That is, the emphasis is not on the line segment, but only on its orientation as a boundary element. This hypothesis allows us to explain the presence, in the primary area of the visual cortex of higher vertebrates, of a large number of detectors of line orientation, and to ascribe to them the role of "quasi-receptors" that perform the same input functions in the analysis of forms that retinal receptors fulfill in the analysis of the spectral composition of light in the retina (Izmailov et al. 2004; Izmailov et al. 2008; Izmailov and Zimachev 2008). The composition of this multilevel "quasi-receptor" includes neurons of the retina and subcortical structures, which conduct a preliminary analysis of the spatial distribution of boundaries in the illumination level of the visual field. This activates detector neurons for lines of differing orientation.

Thus, in the framework of the above-mentioned three-stage neural network to the visual system that is responsible for "restoring" the configuration signal, the first stage is the activation of retinal photoreceptors and "quasi-receptors" – neuron-detectors of line orientation. At the second stage, a limited set of elements is drawn from these lines of orientation, including the line as a segment. In this case, the value is not determined by the orientation of the line, but by the fact that, as a line segment, it is bounded at one or both ends, and is a full-fledged feature of a contour. This is the level at which basic or key elements of configuration are formed, to be used for subsequent construction of the integrated shape of the object. This function is associated with cortical neurons with complex and supercomplex receptive fields. Finally, in the third stage, the various key elements are combined as configurations, which define the basic contours of objects in the visual field, just as the letters of the alphabet are combine to form words (Izmailov and Chernorizov 2005).

9 The Formation of Basic Units, or Key Elements of Configuration

To verify our proposal about the formation of basic elements of a dual-channel modular visual system, a series of studies was carried out on humans and animals, in which "complex" stimuli were formed from various combinations of "simple," one-dimensional stimuli, the perception of each of which is described by a two-dimensional spherical model of discrimination. Experiments with the discrimination of color stimuli may serve as the most obvious example of such combinations, with the stimuli changing their energy characteristics (intensity) and/or spectral composition (color). In extensive studies of human color vision using psychophysical methods(Izmailov and Sokolov 1978; Izmailov 1980; Izmailov 1982; Sokolov and Izmailov 1983; Sokolov and Izmailov 1984; Izmailov and Sokolov 1991; Paramei et al. 1991; Izmailov 1995)and techniques of recording the evoked cortical potentials, (Izmailov et al. 1989; Izmailov and Sokolov 1991; Izmailov et al. 1998; Izmailov et al. 2003; Sokolov and Izmailov 2006; Chernorizov 2008) as well as in studies of color vision in animals, (Zimachev et al. 1991; Chernorizov 1995; Latanov et al. 1997; Izmailov et al. 2006; Izmailov and Zimachev 2008) it has been shown that the differentiation between achromatic and chromatic stimuli, taken separately, is precisely described by a two-dimensional spherical model of signal discrimination. The attributes of a dual-channel neural network which is derived from this model are consistent with the electrophysiological characteristics of photoreceptors and color opponent neurons of the visual system. At the same time, experiments on stimulus differentiation, varying simultaneously in both luminance and spectral composition, have shown that the geometric model of differentiation is a hypersphere in four-dimensional Euclidean space, which combines spherical models of the discrimination separately of achromatic and chromatic stimuli, as two specific two-dimensional sub-spaces. The three spherical coordinates of a stimulus point characterized such subjective color features as hue, saturation, and brightness; and the four Cartesian coordinates of the stimulus points corresponded to two color opponent channels ("red/green" and "blue/yellow") and two neural channels for luminance ("brightness" and "darkness").

Similarly, experiments were conducted on the differentiation of stimuli, consisting of various combinations of "simple" configurational features, whose differentiation fits the structure of the spherical model and the dual-channel neural network. In particular, experiments involving the differentiation of two linear shapes, varied simultaneously as to size of angle and orientation, yielded a solution in the form of a spherical surface in three-dimensional Euclidean space (Izmailov and Chudina 2005). Two spherical coordinates of a stimulus point in this three-dimensional space corresponded to the subjective scale of orientation and size of angle, consistent with the data obtained in the separate scaling of these characteristics. But, unlike the four-dimensional color space, here, the combination of a pair of dual-channel modules yielded a three-dimensional space, and, accordingly, three Cartesian coordinates were represented by a three-channel neural network. In this case, the result showed another kind of interaction between two dual-channel modules.

More interesting results were achieved in experiments on human differentiation of lines that varied both in intensity and orientation, i.e., with a combination of the energy and configurational stimulus characteristics (Izmailov and Edrenkin 2010). The geometrical model that most closely matched the initial matrix of pairwise differences between stimulus lines was a hypersphere in four-dimensional Euclidean space. From a formal point of view, this corresponded to a combination of dual-channel modules of brightness and color, into a four-channel network of color vision. As in the color hypersphere, in the hypersphere that combines differentiation of brightness and orientation, two-dimensional subspaces corresponded to the spherical model of discrimination of these characteristics, analyzed separately. However, in this general spherical model, only two spherical coordinates of the three expressed psychophysical functions of the subjective attributes of brightness and orientation. The third spherical coordinate was uninterpreted and had no direct connection with any subjective stimulus characteristic. This distinguishes a hypersphere of brightness and orientation from a hypersphere of color and brightness, where the third spherical coordinate displayed an unambiguous association with color saturation. This means that here, as in the case of the neural network of color vision, the two-channel networks of brightness and orientation are also combined in a common four-channel network, but in a different way and with a different result.

Yet another difference between a "brightness/orientation hypersphere" and a color hypersphere turned out to be the nature of the interaction between dual-channel modules. In a color hypersphere, the spherical coordinate characterizing the brightness, was dependent only on the luminance of the stimulus and did not depend on the stimulus's spectral composition, whereas the spherical coordinate characterizing the color hue of the stimulus depended both on the spectral composition and on the luminance of the stimulus (Izmailov 1981; Wyszecki and Stiles 1982; Bimler et al. 2009). In psychophysical terms, this means that the "color hypersphere" reproduces the Bezold-Brücke phenomenon, characterizing the hue shift of color when the brightness of the stimulus is changed (Wyszecki and Stiles 1982; Bimler et al. 2009). And in neurophysiological terms, this means that the channels of achromatic modules have an inhibitory effect on the channels of the chromatic module, but not vice versa.

In the "brightness-orientation hypersphere," the pattern is the opposite. The spherical coordinate characterizing the orientation of the stimulus line was only dependent on the slope of the line in the visual field, and not on the luminance of the stimulus, whereas the spherical coordinate characterizing the brightness of the stimulus depended on both the angle of inclination and the luminance of the stimulus (Izmailov and Edrenkin 2010). This agrees with data obtained in the study of the differentiation of lines of varying luminance and orientation, in the frog's visual system (Izmailov and Zimachev 2008). The results recorded by electroretinogram (ERG), using the method of instant change of stimulus lines of varying luminance and orientation, indicate that the V-shaped function of line orientation, which is built upon the amplitudes of the ERG b-wave, parallels the shifts in luminance of the line without changing its shape, whereas the luminance function detects nonlinear changes in brightness depending on the orientation of the stimulus. The retinal function of luminance for lines of different orientation revealed a striking similarity to analogous psychophysical brightness functions. In terms of the neurophysiology of the visual system, this means that the channels of an orientation module have an inhibitory effect on the channels of a brightness module, but not vice versa. In other words, when simultaneously changing both the energy and configurational characteristics of the stimulus, the configuration module takes priority over the brightness module.

The above data show that simple (one-dimensional) stimuli in different modalities are detected by the visual system using the same type of neural network, which we called a dual-channel differentiation module. At the same time, the combination of dual-channel modules in a network for detecting a more complex (multidimensional) stimuli occurs in different ways for the stimulus's energy parameters (wavelength and radiation intensity) and for configuration parameters (line orientation and the angle between two lines). Furthermore, the nature of the combination of an energy module (brightness) and a configuration module (orientation) into one common network also reveals its specificity. This calls into question the idea of the existence of a general principle of combination of individual modules into a more complex multi-channel network, as it is understood in the widespread hierarchical theories of visual perception.

From our perspective, it is more sensible to refer here to the principle of alphabetic language construction, and to propose that the basic elements (dual-channel modules) of the visual system are combined into multi-channel networks analogous to the combination of letters into syllables, morphemes, and words (Izmailov and Chernorizov 2005) In speech, the combination of letters into syllables or morphemes into words is determined by the meaning that is to be conveyed, rather than by physical characteristics or configurational characteristics of these elements. In precisely the same way, in visual perception, the combination of dual-channel modules into a multi-channel network for complex stimulus detection is determined by the subject matter of the stimulus, and not by the physical and configurational characteristics of the light pattern. We should not be misled by the existence of rigid links, in the form of psychophysical functions, between features of light radiation and the subjective features whose terms (luminosity, color, shape, and movement) are used to describe and specify the phenomenology of visual perception.

Psychophysical functions express the specifics of the language of perception. In contrast to the language of speech, where meaning is completely independent of the physical medium of its speech elements, and the very same language can be used in an entirely different physical medium ("Saussure's postulate"), a visual language can only be realized by analysis of the parameters of electromagnetic radiation. Studies of the visual systems of all animals, both vertebrates and invertebrates, show that vision is based on the same photoreceptors ("Adrian's generalization") and, accordingly, no other physical effect except electromagnetic radiation in a very narrow spectral band (380–700 nm) can be perceived by the visual system. And this means that visual language is strictly associated with one unique physical medium.

On the one hand, this aspect of visual language makes the nature of visual perception difficult to understand, because it creates the illusion that perception is determined by stimulation, and that the goal of perception is to represent, as precisely and accurately as possible, a picture of the external environment (Bongard 1967). This was proposed long ago by Aristotle, who asserted that to perceive means to know "what" and "where" (Izmailov and Chernorizov 2005). But taking an information approach instead, the purpose of perception is also to extract information from the environment, filtering it for its importance to the organism, and transferring it to a storage center for later use in solving intellectual tasks (Neisser 1976; Latanov et al. 1997). On the other hand, the psychophysical aspect of visual language facilitates the task of deciphering visual stimuli, because study of the properties of the medium (visual stimulation) and its relationship to the language structures (the subjective characteristics of perception) provide unique information about the nature of these structures. In particular, as shown in the data presented here, the identification of a dual-channel module as the baseline element of visual language turned out to be possible only within the framework of the psychophysical methodology in visual perception studies. In just the same way, this methodology makes it possible to identify the next level of language structures – options for merging the baseline elements into the structural units of the visual language, equivalent to syllables or morphemes. All the results of the experiments examined here were obtained using the spherical model of stimulus discrimination. These studies allowed us to realize that classical psychophysics of perception has exhausted its potential, and that further progress in understanding the nature of perception requires that research include such features of "the meaning of the stimulus," as the categorical characteristics of visual perception.

9.1 *Analysis of Categorical Characteristics of Visual Perception*

The advantage of the approach we propose is that it uses a common methodology for measuring the perceptual differences of not only energy and configurational stimulus features, but also of the categorial. In a special series of experiments, we used different types of categorial distinctions which are associated in different ways with changes in the configurational and energy stimulus variables.

Let us consider as an example the results of experiments in schematic depiction of emotional expression in the human face (Izmailov et al. 1999; Izmailov et al. 2005). In these experiments, oval-shaped images were used, with lines sketching the eyebrows, eyes, nose, and mouth. The face was given an emotional expression by curvature of the mouth, changing from zero (a horizontal line), up and down in increments of 14 degrees, and by the slant of the eyebrows, changing from zero up and down in increments of 6 degrees. In psychophysical experiments, 25 stimulus faces were presented in pairs to subjects and they rated the difference in emotional expressions between each pair of faces, on a scale from 1 to 9 (Izmailov et al. 1999). In psychophysiological experiments 9 basic stimuli from 25 faces were presented in pairs using method of instant substitution. The evoked potential of differences (EPD) in the human visual and temporal cortex was recorded in response to each change (Izmailov et al. 2005). The interpeak amplitude of the P120-N180 and N180-P230 components, as well as the peak amplitude of N180 component, were used to measure the difference. As it was shown in the work of Izmailov et al. (Izmailov et al. 2001), the amplitude of those EPD components corresponds to the subjective estimates of interstimulus differences between the schematic faces.

By combining all pairs of stimuli for each of the four sites of EPD registration, three matrices of interstimulus differences were obtained, expressed by the amplitudes of the three EPD components. The aim of this work was to build a geometric model of the visual differentiation of schematic faces, both according to the amplitudes of evoked potential of differences registered in the human cortex in response to rapid-fire stimulus change, and according to the subjective evaluations of differences between emotional expressions of the same schematic faces. A detailed description of the formal and substantive criteria on which the spherical model for differentiations these stimuli was based on work of Izmailov et al. (Izmailov et al. 2005). Here we consider only one aspect of the solution: the relationship between the configurational and categorial characteristics of visual perception.

The configurational attributes of the face are supplied by a pattern of lines representing the mouth and eyebrows, and categorical – by the emotional expressions (Ekman and Friesan 1978; Izmailov et al. 1999). Let us consider first the data obtained for subjective estimates of interstimulus differences. The system of spherical and Cartesian coordinates of the resultant four-dimensional space was analyzed according to the structure of the spherical model of stimulus discrimination and the dual-channel neural network of the visual system. The analysis revealed that the four Cartesian coordinates are associated with perception of the orientation of the lines forming the eyebrows and mouth of the schematic faces. On this basis, it was concluded that the configurational attributes of the stimulus were detected by the four-channel neural network, composed of dual-channel modules of line orientation. However, the emotional expression of the face takes up only two of the three spherical coordinates of the hypersphere. Thus, the first basic categorial attribute of emotional expression, expressed in terms of six basic emotional categories (happiness, pleasure, surprise, fear, displeasure, disgust, anger), presented in the work of Ekman and Friesan (1978) was depicted in the form of the first spherical coordinate of the stimulus points (measured by the size of the horizontal angle in the

X_1X_2 plane). Such mapping is consistent with the categorical structure of emotions in the form of the Schlossberg circle. By analogy with Newton's color circle for color tone, we have designated this attribute as emotional tone (Izmailov et al. 1999).

Another basic characteristic of emotions, designated as emotional intensity, was expressed by the second spherical coordinate of the four-dimensional space, and measured by the vertical angle of the stimulus point, i.e., the angle between the X_3 axis and the X_1X_2 plane. The model's third spherical coordinate had no apparent relationship to any expressive characteristics of the schematic face.

Additional arguments in favor of this interpretation of the spherical model of schematic faces follow from the EPD analysis, recorded during the abrupt substitution of schematic faces. The model built using EPD analysis has the form of a four-dimensional sphere with the same properties of spherical and Cartesian coordinates as the model constructed from psychophysical data (Izmailov et al. 1999).

The main conclusion to be drawn from these experiments is that the geometric representation of categorial attributes of the stimulus has a simpler, less rigid structure than the representation of configurational attributes of the stimulus, although it is based on the very same mechanism of dual-channel modules of the visual system. On the other hand, the EPD analysis shows that the configurational and categorial attributes of complex stimuli (schematic faces) are detected simultaneously, not sequentially. This demonstrates the essential independence of the categorial description of stimuli from the configurational structure of these stimuli. The transition from the configurational attributes of the stimulus to its categorial properties can be viewed as a transition from a multidimensional metric space (a hypersphere) to two-dimensional topological mapping. Similarly, we have obtained additional confirmation of these findings by studying the visual perception of words denoting colors and emotions (Izmailov et al. 2008).

Acknowledgements

The present research was supported by Russian Humanitarian Science Foundation (07-06-00184a), Research Initiation grants 07-06-00109a, 09-06-00366a, and 10-04-00313 from the Russian Foundation for Basic Research.

References

Biederman, I. 1995. "Higher-level vision." In *Visual Cognition and Action*, vol. 2, ed. D. N. Osherson, S. M. Kosslyn, and M. Hollerbach, 41–72. Cambridge, Mass.: MIT Press.

Bimler, D. L., G. V. Paramey, and C. A. Izmailov. 2009. "Hue and saturation shifts from spatially induced blackness." *Journal of the Optical Society of America* 26, no. 1: 163–172.

Bongard, M. M. 1955. "Colorimetry on animals." *DAN USSR* 103, no. 2: 239–242.

Bongard, M. M. 1967. *The Recognition Problem*. Moscow: Science.

Chernorizov, A. M. 1995. "Chromatic vision of fish as a model of chromatic vision of a person." *Moscow University Herald. Series in Psychology* 14, no. 3: 35–42.

Chernorizov, A. M. 2008. "Vector encoding of color in visual system of human and animals." *International Journal of Psychophysiology* 69, no. 3: 173–174.

Ekman, P., and W. V. Friesan. 1978. *Facial Action Coding System*. Palo Alto, Cal.: Consulting Psychologists Press.

Estevez, O., and H. Spekreijse. 1982. "The 'silent substitution' method in visual research." *Vision Research* 22, no. 6: 681–691.

Fomin, S. V., E. N. Sokolov, and G. G. Vaitkevicius. 1979. *Artificial Sense Organs*. Moscow: Science.

Gibson, J. J. 1979. *An Ecological Approach to Visual Perception*. Boston: Houghton Mifflin.

Gregory, R. L. 1970. *The Intelligent Eye*. New York: McGraw-Hill.

Hartridge, H. 1950. *Recent Advances in the Physiology of Vision*. London: Churchill.

Heggelund, P. 1974. "Achromatic color vision. I. Perceptive variables of achromatic colors." *Vision Research* 14, no. 11: 1071–1078.

Hess, R. F., and C. L. Baker. 1984. "Human pattern-evoked electroretinogram." *Journal of Neurophysiology* 51, no. 5: 939–951.

Hubel, D. N., and T. N. Wiesel. 1962. "Receptive fields, binocular integration and functional architecture in the cat's visual cortex." *Journal of Physiology* 160: 106–154.

Ivanitsky, A. M., V. B. Strelec, and I. A. Korsakov. 1984. *Informational Processes of the Brain and Mental Activity*. Moscow: Science.

Izmailov, C. 1980. *Spherical Model of Colour Distinction*. Moscow: Moscow State University Publishing House.

Izmailov, C. 1981. "Multidimensional scaling of the colour's achromatic component." In *Standard and Descriptive Models of Decision-making: Based on the Soviet-American Seminar Materials*, ed. B. F. Lomov, R. D. Luce, W. K. Estes, V. J. Krylov, and N. V. Krylova, 98–110. Moscow: Science.

Izmailov, C. 1982. "Uniform color space and multidimensional scaling {MDS}." In *Psychophysical Judgement and the Process of Perception*, ed. H. G. Geissler and F. Petsold, 52–62. Berlin: VEB Deutcher Verlag der Wissenschaften.

Izmailov, C. 1995. "Spherical model of discrimination of self-luminous and surface colors." In *Geometric Representations of Perceptual Phenomena*, ed. R. D. Luce, M. D. D'Zmura, and A. K. Romney, 153–168. Mahwah, N.J.: Lawrence Erlbaum Associates Publishers.

Izmailov, C., A. M. Chernorizov. 2005. "Language of perception and brain." *Psychology: Higher School of Economy Magazine* 2, no. 4: 22–52.

Izmailov, C., and U. A. Chudina. 2005. "Configurational and categorical characteristics of visual perception of schematic figures." *Herald of RUDN* 2: 27–41.

Izmailov, C., and I. V. Edrenkin. 2010. "Distinction of bimodal stimuli of the visual system." In *Mathematical Psychology in Russia*, ed. G. M. Golovina. Moscow: IPRAS.

Izmailov, C., S. A. Isaichev, S. G. Korshunova, and E. N. Sokolov. 1998a. "Colour and brightness' components of the person's visual evoked potentials." *HNA Magazine* 48, no. 5: 777–787.

Izmailov, C., S. A. Isaichev, and E. D. Shekhter. 1998b. "Two-channel model of signals' distinction in sensory systems." *Moscow University Herald. Series in Psychology* 14, no. 3: 29–40.

Izmailov, C., S. G. Korshunova, and E. N. Sokolov. 1999. "Spherical model of distinction of the schematically face's emotional expressions." *HNA Magazine* 49, no. 2: 186–199.

Izmailov, C., S. G. Korshunova, and E. N. Sokolov. 2001. "Relationship between visual evoked potentials and subjective differences between emotional expressions in 'face diagrams'." *Neuroscience & Behavioral Physiology* 31, no. 5: 529–538.

Izmailov, C., S. G. Korshunova, and E. N. Sokolov. 2005. "Multidimensional scaling of schematically represented faces based on dissimilarity estimates and evoked potentials of differences (EPD) amplitudes." *The Spanish Journal of Psychology* 8, no. 2: 119–133.

Izmailov, C., S. G. Korshunova, and E. N. Sokolov. 2008. "The semantic component of the evoked potential of differentiation." *The Spanish Journal of Psychology* 11, no. 1: 321–340.

Izmailov, C. A., and E. N. Sokolov. 1978. "Metric characteristics of a colour distinction spherical model." *Moscow University Herald. Series in Psychology* 14, no. 2: 47–61.

Izmailov, C. A., and E. N. Sokolov. 1990. "Multidimensional scaling of lines and angles discrimination." In *Psychophysical Explorations of Mental Structures*, ed. H. G. Geissler, 181–189. Stuttgart, Germany: Hogrefe-Huber Publishers.

Izmailov, C. A., and E. N. Sokolov. 1991. "Spherical model of color and brightness discrimination." *Psychological Science* 2, no. 4: 249–259.

Izmailov, C. A., and E. N. Sokolov. 2004. "Subjective and objective scaling of large color differences." In *Psychophysics beyond sensation. Laws and Invariants of human cognition*, eds. C. Kaernbach, E. Schroger, and H. Muller, 27–42. Mahwah, N.J.: Lawrence Erlbaum Associates, 2004.

Izmailov, C., E. N. Sokolov, and A. M. Chernorizov. 1989. *Psychophysiology of Chromatic Vision*. Moscow: Moscow State University Publishing House.

Izmailov, C., E. N. Sokolov, and I. V. Edrenkin. 2008. "Integration of simple signs of stimulus in neural networks of visual system." *Neural Computers: Design and Application* 3–4: 43–55.

Izmailov, C., E. N. Sokolov, and S. G. Korshunova. 2003. "The colour space of human based on the cortex evoked potentials data." *Sensory Systems* 17, no. 1: 32–44.

Izmailov, C., E. N. Sokolov, S. G. Korshunova, and U. Chudina. 2004. "Geometrical model of distinction of the line orientation, based on the subjective estimation and visual evoked potentials." *HNA Magazine* 54, no. 2: 267–279.

Izmailov, C., and M. M. Zimachev. 2008. "Detection of bimodal stimuli in the frog retina." *Neuroscience and Behavioral Physiology* 38, no. 2: 103–144.

Izmailov, C., M. M. Zimachev, E. N. Sokolov and A. M. Chernorizov. 2006. "Two-channel model of a frog's achromatic sight." *Sensory Systems* 20, no. 1: 1–11.

Julesz, B. 1984. "A brief outline of text on theory of human vision." *Trends in Neuroscience* 7, no. 2: 41–45.

Kruskal, J. B. 1964. "Multidimensional scaling by optimizing goodness of fit to a nonmetric hypothesis." *Psychometrika* 29, no. 1: 1–27.

Latanov, A. B., A. U. Leonov, D. V. Evtikhin, and E. N. Sokolov. 1997. "Comparative neurobiology of chromatic vision of human and animals." *HNA Magazine* 47, no. 2: 308–320.

Lindsay, P. H., and D. A. Norman. 1972. *Human Information Processing*. London: Academic Press.

Maffei, L., and A. Fiorentini. 1990. "Pattern visual evoked potentials and electroretinograms in man and animals." In *Visual Evoked Potentials*, ed. J. E. Desmedi, 25–33. Amsterdam: Elsevier.

Maffei, L., and A. Fiorentini, S. Bisti, and H. Hollander. 1985. "Pattern ERG in the monkey after section of the optic nerve." *Experimental Brain Research* 59, no. 2: 423–430.

Neisser, U. 1976. *Cognition and Reality*. San Francisco: W. H. Freeman and Company.

Paramei, G. V., C. Izmailov, and E. N. Sokolov. 1991. "Multidimensional scaling of large chromatic differences by normal and color-deficient subjects." *Psychological Science* 2, no. 4: 244–248.

Paulus, W. M., V. Homberg, K. Cuningham, A. Halliday, and N. Ronde. 1984. "Colour and brightness components of foveal visual evoked potentials in man." *Electroencephalography and Clinical Neurophysiology* 58, no. 2: 107–119.

Poggio, G. F., F. N. Baker, Y. Lamarre, and E. R. Sanseverino. 1969. "Afferent inhibition at input to visual cortex of the cat." *Journal of Neurophysiology* 32, no. 6: 892–915.

Polanskiy, V. B., D. E. Alimkulov, E. N. Sokolov, and M. G. Radzievskaia. 2008. "Reflexion of changes in orientation and intensity of lines in the evoked potentials of a rabbit's visual cortex." *HNA Magazine* 58, no. 6: 688–699.

Polanskiy, V. B., E. N. Sokolov, and D. V. Evtikhin. 2000. "Reconstruction of the perceptive space of brightness and colour on the basis of the evoked potentials and their comparison with behavioural experiments data." *HNA Magazine* 50, no. 5: 843–854.

Shapley, R. 1990. "Visual sensitivity and parallel retinocortical channels." *Annual Review of Psychology* 41: 635–658.

Shelepin, U. G. 1981. "Orientational selectivity and spatially frequency characteristics of a cat's receptive fields of visual cortex neurons." *Neurophysiology* 13, no. 3: 227–232.

Shepard, R. N. 1962. "The analysis of proximities: Multidimensional scaling with an unknown distance function." *Psychometrika* 27, no. 2: 125–140.

Shepard, R. N. 1987. "Toward a universal law of generalization for psychological science." *Science* 237, no. 4820: 1317–1323.

Shepard, R. N., and J. D. Carroll. 1966. "Parametric representation of nonlinear data structures." In *Multivariate Analysis*, ed. P. R. Krishnaiah, 561–592. New York: Academic Press.

Shevelev, I. A., N. A. Lazareva, and G. A. Sharaev. 1999. "Interrelation of tuning characteristics to bar, cross and corner in striate neurons." *Neuroscience* 88, no. 1: 17–25.

Shvirkov, V. B., and U. I. Alexandrov. 1973. "Information processing, behavioural act and cortical neurons." *DAN USSR* 212, no. 4: 1021–1024.

Sokolov, E. N. 1980. "Principles of psychophysiology." *Soviet Psychology* 18, no. 3: 69–82.

Sokolov, E. N. 1986. "Research strategy in psychophysiology." In *Logic, Methodology and Philosophy of Science*, ed. R. B. Marcus, G. Dorn, and P. Weingartner, 495–502. Amsterdam: North-Holland.

Sokolov, E. N. 2003. *Perception and Conditional Reflex: A New View*. Moscow: Moscow Psychological-Social Institute.

Sokolov, E. N., and C. Izmailov. 1983. "Conceptual reflex arc and color vision." In *Modern Issues of Perception*, ed. H. G. Geissler, 192–216. Berlin: VEB Deutscher Verlag der Wissen.

Sokolov, E. N., and C. Izmailov. 1984. *Chromatic Vision*. Moscow: Moscow State University Publishing House.

Sokolov, E. N., and C. Izmailov. 1988. "Three-stage model of color vision." *Sensory Systems* 2, no. 4: 314–320.

Sokolov, E. N., and C. Izmailov. 2006. "Evoked potentials in spherical model of cognitive processes." *Neural Computers: Design and Application* 4–5: 90–105.

Stevens, S. S. 1961. "To honor Fechner and repeal his law." *Science* 133, no. 3446: 80–86.

Supin, A. I. 1981. *Neurophysiology of Mammals' Vision*. Moscow: Science.

Torgerson, W. S. 1958. *Theory and Method of Scaling*. New York: Wiley.

Winston, P. 1978. "Computer vision." In *Psychology of Machine Vision*, ed. P. Winston. Moscow: Mir.

Wyszecki, G. and W. S. Stiles. 1982. *Color Science: Concepts and Methods, Quantitative Data and Formulae*, 2nd ed. New York: Wiley.

Zimachev, M. M., E. D. Shechter, E. N. Sokolov, and C. Izmaylov. 1986. "A chromatic component of a frog's electroretinogram." *HNA Magazine* 36, no. 6: 1100–1107.

Zimachev, M. M., E. D. Shechter, E. N. Sokolov, R. Naatanen, G. Niman, and C. Izmaylov 1991. "Distinction of colour signals by a retina of a frog." *HNA Magazine* 41, no. 3: 518–527.

CHAPTER 7

Individual Characteristics of Brain Activity and Thinking Strategies

Olga M. Razumnikova and Nina V. Volf

Using multi-channel EEG recording and mapping of the power and coherence of biopotentials in the range of 4–30 Hz, we studied individual features of brain activity as determined by sex, creativity, intelligence, and a number of personality traits (extraversion, neuroticism, psychoticism, rational/irrational mental traits). It was found that creative people are distinguished by their high ability to change the frequency-spatial organization of cortical activity, specific forms of which are dependent on sex, intelligence, and other individual characteristics, especially the person's emotional sensitivity. The basis for sex differences in EEG correlates of creativity may lie in differences in information processing strategies, because for men, integration of cortical ensembles at beta rhythm frequencies is more important, whereas for women, lower-frequency rhythms are more prominent, including left hemisphere frontal control of mental processes. The specific nature of the interaction between the anterior and posterior cortical regions is just as necessary a condition for organizing different thinking strategies, as is the interaction of the two hemispheres, and this interaction is related to the type of problem being solved and to individual distinctions in the regulation of functional brain activity. Clearly expressed intellectual and personality traits are formed as the result of a specific individual mosaic of both activating and inhibitory interactions of cortical and subcortical structures, establishing conditions for future thinking strategies: rational/irrational, logical/intuitive, verbal/figural.

One of the pressing problems of modern neurobiology is the study of individual characteristics of brain activity that underlie different thinking and behavior strategies that are preferred, to one degree or another, by different people. A dual approach is often used in thinking classification, for example, distinguishing between rational and irrational, logical and intuitive, and verbal and figural thinking. From the neurophysiological standpoint, this distinction corresponds to the differentiation of the functionally dominant hemisphere: the left (rational, logical, and verbal) and right (irrational, intuitive, and figural.

The search for parallels between individual thinking characteristics and the distinctive features of brain activity has a long history in Russia. I. P. Pavlov should be considered the founder of this trend; he showed, as far back as the middle of the last century, a link between temperament and distinctive features of higher nervous activity (Pavlov 1951). And the problem of connections between the brain and individual thinking characteristics has long remained relevant, attracting the attention of researchers searching for patterns in these relationships, using new technical means of recording brain activity (Eysenck 1990; Stelmack 1990; Rusalov et al. 1993; Sviderskaya and Korol'kova 1996; Pavlova and Romanenko 1998; Volf 2000; Robinson 2001; Razumnikova 2004c; Razumnikova 2005a).

A significant step in understanding patterns in the formation of neural ensembles that give rise to mental processes was made by N. P. Bekhtereva and associates, who revealed the existence of stable, "rigid" connections among groups of neurons involved in verbal processes, and of individually labile functional interaction among neurons (Bekhtereva et al. 1977). Another fundamental approach influencing the organization of our research was A. M. Ivanitskii's model of "information synthesis." According to his theory, the distinctive character of the mental state is determined by a self-organizing system of neuronal groups of varying lability, which has a rigid core (Ivanitskii 1996; Ivanitskii 1997).

Such a model can also be applied to explain stable thinking strategies. In this case the "rigid" systems reflect the most likely brain structure connections that yield clearly expressed individual patterns of thinking (e.g., structure of intellect and/or cognitive style inherent to the individual). Depending on the situation, additional neural modules are flexibly connected to this "skeleton." The resistance of specific thinking strategies is based on the stability of this "rigid" interaction. A similar approach to explaining individual behavioral diversity is known in psychology as the "personal construct theory" of J. A. Kelly (2000).

Along with numerous studies of EEG correlates of human cognition with respect to personality characteristics (Rusalov et al. 1993; Sviderskaya and Korol'kova 1996; Volf 1998; Aftanas 2000; Volf 2000; Razumnikova 2000b), researchers have paid special attention in recent years to the spontaneous electrical activity of the cerebral cortex. This is connected with the fact that what causes the brain's cognitive activity depends on its baseline state (Sheppard and Boyer 1990; Green et al. 1992; Basar et al. 2000). It has also been established that spontaneous electrical activity of the cortex is determined by particular individual genetic features in the structural and functional organization of the brain (Van Beijsterveldt and van Baal 2002; Begleiter and Porjesz 2006). This suggests a promising comparison of baseline cortical activity with cortical activity when performing a task, searching for the EEG correlates of various cognitive strategies, depending on the psychological characteristics of the individual.

We have conducted a series of such studies over several years to elucidate the significance of sex, creativity, intelligence, and several personality traits (extraversion, neuroticism, psychoticism, rational/irrational mental characteristics) (Volf and Razumnikova 1999; Razumnikova 2003b; Razumnikova 2004a; Razumnikova and Volf 2007; Razumnikova et al. 2007; Razumnikova 2008).

1   Sex Differences in Patterns of Hemispheric Interaction and in Thinking Strategies

Among personal characteristics, sex is a genetically determined factor pertaining to the possible variability of thinking strategies that attracts particular attention. Numerous studies of this problem, however, often yield conflicting results, so that elucidating the sex differences in neurophysiological mechanisms of mental processes remains quite relevant.

Sexual dimorphism in functional hemispheric organization during memorization of verbal information was first demonstrated in Russian neurophysiological studies by N. V. Volf (Volf 1998; Volf 2000). Evidence of qualitative differences between men and women, in the formation of intrahemispheric functional systems and interhemispheric interaction during the processing of verbal information was based on a comparative analysis of behavioral characteristics of memory and their EEG correlates. Our studies were also based upon data showing sex differences in processes of information selection (Meyer-Levy 1989; McGivern et al. 1997) and in the activity of the anterior and posterior functional systems of the cerebral cortex (Goldberg et al. 1994).

We considered, in this connection, the importance of sex in elucidating individual differences in hemispheric thinking strategies, presumably related to other individual characteristics: creativity, intelligence, and a number of personality features (extraversion, neuroticism, psychoticism, rational/irrational traits).

Analysis of the frequency-spatial organization of cortical biopotentials was performed for a baseline state prior to carrying out various cognitive tasks, and during the activity. Indicators of power and coherence of the EEG were used for the analysis; they were computed for six frequency bands: theta1 (4–6 Hz), theta2 (6–8 Hz), alpha1 (8–10 Hz), alpha2 (10–13 Hz), beta1 (15–20 Hz), and beta2 (20–30 Hz). Such specifications of EEG recording and analysis have been described in a number of Russian as well as foreign works (Volf and Razumnikova 1999; Volf and Razumnikova 2002; Razumnikova 2004a; Razumnikova 2004; Volf and Razumnikova 2004; Razumnikova et al. 2007).

Attention control and working memory are the main components of higher cognitive functions. This suggests that sex differences in cognitive abilities may be related to differences in activity of brain systems that support these functions. In the models of memorization of dichotically and monaurally presented verbal information the differences were identified in modulation of theta and alpha EEG activity by variations in task demands. It has been shown that during memorization of dichotically presented words women differed from men by higher coherence increase over the right hemisphere (Volf and Razumnikova 1999). In addition, the females showed more diffuse and massive increases in interhemispheric coherence that the males in association with the task. Negative correlation between retrieval of words and alpha desyhronization performance was found. In dichotic task women outperformed men in memory for words that were addressed to the right hemisphere. Women also tend to engage right hemisphere polymodal cognitive strategies while men tend to use left hemispheric strategies (Figure 7.1) (Volf 2000). In sum, it was suggested that in women concrete nouns may be easier to memorize because more sensory-based features can be simultaneously activated as a result of more co-operation of different functional units of the brain.

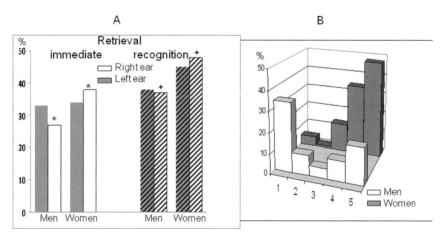

FIGURE 7.1   Retrieval effectiveness (A) and strategies of memorization (B) of dichotically presented words in men and women. Similar signs indicate significant retrieval differences (p<0.05) between men and women. Strategies of memorization: 1 – automatic, 2 – semantic, 3 – rhythmic with other words, integrating in sentences, 5 – integrating in pictures.

Sex differences were found in the hemispheric organization of different forms of selective processes: latent inhibition (Volf and Razumnikova 2004), selective attention in Stroop task (Bryzgalov and Volf 2006), directed and distributed attention in the perception and memorization of laterally presented verbal stimuli (Razumnikova and Volf 1997; Volf and Razumnikova 1999; Volf and Razumnikova 2002; Volf and Razumnikova 2004); Razumnikova and Volf 2007.

Implicit directing of attention during in monaural presentation of verbal stimuli and testing of latent inhibition was associated with predominant involvement of the left hemisphere in women and with the right one in men (Figure 7.2). Explicit directing of attention to the verbal information addressed to the left hemisphere was also associated with higher degree of alpha 2 desynchronization in women in comparison to men (Razumnikova and Volf 2007). The data indicate the left hemisphere in women is more engaged in selection of information.

In this connection it should be noted that attention processes in women may be more subjected to voluntary control. So, changes in testing procedures of latent inhibition from operant learning to explicit classic condition resulted in reduction of latent inhibition in women but not in men (Golosheikin et al. 1997; Volf and Mashukova 2005). Thus, these results suggest that sex differences exist in brain organization and strategies of complex mental functions.

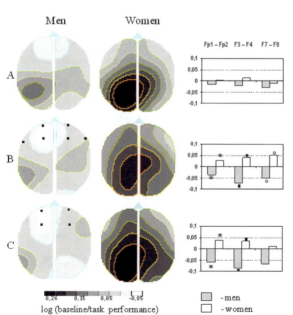

FIGURE 7.2
Maps of alpha2 reactivity in men and women during memorization of laterally presented verbal stimuli. Dichotic (A), monaural in the left ear (B), and in the right ear (C) presentations. In the left column – the maps of task-induced power changes; the light circles indicate the electrode sites where task related desynchronization in women is more pronounced than in men. In the right column – hemispheric differences between men and women in the desynchronization for the sites presented at the top of the picture ($p < 0.05$).

2   The Interconnection between Creativity and the Frequency-Spatial Organization of Cortical Activity

Interest in studying the neurobiological basis of creativity has increased markedly in recent years. This is due, on the one hand, to the psychological knowledge that has been attained about the stages of creative problem solving and the role of intelligence and personality traits in creative productivity, and on the other hand, to the development of multi-channel mapping of electrical cortical activity, and to tomographic methods for analyzing the activity of cortical and subcortical structures. To describe creative thinking, which implies a multitude of solutions to a problem (each of which could be valid), or logical thought (where there is only one answer), Guilford proposed a distinction between divergent and convergent thinking, respectively (Guilford 1967). Analysis of the coherence of an EEG, with its multi-channel registration from different parts of the cortex, makes it possible to clarify the correspondence of originality in problem-solving with the divergent nature of the interaction between different regions of the cortex, and, conversely, of stereotyped solutions with convergent interaction, having more localized representation in the cortex. Given what is known about the functional heterogeneity of EEG rhythms (Robinson 1999; Basar et al. 2000), it seems important to perform such an analysis in a wide range of frequencies. As a model of divergent thinking, we have used a solution to a heuristic type of problem, specially selected due to its suitability for electroencephalographic experiments (Razumnikova 2000b; Razumnikova 2004a; Razumnikova 2004b). The problem was as follows: "The zoo contains hundreds of poisonous snakes. How can the length of each be measured?"

The EEG correlates of divergent thinking were analyzed, taking into account sex and success in solving the heuristic problem. Some maintain that sex differences in creative productivity (whether in science or art) are due to socio-cultural stereotypes, according to which innovative behavior in historically female domains (the household, child-rearing) was not, until recently, considered by society to be creative (Abra and Valentino-French 1991; Vinogradova and Semenov 1993; Simonton 2000; Razumnikova 2002a; Razumnikova 2006). On the other hand, it has been shown that sexual dimorphism in the organization of cognitive processes can be associated not only with the impact of socio-cultural stereotypes, but also with differences in the functional activity of the cerebral hemispheres (Kimura and Harshaman 1984; Haier and Benbou 1995; Volf 1998; Volf and Razumnikova 1999; Volf 2000; Haier et al. 2005), with sex differences in the neural mechanisms of cognition observed when there are equally successful outcomes by men and women (Volf and Razumnikova 1999; Kirkpatrick and Bryant 2005; Halari et al. 2006).

As for a high degree of creative abilities, it is known that they are associated with less pronounced functional brain asymmetry (Atchley et al. 1999; Carlsson et al. 2000; Medvedev et al. 2004), with flexibility of thinking strategies (Martindale 1999; Carlsson et al. 2000), and with low cortical activation (Martindale 1999; Neubauer et al. 2006). At the same time, women tend to demonstrate less pronounced interhemispheric asymmetry (Beamont et al. 1978; Zaidel et al. 1995; Volf and Razumnikova 1999) and greater variability and flexibility of cognitive strategies (Davidson et al. 1976; Hausmann and Gunturkun 1999) in comparison with men, whereas less cortical activation has been observed in men (Robinson 1998).

Based on these data, which reflect the correlation among creativity, sex, and brain activity in different ways, we surmised that defining the role of sex in the specifics of frequency-spatial organization of hemispheric activity as related to solving heuristic problems, would be extremely useful in clarifying the neurophysiological mechanisms that allow successful strategies for creative productivity.

Analysis of the sex differences in EEG correlates of divergent thinking, has shown that high creativity is associated with different patterns of hemispheric activity in men and women: the former solve a problem with a significant increase in the power of the beta2 rhythm, but with local desynchronization of EEG in the alpha1 range; whereas the latter, on the contrary, have a smaller increase in the amplitude of beta2 oscillations and regionally generalized desynchronization of the alpha1 rhythm compared to low-creativity individuals (Figure 7.3). This relation of changes in the power of alpha1 and beta2 rhythms in men and women, engaged in successful, divergent thinking, may reflect different forms of interaction among cortico-subcortical structures in regulating how information is selected when the person is searching for a solution to a given problem (Razumnikova 2000b; Razumnikova 2004a; Razumnikova 2004b).

Beta activity (20–30 Hz) is considered as an indicator of "cortical excitation," in contrast to "cortical inhibition," for which theta and alpha activity are indicators (Lazarev 1998; Neuper and Pfurtscheller 2001). Some people think that a high-frequency beta rhythm (more than 20 Hz) is characteristic of cognitive processes in which the discrete features of the stimuli have to be combined into a unified whole (Pulvermuller et al. 1999). Attention to alpha oscillations (7–13 Hz) in the study of EEG correlates of creative activity, is based on the fact that the power of the alpha rhythm is an indicator of cortical activation, a

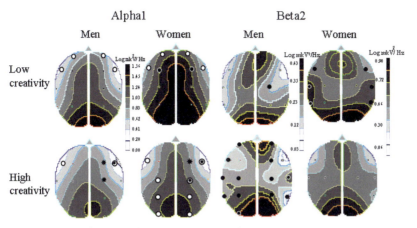

FIGURE 7.3   Changes in the power of alpha1 and beta1 biopotentials associated with carrying out heuristic tasks, in men and women of high or low creativity. The white circles denote the sites for which a significant decrease in power compared to baseline was noted; the black circles show an increase; stars show sex differences ($p < 0.05$).

low level of which, according to C. Martindale, defines the "unfocused" state of attention required for creative activity (Martindale 1999).

One strategy for creative problem-solving is to search multiple hypotheses by systematic analysis of the individual steps of the problem. To come up with such a multitude of ideas, one must retrieve verbal and/or figural traces of memory and use a variety of analogies and metaphors (Costello and Keane 2000). Such operations require engagement of numerous cortical areas, of both the left and right hemispheres, activating neighboring as well as distantly located neural networks. Some believe that individuals of low creativity, when performing a divergent task, use mainly analytical, verbal strategies and semantic memory, whereas highly creative people use a visual-spatial strategy and episodic memory (Carlsson et al. 2000). A great deal of evidence has also been developed for the weakening of functional asymmetry, as the reserves of the right hemisphere are drawn upon for creative thinking (O'Boyle and Benbow 1990; Simonov 1993; Bowden and Beeman 1998; Razumnikova 2004a; Howard-Jones et al. 2005). Right-hemisphere dominance in creative activities is linked to the fact that its functions include not only visual-spatial, but also verbal processes, such as the construction of metaphors or semantic operations that require a wide net of associations (Beeman and Bowden 2000).

These data were confirmed in our study by mapping of coherent connections in the beta2 range: on the one hand, there was more involvement of

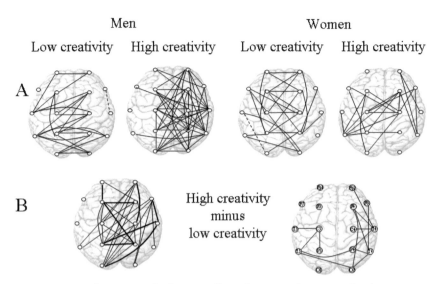

FIGURE 7.4 The increase of coherence of beta2 biopotentials associated with carrying out heuristic tasks, in men and women of high or low creativity compared to baseline (A), and coherence differences between groups of high and low creativity (B). The solid lines connect sites that show a significant increase in the coherence value by comparison with baseline (A) or between groups (B) (p <0.05).

the left hemisphere in divergent thinking among low-creativity people (Cr0) (where the foci of coherent connections was mainly located); and on the other, more pronounced interaction of cortical areas in the right hemisphere among the highly creative (Cr1) (Figure 7.4).

These effects were found to a greater extent among men. However for women, the increased coherence of the right hemisphere in the highly creative group is also observed in the left hemisphere. Thus, coherence patterns connected with performance of the tasks in the low-creativity men can be viewed as an electrographic correlate of a verbal and sequential way of organizing the thinking process, while among the highly creative, a correlate of a visual-spatial and simultaneous approach. For women, apparently, thinking strategies are more changeable, and therefore not so clearly expressed.

In studying cortical activity with a hypothesis based on "neural efficiency," it turned out that weaker activation of the cortex in people of higher intelligence occurs only for women in the testing of verbal abilities, and only for men in the testing of figural abilities (Neubauer et al. 2002; Fink and Neubauer 2006). We can assume that there is a statistically significant pattern in the organization of neural networks for stably expressed thinking strategies. For men, the integration of neural systems required to carry out a complexly organized creative process has more clearly expressed EEG correlates than for women, whose cognitive processes are reflected more weakly, in the changeability of hemispheric connections, and are statistically "vague" as to both topographic and frequency features.

The data cited above, as well as the fact that women demonstrate clearer results with re-testing on visual and verbal tasks (Razumnikova and Volf 1997; Hausmann and Gunturkun 1999), may suggest greater flexibility and variability of the functional organization of neural networks in women than in men, and correspondingly greater variability in their thinking strategies, which complicates their precise delineation.

Comparison of the cortical organization in people who successfully cope with the heuristic problem mentioned earlier with those who fail to do so, shows that men and women achieve the same degree of effectiveness in this activity, but through different types of hemispheric interaction. Successful performance of the task by women is accompanied by relative weakening of hemispheric interaction, compared to low-creativity individuals; whereas, in men, that interaction is significantly strengthened. This interaction between the hemispheres can occur, in creative men, either through the corpus callosum (as evidenced by the increased coherence between homologous sites in the left and right hemispheres), or through subcortical structures (increase of coherent connections between distantly located leads, for example, F3-O2, F3-T6, F4-O2, etc.). This conclusion is based on data concerning the existence of two types of neurons and, accordingly, two systems: a local one and one with more widely distributed cooperation among cortical neurons (Thatcher et al. 1986), and is confirmed by the results of parallel recording of brain activity using MRI and EEG (Hollander et al. 1997).

The observed sex differences in reactivity of the power and coherence of the alpha1 rhythm during divergent thinking (Razumnikova 2004b) may indicate different mechanisms for information selection by men and women. But in this case, it refers to "internal" attention processes aimed at retrieving information from memory and integrating it into complex associative structures. Apparently, for women, the selection of information to solve heuristic problems is based to a large degree on activation processes derived from thalamo-cortical connections, inasmuch as decreasing both the amplitude and coherence of the alpha rhythm can be considered an indicator of the strengthening of these connections (Petsche et al. 1997). In non-creative women, a system of voluntary information selection dominates (activation of the frontal regions), whereas in creative women, it is a system of involuntary attention (the posterior system). Another type of information selection, "differential attention," which has been proposed in the analysis of EEG correlates of creativity (Petsche 1996), may be evidenced by simultaneous interaction of high-frequency cortical oscillators in the beta2 band. This mode of information selection evidently predominates in creative men.

According to some authors (Cowell and Hugdahl 2000; Voyer and Flight 2001), there is a difference in the way men and women select information: the former use more impulsive/global strategies, while the latter use reflective/consistent methods of processing information, thinking it through and adapting it to existing concepts, including to social stereotypes (McGivern et al. 1997). It is possible that the observed high-frequency beta oscillations among creative men, and lower-frequency alpha oscillations among women, are a neurophysiological support of this hypothesis.

It is interesting that the success of divergent thinking among men occurs with close interaction between the hemispheres, while in women there is weaker interaction; this could be linked to the asymmetrical character of interference inhibition among the former, and its more symmetrical character among the latter (Hetrick et al. 1996). Proceeding from this hypothesis, we may suggest that the more pronounced interhemispheric connections among men facilitate a longer period of intuitive thinking and generation of right-hemispheric metaphorical conceptions, by blocking the expression of inhibitory processes from the left hemisphere to the right. For women, the interhemispheric organization optimal for creative thinking is realized with looser interaction between left and right hemispheres, and is probably accompanied by relatively greater lateralization of mental processes, compared to the "normal" state, in which women are observed to have greater integration of hemispheric functions than men (Zaidel et al. 1995; Volf 1998, Volf 2000; Volf and Razumnikova 2002; Westerhausen et al. 2004). Such a relative "disconnection" of the hemispheres can block the emergence into consciousness of "crude" stereotyped solutions, and thus lead to greater creativity among women (Razumnikova 2004b).

Another model that we used to clarify individual features of the frequency-spatial organization of hemispheric activity associated with creativity, was a well-known verbal task proposed by Mednick: the remote association task (RAT) (Mednick 1962; Druzhinin 1999; Razumnikova 2002a). In our experimental conditions, the participants had to think of an association, as original as possible, to a triad of stimulus words. Quantitative assessment of the originality of the responses was determined on the basis of a previously created computerized database (Razumnikova and Petrov 1999; Razumnikova 2002a). Starting from indicators of originality obtained using this assessment, subjects were grouped according to high and low creativity, to compare the EEG correlates in carrying out this naturally divergent task with those obtained for simpler verbal problems: the generation of words starting with a given letter and a chain of simple associations (Razumnikova and Larina 2005; Razumnikova 2007a; Razumnikova 2007b; Razumnikova and Bryzgalov 2007).

For the remote associations task, domination of right hemisphere activation processes was observed, based on statistical analysis of the total power of the biopotentials. However, when comparing the patterns of functional changes in coherence, the left hemisphere was represented to a greater extent in the search for associations than for solving a heuristic problem, apparently due to the verbal nature of the task. This corresponds to published data, because it is known that the left hemisphere takes priority in the conceptual analysis of verbal stimuli, whereas the right hemisphere is involved in processes of more complex symbolic and metaphorical associations between words, as well as the search for words from lexically unrelated categories, and from unusual remote associations (Bowden and Beeman 1998; Grossman et al. 2002).

While there were no sex differences in the originality of the participant's associations, such differences were found in the factor structure of indicators for different types of verbal activity (the originality of associations and the time required to come up with them, the number of words thought of for a given letter, and the number of associations in a chain), and also were found in the dynamics of cortical activity changes. For men, the search for remote associations is accompanied by increased power of the beta2 rhythm in both hemispheres at the beginning of the task, and by concentration of this effect in the central regions of the cortex by the end of testing. For women, the initial period showed a large right hemisphere increase in the power of the beta2 rhythm, and, in the final stage, a relative decrease in beta activity in the parieto-temporal cortical regions along with an increase in the left prefrontal regions. Along with it, positive correlations were achieved between the alpha1,2 power and the originality of generated words; these correlations were widely represented topographically in the female group, but were not present among the males.

Factor analysis of verbal fluency, the time required for deliberation, and the originality of the associations, identified two factors differentiating men and women, which we interpreted as reflecting an "insightful" or "intellectual" strategy of searching for a new solution to a problem (Razumnikova and Bryzgalov 2007). Comparison of these factors with the observed hemispheric activation patterns allows us to propose that the search for original word associations takes place, with men, primarily by an insightful strategy, whereas women, while using both strategies, put a greater emphasis on "intellectual" strategies (i.e., on choosing a solution based on critical evaluation of a multitude of generated words).

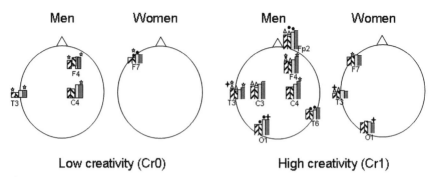

FIGURE 7.5 Changes in the total values of interhemispheric coherence of the beta2 rhythm associated with performance of verbal tasks, compared with baseline for men and women of high or low creativity. ▨ – generating words beginning with a given letter (Exs1), ▬ – making a chain of associations (Exs2), ▭ and ■ the beginning and end, respectively (Exs3n and Exs3f), of a search of remote associations; significant differences (p<0.05) between values of coherence are marked ☆ – between Cr1 and Cr0, △ – Exs2 and Exs1, ● – Exs3f and Exs3n, ✚ – men and women.

By studying changes in the coherence of biopotentials associated with the search for remote associations in comparison with the verbal control tasks, we found a link both to the level of verbal creativity and the sex of the participants (Razumnikova and Larina 2005). In comparison with non-creative people, creative people were distinguished by more pronounced changes in the interaction of cortical areas in the transition from one verbal task to another. In a highly creative group of women, these effects were localized in the left hemisphere, whereas for men, they also encompass the right (Figure 7.5). Creative men differed from the non-creative in their high values for interhemispheric and intrahemispheric coherence, and were similar to women in the level of interhemispheric interaction. An increase in interhemispheric beta2 rhythm coherence, and in the sums of all the connections for each lead at the initial stage of the search for remote associations, was observed for the frontal and temporal regions of the right hemisphere and for the left occipital region. Increased coherence of beta2 biopotentials in creative women was locally represented in the left temporal cortex only during the early stages of the simple verbal tasks, but only the low-creativity participants displayed an additional increase in the left frontal cortex when searching for remote associations. Comparison of these results with sex differences in selection processes found by us and by other researchers (Goldberg et al. 1994; Voyer and Flight 2001) suggests that these findings may very well constitute the neurophysiological basis for sexual dimorphism in the interaction of the hemispheres during creative thinking. For men, selection of information involves to a greater extent the anterior right hemisphere's system of involuntary attention, whereas for women, the left hemispheric frontal system is more significant for voluntary information selection (Razumnikova 2004c).

The focal points of functional reactivity giving rise to coherence while solving various verbal tasks, which is regionally distributed in creative people, evidently may reflect their greater verbal flexibility, with relatively precise neural organization corresponding to the activity. The greater value of interhemispheric coherence in the fronto-lateral regions of the left hemisphere among creative women, compared to the non-creative, even at the stage of simple associative thought, suggests that the subsequent search for original associations occurs for them during the "baseline" testing of verbal functions, and this is sufficient for their effective organization. Additional strengthening of activity in this cortical region in order to perform more complex tasks is necessary only (and only occurs) in the group of non-creative women.

Changes in cortical activity during performance of different verbal tasks that are less pronounced in women than in men may reflect the relative ease with which women perform verbal operations by comparison with men. In support of this conclusion, we have established that there are no sex differences in originality or in the number of associations, and greater verbal flexibility for women (Razumnikova and Bryzgalov 2007). Women also display the best indicators of verbal activity, including word-generation and verbal memory, according to the data of other authors (Halpern 2000; Volf 2000). This advantage can occur because of the closer interhemispheric interaction, compared to men, which facilitates use of the right hemisphere in speech (Shaywitz et al. 1995; Volf 2000). In our experimental conditions, sex differences at the level of total interhemispheric coherence, with large values for women, were characteristic only of those less successful in the search for individual associations, while the creative men and women did not differ on this indicator. At the final stage of creativity testing, the increase in hemispheric interaction in the left occipital cortex was more strongly evidenced by creative men than by women (see Figure 7.3). Closer interhemispheric interaction for creative men was also shown in values – that were greater than for women – for interhemispheric coherence, focused in the left temporal site, during simple verbal activity: word generation.

In the study of EEG correlates of intellectual abilities, we have shown that high intellectual abilities are characterized by a certain "presetting" of the interaction of cortical areas specialized for verbal, arithmetic, or figural operations (Razumnikova 2003b) (results of these studies are provided below in more details). Consequently, more pronounced interhemispheric connections of the left temporal region in creative men may be considered a result of such a "presetting" of the verbal zones of the cortex, which creates the conditions for successful performance of simple verbal operations, as evidenced by the absence of sex differences in verbal flexibility indicators for the creative groups. However, this identical verbal ability in men and women is associated with different hemispheric strategies for the selection of processed information.

3 The Interconnection between Intelligence and the Frequency-Spatial Organization of Cortical Activity

Intellectual giftedness is one of the individual characteristics whose neurobiological foundations have been studied for a long time, but especially intensely in recent years, drawing upon tomographic, genetic, and electrophysiological methods (Anokhin and Vogel 1996; Doppelmayr et al. 2000; Haier et al. 2004; Plomin and Spinath 2004; Haier et al. 2005; Geake and Hansen 2005). Our research was designed to determine the interconnections of baseline EEG (the power and coherence of biopotentials in six frequency bands from 4 to 30 Hz) and indicators of figural, verbal, and arithmetic components of intelligence as measured by the Amthauer test, taking account of gender (Razumnikova 2003b, Razumnikova 2004b). This was based on our views that sex differences are present in the hemispheric organization not only of verbal processes, but also of other complex cognitive functions (Volf 2000; Razumnikova 2004c; Volf and Razumnikova 2004). The question of whether sex differences in intellectual ability exist was posed at the very outset of the development of psychometric techniques to assess IQ. However, through analysis of multiple, often contradictory publications on this problem, we conclude that although sex differences are substantially yet smaller than individual differences within each group, it should be recognized that men predominate in performing visual-spatial tasks and women – in verbal and fine-motor operations. (Hyde and Linn 1988; Halpern 2000; Hyde 2005).

Correlation analysis between intelligence scores and power of biopotentials found a significant link between them, primarily for the high-frequency beta2 band. Verbal intelligence (IQv) was positively correlated with the power of biopotentials in the right hemisphere (Figure 7.6A), topographically this relationship was presented in the posterior cortex ($0.34<r<0.43$; $0.004<p<0.03$) (Figure 7.6B). Arithmetic intelligence (IQa), by contrast, was negatively correlated with the power of the biopotentials in the anterior temporal region of the left hemisphere ($r=0.33$; $p=0.03$ for sites F7 and T3) (Figure 7.4C). No significant relationships were found between the power of the EEG and figural intelligence.

Given the possible differences between intellectual abilities and cortical activation, depending on the sex of the participants, a correlation analysis was also performed separately for each group. It was found that in the male group, a positive correlation between IQv and the power of the beta2 rhythm was significant for the right posterior cortex (sites P4 and O2), and a negative correlation of IQa for the left anterior cortex (Figures 7.6B & 7–6C). In the female group, the correlation between IQv and the power of the beta2 biopotentials was topographically more extensive: and appeared bilaterally in the posterior cortex and at the left prefrontal site (Figure 7.6B); for IQf, no significant correlations were found.

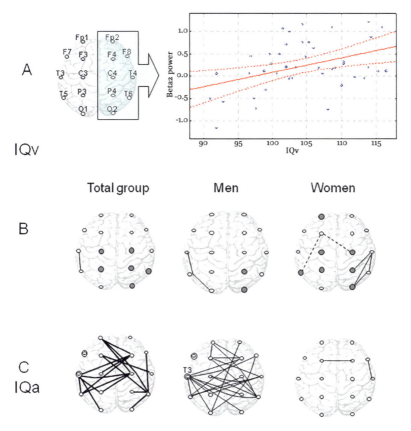

FIGURE 7.6 The relationships between intelligence and beta2 rhythm. A – the correlation of verbal intelligence (IQv) with the total power of the beta2 rhythm in the right hemisphere, B – maps of the coherence and power of the beta2 rhythm, whose values are correlated with IQv, C – maps of the coherence and power of beta2 rhythm whose values are correlated with arithmetic intelligence (IQa); black circles and solid lines indicate positive correlations; white circles and the dotted line indicate negative correlations (p <0.05).

The results of the correlation analysis of intelligence and coherence of biopotentials in the beta2 band, performed for the total group and for men and women separately, are shown in the form of schematic diagrams in Figure 7.6B & 7.6C. The lines connecting pairs of electrodes indicate a significant correlation between the corresponding coherence values and IQ ($0.30 < r < 0.54$; $0.005 < p < 0.05$). IQv was positively correlated with values for intrahemispheric coherence: for men in the left temporal region, and for women in the right (Figure 7.6B). Multiple correlations were typical of IQa: the higher the level of arithmetic intelligence, the greater the coherence of the beta2 rhythm recorded in the left frontal area and the temporal regions of the cortex (Figure 7.6C). However, this pattern was only characteristic of men; for women there are effectively no significant correlations between IQa and coherence. For figural intelligence (IQf), only isolated positive connections were found with the coherence of the beta2 rhythm (pairs F7-T4, F7-T5, F8-T4, and T3-C4) in the total group. Multiple correlations of IQf with coherence scores were characteristic of the low-frequency theta range: for men, they showed increased interaction of the anterior areas of the right hemisphere with posterior cortical regions as IQf increased; whereas for women, on the contrary, there was a weakening of connections of the left frontal cortex with the right hemisphere. Because of these multi-directional changes there was also an apparent lack of significant correlations between the values for IQf and coherence in the total group.

The decrease (or increase) of the coherence of biopotentials in two parts of the cortex are viewed as evidence of weakening (or strengthening) of the interaction of these cortical areas. Figure 7.6C shows that the increase of IQa corresponds to the integration of cortical neural ensembles, at a beta2 rhythm frequency, the locus of their interaction being located at Fp1, T3, T5, and F4, C4, T6. This effect is characteristic only for the male group. IQv is more weakly reflected in changes of cortical interactions, while being connected more with the power of high-frequency beta2 oscillations, especially in women.

Thus the electroencephalographic data show that each type of intellectual giftedness is characterized by its own "presetting" in a frequency-spatial organization of cortical neural ensembles, which may facilitate their subsequent functional combination to solve tasks of a figural, verbal, or numerical nature. The special significance of the beta2 rhythm in the relationships between IQv and IQa and the patterns of activation and interaction of cortical regions, indicates that successful processing of numerical and verbal information relies on high-frequency organization of neuronal activity in brain structures. In support of this conclusion, we can cite data from the literature showing that cortical rhythms in the beta band, especially in the temporoparietal areas, are associated with multimodal semantic integration of diverse information (Pulvermuller et al. 1997; von Stein and Sarnthein 2000). The regional characteristics of the beta2 coherence patterns that we found, whose values are correlated with IQ level, can be viewed as a reflection of the ability to use different strategies to informational process: in the left hemisphere, in sequential analytical operations, especially delineated by "presetting" for numerical operations in men; and in the right hemisphere, in a parallel synthesis of information, which is more characteristic of women of high verbal intelligence. These results, as well as recently published information about the positive correlations of intelligence in men with a greater volume of gray matter, and in women with a greater volume of white matter (Haier et al. 2005), lead to the conclusion that sex differences exist in the functional organization of both left and right hemispheres.

4 The Interconnection between Character Traits and the Frequency-Spatial Organization of Cortical Activity

Not only intellectual traits, but also many other personal characteristics are associated with special patterns of the frequency-spatial organization of cortical activity (Stelmack 1990; Rusalov et al. 1993; Sviderskaya and Korol'kova 1996; Razumnikova 2000a; Razumnikova 2001; Robinson 2001; Razumnikova 2002a; Razumnikova 2002b; Razumnikova 2003a; Razumnikova 2003b; Razumnikova 2004a; Knyazev 2007). Given that it is stable personality traits that determine stable forms of behavior, we can assume that the observed intensity of individual psychological traits is a reflection of the "rigidity" or "flexibility" of neural connections that appear in the pattern of baseline activity of neural ensembles, and determine their subsequent functional interaction in performing various cognitive operations. Researchers' attention has most frequently been drawn to the structure of personality according to the three main factors (extraversion, neuroticism, and psychoticism) proposed by H. Eysenck. This is based on the fact that, according to H. Eysenck's hypothesis, the tendency to extraversion/introversion is determined by the baseline level of tonic cortical activation and the related excitation threshold, which is higher in extraverts due to lower tonic activation, than in introverts (Eysenck 1990). Numerous studies designed to test this hypothesis have yielded contradictory results about the relationship between the degree of extraversion and activation of the cortex. We too failed to detect significant differences in baseline indicators of the power of biopotentials when comparing groups of introverts and extraverts. However, correlation analysis showed a significant association between the values for the power of beta2 and extraversion in the total group (79 subjects): a higher level of extraversion was accompanied by an increase in the power of beta biopotentials in the frontal part of the cortex (sites Fp2, F4, F7; $0.24 < r < 0.37$; $0.004 < p < 0.03$). For psychoticism and neuroticism, no significant correlations with power scores were found.

Multiple correlations, primarily for the biopotentials of the theta and beta2 bands, were identified in a separate analysis of coherence indicators and values for extraversion or neuroticism in groups of men and women (Razumnikova 2001; Razumnikova 2004b). These indicators differed as to both sign and topographical representation. For example, in neuroticism, opposite correlations were obtained for the coherence of the beta2 rhythm in men and women: for men, an increase in cortical interactions, primarily in the anterior part of the cortex, corresponded to increased neuroticism, while for women, a focus of coherent connections that correlated negatively with neuroticism was present in the right occipital region (Figure 7.7A). Correlation dependencies of opposite sign also characterized the comparison of extraversion and coherence of the theta2 rhythm for men and women (Figure 7.7B). Significant correlations with psychoticism were found for men only, whereas correlations with social conformity were present in women only; however, both cases pointed to the precedence of the left hemisphere, where the interaction of cortical areas was linked to the intensity of these personal characteristics (Figure 7.7C). Based on concepts of a weakening long-distance coherence that coincides with strengthening of cortical/subcortical interactions (Petsche 1996; Petsche and Etlinger 1998), the changes found in women in the interaction of cortical areas as a function of these three personality traits can be regarded as evidence of a more pronounced influence of subcortical structures on the functional integration of cortical neural ensembles. For men, the association between coherence indicators and extraversion/neuroticism has been shown more in the anterior parts of the cortex, indicating particular significance of those areas for the variability of interaction among neural ensembles, which depends on the psychological characteristics mentioned above.

Using variance analysis of coherence indicators with the factors of sex and group (high or low value of character traits), it was found that for men, the values for total intrahemispheric coherence were associated with psychoticism: at high values, left hemispheric coherence in men was greater than in women, and higher than in the right hemisphere (Razumnikova 2004b). For women, the neuroticism effect was more pronounced: the group with a high value for neuroticism was characterized by lower right hemispheric coherence both as compared to men, and as compared to women with low neuroticism levels. Because the groups did not differ significantly by intelligence, the

INDIVIDUAL CHARACTERISTICS OF BRAIN ACTIVITY

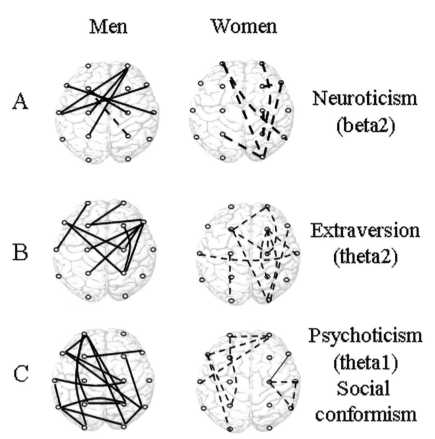

FIGURE 7.7 Maps of the coherence of biopotentials whose values are correlated with neuroticism (A), extraversion (B), psychoticism (in men), or social conformity (in women) (C). Symbols as in Fig. 1.6.

observed effects could be linked to the person's personality traits. Thus, character traits, classified according to H. Eysenck's typology, are reflected in the "presetting" of the functional connections of cortical ensembles at different frequencies, which serves as the basis for later formation of a variety of strategies of cognitive activity.

To further clarify the patterns of such "presetting," we studied the EEG correlates of psychological traits according to C. Jung's personality typology. His introduction of rational mental functions (thinking and feeling) and irrational ones (sensation and intuition) makes it possible to explain the differences in people's perception of the outside world and their judgments of events, based on strategies of information-processing that correspond to each function (Jung 1995). Dominance of the thinking function reflects the fact that the individual, in assessing information, relies on arguments and facts, and uses logic to explain them. If feeling dominates – the function that is the opposite of the thinking function – then evaluation of the meaning of an event is based primarily on emotions, and judgments are formed by comparison with pleasant or unpleasant experience. Irrational functions, in Jung's view, reflect a "passive" perception of the world. This means that sensation is a characteristic of the perception of the external world, while intuition is a characteristic of the unconscious perception of the essence or hidden meaning of the same objects. In each pair, one of the functions can become primary, and these aspects of psychological functions can be associated with the functional asymmetry of the hemispheres; we may predict that sustained dominance of the rational function of thought will correspond to dominance of the left hemisphere, and the irrational function of intuition to the right hemisphere.

Using this classification of personality traits, adopted in the psychoanalytic typology, numerous positive correlations were found for men between indicators for power and coherence, and the irrational function of "sensation:" the higher the preference for this function (i.e., the less the intuition), the greater the power of the $theta_{1, 2}$ rhythm for sites in the right hemisphere (F8, T4), and the stronger the interhemispheric connections in the anterior part of the cortex (Figure 7.8) (Razumnikova 2003b; Razumnikova 2004a; Razumnikova 2004b). For women, on the contrary, analysis of irrational features established negative correlations between "sensation" and interhemispheric coherence, for both the low-frequency $theta_2$ and the high-frequency $beta_2$ rhythms. For women, the modulating effect of rational functions was the most pronounced: the preponderance of "feeling" was associated with a generalized increase in the power of the $alpha_1$ rhythm and with increased coherence, mainly with foci in the anterior part of the cortex of the left hemisphere (Figure 7.6B). For men, correlations between "feeling" and indicators of coherence were most pronounced for the $beta_2$ range, and indicated a weakening of the interaction between the anterior and posterior regions of the cortex.

On the basis of variance analysis of the data, it was established that at high values for intuition (low sensation, GR_S0), women tend to have higher-power $theta_1$ and $theta_2$ rhythms than men; while at low values (GR_S1), men demonstrate greater power of the biopotentials in the theta and alpha bands (Figure 7.9A). Sex differences in the power features linked to irrational functions were shown regionally on the frontal sites: at high values of intuition, the power of the biopotentials is higher for women than for men; while at low values, the power is lower. Furthermore, for men for whom the sensation function predominates, it is characteristic to have not only a frequency gradient, but also a regional gradient of changes in the power of the biopotentials in the

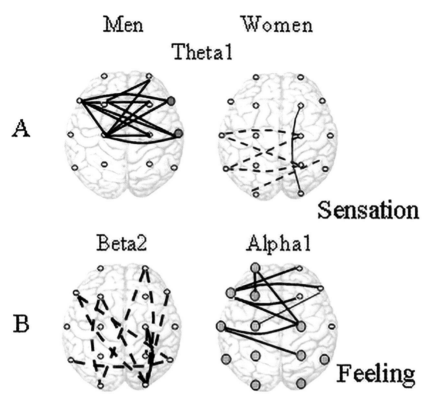

FIGURE 7.8 Maps of the coherence of biopotentials whose values are correlated with irrational (A) and rational (B) personal characteristics of men and women. Symbols as in Fig. 7.1.

frontal and occipital leads (Figure 7.9B). In analyzing the interaction of the factors sex × group × frequency range for thinking/feeling functions, sex differences were significant when "feeling" was predominant (GR_To) (with higher values of the power of theta1-alpha2 biopotentials in men than in women), but were smoothed out when "thinking" was predominant (Figure 7.9C).

Consequently, rational/irrational mental functions, complementing each other, reflect the general "presetting" of neural cortical oscillators at different frequency bands, which affects the subsequent perception and processing of sensory signals and the preference for verbal or figural, simultaneous or successive cognitive strategies. Thus, personality traits pertaining both to intelligence and character, reflecting the most stable connections of the brain's neural systems, determine features of human behavior, including creative work and the diversity (or stereotyped nature) of the thinking strategies used to carry it

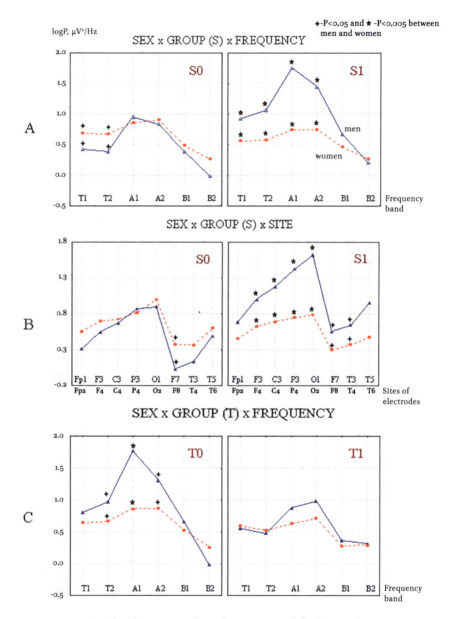

FIGURE 7.9 Results of variance analysis of EEG power and the factors of SEX, PSYCHOLOGICAL GROUP, FREQUENCY BAND, and SITES. S0 – low sensation (high intuition); S1 – high sensation; T0 – low thinking (high feeling); T1 – high thinking. Signs mark significant differences between men and women ($0.005 < p < 0.05$).

out. Complex recording and comparison of psychometric and neurobiological indices of cognitive processes in different models of creative work make it possible to identify patterns in the formation of such strategies, and "weak" links that should be taken into account, to achieve more creative productivity.

5   The Interconnections of Creativity, Intelligence, Character Traits and the Frequency-Spatial Organization of Hemispheric Activity

Representation of the "intellectual" model of creative thinking, according to which it is the volume of existing knowledge that is of primary significance in the search for an original solution to a problem (Heilman et al. 2003; Geake and Dodson 2005), calls for clarifying the relationship between creative and intellectual abilities, as reflected in the frequency-spatial organization of cortical activity. Investigation of the contribution of creativity, intelligence, and character traits to the frequency-spatial organization of hemispheric activity was conducted only with men. The characteristics of the separate groups that were used for variance analysis of the baseline power and coherence of biopotentials are shown in Table 7.1. The participants were divided into high- and low-creativity groups, on the basis of successful solution of the heuristic problem described previously.

TABLE 7.1   The characteristics of groups by strength of personality traits

Characteristics	GR1 – high score			GR0 – low score		
	n	Median	±	n	Median	±
Intelligence						
IQ verbal (IQv)	13	111.0	2.8	18	99.6	3.9
IQ figural (IQf)	18	115.0	6.5	13	105.0	4.1
Eysenck's personality traits						
Extraversion	25	14.6	2.8	15	7.4	5.5
Neuroticism	21	13.9	4.3	19	7.1	2.0
Psychoticism	20	6.3	1.6	20	3.1	2.0
Jung's personality traits						
Sensation	16	13.0	1.5	15	7.1	3.0
Thinking	11	13.5	1.3	20	8.5	2.9

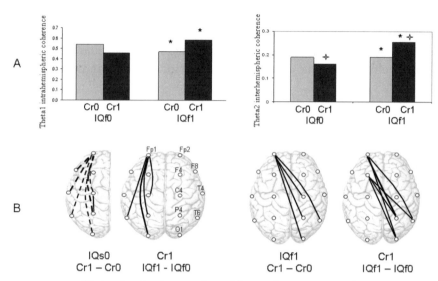

FIGURE 7.10 The results of variance analysis of factors of CREATIVITY and INTELLIGENCE and the total intrahemispheric coherence of the theta1 rhythm or the interhemispheric coherence of the theta2 rhythm (A), and maps of the differences in the coherence of theta rhythms, as a function of creativity and intelligence (B). IQf0 – low figural intelligence, IQf1 – high intelligence, Cr0 – low creativity, Cr1 – high creativity. Signs mark significant differences between groups (p<0.05).

Interaction of the factors of creativity and intelligence were found for biopotentials in the theta1, theta2, alpha 2, beta1, and beta2 bands (Razumnikova 2008). The most pronounced effects involved creativity-related changes in inter- and intrahemispheric coherence, and pointed to greater specialization in the interaction of cortical regions for subjects with high IQ. Creative individuals with high intelligence (Cr1 & IQf1) were distinguished by greater integration of neural ensembles in the frontal cortex of the left hemisphere, and by their close connections with the temporo-parieto-occipital cortical areas (Figure 7.10). The combination of high creativity and relatively low intelligence (Cr1 & IQf0) was accompanied, on the contrary, by weakening of the connections in the frontal cortex. These features of the frequency-spatial organization of cortical neural ensembles can be regarded as "presetting," for future use of various strategies for creative thinking: "intellectual" (close connections of the frontal cortex with the posterior regions) or "insightful" (weakened connections of the frontal cortex). Consequently, the selective inclusion of those brain structures which are used to solve relevant problems differs, depending on the ratio between intellectual and creative abilities, while to a large degree the contribution of intelligence occurs in the functions of the left hemisphere.

Although inconsistencies in the known data have prevented definite conclusions about the relationship of creativity and personal traits (Druzhinin 1999; Bogoyavlenskaya 2002), still, the reflection not only of intellectual, but also of character traits in the structure and functions of the brain (Stelmack 1990; Robinson 2001; Razumnikova 2003b), provide the basis for the existence of such a relationship. According to the H. Eysenck hypothesis, creative individuals must be characterized by a high level of psychoticism (Eysenck 1994). This hypothesis was supported by the positive correlations between level of psychoticism and figural or verbal creativity (Upmanyu et al. 1996; Abraham et al. 2005), although in other studies, using a complex battery of creativity tests, no such relationship was found (Kline and Cooper 1986; Reuter et al. 2004).

We found an interaction of the factors of creativity and psychoticism only for indicators of coherence of the theta1 rhythm, and for creativity and extraversion at frequencies of the alpha1, and beta1 and beta2 rhythms. Most broadly: in the theta1, alpha2, and beta2 bands, there were interactions between creativity and neuroticism (Razumnikova 2008). The asymmetry of the power of theta1 biopotentials and the gradient between the central-temporal and occipital cortical areas, as well as the total value of interhemispheric coherence of theta1 biopotentials in the anterior and posterior cortical areas in the highly creative group, were dependent on the participant's level of neuroticism: the high-neuroticism group differed from the others by having the greatest power of right occipital rhythm, while for those with low neuroticism, the largest value for coherence was in the left posterior part of the cortex. Creative individuals with a high degree of neuroticism also differed from the other groups by having more alpha 2 rhythm power and by a gradient of beta2 oscillations, with large values for power in the occipital, as compared to the frontal and temporal regions of the cortex.

Interaction of the factors of creativity and "feeling" was found with analysis of the power of EEG rhythms, using Jungian typology for the classification of mental traits. The high power of the theta2 rhythm in the left hemisphere compared to the right in low-creativity individuals, and the lack of functional asymmetry in the baseline activity of the cortex in the highly creative, was detected where the "feeling" function was predominant. In the alpha 2 range, changes in cortical activity associated with creativity and rational personality characteristics were represented mainly in the posterior part of the cortex, without lateral features. When the "feeling" function predominated, the alpha2 power was higher among creative than uncreative students, yet when the "thinking" function predominated the opposite was true.

The irrational properties of "sensation/intuition" were found, to a greater extent, to be associated with the power of a low-frequency alpha1 rhythm in creative people: in the frontal and occipital cortical regions, the power of biopotentials was higher in the group for which sensation was predominant, compared to the group where intuition was predominant. In studying the functional significance of the alpha rhythm, the low-frequency range is associated with generalized activation through reticulo-cortical and thalamo-cortical neural pathways (Hari and Salmelin 1997; Robinson 1999) and the organization of selective attention (Cooper et al. 2003; Palva and Palva 2007), while the high-frequency range is mainly associated with retrieving information from semantic memory (Klimesch 1999; Klimesch et al. 2006). Consequently, the results are consistent with the views of C. Jung on the participation of his proposed mental functions of individual aptitudes in the processing of information, and they also indicate various strategies to enable similar creative productivity by people with different personality traits. The observed differences in the power of the alpha 1 and alpha 2 rhythm can be viewed as evidence that the processing of external stimuli and the degree of utilization of semantic memory differ in highly creative individuals, depending on which mental functions predominate: sensation/intuition, and feeling/thinking, respectively.

Thus, creative people commonly have a distinctive functional plasticity in the frequency-spatial organization of activity in cortical neural ensembles and of hemispheric asymmetry. Intelligence and character traits influence both the interaction of the anterior and posterior cortical regions, and hemispheric asymmetry. Perhaps this is because the preconditions for the successful search for an original idea are the speed of information processes in the brain (for which intelligence is an indicator), emotional support for that search (i.e., emotional sensitivity), and the optimal relationship of control functions of the frontal cortex and activity of the posterior regions of the cortex, which are viewed as knowledge resources. A hypothetical model of the interaction among all the EEG correlates of individual characteristics mentioned above, created as a result of summation of the effects of activation/inhibition in the thalamo-cortical, limbic-cortical, and fronto-temporo-parieto-occipital system, is represented schematically in Figure 7.11. This schema reflects our interpretation of the observed individual characteristics in the patterns of frequency-spatial interactions of cortical neural ensembles.

Considering the functional significance of the separate brain structures in creative thinking, it is worth mentioning that there is no single necessary and sufficient area of the brain that ensures the final result, but instead a topographically extensive neural network, which dynamically changes its characteristics depending on the stage of the creative process or its character. Ideas about the fronto-parietal system underlying intelligence (Heilman et al. 2003), or concepts about the interaction of the anterior and posterior cortical

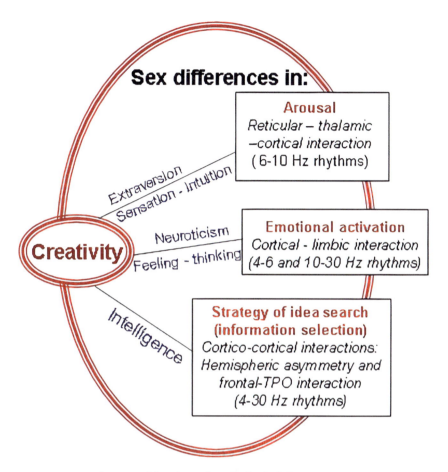

FIGURE 7.11 Schematic of the relationship of individual characteristics (sex, creativity, intelligence and personality traits) and the activity of the cerebral cortex that is determined by the thalamo-cortical, limbic-cortical, and fronto-temporo-parieto-occipital systems.

areas during a spontaneous or deliberative search for a creative solution to a problem (Dietrich 2004) seem promising for further study of the patterns of the neurobiological bases of creative abilities. The parietal system, in this case, represents the "searching" part of the creative process and provides the generation of multiple ideas through a variety of associations of visual, auditory, and symbolic representations. The frontal system performs a "critical/initiating" function and, according to individual goals and interests, selects ideas received from the parietal system by developing those that are acceptable and suppressing those that do not seem necessary.

6   Conclusion

Comparative analysis of the EEG correlates of cognitive activity such as memory and creative thinking allows us to conclude that the functional properties of the frequency-spatial organization of cortical neural oscillators in men and women may be the basis for different strategies of information processing. For men, the integration of cortical ensembles at beta rhythm frequencies is of greater significance, while for women, lower frequency rhythms are predominant, with the inclusion of left hemispheric frontal control of mental processes.

Clearly expressed features of the intellect and personality traits are formed as the result of a specific individual mosaic of both activation and inhibition interactions of cortical and subcortical structures, defining their "presetting" for future corresponding strategies of thinking: rational/irrational, logical/intuitive, verbal/figural. Creative individuals are distinguished by a high capacity for change in the frequency-spatial organization of cortical activity, depending on the level of intelligence and other personality traits, especially emotional sensitivity (neuroticism or the profile of rational//irrational traits). The specific nature of the interaction of the anterior and posterior cortical regions is just as necessary a condition for creativity as is the nature of the interaction of the two hemispheres. The degree to which these brain areas are included in creative activity is determined by the type of problem to be solved and is related to individual features in the regulation of functional activity in the brain.

Defining the personality profile of an individual makes it possible to predict his success in solving problems that require specific thinking strategies in professional work. The interaction of the left hemispheric frontal with the parietal part of the attention system, which is more pronounced in women, may indicate that conscious control of such activity is more important for women than for men. Consequently, increasing the significance attributed to intellectual abilities in modern professional work, as well as the prestige of innovative forms of behavior, should be seen as a most significant step toward increasing the creativity of women.

References

Abra, J. and S. Valentino-French. 1991. "Gender differences in creative achievement: survey of explanation." *Genetic, Social & General Psychology Monographs* 117, no. 3: 233–238.

Abraham, A., S. Windmann, I. Daum, and O. Güntürkün. 2005. "Conceptual expansion and creative imagery as a function of psychoticism." *Consciousness and Cognition* 14, no. 3: 520–534.

Anokhin, A. and F. Vogel. 1996. "EEG alpha rhythm frequency and intelligence in normal adults." *Intelligence* 23, no. 1: 1–14.

Atchley, R. A., M. Keeney, and C. Burgess. 1999. "Cerebral hemispheric mechanisms linking ambiguous word meaning retrieval and creativity." *Brain and Cognition* 40, no. 3: 479–499.

Basar, E., C. Basar-Eroglu, S. M. Karakas, and M. Scurmann. 2000. "Brain oscillations in perception and memory." *International Journal of Psychophysiology* 35, no. 2–3: 95–124.

Beamont, J., A. R. Mayes, and M. D. Rugg. 1978. "Asymmetry in EEG alpha coherence and power: effects of task and sex." *Electroencephalography and Clinical Neurophysiology* 45, no. 3: 393–401.

Beeman, M. J. and E. M. Bowden. 2000. "The right hemisphere maintains solution-related activation for yet-to-be-solved problems." *Memory and Cognition* 28, no. 7: 1231–1241.

Begleiter, H. and B. Porjesz. 2006. "Genetics of human brain oscillations." *International Journal of Psychophysiology* 60, no. 2: 162–171.

Bekhtereva, N. P., P. V. Bundzen, and Y. Gogolitsyn. 1977. *The Brain's Encoding of Mental Activity*. Leningrad: Nauka.

Bogoyavlenskaya, D. B. 2002. *The Psychology of Creativity*. Moscow: AKADEMA.

Bowden, E. M. and M. J. Beeman. 1998. "Getting the right idea: Semantic activation in the right hemisphere may help solve insight problems." *Psychological Science* 9, no. 6: 435–440.

Bryzgalov, A. O. and N. V. Volf. 2006. "Sex differences in EEG coherence during Stroop task performance." *Journal of Higher Nervous Activity* 56, no. 4: 464–471.

Carlsson, I., P. E. Wendt, and J. Risberg. 2000. "On the neurobiology of creativity. Differences in frontal activity between high and low creative subjects." *Neuropsychologia* 38, no. 6: 873–885.

Cooper, N. R., R. J. Croft, S. J. Dominey, A. P. Burgess, and J. H. Gruzelier. 2003. "Paradox lost? Exploring the role of alpha oscillations during externally vs. internally directed attention and the implications for idling and inhibition hypotheses." *International Journal of Psychophysiology* 47, no. 1: 65–74.

Costello, F. J. and M. T. Keane. 2000. "Efficient creativity: constraint-guided conceptual combination." *Cognitive Science* 24, no. 2: 299–348.

Cowell, P. and K. Hugdahl. 2000. "Individual differences in neurobehavioral measures of laterality and interhemispheric function as measured by dichotic listening." *Developmental Neuropsychology* 18, no. 1: 95–112.

Davidson, R. J., G. E. Schwartz, E. Pugash, and E. Bromfield. 1976. "Sex differences in patterns of EEG asymmetry." *Biological Psychology* 4, no. 2: 119–138.

Dietrich, A. 2004. "The cognitive neuroscience of creativity." *Psychonomic Bulletin & Review* 11, no. 6: 1011–1026.

Doppelmayr, M., W. Klimesch, W. Stadler, D. Pollhuber, and C. Heine. 2000. "EEG Alpha Power and Intelligence." *Intelligence* 30, no. 3: 289–302.

Druzhinin, V. N. 1999. *The psychology of general abilities*. Saint Petersburg: Peter Kom.

Eysenck, H. J. 1990. "Biological dimensions of personality." In *Handbook of personality: Theory and research*, ed. L. Pervin, 244–276. New York: Guilford.

Eysenck, H. J. 1994. "Creativity and personality: Word association, origence, and psychoticism." *Creativity Research Journal* 7, no. 2: 209–216.

Fink, A. and A. C. Neubauer. 2006. "EEG oscillations during performance of verbal creativity tasks: Differential effects of sex and verbal intelligence." *International Journal of Psychophysiology* 62, no. 1: 46–53.

Geake, J. G. and C. S. Dodson. 2005. "A neuro-psychological model of the creative intelligence of gifted children." *Gifted & Talented International* 20, no. 1: 4–16.

Geake, J. G. and P. Hansen. 2005. "Neural correlates of intelligence as revealed by fMRI of fluid analogies." *NeuroImage* 26, no. 2: 555–564.

Goldberg, E., R. Harner, M. Lovell, K. Podell, and S. Riggio. 1994. "Cognitive bias, functional cortical geometry, and the frontal lobes: laterality, sex, and handedness." *Journal of Cognitive Neuroscience* 6, no. 3: 276–296.

Golosheikin, S. A., N. V. Volf, and O. M. Razumnikova. 1997. "Significance of laterality and sex in the processes of selective attention." *Journal of Higher Nervous Activity* 47, no. 4: 740–742.

Green, J., R. Green, and C. Epstein. 1992. "Assessment of the relationship of cerebral hemisphere arousal asymmetry to perceptual asymmetry." *Brain and Cognition* 20, no. 2: 264–279.

Grossman, M., E. Smith, and P. Koenig. 2002. "The neural basis for categorization in semantic memory." *NeuroImage* 17, no. 3: 1549–1561.

Guilford, Y. P. 1967. *The Nature of Human Intelligence*. New York: McGraw Hill.

Haier, R. J. and C. P. Benbou. 1995. "Sex differences and lateralization in temporal lobe glucose metabolism during mathematical reasoning." *Developmental Neuropsychology* 11, no. 4: 405–414.

Haier, R. J., R. E. Jung, R. A. Yeo, K. Head, and M. T. Akire. 2004. "Structural brain variation and general intelligence." *Neuroimage* 23, no. 1: 425–433.

Haier, R. J., R. E. Jung, R. A. Yeo, K. Head, and M. T. Akire. 2005. "The neuroanatomy of general intelligence: sex matters." *Neuroimage* 25, no. 1: 320–328.

Halari, R., T. Sharma, M. Hines, C. Andrew, A. Simmons, and V. Kumari. 2006. "Comparable fMRI activity with differential behavioral performance on mental rotation and overt verbal fluency tasks in healthy men and women." *Experimental Brain Research* 169, no. 1: 1–14.

Halpern, D. F. 2000. *Sex Differences in Cognitive Abilities*. New York: Lawrence Erlbaum Associates.

Hari, R. and R. Salmelin. 1997. "Human cortical oscillations: a neuromagnetic view through the skull." *Trends in Neuroscience* 20, no. 1: 44–49.

Hausmann, M. and O. Gunturkun. 1999. "Sex differences in functional cerebral asymmetries in a repeated measures design." *Brain and Cognition* 41, no. 3: 263–275.

Heilman, K. M., S. E. Nadeau, and D. O. Beverdor. 2003. "Creative innovation: possible brain mechanisms." *Neurocase* 9, no. 5: 369–379.

Hetrick, W. P., C. A. Sandman, W. Bunney, and Y. Jin. 1996. "Gender differences in gating of the auditory evoked potentials in normal subjects." *Biological Psychiatry* 39, no. 1: 51–58.

Hollander, I., H. Petsche, L. Dimitrov, and O. Filz. 1997. "The reflection of cognitive tasks in EEG and MRI and a method of its visualization." *Brain Topography* 3, no. 177–189: 9.

Howard-Jones, P. A., S. J. Blakemore, E. A. Samuel, I. R. Summers, and G. Glaxton. 2005. "Semantic divergence and creative story generation: An fMRI investigation." *Cognitive Brain Research* 25, no. 1: 240–250.

Hyde, J. S. 2005. "The gender similarities hypothesis." *American Psychologist* 60, no. 6: 581–592.

Hyde, J. S. and M. C. Linn. 1988. "Gender differences in verbal ability: A meta-analysis." *Psychological Bulletin* 104, no. 1: 53–69.

Ivanitskii, A. M. 1996. "The cerebral basis of subjective experiences: a hypothesis of information synthesis." *Journal of Higher Nervous Activity* 46, no. 2: 241–252.

Ivanitskii, A. M. 1997. "Synthesis of information in key regions of the cortex as the basis of subjective experiences." *Journal of Higher Nervous Activity* 47, no. 2: 209–225.

Jung, C. 1995. *Psychological Types*. Saint Petersburg: Yuventa, Progress-Univers.

Kelly, G. A. 2000. *The Theory of Personality. Psychology of Personal Constructs*. Saint Petersburg: Speech.

Kimura, D. and R. A. Harshaman. 1984. "Sex differences in brain organization for verbal and non-verbal function." *Progress in Brain Research* 61, no. 1: 423–441.

Kirkpatrick, B. and N. L. Bryant. 1995. "Sexual dimorphism in the brain: it's worse than you thought." *Biological Psychiatry* 38, no. 6: 347–348.

Klimesch, W. 1999. "EEG alpha and theta oscillations reflect cognitive and memory performance: a review and analysis." *Brain Research Reviews* 29, no. 2–3: 169–195.

Klimesch, W., M. Doppelmayr, and S. Hanslmayer. 2006. "Upper alpha ERD and absolute power: their meaning for memory performance." *Progress in Brain Research* 159, no. 1: 151–165.

Kline, P. and C. Cooper. 1986. "Psychoticism and creativity." *Journal of Genetic Psychology* 147, no. 2: 183–188.

Knyazev, G. 2007. "Motivation, emotion, and their inhibitory control mirrored in brain oscillations." *Neuroscience & Biobehavioral Reviews* 31, no. 3: 377–395.

Lazarev, V. 1998. "On the intercorrelation of some frequency and amplitude parameters of the human EEG and its functional significance." *International Journal of Psychophysiology* 28, no. 1: 77–98.

Martindale, C. 1999. "Biological bases of creativity." In *Handbook of Creativity*, ed. R. Sternberg, 137–152. Cambridge, UK: Cambridge University Press.

McGivern, R. F., J. P. Huston, D. Byrd, and T. King. 1997. "Sex differences in visual recognition memory: support for sex-related differences in attention in adults and children." *Brain and Cognition* 34, no. 3: 323–336.

Mednick, S. A. 1962. "The associative basis of the creative process." *Psychological Review* 69, no. 3: 220–232.

Medvedev, S. V., N. P. Bekhtereva, S. G. Danko, M. G. Starchenko, N. V. Shemyakina, and S. V. Pakhomov. 2004. "PET and EEG studies of brain maintenance of verbal creative activities." *International Journal of Psychophysiology* 54, no. 1: 34–44.

Meyer-Levy, J. 1989. "Gender differences in information processing: a selectivity interpretation." In *Cognitive and Affective Responses to Advertising*, ed. P. Cafferata and A. Tybout, 219–260. Lanham Md.: Lexington Books.

Neubauer, A. C., A. Fink, and R. H. Grabner. 2006. "Sensitivity of alpha band ERD to individual differences in cognition." *Progress in Brain Research* 159, no.: 167–178.

Neubauer, A. C., A. Fink, and D. G. Schrausser. 2002. "Intelligence and neural efficiency: The influence of task content and sex on the brain-IQ relationship." *Intelligence* 30, no. 6: 515–536.

Neuper, C. and G. Pfurtscheller. 2001. "Event-related dynamics of cortical rhythms: frequency-specific features and functional correlates." *International Journal of Psychophysiology* 43, no. 1: 41–58.

O'Boyle, M. W. and C. P. Benbow. 1990. "Enhanced right hemisphere involvement during cognitive processing may relate to intellectual precocity." *Neuropsychology* 28, no. 2: 211–216.

Palva, S. and J. M. Palva. 2007. "New vistas for alpha frequency band oscillations." *Trends in Neuroscience* 30, no. 4: 150–158.

Pavlov, I. P. 1951. *The physiological theory of nervous system types as well as temperaments. Poln. sobr. soch.* Leningrad: Academy of Sciences of the USSR Press.

Pavlova, L. I. and A. F. Romanenko. 1998. *A Systems Approach to the Psychophysiological Study of the Human Brain.* Saint Petersburg: Nauka.

Petsche, H. 1996. "Approaches to verbal, visual and musical creativity by EEG coherence analysis." *International Journal of Psychophysiology* 24, no. 1–2: 145–159.

Petsche, H. and S. C. Etlinger. 1998. "EEG aspects of cognitive processes: A contribution to the proteus-like nature of consciousness." *International Journal of Psychology* 33, no. 3: 199–212.

Petsche, H., S. Kaplan, A. von Stein, and O. Filz. 1997. "The possible meaning of the upper and lower alpha frequency ranges for cognitive and creative tasks." *International Journal of Psychophysiology* 26, no. 1–3: 77–97.

Plomin, R. and F. M. Spinath. 2004. "Intelligence: genetics, genes, and genomics." *Journal of Personality and Social Psychology* 86, no. 1: 112–129.

Pulvermuller, F., N. Birbaumer, W. Lutzenberger, and B. Mohr. 1997. "High-frequency brain activity: its possible role in attention, perception and language processing." *Progress in Neurobiology* 52, no. 5: 427–445.

Pulvermüller, F., A. Keil, and T. Elbert. 1999. "High-frequency brain activity: perception or active memory." *Trends in Cognition Neuroscience* 3, no. 7: 250–252.

Razumnikova, O. M. 2000a. "Features of spatial organization of EEG in people of various personality characteristics." *Journal of Higher Nervous Activity* 50, no. 6: 921–932.

Razumnikova, O. M. 2000b. "Gender differences in hemispheric organization during divergent thinking: an EEG investigation in human subjects." *Neuroscience Letters* 362, no. 3: 193–195.

Razumnikova, O. M. 2001. "Features of spatial organization of EEG as a function of temperament." *Physiology of Man* 4, no. 1: 34–41.

Razumnikova, O. M. 2002a. "Sex and professional orientation of students as factors in creativity." *Voprosy psikhologii* 1, no. 1: 111–125.

Razumnikova, O. M. 2002b. *Methods of Creativity Assessment*. Novosibirsk: Novosibirsk State Technical University Press.

Razumnikova, O. M. 2003a. "Reflection of the structure of intelligence in the spatial-temporal characteristics of baseline EEG." *Physiology of Man* 4, no. 1: 44–51.

Razumnikova, O. M. 2003b. "Interaction of personality and intelligence factors in cortex activity modulation." *Personality and Individual Differences* 35, no. 1: 135–162.

Razumnikova, O. M. 2004a. "Functional organization of different brain areas during convergent and divergent thinking: An EEG investigation." *Cognitive Brain Research* 10, no. 1–2: 11–18.

Razumnikova, O. M. 2004b. "Gender-dependent frequency-spatial organization of the brain cortex activity during convergent and divergent thinking: I. Analysis of the EEG power coherence." *Human Physiology* 30, no. 6: 637–647.

Razumnikova, O. M. 2004c. *Thought and Functional Brain Asymmetry*. Novosibirsk: Siberian Division, Russian Academy of Medical Sciences Press.

Razumnikova, O. M. 2007a. "The functional significance of alpha2 frequency range for convergent and divergent verbal thinking." *Human Physiology* 33, no. 2: 146–156.

Razumnikova, O. M. 2007b. "Creativity related cortex creativity in the remote associates task." *Brain Research Bulletin* 73, no. 1–3: 96–102.

Razumnikova, O. M. 2008. "Intelligence and personality as modulator of divergent thinking." *International Journal of Psychophysiology* 69, no. 1: 170.

Razumnikova, O. M. and A. O. Bryzgalov. 2007. "Frequency-spatial organization of brain electrical activity in creative verbal thought: The role of the gender factor." *Neuroscience and Behavioral Physiology* 36, no. 6: 645–653.

Razumnikova, O. M. and E. H. Larina. 2005. "Hemispheric interaction in the search for original verbal associations: features of the coherence of biopotentials in the cortex of creative men and women." *Journal of Higher Nervous Activity* 6, no. 3: 785–795.

Razumnikova, O. M. and R. V. Petrov. 1999. "Quantity determination of the cognitive style characteristics by means the computerized metohodics." Paper presented at the Third Russian-Korean International Symposium of Science and Technology, Novosibirsk, Russia, June 22–25.

Razumnikova, O. M. and N. V. Volf. 2007. "Gender differences in interhemispheric interactions during distributed and directed attention." *Neuroscience and Behavioral Physiology* 37, no. 5: 429–434.

Razumnikova, O. M. and N. V. Volf. 1997. "Sex differences in the temporal dynamics of interhemispheric asymmetry in the perception of verbal information." *Bulletin of the Siberian Division, Russian Academy of Medical Sciences* 2, no. 1: 87–90.

Razumnikova, O. M., N. V. Volf, and I. V. Tarasova. 2007. "Gender differences in creativity: A psychophysiological study." In *Aesthetics and Innovation*, ed. C. Martindale, V. Petrov, and L. Dorfman, 445–468. Cambridge, UK: Cambridge Scholars Press.

Reuter, M., J. Panksepp, N. Schnabel, N. Kellerhoff, P. Kempel, and J. Hennig. 2004. "Personality and biological markers of creativity." *European Journal of Personality* 19, no. 2: 83–95.

Robinson, D. L. 1998. "Sex differences in brain activity, personality and intelligence: a test of arousability theory." *Personality and Individual Differences* 26, no. 6: 1133–1152.

Robinson, D. L. 1999. "The technical, neurological and psychological significance of 'alpha', 'delta' and 'theta' waves confounded in EEG evoked potentials: A study of peak amplitudes." *Personality and Individual Differences* 28, no. 4: 673–693.

Robinson, D. L. 2001. "How brain arousal systems determine different temperament types and the major dimensions of personality." *Personality and Individual Differences* 31, no. 8: 1233–1259.

Rusalov, V. M., M. N. Rusalova, and I. G. Kalashnikova. 1993. "Bioelectrical activity of the human brain in people of different temperament types." *Journal of Higher Nervous Activity* 3, no. 4: 530–538.

Shaywitz, B. A., S. E. Shaywitz, and K. R. Pugh. 1995. "Sex differences in the functional organization of the brain for language." *Nature* 373, no. 6515: 607–609.

Sheppard, W. D. and R. W. Boyer. 1990. "Pretrial EEG coherence as a predictor of semantic priming effects." *Brain and Language* 39, no. 1: 57–68.

Simonov, P. V. 1993. *The Creating Brain. Neurobiological Foundations of Creativity*. Moscow: Nauka.

Simonton, D. K. 2000. "Creativity. Cognitive, personal development, and social aspects." *American. Psychologist* 55, no. 1: 151–158.

Stelmack, R. M. 1990. "Biological bases of extraversion: psychophysiological evidence." *Journal of Personality* 58, no. 1: 293–311.

Sviderskaya, N. E. and T. A. Korol'kova. 1996. "Spatial organization of EEG and individual psychological characteristics." *Journal of Higher Nervous Activity* 4, no.: 689–698.

Thatcher, R. W., P. J. Krause, and M. Hrybyk. 1986. "Cortico-cortical associations and EEG coherence: a two-compartmental model." *Electroencephalography and Clinical Neurophysiology* 64, no. 2: 123–143.

Upmanyu, V. V., S. Bhardwaj, and S. Singh. 1996. "Word-association emotional indicators: associations with anxiety, psychotism, neuroticism, extraversion, and creativity." *Journal of Social Psychology* 136, no. 4: 521–529.

Van Beijsterveldt, C. E. and G. C. van Baal. 2002. "Twin and family studies of the human electroencephalogram: a review and a meta-analysis." *Biological Psychology* 61, no. 1–2: 111–138.

Vinogradova, T. V. and V. V. Semenov. 1993. "Comparative study of cognitive processes in males and females: the role of biological and social factors." *Voprosi Psichologii* 2, no. 1: 63–71.

Volf, N. V. 1998. "Sex differences in interhemispheric interference interaction in memorization of verbal information." *Journal of Higher Nervous Activity* 3, no. 4: 551–553.

Volf, N. V. 2000. *Sex Differences in Functional Organization of Hemispheric Processing of Verbal Information*. Rostov-on-Don: Russian Educational Research Center for Valeology Press.

Volf, N. V. and A. V. Mashukova. 2005. "Alignment of differences in latent inhibition between males and females at use of classical conditioning in a testing procedure." *Bulletin of the Siberian Division, Russian Academy of Medical Sciences* 2, no. 1: 143–146.

Volf, N. V. and O. M. Razumnikova. 1999. "Sex differences in EEG coherence during a verbal memory task in normal adults." *International Journal of Psychophysiology* 34, no. 2: 113–122.

Volf, N. V. and O. M. Razumnikova. 2002. "EGE asymmetry in perception of speech information in women and men." *Journal of Higher Nervous Activity* 3, no. 4: 310–314.

Volf, N. V. and O. M. Razumnikova. 2004. "Sexual dimorphism in the functional organization of the brain in the processing of verbal information." In *Functional Interhemispheric Asymmetry: A Reader*, 386–410. Moscow: Scientific World.

von Stein, A. and J. Sarnthein. 2000. "Different frequencies for different scales of cortical integration: from local gamma to long range alpha/theta synchronization." *International Journal of Psychophysiology* 38, no. 3: 301–313.

Voyer, D. and J. Flight. 2001. "Gender differences in laterality on dichotic task: the influence of report strategies." *Cortex* 37, no. 3: 345–362.

Westerhausen, R., F. Kreuder, S. Dos Santos Sequeira, C. Walter, W. Woerner, R. A. Wittling, et al. 2004. "Effects of handedness and gender on macro- and microstructure of the corpus callosum and its subregions: a combined high-resolution and diffusion-tensor MRI study." *Cognitive Brain Research* 21, no. 3: 418–426.

Zaidel, E., F. Aboitiz, and J. Clark. 1995. "Sexual dimorphism in inter-hemispheric relations: anatomical-behavioral convergence." *Biological Research* 28, no. 1: 27–43.

SECTION 2 COMMENTARY

Neuroscience of Cognitive Skills and Abilities

Gabriel A. Radvansky and Chris Forsythe

The chapters in this section present explorations of various individual skills and abilities as they emerge from the underlying neurophysiology. This stretches from perceptual processes in the visual system, as described by Izmailov, Chernorizov, and Polyanskii, through the processing of facial features and expressions as described by Kostandov, and moving on to sex differences in creativity as conveyed by Razumnikova and Volf. In each of these cases, we see the basic themes of the Russian approach to neuroscience and psychology, and how they have adopted various constructs from other areas of the world to produce a distinctive approach to these subjects that is both insightful and valuable. In all of these cases, there is a broader consideration of the influences on skills and abilities that cuts across levels of processing that is typically not found in the West. Rather than focusing on one level of processing, there is a greater acknowledgement of the idea that both micro and macro levels of analysis are needed.

One of the major aims of psychology and neuroscience is to understand how various skills emerge, operate, and develop, and to understand the sources of any individual variation. The nervous system is highly complex, but functions so that principled operations emerge. These are the skills that develop in an individual. Coupled with this inherent bias towards the systematic processing of information from the world, the complexity of the system allows for variation in how well different types of processing are done. This is one of the sources of individual differences seen across people, which emerge from the fundamental nature of the underlying neurophysiology. This respect for processing complexity is more likely to provide a complete and satisfactory explanation because so many different facets of cognitive processing are considered, as is accomplished by the Russian approach.

A good example of this wide-ranging approach to neuroscience is Sokolov's Man-Neuron-Model approach that combines efforts from research with human beings, animals, and computational models. This approach reaches across a wide range of situations, data types, and means of analysis. That said, some readers may find it unusual, because this model still places a strong emphasis on the reflex arc, as noted in the earlier chapters of this volume. Again, while there is a vertical emphasis on many levels of processing, such modeling still reflects the history of this tradition. Moreover, the use of multidimensional scaling (MDS) as part of the modeling process is atypical. Typically MDS is used to acquire an understanding of the organization to the data set, and its use as a modeling tool has value. However, each of these aspects of the approach to understanding lends insight into the problem at hand.

Consistent with this approach of assessing system-wide changes and functions, various approaches are used to study patterns of neural oscillations across wider regions to assess individual performance. These sorts of measures look at how whole collections of neurons are working together in the service of a particular cognitive task. This is an approach also linked to the early studies and philosophies of Pavlov. This broad approach to neuroscience is captured in this section by Razumnikova and Volf in their account of creativity, and how expressions of creativity in males and females differ in the change of patterns of cortical oscillations. There is no skill where individual differences are more clearly noted and valued than that of creativity. For many skills and abilities, people work to achieve high levels of performance by imitating the actions and techniques of others. For creativity, the more distinct and separate one is from everyone else, the better.

The act of perception itself is guided by more complex and goal-oriented processes, which necessarily bias and alter one's perceptions. Both Izmailov, Chernorizov, and Polyanskii, as well as Kostandov, make a point of noting the importance to perceiving facial expressions. Recognizing facial expressions should not be regarded as the result of simple bottom-up processes, nor as the result of some face-specific processing region. Instead, the fundamental role of emotion is integrated deeply into theoretical views. Facial perception is viewed as critically dependent on, while influencing the process of, evaluating the emotional states of another person. It is of great interest to us not only to identify faces of people we may know, but to also identify the emotional states of people we encounter. This ability allows us to better predict what sort of interactions we will have with people and how we should behave ourselves. For example, is this someone we should approach, or avoid, or run from?

Accounting for individual predispositions to act in one way or another is again explained in terms of the concept of the dominant, which was also highlighted in earlier chapters. Understanding the underlying neurophysiological processes, along with the current dominant, makes it possible to understand the goal-directed behavior of an organism. Cognitive and neural processing is done in the service of some organism-based aim, which prioritizes various processes and actions.

The importance of understanding the fundamental neuroscientific and cognitive principles that underlie the development of skills and abilities can be seen in the wide range of issues relating to mental life that depend in one way or another on this understanding. For example, a wide range of pathologies are difficult to treat because individualized regiments need to be developed for handling the broad range of cases that are encountered. Why does one person have the mental resiliency to avoid psychopathology and another does not? Research into relevant human factors must take into account the range of skills required for operating devices and machinery, recognizing how operators vary in their level of expertise. Most of us are not professional drivers or mechanics, and our cars must be usable by 16-year-olds nervously taking the road for the first time, as well as professional racers pushing cars to their limits. The goal of educators and trainers is to implant in the minds of novices the requisite skills and knowledge needed to perform a wide array of tasks. What are ways that we can take advantage of the basic abilities of the individual and their current level of skill to better provide them with the knowledge they need to succeed?

Acknowledgement

Sandia National Laboratories is a multiprogram laboratory operated by Sandia Corporation, a Lockheed Martin Company, for the United States Department of Energy's National Nuclear Security Administration under contract DEAC04-94AL85000.

SECTION 3

Russian Electrophysiological Research

∴

CHAPTER 8

Brain Oscillations and Personality from an Evolutionary Perspective

Gennady G. Knyazev

Contemporary science is an international enterprise. Owing to the internet and international journals, scientists may share ideas and empirical findings independent of their geographical place of origin. That may cast doubt on the value of national scientific schools. One may think that scientific ideas only survive due to their fruitfulness, with all other concomitants being mere noise that should be ignored. The history of science, however, shows that the matter is far from being so simple. Many very interesting and potentially fruitful ideas were buried for many years (or sometimes maybe forever) just because they were suggested by the wrong person, in the wrong place, or at an inappropriate time. There is another reason why we should not ignore cultural contexts. Scientists are human beings, and the way they approach a scientific problem (let alone which problem they choose to approach) is highly affected by such concomitants as cultural context, education, available financial support, and, certainly, other people, particularly those who reared, educated, and taught him or her to be a scientist. In that train of thought, a brief overview of those who influenced my own way of thinking would be a fair way to begin this chapter.

During the start of my career, Rostislav Illjutchenok and Alexander Nikiforov were my supervisors. In some sense, their influences were opposed. On the one hand, the main message I obtained from Illjutchenok was to look to the front line in the field. In his opinion, the only criterion of a good job would be a high level of methodological sophistication and publications in prestigious journals. On the other hand, Nikiforov considered that tradition and school should be taken into account. At that time I did animal research in the field of neurochemistry of monoamines and neuropeptides. About twelve years ago, under the influence of my wife and co-worker Helena Slobodskaya, I made a sharp turn in my career and started research on humans, looking for psychophysiological (mostly EEG) correlates of personality-related individual differences. Helena Slobodskaya also was the one who directed my attention to Jeffrey Gray's Reinforcement Sensitivity Theory. Hence, my current interest and most of my papers published in international journals relate to two interconnected issues: (1) Behavioral Inhibition and Behavioral Activation as biologically founded personality traits – their psychophysiological correlates and association with psychological adjustment and health; and (2) brain oscillations from an evolutionary perspective and their relation to personality and behavior. The rest of the chapter will be devoted to a brief discussion of these issues.

1 Hierarchical Structure of Personality

In the past decades, two models have dominated in the area of personality research. The first is the Eysenck's hierarchical three factor model, recently described as the "Giant Three" (Eysenck 1994). The second model assumes that personality is best described by five factors, and is usually referred to as the "Big Five" model (Costa and McCrae 1992). Initially, Eysenck distinguished two basic dimensions of personality, which he labeled Extraversion and Neuroticism. Subsequently, a third dimension, labeled Psychoticism, was added. In the Big Five model, Extraversion and Neuroticism retained their status of fundamental personality dimensions but Psychoticism gave way to three other dimensions, namely Agreeableness, Conscientiousness and Openness. Several methods have been applied to examine whether three or five factors best represent the basic dimensions of personality and to what extent Psychoticism should be regarded as a combination of Agreeableness, Conscientiousness and Openness as Eysenck (1991) claimed. Both models are hierarchical and proponents of both models assert that their three- or five-factor model constitute the highest level of the hierarchy. There is consistent evidence however that these dimensions are not independent. Confirmatory factor analysis studies of the Eysenck Personality Profiler usually find a negative correlation between Extraversion and Neuroticism (Eysenck et al. 2000; Moosbrugger and Fischbach 2003; Knyazev et al. 2004a). Studies of the NEO Personality Inventory and the NEO Five Factor Inventory also detect appreciable intercorrelations between the Big Five factors (Block 1995). From a hierarchical perspective, these correlations are understandable if the Giant Three and the Big Five do not, as claimed, represent the highest point of the hierarchy.

Digman (1997) proposed that correlations between the Big Five give rise to two broader dimensions at a higher level of abstraction. Exploratory and confirmatory factor analyses consistently supported the hypothesis of two higher order factors, labeled Alpha and Beta. The Alpha factor was defined by high loadings of Agreeableness, Emotional stability, and Conscientiousness. The Beta factor was defined by high loadings of Extraversion, Openness, Emotional stability, and Conscientiousness. Digman (1997) proposed that Alpha seems to reflect the development of impulse restraint and the reduction of hostility, aggression, and neurotic defense. Beta seems related to self-actualization versus personal constriction. Two higher order factors, labeled Impulsivity and Withdrawal, also underlie the scales of the Antisocial Personality Questionnaire. Using structural equation modeling, Blackburn et al. (2004) have recently shown that the Big Five's Alpha and Beta divisions correspond to the Impulsivity and Withdrawal dimensions of the Antisocial Personality Questionnaire. Therefore, it could be concluded that each of the two most popular personality models could be collapsed into just two super dimensions representing impulsive and antisocial tendencies and neurotic introversion, respectively.

Research on temperament is an alternative approach to the study of individual differences. It has been shown that a two-factor model explains much of the variance in temperament (Halverson 2004). These two factors were identified with impulsivity and inhibition. In recent years, empirical studies using either Q-factor or cluster analyses have found evidence that three personality types, which have been labeled Resilients, Overcontrollers, and Undercontrollers. These can be replicated across methods, languages and ages. Recently we have shown that Undercontrollers are high on Behavioral activation, Overcontrollers are high on Behavioral inhibition, and Resilients are low on both dimensions (Knyazev 2006; Knyazev and Slobodskaya 2006).

It could be concluded therefore that all the three approaches to the study of individual differences, namely personality, temperament, and typology research, point to the existence of two super dimensions, which could be labeled Impulsivity and Inhibition. It should be emphasized that these dimensions do not explain all of personality. Each of the Big Five or Giant Three factors preserves a considerable amount of unique variance which is not accounted for by the two super dimensions. But these Really Big Two (Halverson 2004) lie at the highest level of abstraction and probably reflect some common causes, which somehow reveal themselves in all lower level personality traits.

2 Theories Linking Personality with Activity of Brain Structures

It is generally accepted that fundamental personality dimensions are somehow linked with the activity of brain structures. Several theoretical models have been put forward to explain the neuropsychological underpinning of personality. Gray (1987) proposed three major neuropsychological systems, the Behavioral Activation System (BAS), the Behavioral Inhibition System (BIS), and the Fight/Flight system (FFS). BIS mostly depends on activity of the limbic system, promoting avoidance behavior and feelings of anxiety. BAS depends on ascending motivational pathways from the brainstem, mostly dopaminergic, promoting appetitive motivation and approach behavior. FFS depends on activity of brainstem structures such as the periacqueductal gray region, promoting reactions to unconditional aversive stimuli. Gray (1987) claimed that activity of the BAS and the BIS underlie personality dimensions of Impulsivity and Trait Anxiety, respectively, whereas FFS activity is probably somehow associated with Psychoticism.

In psychometric and experimental studies, only two of the three proposed systems have received some support. Particularly, psychometric evidence disputes the existence of FFS as a distinct dimension, orthogonal to the BIS and BAS dimensions (Wilson et al. 1990; Wilson et al. 1995; Slobodskaya et al. 2001; Knyazev et al. 2004d). Another problem, which reveals itself in psychometric studies, is that Behavioral Activation or Impulsivity proved to be a non-homogenous construct. There are different kinds of impulsive behavior. Dickman (1992) suggested distinguishing between Functional and Dysfunctional Impulsivity. The former refers to individual differences in appropriate spontaneity, the later to the more widely-used construct of impulsivity focusing on potentially problematic disinhibition. Performing a factor analysis of the Gray-Wilson Personality Questionnaire, Knyazev et al. (2004d) have also found that BAS is best represented by two lower-level factors. The first one is mostly composed of items measuring aggressiveness and lack of conscientiousness, the second one is composed of items measuring impulsive approach behavior. We have shown that the BIS and the BAS, as measured by the Gray-Wilson Personality Questionnaire, are good predictors of emotional and behavioral problems and substance use in adolescents (Knyazev 2004; Knyazev and Wilson 2004; Knyazev et al. 2004c).

Cloninger (1987) proposed a biological model of personality derived from animal research. He suggests that three personality traits: Harm Avoidance, Reward Dependence, and Novelty Seeking are heritable and relate to monoamine systems: serotonin, noradrenaline, and dopamine, respectively. The dimension of Harm Avoidance is similar to BIS because it is characterized by a heritable susceptibility to anxiety and behavioral inhibition in the presence of punishment cues. The two other dimensions are similar to Behavioral activation and relate to potentially more (Novelty Seeking) or less (Reward Dependence) problematic aspects of reward-driven acting out behavior.

Zuckerman et al. (1993) point out that personality could be described by a three-factor model similar to Eysenck's Giant Three. Like Cloninger, Zuckerman focused on monoamine neurotransmitter systems as the bases for fundamental personality traits, although they differ on the relationships between particular monoamines and personality traits and in the relative specificity of the relationships (Zuckerman 1996).

There is also research linking asymmetrical activity over the frontal cortex with the experience and expression of emotions and motivations (e.g., Davidson 1992; Tomarken et al. 1992). Although these researchers do not attempt to explain personality and conceptualize their findings in terms of positive and negative affect, it has been shown that these findings are best explained in terms of approach and withdrawal behaviors (Harmon-Jones 2003) which closely match the constructs of Impulsivity and Inhibition.

In summary, biologically oriented personality theorists tend to propose two or three brain systems, and corresponding behavioral patterns. A dimension resembling Inhibition most consistently appears in all theoretical models and enjoys the most empirical support. Other dimensions differ in different models but all of them describe different aspects of acting-out, reward-dependent behavior which could be identified with different facets of Impulsivity. Thus, these constructs overlap conceptually with Impulsivity and Inhibition, which have emerged at the highest level of the hierarchy as global personality and temperament dimensions. Inhibition seems to be a more homogenous construct whereas Impulsivity tends to break down into at least two components. It could be concluded that empirical evidence votes for existence of two presumably biologically-rooted factors which underlie residual covariance of fundamental personality dimensions. One of these factors is homogenous; another one conceivably includes at least two correlated components. As for their biological underpinning, different theorists propose different mechanisms and brain systems, but none of them takes into account oscillatory brain activity.

3 Brain Oscillations from an Evolutionary Perspective

One of pioneers in electroencephalography (EEG) research once noted that EEG signal may not be a meaningful representation of brain events and should be treated as noise (Jasper 1991). The first human EEG pattern described was an 8 to 12 Hz rhythm, the alpha waves of Berger (1929). From scalp recordings, investigators identified various other oscillatory patterns that were particularly obvious during rest and sleep. However, the scalp EEG during conscious, waking behavior demonstrated low amplitude, "desynchronized" patterns. Therefore, the motivation to relate these "idling" rhythms to complex cognitive brain operations was diminished. In the first volume of the Electroencephalography and Clinical Neurophysiology, an article by Moruzzi and Magoun (1949) established the consequences of reticular stimulation on cortical EEG. Following stimulation of the brainstem reticular formation in cats, widespread reduction of cortical EEG was observed. This helped to establish a role for EEG measures in the assessment of arousal but also had the unwitting effect of reinforcing the view that EEG could not provide useful information of cognitive brain operations. This idea was championed by some and led to the development of general arousal theory (e.g. Duffy 1962; Thayer 1989) in which the EEG is considered to be useful only for making inferences about global states of sleep and wakefulness.

The recent resurgence of interest in neuronal oscillations is a result of several parallel developments, which showed that mammalian cortical neurons form behavior-dependent oscillating networks of various sizes. These oscillations are phylogenetically preserved, suggesting that they are functionally relevant. Recent findings indicate that network oscillations bias input selection, temporally link neurons into assemblies, and facilitate synaptic plasticity, mechanisms that cooperatively support temporal representation and long-term consolidation of information (Buzsaki and Draguhn 2004). The synchronous activity of oscillating networks is now viewed as the critical "middle ground" linking single-neuron activity to behavior. Although it is unknown how the neural code is integrated in spontaneous and evoked brain oscillations, synchrony has been largely viewed as a potentially valid mechanism for cerebral integration (Salinas and Sejnowski, "Correlated neuronal activity and the flow of neural information," 539–550; Singer, "Neuronal synchrony," 49–65). A growing body of evidence suggests that different levels of cerebral integration mediated by spatial and temporal synchrony over multiple frequency bands could play a key role in the emergence of percepts, memories, emotions, thoughts, and actions (Nunez 2000; Varela et al. 2001; Cantero and Atienza 2005).

The brain's average connection density must decrease with increasing brain size; otherwise the number of axons would increase explosively with number of neurons, racking up enormous costs of space and metabolic energy (Ringo 1991). This decrease in average connection density implies that brains need to become more modular, both structurally and functionally, as they increase in size (Jacobs and Jordan 1992). That places major constraints on global synchrony in growing brains. In the cortex, the densely connected local neuron networks are supplemented by a small fraction of long-range connections (Braitenberg and Schutz 1998) which keeps the synaptic path lengths short and maintains fundamental functions in growing brains without excessive wiring. Despite the progressively decreasing fraction of long-range connections in larger brains, synchronization of local and distant networks can be readily accomplished by oscillators because of the low energy costs involved in coupling rhythms (Buzsaki and Draguhn 2004). Synchronous fluctuations of membrane potentials bias input selection, temporally linking neurons into assemblies, and facilitating synaptic plasticity. These mechanisms cooperatively support temporal representation and the long-term consolidation of information. Temporary hard-wired connections could occur via the rhythmic modulation of electrical coupling among subsets of functionally related neurons. This makes possible the reversible formation of sub-circuits that are capable of dealing with specific situations. Such integration can exist across a number of functional domains, with different frequency rhythms associated with each domain (Newman and Grace 1999). Thus, each frequency oscillations may, in a way, "tune" distant brain regions for a specific function.

Such a mechanism of spatial neuronal integration is only needed in the sufficiently large brains which appeared in vertebrates. Comparative studies by Bullock indicate that invertebrates have much more obvious unit spiking than vertebrates, but much less relative amplitude of slow waves (Bullock 1993). Among vertebrates, the degree of synchronization also increases during evolution. There is evidence of less synchrony or more rapid coherence decline with distance in reptiles, amphibians, and fish than in mammals (Bullock 1997). There is also an important distinction between reptiles, lower mammals and humans in what frequency dominates in the scalp EEG. Alpha is the dominant frequency in adult humans, while theta dominates in the EEG of lower mammals (Sainsbury 1998; Klimesch 1999) and delta in the reptilian EEG (Gaztelu et al. 1991; Gonzalez et al. 1999). We have proposed an evolutionary hypothesis linking brain oscillations with behavior (Knyazev and Slobodskaya 2003; Knyazev et al. 2004b; Knyazev et al. 2004c; Knyazev 2007). This hypothesis posits that *the oscillatory system, which dominates the EEG of particular species, should be linked with functions and behavioral patterns that dominate the behavior of these species*. From such a standpoint, alpha oscillations represent the newest and most advanced mode of processing, which was acquired later in the evolution of mammals.

4   Brain Oscillations and Behavior

In lower vertebrates with dominant delta oscillations, behavior oriented to the acquisition of biologically important goals such as physical maintenance, survival, dominance and mating predominates. Sensitivity to internal stimuli is important for the organization of behavior which is oriented to satisfaction of basic biological needs. Hence, delta activity is expected to be sensitive to internal stimuli signaling disturbance of homeostasis (such as hypoxia, hypoglycemia, fatigue, sustained pain), as well as to the stimuli signaling a need for sexual activity (e.g. the level of sexual hormones). It should be implicated in monitoring of autonomic functions, such as breathing and heartbeat. That does not imply participation in the on-line regulation of autonomic functions, but rather a synchronization of brain activity with autonomic patterns. Ample evidence suggests that behavior which is oriented to satisfaction of basic biological needs mostly depends on activity of the brain reward systems such as the brain opiate system and the dopaminergic mesolimbic pathways. Delta oscillations are expected to be modulated by these systems' activity. That should be most evident with respect to drugs of abuse which directly influence the brain reward systems. Furthermore, delta activity is expected to be associated with primitive defense mechanisms which in humans are mostly rudimentary. Because detection of the motivational salience of environmental stimuli is supposed to be the main function of the brain motivational systems (Gray 1987), delta activity is expected to play a leading part in this process.

The theta system is hypothesized to be associated with the most advantageous achievements which distinguish mammals' behavior from that of lower vertebrates. Above all it is the highly developed ability to learn. Besides, although typical mechanisms of emotional response for mammals are based on motivational drives which they share with lower vertebrates, these mechanisms represent a much more flexible and advantageous way of behavioral regulation. Hence, the theta system is expected to be associated with memory processes and emotional regulation. Together with delta, theta activity is expected to participate in the process of salience detection. Since behavioral patterns, which in lower animals were sufficient and appropriate for satisfaction of basic needs and acquisition of biologically important goals, would not fit in the modern human society, the relative prevalence of delta and theta oscillations is expected to correlate with maladaptive and deficient behaviors. Prevalence of delta activity is expected to correlate with delinquent and antisocial behavior, whereas prevalence of theta activity with a more benign kind of impulsive behavior.

In humans, the alpha system is expected to play the leading part in the organization of conscious, distinctly human interactions with the environment. The most prominent feature of human behavior which distinguishes it from that of lower mammals is reliance not only with instinctive behavioral patterns and subjective experience acquired during life, but also on the knowledge that is stored in the long-term semantic memory. Hence, the alpha system is expected to participate in instantaneous recognition of environmental patterns by means of matching them with categorized knowledge stored in semantic memory. To accomplish such a function, the alpha system has to participate in attention and memory operations with the latter ones being of a different quality than those which are associated with theta activity. Characteristics of alpha activity are expected to correlate with cognitive performance. Alpha activity should be in reciprocal relationship with the low-frequency oscillations of delta and theta ranges because they should be linked with largely opposite processing modes.

Review of the relevant literature (Knyazev 2007) shows that most of these predictions are in line with existing empirical evidence. Delta power increases in motivationally relevant states, such as hunger, fatigue, sexual arousal, pain, and craving for drugs in drug addicts. It is sensitive to signals from the respiratory and cardiovascular systems. It plays the main part in the so-called P300 response to salient and motivationally relevant stimuli. Delta is the only oscillatory system which is active even in deep sleep, presumably because it is involved in the monitoring of metabolic and autonomic functions.

In lower mammals, hippocampal theta has been shown to correlate with a number of processes, such as the orienting response, voluntary movement, learning and attention, arousal, and behavioral inhibition. A host of studies have been conducted to establish a link between theta oscillations and memory. Many recent theoretical accounts and reviews emphasize involvement of theta oscillations in the encoding of information particularly during active exploratory movements and spatial navigation (see Knyazev 2007 for a review). In mammals, memory is closely associated with emotion. Existing evidence confirms a link between theta activity and emotional states both in animals and humans.

Starting from Berger's (1929) pioneering works, many studies have noted a task-related decrease in alpha power. This finding was so pervasive that alpha power has come to be considered as a reverse measure of activation. More recently this idea has been reconceptualized with alpha as a mechanism for increasing signal to noise ratios within the cortex by means of inhibiting unnecessary or conflicting processes to the task at hand. Many studies have shown that alpha oscillations are involved in inhibitory control of motor programs, selective attention, and memory operations. In a series of reviews, Klimesch (1999) discussed experimental findings supporting the hypothesis that short-term (episodic) memory demands lead to synchronization in the theta band, whereas long-term (semantic) memory demands lead to a task-specific desynchronization in the upper alpha band. EEG measures of alpha activity correlate with cognitive performance. Changes in the EEG alpha rhythm in response to manipulations of task practice and load discriminated between subjects with high- and low-ability, younger and older, and with and without Alzheimer's disease. Moreover, artificial enhancement of alpha power by means of repetitive transcranial magnetic stimulation at the individual upper alpha frequency (Klimesch et al. 2003) or neurofeedback training (Hanslmayr et al. 2005) can enhance task performance. It has been proposed recently that alpha oscillations are involved in top-down regulation (Klimesch et al. 2007).

In sum, this evidence seems generally to be in line with the predictions derived from the evolutionary interpretation of brain oscillations. Delta and theta power correlates with more "basic" and evolutionary old processes of motivation, emotion, and procedural learning; alpha power correlates with inhibitory control and top-down regulation which are implicated in many cognitive operations including semantic memory and fine-grained control of motor programs.

In accord with the principle that ontogeny recapitulates phylogeny, the alpha system develops more slowly than delta and theta oscillatory systems. It is also more sensitive to a variety of detrimental influences. In a number of developmental stages and pathological conditions, a deficient alpha and/or increased slow-wave activity are associated with cognitive deficits and a lack of inhibitory control (Knyazev 2007). It has been shown that slow-wave and alpha oscillations are reciprocally related to each other (Klimesch 1999; Robinson 1999; Klimesch et al. 2003; Knyazev and Slobodskaya; Knyazev et al. 2004c; Knyazev 2006). This reciprocal relationship may reflect a conscious inhibitory control over motivational and emotional drives (Knyazev 2007).

Evidence about so-called altered states of consciousness (ASC) supports such a view. The multitude and heterogeneity of ASC makes the search of a common mechanism unfeasible but all of them could be characterized by a detachment from reality and predominance of the unconscious (Freud 1900). Most of these states imply suppression of rational thinking and disinhibition of subconscious emotional and motivational drives. Most interesting, in terms of EEG power measures, most ASC are characterized by a decrease of alpha and an increase of slow-wave activity (see Vaitl et al. 2005). The similarity of EEG power changes during ASC of largely varying origins is striking. This similarity implies that independent of causes leading to ASC, the disinhibition of the unconscious inherent to these states has a clear EEG signature: an increase of slow waves and relative decrease of alpha oscillations.

There is also evidence confirming the idea that slow waves are more associated with the subconscious, whereas alpha waves are more associated with conscious processes. One example of subconscious perception of external stimuli would be during sleep. It has been shown that both in cats and humans, EEG responses to external stimuli during slow-wave sleep are predominantly evident in the delta range of frequencies (Basar 1999). It is possible that the delta system, which dominates the EEG in this state, may be "on guard" for motivationally relevant external stimuli. Study of evoked oscillations on the hearing threshold in awake humans gives another example of subconscious or borderline perception. These studies demonstrated that stimulus intensity is one of the factors determining which frequency component of the auditory Evoked Potential is dominant. At high stimulation intensities, the dominant frequency component is in the alpha to theta range. At 40–20 dB stimulation, the dominant frequency component is in the theta range. At threshold stimulation, the frequency characteristics are dominated by distinct delta activity (Parnefjord and Basar 1999). Interestingly, for near-threshold visual stimuli, it has been shown that the pre-stimulus state of alpha oscillations determines whether the stimulus will be consciously perceived or not (Ergenoglu et al. 2004). Thus, conscious perception depends on alpha activity, whereas subconscious perception depends more on the low frequency oscillations.

5   Brain Oscillations and Personality

In earlier sections, it is suggested that low frequency oscillations are associated with evolutionary older motivational and emotional processes, which dominate the unconscious. Alpha oscillations are associated with inhibitory control and top-down regulation, which contribute to a variety of cognitive processes and prevail during conscious states. It may be asked, how this evidence and these ideas may be applied to human behavior and personality?

Abundant empirical evidence which comes from clinical and forensic EEG research suggests a straightforward answer. This evidence shows the prevalence of slow waves and/or a deficit of alpha oscillations in the resting EEG is associated with impulsive and disinhibited behavior (see Barry et al. 2003; Knyazev 2007). It appears that a prevalence of delta oscillations is associated with a more malignant aggressive and antisocial kind of impulsivity, whereas prevalence of theta is associated with hyperactivity and pure impulsivity (Knyazev 2007). The relative prevalence of alpha oscillations, on the other hand, could be associated with exaggerated inhibitory control which is peculiar to high trait anxiety individuals or patients with anxiety disorder (Herrmann and Winterer 1996; Knyazev and Slobodskaya 2003; Knyazev et al. 2004a). This latter association has been shown to be state-dependant (Herrmann and Winterer 1996; Knyazev et al. 2004b) and probably reflects inhibitory reactions in a novel situation which are inherent to anxious individuals (Gray 1987). Such a state of vigilance and preparatory inhibition of ongoing activities is associated with increased reaction to upcoming stimuli which is evident in higher event-related alpha band desynchronization (Knyazev et al. 2006b; Knyazev et al. 2008b).

Thus, it appears that the two higher order dimensions of personality, Impulsivity and Inhibition, may have a clear manifestation in the electrical oscillatory activity of the brain. Impulsivity is associated with higher activity of delta and theta oscillatory systems, the former correlating with aggressive and antisocial behavior, the latter with hyperactivity and pure impulsivity. Both patterns frequently co-occur and both imply a deficit of inhibitory control from higher centers, such as prefrontal cortex (Knyazev 2007). Inhibition is associated with relatively higher activity of the alpha oscillatory system.

These associations are frequently evident even in resting EEG measures obtained in non-pathological samples. Using structural equation modeling, we found a good fit for models linking spontaneous activity of the three oscillatory systems with the three kinds of behavior (Knyazev 2007; Knyazev et al. 2008c). But generally, spontaneous activity of the brain is subject to a host of influences that are difficult to control. Study of oscillatory responses to relevant stimuli may provide more solid evidence about associations with impulsivity and inhibition properties of respective oscillatory systems. It could be predicted that an emotional response to relevant stimuli should predominate in subjects with higher scores on Impulsivity and Aggressiveness. This should show up as a higher event-related synchronization in the theta and delta frequency ranges. On the other hand, in those who score high on Behavioral Inhibition and Trait Anxiety, exaggerated preparatory reactions would reveal itself as increased alpha band synchronization during the inter-stimulus interval, whereas higher investment of cognitive resources into stimuli processing would show up as a higher event-related alpha band desynchronization. We have shown that these tendencies could be noticed even in reactions to emotionally neutral auditory stimuli (tone) in the so-called stop-signal experimental paradigm (Knyazev et al. 2008b). They were also evident in reactions to emotionally laden socially significant stimuli, such as emotional facial expressions (Knyazev et al. 2008a).

In subjects with high scores on Hostility, as measured by the Buss and Perry aggression scales, as compared to low scorers, face presentation evoked stronger theta band synchronization and lower alpha band desynchronization. This effect was most pronounced during presentation of angry faces and was least pronounced during presentation of neutral faces (Figure 8.1). In this experiment, subjects were instructed to evaluate the level of hostility in presented faces, hence, their attention was explicitly directed towards emotional content of the stimulus. In another (not yet published) experiment, the subjects performed the gender discrimination task. Hence, the emotional content of the

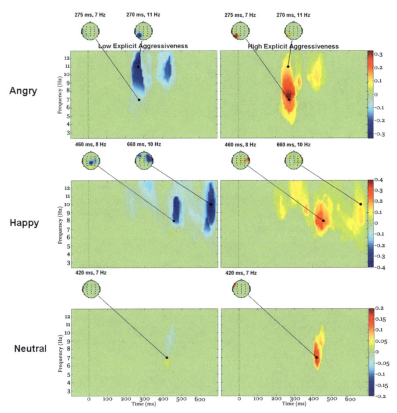

FIGURE 8.1 Averaged across all cortical sites event-related spectral perturbations during explicit presentation of angry, happy, and neutral faces to low and high Aggressiveness (measured by the Buss and Perry's Hostility scale) scorers. Areas with no significant between-group differences (p<0.05 after FDR correction for multiple comparisons – see Knyazev et al., 2008 for details of statistical analysis) are zeroed out and showed in green. Red color shows synchronization, blue color – desynchronization. Cortical maps at the top of each panel show cortical distribution of most pronounced effects.

stimulus was not consciously attended to and was perceived subconsciously. In this case, the distinction between high and low Hostility scorers was limited to delta and low theta bands, which again showed stronger synchronization in high Hostility scorers (Figure 8.2).

The effect of Trait Anxiety during explicit presentation of emotional facial expressions is shown in Figure 8.3. Again, this effect was most pronounced during presentation of angry faces. It consisted of stronger alpha band desynchronization and weaker theta band synchronization in high than in low Trait

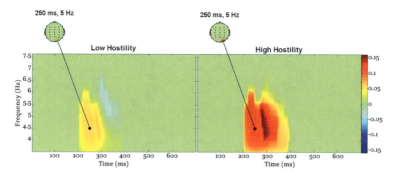

FIGURE 8.2 Averaged across all cortical sites and all face categories event-related spectral perturbations during implicit presentation of emotional facial expressions (the gender discrimination task) to low and high Aggressiveness scorers.

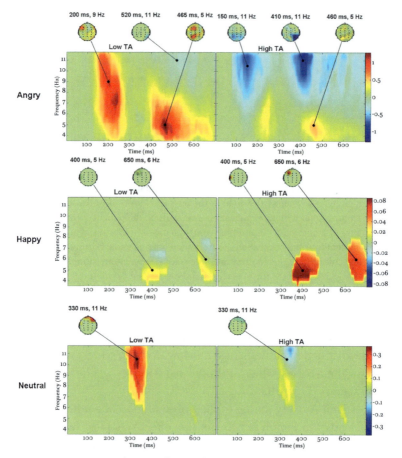

FIGURE 8.3 Averaged across all cortical sites event-related spectral perturbations during explicit presentation of angry, happy, and neutral faces to low and high Trait Anxiety (TA) scorers.

Anxiety subjects. A similar, but much weaker, effect could be noticed during presentation of neutral faces. However, presentation of happy faces evoked stronger theta synchronization in high than in low Trait Anxiety subjects, with no differences in the alpha band of frequencies. Interestingly, during implicit presentation of emotional facial expressions (that is, gender discrimination task) effect of Trait Anxiety was virtually opposite – theta band synchronization was more pronounced in high than in low Anxiety subjects, whereas alpha desynchronization was present in the latter but was replaced by synchronization in the former case (Figure 8.4).

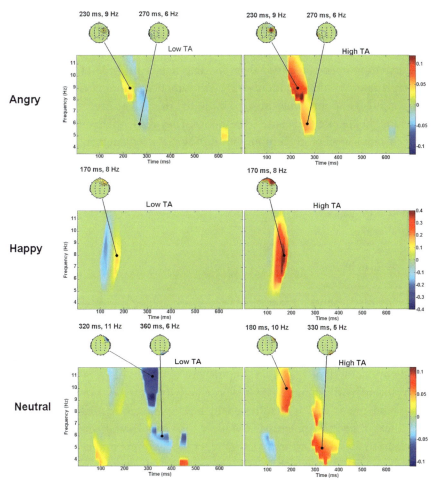

FIGURE 8.4 Averaged across all cortical sites event-related spectral perturbations during implicit presentation of angry, happy, and neutral faces to low and high Trait Anxiety (TA) scorers.

These data show that effects of hostility and anxiety show up differently during subconscious and conscious processing of emotional information. In the former case both traits predispose to a higher synchronization in the theta band, which could be interpreted as a sign of stronger emotional response. However, when conscious processing takes place, effects of the two traits become opposite. Hostility still predisposes to a stronger theta synchronization which is accompanied by a diminished alpha desynchronization. I interpret this pattern as an indicator of predominantly emotional processing (cognitive processing could be even inhibited due to alpha synchronization). In anxious individuals, on the other hand, cognitive processing (indexed by alpha desynchronization) clearly prevails during presentation of angry and neutral faces, whereas emotional processing (theta synchronization) is diminished. This latter effect seems counterintuitive, but it should be borne in mind that extemporaneous emotional responding needs a degree of disinhibition which is alien to anxious individuals. Emotional responding is fraught with rash impulsive actions that must be inhibited in anxious individuals in favor of a more deliberate and cautious response. They respond emotionally on the subconscious level of perception, but during conscious perception of potentially threatening stimuli (angry and neutral faces) anxiety predisposes them to thorough cognitive evaluation which shows up in abundant alpha desynchronization. They may take liberty to respond emotionally only to explicitly friendly happy faces.

6   Conclusion

This chapter presents a theoretical framework linking personality with brain oscillations. It is shown that two personality dimensions, which appear at the highest level of the personality hierarchy and could be labeled Impulsivity and Inhibition, may have a clear manifestation in spontaneous and event-related oscillatory activity of the brain. Impulsivity is associated with disinhibition of evolutionary old brain systems whose activity underlies motivational and emotional drives and is manifested in low frequency oscillations of delta and theta ranges. Impulsive individuals may have higher delta and theta power in the resting EEG and tend to react to environmental challenges with emotional excitation which in EEG shows up as an event-related increase of theta and delta power. Inhibition is associated with exaggerated inhibitory control over behavior and a tendency to invest more cognitive resources in the processing of potentially threatening information. In EEG, this shows up as a preparatory increase of alpha power in the background or pre-stimulus EEG and a marked event-related alpha band desynchronization. It should be emphasized that the proposed associations between personality and spontaneous EEG are state-dependant and may not always be observed in the main-stream population. Event-related changes in oscillatory activity should be more uniformly linked to personality, but they depend on experimental context, particularly on whether emotional stimuli are presented explicitly or implicitly.

Acknowledgements

While working on the paper, the author was supported by grants of the Russian Foundation for Basic Research (RFBR) No. 08-06-00016-a and No. 08-06-00011a. I am grateful to my colleagues Helena Slobodskaya, Evgenij Levin, Alexander Savostyanov, Andrey Bocharov, Jaroslav Slobodskoj-Plusnin, and Margarita Safronova for data collection and discussion of presented ideas and findings.

References

Barry, R. J., A. R. Clarke, and S. J. Johnstone. 2003. "A review of electrophysiology in attention-deficit/hyperactivity disorder: I. Qualitative and quantitative electroencephalography." *Clinical Neurophysiology* 114, no. 2: 171–183.

Basar, E. 1999. *Brain Function and Oscillations, Volume II: Integrative Brain Function, Neurophysiology and Cognitive Processes.* Berlin: Springer.

Berger, H. 1929. "Uber das elecktroenzephalogramm des menschen I." *Archive Psychiatrie* 87: 527–570.

Blackburn, R., S. J. D. Renwick, J. P. Donnelly, and C. Logan. 2004. "Big five or big two? Superordinate factors in the NEO five factor inventory and the antisocial personality questionnaire." *Personality and Individual Differences* 37, no. 6: 957–970.

Block, J. 1995. "A contrarian view of the five-factor approach to personality description." *Psychological Bulletin* 117, no. 2: 187–215.

Braitenberg, V., and A. Schutz. 1998. *Cortex: Statistics and Geometry of Neuronal Connectivity.* Heidelberg, Germany: Springer-Verlag.

Bullock, T. H. 1993. *How Do Brains Work?* Boston: Birkhouser.

Bullock, T. H. 1997. "Signals and signs in the nervous system: The dynamic anatomy of electrical activity is probably information-rich." *Proceedings of the National Academy of Sciences* 94, no. 1: 1–6.

Buzsaki, G., and A. Draguhn. 2004. "Neuronal oscillations in cortical networks." *Science* 304, no. 5679: 1926–1929.

Cantero, J. L., and M. Atienza. 2005. "The role of neural synchronization in the emergence of cognition across the wake-sleep cycle." *Reviews in the Neurosciences* 16, no. 1: 69–83.

Cloninger, C. R. 1987. "A systematic method for clinical description and classification of personality variants. A proposal." *Archives of General Psychiatry* 44, no. 6: 573–588.

Costa, P. T. Jr., and R. R. McCrae. 1992. "Four ways five factors are basic." *Personality and Individual Differences* 13, no. 6: 653–665.

Davidson, R. J. 1992. "Anterior cerebral asymmetry and the nature of emotion." *Brain and Cognition* 20, no. 1: 125–151.

Dickman, S. J. 1990. "Functional and dysfunctional impulsivity: Personality and cognitive correlates." *Journal of Personality and Social Psychology* 58, no. 1: 95–102.

Digman, J. M. 1997. "Higher-order factors of the big five." *Journal of Personality and Social Psychology* 73, no. 6: 1246–1256.

Duffy, E. 1962. *Activation and Behavior*. New York: Wiley.

Ergenoglu, T., T. Demiralp, Z. Bayraktaroglu, M. Ergen, H. Beydagi, and Y. Uresin. 2004. "Alpha rhythm of the EEG modulates visual detection performance in humans." *Cognitive Brain Research* 20, no. 3: 376–383.

Eysenck, H. J. 1991. "Dimensions of personality: 16, 5 or 3? – criteria for a taxonomic paradigm." *Personality and Individual Differences* 12, no. 8: 773–790.

Eysenck, H. J. 1994. "The Big Five or Giant Three: criteria for a paradigm." In *The Developing Structure of Temperament and Personality from Infancy to Adulthood*, ed. C. F. Halverson, G. A. Cohnstamm, and R. P. Martin, 37–51. Hillsdale, N.J.: Erlbaum.

Eysenck, H. J., G. D. Wilson, and C. J. Jackson. 2000. *Eysenck Personality Profiler (Short V6)*. Worthing, UK: Psi-Press.

Freud, S. 1900. *Die Traumdeutung* (The Interpretation of Dreams). Berlin: Deuticke.

Gaztelu, J. M., E. Garcia-Austt, and T. H. Bullock. 1991. "Electrocorticograms of hippocampal and dorsal cortex of two reptiles: comparison with possible mammalian homologs." *Brain, Behavior and Evolution* 37, no. 3: 144–160.

Gonzalez, J., A. Gamundi, R. Rial, M. C. Nicolau, L. De Vera, and E. Pereda E. 1999. "Nonlinear, fractal, and spectral analysis of the EEG of lizard, Gallotia galloti." *American Journal of Physiology* 277, no. 1: 86–93.

Gray, J. A. 1987. *The Psychology of Fear and Stress*. Oxford: Oxford University Press.

Halverson, C. F. 2004. "Hierarchical models of the temperament-personality interface." Paper presented at the 15th Occasional Temperament Conference, Athens, Georgia. October 28–31.

Hanslmayr, S., P. Sauseng, M. Doppelmayr, M. Schabus, and W. Klimesch. 2005. "Increasing individual upper alpha power by neurofeedback improves cognitive performance in human subjects." *Applied Psychophysiology and Biofeedback* 30, no. 1: 1–10.

Harmon-Jones, E. 2003. "Clarifying the emotive functions of asymmetrical frontal cortical activity." *Psychophysiology* 40, no. 6: 838–848.

Herrmann, W. M., and G. Winterer. 1996. "Electroencephalography in psychiatry-current status and outlook." *Nervenarzt* 67, no. 5: 348–359.

Jacobs, R. A., and M. I. Jordan. 1992. "Computational consequences of a bias toward short connections." *Journal of Cognitive Neuroscience* 4, no. 4: 323–336.

Jasper, H. H. 1991. "History of the early development of electroencephalography and clinical neurophysiology at the Montreal Neurological Institute: The first 25 years 1939–1964." *Canadian Journal of Neurological Sciences* 18, no. 4: 533–548.

Klimesch, W. 1999. "EEG alpha and theta oscillations reflect cognitive and memory performance: a review and analysis." *Brain Research Reviews* 29, no. 2–3: 169–195.

Klimesch, W., P. Sauseng, and C. Gerloff. 2003. "Enhancing cognitive performance with repetitive transcranial magnetic stimulation at human individual alpha frequency." *European Journal of Neuroscience* 17, no. 5: 1129–1133.

Klimesch, W., P. Sauseng, and S. Hanslmayr. 2007. "EEG alpha oscillations: The inhibition–timing hypothesis." *Brain Research Reviews*. 53, no. 1: 63–88.

Knyazev, G. G. 2004. "Behavioural activation as predictor of substance use: Mediating and moderating role of attitudes and social relationships." *Drug and Alcohol Dependence* 75, no. 3: 309–321.

Knyazev, G. G. 2006. "EEG correlates of personality types." *Netherlands Journal of Psychology* 62, no. 2: 82–90.

Knyazev, G. G. 2007. "Motivation, emotion, and their inhibitory control mirrored in brain oscillations." *Neuroscience & Biobehavioral Reviews* 31, no. 3: 377–395.

Knyazev, G. G. 2008. "Brain oscillations and biological roots of personality." *Brain Research Journal* 2, no. 1–2: 79–101.

Knyazev, G. G., I. V. Belopolsky, M. V. Bodunov, and G. D. Wilson. 2004a. "The factor structure of the Eysenck personality profiler in Russia." *Personality and Individual Differences* 37, no. 8: 1681–1692.

Knyazev, G. G., A. V. Bocharov, E. A. Levin, A. N. Savostyanov, and J. Y. Slobodskoj-Plusnin. 2008a. "Anxiety and oscillatory responses to emotional facial expressions." *Brain Research* 1227: 174–188.

Knyazev, G. G., A. N. Savostyanov, and E. A. Levin. 2004b. "Alpha oscillations as a correlate of trait anxiety." *International Journal of Psychophysiology* 53, no. 2: 147–160.

Knyazev, G. G., A. N. Savostyanov, and E. A. Levin. 2006a. "Alpha synchronization and anxiety: implications for inhibition vs. Alertness hypotheses." *International Journal of Psychophysiology* 59, no. 2: 151–158.

Knyazev, G. G., A. N. Savostyanov, and E. A. Levin. 2008b. "Impulsivity, anxiety, and individual differences in evoked and induced brain oscillations." *International Journal of Psychophysiology* 68, no. 3: 242–254.

Knyazev, G. G., A. N. Savostyanov, and E. A. Levin. 2008c. "Resting EEG power and personality." *Brain Research Journal* 2, no. 1–2: 38–59.

Knyazev, G. G., D. J. L. Schutter, and J. van Honk. 2006b. "Anxious apprehension in-creases coupling of delta and beta oscillations." *International Journal of Psychophysiology* 61, no. 2: 283–287.

Knyazev, G. G., and H. R. Slobodskaya. 2003. "Personality trait of behavioral inhibition is associated with oscillatory systems reciprocal relationships." *International Journal of Psychophysiology* 48, no. 3: 247–261.

Knyazev, G. G., and H. R. Slobodskaya. 2006. "Personality types and behavioural activation and inhibition in adolescents." *Personality and Individual Differences* 41, no. 8: 1385–1395.

Knyazev, G. G., H. R. Slobodskaya, I. I. Kharchenko, and G. D. Wilson. 2004c. "Personality and substance use in Russian youths: The predictive and moderating Role of Behavioural activation and Gender." *Personality and Individual Differences* 37, no. 4: 827–843.

Knyazev, G. G., H. R. Slobodskaya, and G. D. Wilson. 2004d. "Comparison of the construct validity of the Gray-Wilson personality questionnaire and the BIS/BAS scales." *Personality and Individual Differences* 37, no. 8: 1565–1582.

Knyazev, G. G., H. R. Slobodskaya, and G. D. Wilson. 2004e. "Personality and brain oscillations: Developmental aspects." In *Advances in Psychology Research*, ed. S. P. Shohov, 3–34. New York: Nova Science Publishers.

Knyazev, G. G., and G. D. Wilson. 2004. "The Role of personality in the co-occurrence of emotional and conduct problems in adolescents: A confirmation of Corr's 'joint subsystems' hypothesis." *Personality and Individual Differences* 37, no. 1: 43–63.

Knyazev, G. G., G. D. Wilson, and H. R. Slobodskaya. 2007. "Behavioural activation and inhibition and social adjustment." In *The Reinforcement Sensitivity Theory of Personality*, ed. P. Corr, 415–430. Oxford: Oxford University Press.

Moosbrugger, H., and A. Fischbach. 2002. "Evaluating the dimensionality of the Eysenck Personality Profiler-German version (EPP-D): a contribution to the Super Three vs. Big Five Discussion." *Personality and Individual Differences* 33, no. 2: 191–211.

Moruzzi, G., and H. W. Magoun. 1949. "Brain stem reticular formation and activation of the EEG." *Electroencephalography and Clinical Neurophysiology* 1, no. 4: 455–473.

Newman, J., and A. A. Grace. 1999. "Binding across time: The selective gating of frontal and hippocampal systems modulating working memory and attentional states." *Consciousness and Cognition* 8, no. 2: 196–212.

Nunez, P. L. 2000. "Toward a quantitative description of large-scale neocortical dynamic function and EEG." *Behavioral and Brain Sciences* 23, no. 3: 371–398.

Parnefjord, R., and E. Basar. 1999. "Evoked delta oscillations on the hearing threshold." In *Brain Function and Oscillations. Vol. II: Integrative Brain Function, Neurophysiology and Cognitive Processes,* ed. E. Basar, 161–176. Berlin: Springer.

Ringo, J. L. 1991. "Neuronal interconnection as a function of brain size." *Brain, Behavior and Evolution* 38, no. 1: 1–6.

Robinson, D. L. 1999. "The technical, neurological and psychological significance of 'alpha', 'delta' and 'theta' waves confounded in EEG evoked potentials: a study of peak latencies." *Clinical Neurophysiology* 10, no. 8: 427–1434.

Sainsbury, R. S. 1998. "Hippocampal theta: a sensory-inhibition theory of function." *Neuroscience & Biobehavioral Reviews* 22, no. 2: 237–241.

Salinas, E., Sejnowski T. J. "Correlated neuronal activity and the flow of neural information." *Nature Reviews Neuroscience* 2 (2001):539–550.

Singer, W. 1999. "Neuronal synchrony: a versatile code for the definition of relations?" *Neuron* 24 no. 1: 49–65.

Slobodskaya, H. R., M. V. Safronova, G. G. Knyazev, and G. D. Wilson. 2001. "Reactions of Russian adolescents to reward and punishment: a cross-cultural study of the Gray-Wilson Personality Questionnaire." *Personality and Individual Differences* 30, no. 7: 1211–1224.

Thayer, R. E. 1989. *The Biopsychology of Mood and Arousal.* New York: Oxford University Press.

Tomarken, A. J., R. J. Davidso, R. E. Wheeler, and R. Doss. 1992. "Individual differences in anterior brain asymmetry and fundamental dimensions of emotion." *Journal of Personality and Social Psychology* 62, no. 4: 676–687.

Vaitl, D., N. Birbaumer, J. Gruzelier et al. 2005. "Psychobiology of Altered States of Consciousness." *Psychological Bulletin* 131, no. 1: 98–127.

Varela, F., J. P. Lachaux, E. Rodriguez, and J. Martinerie. 2001. "The brainweb: phase synchronization and large-scale integration." *Nature Reviews Neuroscience* 2, no. 4: 229–239.

Wilson, G. D., P. T. Barrett, and S. Iwawaki. 1995. "Japanese reactions to reward and punishment: a cross-cultural personality study." *Personality and Individual Differences* 19, no. 1: 198–112.

Wilson, G. D., J. A. Gray, and P. T. Barrett. 1990. "A factor analysis of the Gray-Wilson Personality Questionnaire." *Personality and Individual Differences* 11, no. 10: 1037–1045.

Zuckerman, M. 1996. "Good and bad humors: Biochemical bases of personality and its disorders." *Psychological Science* 6, no. 6: 325–332.

Zuckerman, M., D. M. Kuhlman, P. Teta, J. Joireman, and M. Kraft. 1993. "A comparison of three structural models of personality: The big three, the big five, and the alternative five." *Journal of Personality and Social Psychology* 65, no. 4: 757–768.

CHAPTER 9

Oscillatory Dynamics of Spiking Neurons and the Modeling of Memory Functions

V. I. Nekorkin and V. B. Kazantsev

1   Introduction

Modeling cells, networks, and functions of the brain has become one of the important aspects of modern theoretical and experimental neuroscience (Abeles 1991; Kock 1998; Haken 2000; Scott 2002; Kazantsev, et al. 2003; Izhikevich 2005; Rabinovich et al. 2006). Significant progress in the development of experimental methods and techniques has opened the possibility to explore the intrinsic structure, morphology, and functions of the brain at molecular, cellular, and cognitive levels. However, it is still impossible experimentally to bridge together these two different levels of consideration (in methods and even conceptually) to uncover the mechanisms underlying higher brain functions. Even single cells can generate a huge variety of signals and processes (Izhikevich 2005). The cells represent *nonlinear analog dynamical systems* which generally permits them to generate an infinite number of responses. At the cognitive level, signals are recorded as integral activity averaged over a huge number of cells, and there is no direct correspondence between local cell dynamics and the observed average activity associated with cognitive function. To overcome the gap between different levels of consideration, a modeling approach could be helpful. The models are constructed to fit experimentally observed dynamics and generally do not require full information (parameters) on the underlying network system. Using even indirect knowledge, the models of cells and cellular networks can reproduce the activity of corresponding functional circuits of the brain. Appropriately constructed and tuned, such models permit activity at any level to be monitored and can illustrate the mechanisms underlying nonlinear dynamical transformations of local cell dynamics to reproducible and robust patterns of collective activity (Kazantsev, et al. 2003; Klinshov and Nekorkin 2008a).

The role of intrinsic oscillatory rhythms of the brain in information processing and cognitive functions is intensively discussed in modern neuroscience (Kandel et al. 1991; Llinas 2002). Oscillations in the frequency range of 1–200 Hz are registered in many brain areas and can be associated with different functions. For example, relatively fast processes (~40 Hz) formed in thalamo-cortical circuits (Llinas 2002; Behrendt 2003; Llinas 2003) are responsible for spatio-temporal binding of sensorial signals into unique information contexts, what underlies perceptual functions. Oscillations in the range of 8–12 Hz play a key role in the dynamics of the olivo-cerebellar neuronal circuit and are responsible for the formation of pre-motor patterns in the motor control system of the brain (Llinas and Yarom 1986; Welsh et al. 1995; Welsh and Llinas 1997; Lang et al. 1999; Llinas 2002). Oscillatory rhythms in hippocampus (5–10, and 40 Hz) are associated with short-term memory, body coordination and navigation in space (Lisman and Idiart 1995; Henze and Buzsaki 2003; Magee 2003; Jensen and Lisman 2005).

The intrinsic oscillatory rhythms are generated and persist due to the two following basic dynamical mechanisms: (1) due to local activity, cells can exhibit local oscillations. Such oscillations (e.g., pacemakers) can drive and synchronize the activity of the whole network; and (2) another case arises when the oscillations emerge from collective dynamics providing global feedback/feedforward neuronal loops, while the local cells constituting the network may not be true oscillators. In both cases, the evolution is governed by nonlinear mechanisms and results in the formation of self-sustained and reproducible oscillatory activity patterns. Such patterns are believed to be key elements for information representation in the brain (Llinas 2002). However, the question on how the brain operates with such elements (a brain "computing algorithm") is still open and represents a fundamental problem of information theory and neuroscience. It has become obvious that not only the presence of complex (non-local) network topology is responsible for information processing, but also the internal cell activity and particularly oscillatory rhythms (Llinas and Yarom 1986; Welsh et al. 1995; Welsh and Llinas 1997; Lang et al. 1999; Llinas 2002; Jensen and Lisman 2005).

In this chapter we focus on two particular examples of networks, beginning with consideration of cellular dynamics and progressing to emergent networks functions. For this purpose, we will use the simplified models of nonlinear dynamics reproducing only the specific features of real neuronal cells and real network topologies (Kazantsev, et al. 2003; Klinshov and Nekorkin 2008a).

We consider the oscillatory models of inferior olive networks and the olivocerebellar neuronal circuit which is responsible for the higher-level control of motor pattern generation (Welsh et al. 1995; Welsh and Llinas 1997). The second example is the hippocampal network with inhibitory feedback implementing short-term working memory in the form of oscillatory cluster sequences (Lisman and Idiart 1995; Jensen and Lisman 1996; Jensen and Lisman 2005).

2 Olivo-Cerebellar Neuronal Circuit and Motor Pattern Formation

The olivo-cerebellar system represents one of the key neuronal circuits in the brain. It is the motor control center providing highly coordinated activation of muscles to execute faithfully any movement of the body (Welsh et al. 1995; Welsh and Llinas 1997). It involves the inferior olive nucleus (ION) whose neurons project their axons (the climbing fibers), providing strong excitatory input to the Purkinje cell layer of the cerebellar cortex. The Purkinje cells send their axons to the cerebellar nuclei, which also receive collateral input from ION. Subgroups of these nuclear cells relay back to the ION completing the inhibitory neuronal loop (o). The ION neurons display rhythmic activity with the spikes occurring at the top of *quasisinusoidal* subthreshold oscillations with a *10 Hz* limit frequency (Llinas and Yarom 1986). The dendrites of the ION cells form gap junction couplings synchronizing cell oscillations. The couplings have been shown to be mainly local affecting about 50 neighboring cells (Llinas et al. 1974). The ION spikes activate the inhibitory loop leading to repetitive blocking of the gap junctions and desynchronizing cells. These two mechanisms of internal synchronization and desynchronization together with sensory and muscle reflex input result in the formation of spatio-temporal oscillatory clusters in the ION (Llinas et al. 1974; Welsh et al. 1995). Such clusters were monitored from the Purkinje cell layer with multiple electrode recordings (Lang et al. 1999). With temporally appropriate timing, the clusters control the sequence of pre-motor patterns to be processed by the motor execution system. The clusters implement motor intention patterns that are ultimately conveyed to the motor execution system (muscles) (Welsh et al. 1995). Given the biological necessity for rapid motor coordination, ION cluster configuration must be easily resettable in response to sensory stimuli. Recent *in vitro* experiments in rodent brainstem slices have shown that the ION oscillations have the amazing property of stimulus phase resetting, to an expected value, which is independent of the initial oscillatory phase (Leznik et al. 2002). Thus, neurons in the ION can be independently phase synchronized by a given stimulus.

3 Dynamical Model of Single ION Neuron

The ION neuron dynamics can be modeled by a behavior-based nonlinear dynamical system comprising two inter-acting FitzHugh-Nagumo subsystems (FitzHugh 1961; Kazantsev, et al. 2003) (Figure 9.1):

$$\varepsilon_{Na}\frac{du}{d(kt)} = f(u) - v;$$

$$\frac{dv}{d(kt)} = u - (z - I_{Ca}) - I_{Na};$$

$$\frac{dz}{dt} = f(z) - w;$$

$$\frac{dw}{dt} = \varepsilon_{Ca}(z - I_{Ca} - I_{ext}(t)).$$

(1)

The first subsystem (variables z and w) is responsible for the subthreshold oscillations and low-threshold (Ca^{2+}/K-dependent) spiking (mostly defined by the dendritic compartment of the ION cell membrane), whereas the variables u and v describe the higher-threshold (Na^+-dependent) somatic spiking. The parameters ε_{Ca} and ε_{Na} control the oscillation time scales. The parameters I_{Ca} and I_{Na} drive the depolarization level of the two compartments. Function $f(x)$ is a cubic shape nonlinear function of the form $f(x) = x(x - a_{Ca,Na})(1- x)$. The parameters $a_{Ca,Na}$ controls the shape of the nonlinear function (in particular the excitation threshold) and the shape of the excitation pulse for a particular subsystem. The parameter k adjusts the relative time scale of the oscillations between the two compartments. The function $I_{ext}(t)$ describes the extracellular stimulus.

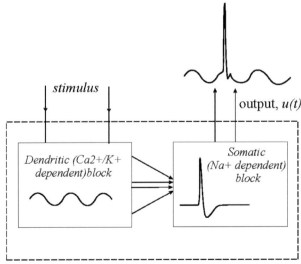

FIGURE 9.1   Schematic diagram of the two-block ION neuron model. The output spikes are generated on peaks of the low-amplitude subthreshold oscillations.

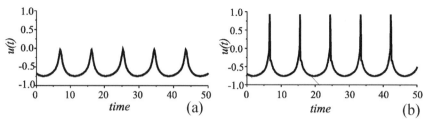

FIGURE 9.2 (a) Subthreshold oscillation of the ION neuron membrane potential, $u(t)$, induced by the dendritic compartment, e.g. by (z,w) subsystem. Parameter values: $\varepsilon_{Na} = 0.001$; $\varepsilon_{Ca} = 0.02$; $k = 0.1$; $I_{Ca} = 0.018$; $I_{Na} = -0.61$; $a_{Ca,Na} = 0.01$. (b) Na+ dependent spiking when (u,v) subsystem of the model (1) is activated at the oscillation peaks. Parameter values: $\varepsilon_{Na} = 0.001$; $\varepsilon_{Ca} = 0.02$; $k = 0.1$; $I_{Ca} = 0.018$; $I_{Na} = -0.59$; $a_{Ca,Na} = 0.01$. All variables, time and parameters are dimensionless.

When $I_{ext}(t)=0$, the model displays two basic dynamical modes depending on the depolarization parameters I_{Ca} and I_{Na}. For low-amplitude subthreshold oscillations generated by the (z,w) subsystem, the excitable (u,v) block is inactive and no spikes are fired (Figure 9.2A). With increasing I_{Ca}, the amplitude grows and reaches the excitation threshold, specifically on peaks of the (z,w) oscillation (Figure 9.2B).

The relative time scale between the two subsystems is set so that only one spike is generated at each peak. Note that due to the nonlinear dynamics of the FitzHugh-Nagumo model, the shape of the subthreshold (z,w) oscillations have quite sharp peaks. Therefore the output spikes synchronized with peak times acquire very precise timing defined by the 10 Hz subthreshold signal. It is also obvious that the spiking times (e.g. time instants when the spikes are generated) are defined by the phase of the subthreshold signal. Since we have assumed that there is no feedback from the (u,v) to (z,w) subsystem (e.g., we neglect backpropagation) the subthreshold dynamics of the (z,w) subsystem uniquely defines the phase of the ION neuron action potentials.

4 Self-referential Phase Reset

It has been found experimentally that phase dynamics of the ION oscillator has a specific property *called self-referential phase reset* (SPR) (Leznik et al. 2002; Kazantsev, et al. 2004). This means that when the neuron is stimulated by a sufficiently strong extracellular stimulus, its phase resets to a value independent of the initial phase and defined only by the stimulus intensity.

To show that model (1) can describe this property we consider in detail the dynamics of the oscillatory component (Ca^{2+}/K^+ dependent) of the ION neuron model stimulated by pulses with controllable amplitude and duration:

$$I_{ext}(t) = \langle A_{st}; t \in [t_j; t_j + \tau_{st}]; 0 \text{ otherwise} \rangle$$

where A_{st} and τ_{st} are stimulus amplitude and duration, respectively, and t_j is the time instants when the j-th pulse from an input sequence is applied. We fix the parameters of Equation (1) ($a_{Ca} = 0.01$; $\varepsilon_{Ca} = 0.02$; $I_{Ca} = 0.01$) in the neighborhood of a supercritical Andronov-Hopf bifurcation when the limit cycle appears on the phase plane of the (z,w) subsystem for $I_{ext}(t) = 0$ (Figure 9.3). The limit cycle is located near the minimum of $f(z)$. Then, the oscillation has a quasisinusoidal shape, while other motions on the phase plane have fast and slow features. A reference signal, $x(t)$, is taken to have the same period, T, as the control oscillator (1). That is, it can be described by Equation (1) in the autonomous case, $I_{ext} = 0$. And so, we define relative phase as the phase shift with respect to the reference signal using the peak times as a descriptor:

$$\varphi = 2\pi \frac{p_u - p_x}{T} \mod 2\pi \qquad (2)$$

where p_u and p_x ($p_u > p_x$) are the peak times of $u(t)$ and $x(t)$, respectively. Then, the phase, φ, is defined within the interval $[0, 2\pi]$. Note that the peak time phase definition is motivated by ION dynamics since it corresponds to the time instants of action potential generation. We also assume that the input signal, I_{ext}, satisfies the two following conditions: (A) The input pulse times, t_i, are synchronized with the reference signal, $t_i = p_x + mT$; $m \in Z$. (B) The interval between two neighboring input pulses, $t_{i+1} - t_i = nT$; $n \in Z$, is sufficiently long, i.e.

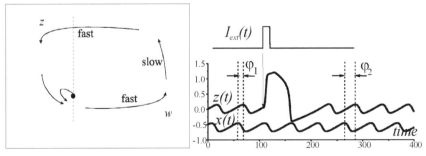

FIGURE 9.3   Qualitative view of the phase plane of autonomous FitzHugh-Nagumo model ((z,w) subsystem), $I_{ext} = 0$ in Equation 1. (b). Phase definition using peak times relative to the reference oscillator.

$n \gg 1$. The second assumption allows us to use the *phase response curve* (PRC) to characterize the dynamics of a multiple pulse stimulus.

Let us investigate the dynamics of phase variable (2) when the pulse stimulus is applied in Equation (1). Let φ_n be the initial phase shift between the control and reference signals. At the arrival time of the stimulus pulse the system dynamics is described by the autonomous FitzHugh-Nagumo model with effective depolarization parameter, $I_{eff} = I_{Ca} + A_{st}$. In particular, it can be shifted along the u-nullcline to its positive slope compartments where the oscillations disappear. Thus, trajectories originating at the limit cycle circle may have a long excursion in the phase plane during the stimulus. Following stimulus termination, the oscillation recovers its shape and frequency with the new phase φ_{n+1}. Assumption (B) requires sufficient elapsed time for the trajectory to return to the neighborhood of the invariant cycle before the next stimulus pulse comes. At that point, the phase dynamics can be characterized approximately by a 1D point map

$$\varphi_{n+1} = \Pi \varphi_n \qquad (3)$$

Equation (3) represents the relative phase circle map. The phase is invariant in the absence of a stimulus. Iterating the map in the presence of a stimulus one can follow the oscillator phase evolution. The function $\Pi(\varphi)$ represents the PRC for model (1).

Let the stimulation be sufficiently strong ($A_{st} \sim 1$, $\tau_{st} \sim T$), then, the $\Pi(\varphi)$, for this case (Figure 9.4A) is close to a constant line. This means that a single stimulation pulse maps all initial phases from the interval $[0,2\pi]$ to the small interval $\Delta \varphi \ll 2\pi$ located in the neighborhood of the stable (*superstable*) fixed point φ^*. That is, after stimulation, all points, initially distributed along the limit cycle, return to being close to in-phase. The dependence of the phase compression factor defined as $\delta \varphi = \Delta \varphi / 2\pi$ on the stimulus amplitude for single and doublet stimuli satisfying (A) and (B) is shown in Figure 9.4B. Figure 9.4C illustrates $N=20$ superimposed oscillations with initial phases uniformly distributed in the $[0;2\pi]$ interval (i.e., along the limit cycle) in Figure 9.4A. Note that the reset is remarkably similar to the ION neurons experimental data (Leznik et al. 2002). Note also that along with excitatory stimulus ($A_{st} > 0$), the reset also takes place after inhibitory potentials ($A_{st} < 0$) (Figure 9.4D), and that the reset occurs rather fast. It takes only a few oscillation periods ($\sim 2T$ for excitatory stimulus and $\sim 1.5T$ for inhibitory pulse) to recover the oscillation shape.

It is important that the reset phase in the SPR effect can take any value within the interval $[0,2\pi]$. So that, by varying the stimulus intensity in the model (1),

OSCILLATORY DYNAMICS OF SPIKING NEURONS

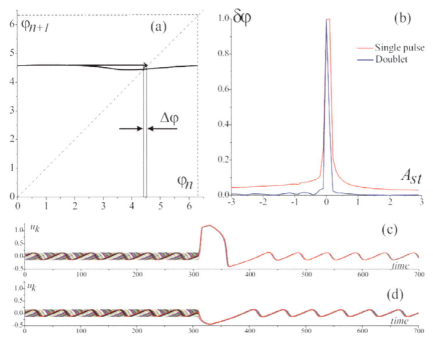

FIGURE 9.4 Self-referential phase reset in the model (1). (a) The PRC calculated for $A_{st}=3$; $\tau_{st}=0.5T$; $T=51.11$. (b) The dependence of the compression factor $\delta\varphi$ on the stimulus amplitude for fixed $\tau_{st} = 0.5T$. (c) Superimposed oscillation traces from $N=20$ initial phases, $A_{st}=1.15$; $\tau_{st} = 0.4T$. (d) The reset due to inhibitory stimulus, $A_{st}=-1$; $\tau_{st}=0.4T$. All units are dimensionless.

one can set any desired phase independently of the initial phase at which the pulse has been applied. The neuron, in fact, forgets the previous (initial) state. Similar to the concept of *auto-oscillations* (e.g., the oscillations with stable and "self-recovered" shape, e.g. amplitude and frequency) in nonlinear dissipative systems, the SPR can be treated as an *auto-reset*. The phase control diagram is illustrated in Figure 9.5.

5 Phase Sequences and Spiking Phase Information Encoding

Many interesting properties of phase map (3) appear with shorter stimulation pulses ($\tau_{st}<<T$)o (Kazantsev, et al. 2004). This case is also biologically relevant since a stimulus may arrive at a neuron via many synaptic couplings or as a sequence of action potentials. For example, ION spikes are about hundred times shorter than the period of subthreshold oscillations. Let us fix the

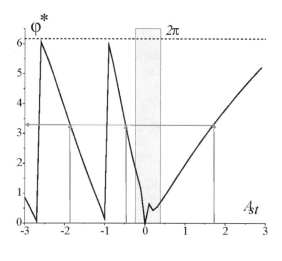

FIGURE 9.5 The dependence of the reset phase on the stimulus amplitude for fixed duration $\tau_{st}=0.4T$

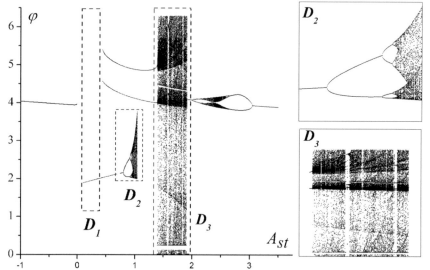

FIGURE 9.6 Bifurcation diagram of the reset phase for $\tau_{st}=0.01T$. The map (3) was iterated for different initial conditions. For each value of A_{st} the set of *100* limit points was depicted on the diagram after *1000* transient iterations.

stimulus duration $\tau_{st}=0.01T$. We also suppose that the model (1) is stimulated by a sequence of pulses satisfying the assumptions (A) and (B). Then, the evolution of the oscillation phase is defined by the sequential iterations of the PRC. Map attractors describe the stationary phase states that may appear for different initial conditions. Different attractors that respond to changing stimulus amplitude, A_{st}, are illustrated in the bifurcation diagram shown in Figure 9.6.

OSCILLATORY DYNAMICS OF SPIKING NEURONS   251

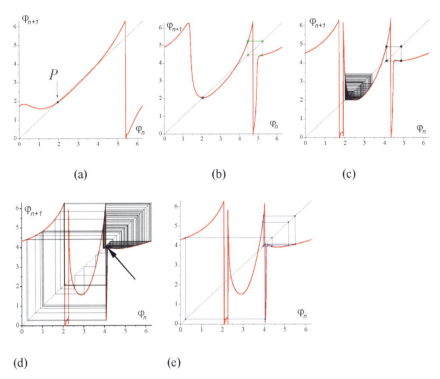

FIGURE 9.7   Phase map (e.g. phase reset curves) (3) for fixed $\tau_{st}=0.01T$. (a) $A_{st}=0.15$. P- is the stable fixed point. (b) $A_{st}=0.5$. Coexistence of stable fixed point and period 2 map cycle. (c) $A_{st}=1.02$. Coexistence of period 2 cycle and chaotic attractor. (d) $A_{st}=1.62$. Chaotic attractor with intermittency. (e) $A_{st}=1.66$. A periodic window inside the region D_3

Obviously, for $A_{st}=0$ the PRC coincides with the diagonal, so that any initial phase remains unchanged. For illustration purposes, we describe only a few important types of behavior in the regions shown in Figure 9.6. In region D_1, the stable fixed point appears to attract all map trajectories with $n \to \infty$. In this case, the map derivative $\Pi'(\varphi)$ is close to 1, hence the map trajectories have quite a long transition before reaching the fixed point (Figure 9.7A). In other words, the SPR also occurs, but it takes a long time for the system to "forget" the initial state. When increasing the stimulus amplitude (between the regions D_1 and D_2), the stable fixed point coexists with period 2 stable cycles (Figure 9.7B), i.e. the phase map displays *multistability*. In other words, for a different initial state the system is reset to different attractors. Now we focus on two regions D_2 and D_3 (enlarged in Figure 9.6). A classical period doubling bifurcation cascade occurs in D_2 and the map exhibits chaotic behavior (Figure 9.7C) coexisting with a period 2 stable limit cycle. Theoretically, all 2^m, $m=1,2,...,\infty$ orbits may co-exist. Each orbit can be stabilized by changing the stimulus amplitude. Then, after each stimulus pulse the oscillation phase jumps along the orbit. Furthermore, spiking behavior of the ION neuron displays the spike sequences encoded by the orbits. This could be viewed as a built-in mechanism for information encoding in the oscillatory neurons when the spike timings are associated with a well-defined stimulus-dependent phase reset. Another interesting behavior appears in region D_3. Here the attractors are characterized by intermittent behavior (Figure 9.7D). The map trajectories remain for a long time near the saddle-node bifurcation point followed by long excursions in the whole invariant $[0,2\pi]$ region. The regions of chaotic behavior alternate with regular windows where stable periodic orbits exist (Figure 9.7E). Each orbit also represents the encoded phase sequences realized for particular values of stimulus amplitude.

Figure 9.8 shows typical time dynamics of the phase variable that defines the spiking times in the ION neuron model (1). Thus, under pulse stimulation, the ION neurons (1) are capable of generating spiking activity patterns with controllable (predicted) spiking time behavior. The patterns are associated with phase sequences defined by the phase map (3). In turn, the phase values determine relative time moments when the spikes are generated in the ION neuron model. In other words, the phase sequences can be treated as the elements of a dynamic code where the parameters of the input stimulus (amplitude and duration) are transformed into the phases of the output spikes.

6   Network Model of the Olivo-Cerebellar Neuronal Loop

As noted in previously, ION neurons are inter-coupled by gap junctions. These junctions can be modeled by the addition of a linear difference term to the dendritic compartment of the model (1) as a coupling current proportional to the difference between the membrane potentials of the dendrites of neighboring ION neurons:

$$I_{gap} = d(z_2 - z_1) \tag{4}$$

where d accounts for the coupling strength (e.g. the integral conductance of the gap junctions). When an ION fires a spike, the olivo-cerebellar feedback is activated. Propagating via Purkinje cells and cerebellar nuclei the signals activate the inhibitory synapses that block the gap junctions. In terms of

OSCILLATORY DYNAMICS OF SPIKING NEURONS 253

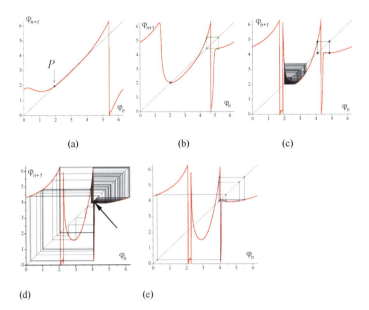

Phase map (e.g. phase reset curves) (3) for fixed $\tau_{st} = 0.01T$. (a) $A_{st} = 0.15$. P- is the stable fixed point. (b) $A_{st} = 0.5$. Coexistence of stable fixed point and period 2 map cycle. (d) $A_{st} = 1.02$. Coexistence of period 2 cycle and chaotic attractor. (e) $A_{st} = 1.62$. Chaotic attractor with intermittency. (e) $A_{st} = 1.66$. A periodic window inside the region D_3.

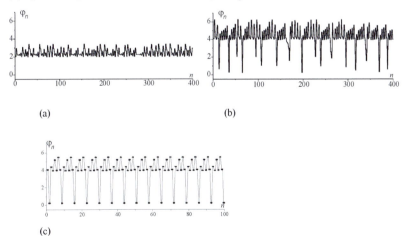

FIGURE 9.8 Phase sequences corresponding to the map (3). (a), (b) Chaotic trajectories corresponding to the attractors shown in Figures 9.7 (c) and (d), respectively. (c) Stable periodic sequence corresponding to the periodic cycle Figure 9.7 (e)

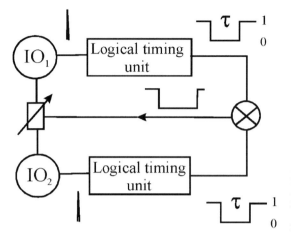

FIGURE 9.9
Block-diagram of the pulse-controlled coupling between two neighboring ION neurons

mathematical models (1) and (4), this means that the coupling coefficient d decreases when the olivo-cerebellar loop is active. The schematic diagram of such a *pulse controlled coupling* is illustrated in Figure 9.9.

The duration of the coupling inhibition induced by a single spike is less than 100 msec, e.g. the ION neurons oscillation period. Moreover, the durations are summarized if the neighboring neurons fire asynchronously. This feature is principally important for the sustainability of the inter-unit phase locking modes. In other words, if the ION spikes are fired synchronously, the neurons tend to sustain their synchronization. However, if the spikes are generated with a certain phase lag, its duration is added to the inhibition period and, hence, to the interval when the neurons are effectively uncoupled with no locking. Typical signals generated by the two ION neurons (1), (4) with pulse inhibition are illustrated in Figure 9.10.

7 Phase Clusters in the IONs Network

Let us now consider the activity of the network of ION neurons coupled by gap junctions with inhibitory feedback. Nonlinear equations for the network based on (1) and (4) can be written in the following form:

OSCILLATORY DYNAMICS OF SPIKING NEURONS

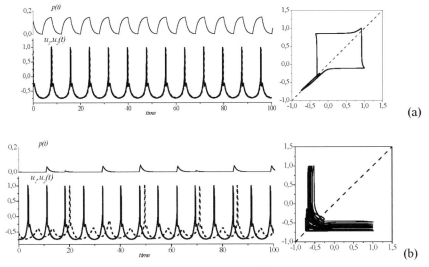

FIGURE 9.10 (a) Synchronization with spiking phase locking, $a_{Ca}=0.01$, $\varepsilon_{Ca}=0.02$, $\varepsilon_{Na}=0.001$, $I_{Ca(1)}=0.014$, $I_{Na}=-0.55$, $\delta I_{Ca}=0.15$, $d=0.015$, $\tau=4$, $\alpha=1$. (b) Asynchronous oscillations (no phase locking) $a_{Ca}=0.01$, $\varepsilon_{Ca}=0.02$, $\varepsilon_{Na}=0.001$, $I_{Ca(1)}=0.014$, $I_{Na}=-0.55$, $\delta I_{Ca}=0.15$, $d=0.015$, $\tau=7$, $\alpha=1$. $p(t)\sim d$ is the time varying coupling strength.

$$\begin{cases} \varepsilon_{Na}\dfrac{du_{j,k}}{dt} = f(u_{j,k}) - v_{j,k}; \\[4pt] \dfrac{dv_{j,k}}{dt} = u_{j,k} - (z_{j,k} - I_{Ca}) - I_{Na}; \\[4pt] \dfrac{dz_{j,k}}{d(kt)} = f(z_{j,k}) - w_{j,k} + d(\Delta_p z)_{j,k}; \\[4pt] \dfrac{dw_{j,k}}{d(kt)} = \varepsilon_{Ca}(Z_{j,k} - I_{Ca}); \end{cases} \qquad (5)$$

where d is the constant coupling coefficient (e.g. maximal gap junction conductance) when the olivo-cerebellar loop is blocked,

$$\begin{aligned}(\Delta_p z)_{j,k} = \ & P(u_{j,k})P(u_{j+1,k})P_{st}(|\psi_{j,k}-\psi_{j+1,k}|)(z_{j+1,k}-z_{j,k})+ \\ & +P(u_{j,k})P(u_{j-1,k})P_{st}(|\psi_{j,k}-\psi_{j-1,k}|)(z_{j-1,k}-z_{j,k})+ \\ & +P(u_{j,k})P(u_{j,k+1})P_{st}(|\psi_{j,k}-\psi_{j,k+1}|)(z_{j,k+1}-z_{j,k})+ \\ & +P(u_{j,k})P(u_{j,k-1})P_{st}(|\psi_{j,k}-\psi_{j,k-1}|)(z_{j,k-1}-z_{j,k}).\end{aligned} \qquad (6)$$

Here the function P describes the action of the inhibitory feedback. The simplest implementation of P is a binary function switched on/off by the IONs spikes. It can be written in the form:

$$P(u) = \begin{cases} 1, & \text{if } t < t_{IO}(u); \\ 0, & \text{if } t_{IO}(u) < t < t_{IO}(u) + \tau, \end{cases} \quad (7)$$

where $t_{IO}(u)$ is the time moments when the somatic ION spikes are generated, τ is the duration of the inhibition pulse. The function $P_{st}(x)$ describes the action of an external stimulus coming to the ION network from cerebellar nuclei and, hence, blocking the gap junctions according to a certain spatial distribution. For illustration, we assume that the stimulus represents a two-dimensional gray-scale picture in the form of squares with different color intensities from black to white. We introduce the stimulus function, $P_{st}(x)$, in the form:

$$P_{st}(x) = \begin{cases} 1, & \text{if } x < \delta; \\ 0, & \text{if } x < \delta, \end{cases} \quad (8)$$

where δ is a small positive quantity defining the resolution of the model (5) with the system implementing a given stimulus as phase clusters. The function P_{st} blocks the coupling in the ION network along the interfaces between different stimulus intensities, that is, between the groups of synchronized cerebellar nuclei projecting the stimulus into the ION. The ION neurons within the same "color grade" δ become effectively uncoupled with the other groups. Within each group, the dynamics is governed by the internal feedback loop sustaining phase-locked synchronized spiking (the function P).

Let us first consider spontaneous dynamics when no stimulus is presented. Evolution of spiking phases is illustrated in Figure 9.11. Starting from an initially random phase distribution, the network evolves to a certain phase cluster state. It may be noted that the spatial configuration of the clusters is sustained for quite a long period of time. This happens due to inhibitory feedback mechanisms which stabilize synchronous spiking events. The actual distribution of the phase clusters depends on the initial conditions. When a certain stimulus is applied using (8), the contours of the resulting state are defined by the interfaces between different intensity levels (differed on values more than δ). The profile of stimulus-induced cluster formation is shown in Figure 9.12. It may be

OSCILLATORY DYNAMICS OF SPIKING NEURONS 257

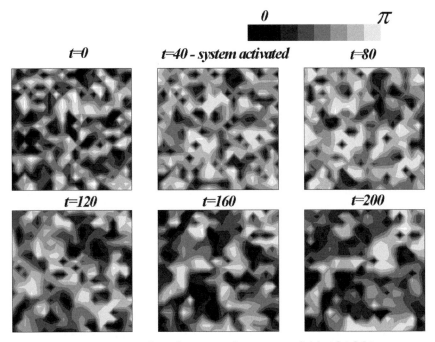

FIGURE 9.11   Spontaneous phase clustering in the ION network (5) with inhibitory feedback. Parameter values: $a=0.01$, $\varepsilon_{Ca}=0.02$, $\varepsilon_{Na}=0.001$, $I_{Ca(1)}=0.014$, $I_{Na}=-0.55$, $\delta II_{Ca}=0.15$, $d=0.14$, $\tau=0.9T$, $T=7.4$.

noted that only the contours of the desired pattern have been implemented, while inside the group, the dynamics is defined by the internal coupling break mechanism. Due to the small initial frequency difference (I_{Ca} is randomly distributed within $[I_{Ca}, I_{Ca}+\delta I_{Ca}]$ for the ION neurons), the inter-cluster phase shift relations slowly evolve. Once more, it may be noted that the phase pattern uniquely defines the spiking times in the ION network.

8   Reset of the Clusters in the IONs Network

To reset the spiking phases of the oscillators to the correct (desired) values, we use the self-referential phase reset in the ION neurons that occurs when they are stimulated by the *direct* pulse input. Since the reset phase does not depend on the initial state, the direct stimulus can be encoded by the intensities of the stimulation pulse (Figure 9.5). We add to the *ION* network model (5) the direct stimulus, so that the complete mathematical model is written as follows:

$$\begin{cases} \varepsilon_{Na}\dfrac{du_{j,k}}{dt}=f(u_{j,k})-v_{j,k};\\ \dfrac{dv_{j,k}}{dt}=u_{j,k}-(z_{j,k}-I_{Ca})-I_{Na};\\ \dfrac{dz_{j,k}}{d(kt)}=f(z_{j,k})-w_{j,k}+d(\Delta_p z)_{j,k};\\ \dfrac{dw_{j,k}}{d(kt)}=\varepsilon_{Ca}(z_{j,k}-I_{Ca}-I^{st}_{j,k}(\psi,t)); \end{cases} \qquad (9)$$

where $I^{st}_{j,k}$ is given by:

$$I^{st}_{j,k}(\Psi,t)=\begin{cases} A_o+(A_1-A_o)\dfrac{\psi_{j,k}-\psi_{min}}{\psi_{max}-\psi_{min}}, & \text{if } t_{st}<t<t_{st}+\tau_{st}\\ 0, & \text{if } t<t_{st}\end{cases} \qquad (10)$$

The matrix $\Psi=\{\psi_{j,k}\}$ describes the intensities of the stimulus pattern. For convenience, we express its values in phase terms, that is, the matrix values represent the desired phase shift to be set and sustained in the given ION neuron. We assume that the elements are scaled within some interval $\{\psi_{j,k}\}\in[\psi_{min},\psi_{max}]$. According to (10), this interval is mapped to the interval of amplitudes of the input pulses, $A_{st}\in[A_o,A_1]$. The latter, in turn, determines the interval of the reset phases $A_{st}\in[A_o,A_1]$. (Fig. 9.5). The time moment t_{st} defines the stimulation time. It may be noted that the stimulus must be applied simultaneously

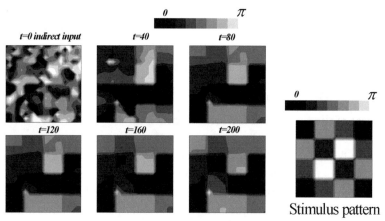

FIGURE 9.12 Phase clusters the ION network (5) induced by an "indirect" stimulus coming from cerebellar nuclei and blocking the ION gap junctions. Parameter values: $a=0.01$, $\varepsilon_{Ca}=0.02$, $\varepsilon_{Na}=0.001$, $I_{Ca(1)}=0.014$, $I_{Na}=-0.55$, $\delta I_{Ca}=0.15$, $d=0.14$, $\tau=0.9T$, $T=7.4$.

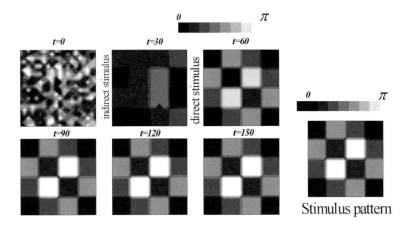

(a)

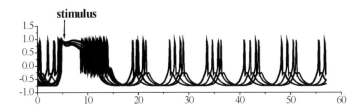

(b)

FIGURE 9.13 Phase clusters in the ION network (9) induced by the self-referential phase reset. The stimulus pattern is encoded according to (10) with $\psi_{min}=0$, $\psi_{max}=\pi$. Parameter values: $a=0.01$, $\varepsilon_{Ca}=0.02$, $\varepsilon_{Na}=0.001$, $I_{Ca(1)}=0.014$, $I_{Na}=-0.55$, $\delta I\, I_{Ca}=0.15$, $d=0.14$, $\tau=0.9T$, $T=7.4$. (a) Sequence of snapshots of subthreshold oscillation phases. (b) Spiking oscillations with phase locking (u-variable).

(or with precise timing defined by the subthreshold oscillation period) to achieve correct phase locking. All the phases may be accounted for relative to a base or reference oscillator with 10 Hz frequency.

Figure 9.13 illustrates the process of stimulus representation as a self-sustainable spiking pattern in the ION network. It may be noted that the process of cluster formation in the case of a direct stimulus is quite fast. It takes one or two periods to achieve the final distribution. Thus, the ION network can be easily rearranged if another command has arrived. Due to internal inhibitory feedback, the current distribution can be conserved for an extended duration since the synchronized spiking clusters do not effectively interact. The resulting phase distribution reproduces the stimulus profile quite precisely. The model can resolve up to $M=\pi/\delta$ stimulus intensity grades (phases).

Here, the parameter δ introduced in (8) can be treated as the precision of the SPR effect (phase compression factor, Figure 9.5).

Furthermore, we note that according to the results described above, the direct input can also provide temporal spiking phase encoding for lower stimulus intensities. In particular, the direct input to the ION network together with the internal inhibitory feedback, may provide spatio-temporal spiking pattern sequences which implement dynamically encoded pre-motor pattern search predictions.

9 Neuronal Network Model for Hippocampal Short-term Memory

Temporary storage of information is one of the key features of neuronal systems (Baddeley 1996). The system used for this purpose is referred to as *short-term memory*, or *working memory*. The existence of short-term memory as an important component of memory in living systems was postulated by Hebb (1949). Atkinson and Shiffrin defined short-term memory as a system where information is stored while it is being used (Atkinson and Shiffrin 1968). After which the information can be forgotten or saved into the so-called long-term memory. Information storage for different types of memory involves various neural systems and different neural mechanisms (Abeles 1991; Kandel et al. 1991; Lisman and Idiart 1995; Haken 2000).

The study of short-term memory functions of the brain is an important and very exciting problem within neuroscience that has been intensively investigated from the 1950s until the present. There are a great number of experiments shedding light on the features of working memory. Since the early 1970s, there has been evidence that cortex, and especially prefrontal cortex, plays a crucial role in working memory (Fuster and Alexander 1971; Goldman-Rakic 1987; Fuster 1989; Goldman-Rakic 1995; D'Esposito et al. 1998; Bisley et al. 2001). Working memory fractionation has been demonstrated (Baddeley 1996), and its different components such as a verbal system or a visual-spatial system have been shown to be independent, corresponding to separate "processing streams" (Ruchkin et al. 1997). The duration of information storage in working memory is limited to about 1–100 seconds (Peterson and Peterson 1959; Lisman and Idiart 1995) and its capacity is sufficient to store about 5–9 symbols or "chunks" of information simultaneously (Miller 1956; Lisman and Idiart 1995; Cowan 2000). Working memory is characterized by the appearance of persistent neural activity associated with retention of the information after a transient input. There are two main concepts explaining the neural mechanisms for this phenomenon. The first supposes the presence of locked synaptic loops, and data storage corresponds to reverberatory excitation in these loops (Wang 2001). The second concept links data storage with the emergence of persistent neural activity in the cortex representing the encoding of information (Lisman and Idiart 1995; Haken 2000; Jensen and Lisman 2005). It is believed that simple signals can be stored in the brain using reverberation in locked synaptic loops, but more complex information (for example, visual images) is stored in the form of structures of sustained neural activity. When data is loaded into the memory, such structures, or clusters, appear in the cortex and exist for some time in conjunction with the retention of information.

Lisman and colleagues (Lisman and Idiart 1995; Jensen and Lisman 1996; Jensen and Lisman 2005) proposed a short-term memory circuit based on a specific property of certain neurons called *afterdepolarization* (ADP), or *delayed after-potenital-*. This property involves a temporary increase of membrane excitability after neuronal firing. The ADP-based memory system represents a network of pyramidal neurons with ADP residing in the cortex. The network is under the influence of subthreshold oscillatory signals within the theta (5–8 Hz) frequency range. This network also receives data from the outside in the form of transient pulses. Then, a subset of neurons appears, firing in synchrony and representing encoded information. This subset of neurons fires periodically in every cycle of the oscillatory signal, and data storage is maintained. The pyramidal neurons also make synapses onto the interneurons which inhibit them. This inhibitory feedback produces several gamma-frequency (30–80 Hz) subcycles and one theta-frequency cycle. Several subsets of pyramidal neurons can fire in different subcycles, which means storage of several memories simultaneously.

10   Basic Unit of the Network

ADP is a well-known property of some neurons (Izhikevich 2005; Lisman and Idiart, "Storage of 7±2 short-term memories in oscillatory subcycles," 1512–15). It consists of a temporary increase in membrane excitability after the neuron's firing. Initially the neuron is at rest and has a normal excitation threshold. After being stimulated by a transient pulse, the neuron produces an action potential, and after a short refractory period, the membrane potential rises and becomes larger than the initial value. This means that the excitation threshold becomes lower. After some time, the membrane potential and the excitation threshold regain their normal values, and the neuron comes back to rest.

In this chapter we propose the following model of a neuron with ADP (Klinshov and Nekorkin 2005; Klinshov and Nekorkin 2008a; Klinshov and Nekorkin 2008b).

$$\begin{cases} \varepsilon \dfrac{du}{dt} = v - f(u), \\ \dfrac{dv}{dt} = w - g(u) + x(t), \\ \dfrac{dw}{dt} = -\beta w + \gamma \left[p\left(u - \dfrac{1}{2}\right) - p(w - w_o) \right], \end{cases} \qquad (11)$$

where variable u describes the membrane potential of the neuron, v is the recovery variable, w describes excitability of the membrane, and $x(t)$ is an external input. Function $f(u)$ is the piecewise cubic-shaped nonlinearity

$$f(u) = \begin{cases} u, & u < \sigma \\ \sigma - 2\sigma \dfrac{u - \sigma}{1 - 2\sigma}, & \sigma \leq u \leq 1 - \sigma, \\ u - 1, & u \geq 1 - \sigma, \end{cases}$$

function $g(u)$ is defined as

$$g(u) = \begin{cases} u, & u \leq \dfrac{1}{2}, \\ \dfrac{1}{2} + \alpha\left(u - \dfrac{1}{2}\right), & u \geq \dfrac{1}{2}, \end{cases}$$

and parameters α and σ determine the form of these functions. Function $p(u)$ is a step function

$$p(u) = \begin{cases} 0, & u \leq 0, \\ u/\varkappa, & 0 \leq u \leq \varkappa, \\ 1, & u \geq \varkappa \end{cases}$$

OSCILLATORY DYNAMICS OF SPIKING NEURONS 263

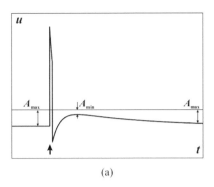
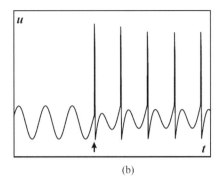

FIGURE 9.14 Dynamics of system (11) after stimulation by a short pulse. Note that the dynamics of the model is similar to the dynamics of a living neuron (Lisman and Idiart 1995). Dynamics of system (11): the transient pulse switches subthreshold oscillations to the mode of periodical firing.

and parameter $\varkappa \ll 1$ characterizes its slope. Parameter $\varkappa \ll 1$ characterizes electrical capacity of the membrane, parameters γ and β denote the excitability growth and recovery rates, respectively. Parameter w_0 is the maximal value of excitability.

Typical regimes of temporal behavior of the system (11) are shown in Figure 9.14.

11 Memory Function

The memory of a single unit. Let us set the signal $x(t)$ to be a sum of a subthreshold sinusoidal input and a short exciting (information) stimulus, so that

$$x(t) = V \cos \frac{2\pi t}{T} + A\delta(t - \tau), \qquad (12)$$

where V is the amplitude of the sinusoidal signal, T is its period, A is the amplitude of the information stimulus and $\delta > 0$ is the moment of its action. If the neuron was initially at rest ($u = v = w = 0$ for $t = 0$), it oscillates under the threshold for $0 < t < \tau$. At $t = t_i$ the neuron is excited, and for $t > t_i$ it starts producing spikes periodically (Figure 9.14). Since spike activity begins after the external pulse, there must be retention of information concerning this input. This means that the system exhibits a memory function, retaining information concerning the pulse arrival.

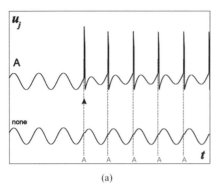 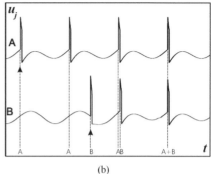

FIGURE 9.15 Dynamics of an ensemble of non-interacting neurons. Different curves correspond to different subsets (clusters) of neurons. The curves are shifted vertically for convenience. (a) Storage of the information item A in the network of non-interacting neurons. The cluster of periodic neural activity appears and represents the loaded item. (b) An unsuccessful attempt to input two items A and B: after a short transient process, we get the cluster representing both items merged together (A+B).

The memory of an ensemble of non-interacting units. As it was shown above, one neuron can store 1 bit of information. If one wants to store more data, a number of such units should be used. N independent neurons can store information about N applied pulses (i.e., N bits of information). For example, consider a digitized black-and-white image consisting of N pixels. If we have an ensemble of N units, each of them can "remember" the color of one pixel. To load the image into memory, exciting pulses must be applied only to the units corresponding to white pixels of the image (i.e., $A=A_0>0$ for the "white" elements, and $A=0$ for the "black" ones). After arrival of the pulses, a cluster of periodic spiking activity appears. The shape of the cluster corresponds to the loaded image (Figure 9.15), with it saved in memory.

Information erasing. The memory system must realize not only data storage, but data erasing too. In our system it can be achieved in two ways: the first way (active) is to apply pulses of negative polarity to all the units (or to firing units only), then after some time they return to the mode of subthreshold oscillations. The second way (passive) is to terminate the sinusoidal signal or to weaken its amplitude. Then, all the units go to rest or start subthreshold oscillations. In both the cases, the ensemble reaches the unexcited state and the data is erased. If the first way is erasing in the true sense, the second can be named 'oblivion'. Accordingly, the presence of the oscillatory input $x(t)$ can be treated as an attention mechanism: when it is present, information retention continues, but when it terminates or weakens, the information is forgotten.

12 A Network with Inhibitory Feedback

We have shown that a network of non-interacting neurons is capable of information storage. But this system has a serious disadvantage, because it can store only *one* data item, whereas, for example, human memory can store about seven different memories simultaneously (Lisman and Idiart 1995). If we sequentially load several items into the studied network we will get a cluster corresponding to *all of them* merged (Figure 9.15B). For example, if we load several black-and-white images, we will get a cluster containing the "white" elements of all the pictures.

Below we show that this defect can be corrected by adding global inhibitory feedback into the network. We modify the network so it can store several items simultaneously. Each item corresponds to some subset, or cluster of neurons. The modified working memory circuit is the following (Figure 9.16A). It is based on a set of N neurons, each having two inputs: a common sinusoidal input and an individual information input. The oscillatory signal plays the role of the attention mechanism providing a possibility of data storage, and transient information pulses load the data, as if an ensemble of non-interacting neurons. In addition, an inhibitory circuit ("interneuron") is present. It is activated when at least one of N neurons is excited and prevents excitation of all the others. The modified system with feedback has the following form:

$$\begin{cases} \varepsilon \dfrac{du_j}{dt} = v_j - f(u_j), \\ \dfrac{dv_j}{dt} = w_j - u_j + x_j(t) - \lambda F, \\ \dfrac{dw_j}{dt} = -\beta w_j + \gamma \left[p\left(u_j - \dfrac{1}{2}\right) - p(w_j - w_o) \right], \end{cases} \quad (13)$$

where $j=1,\ldots,N$ is the number of the unit, u_j, v_j, w_j and $x_j(t)$ are similar to u, v, w and $x(t)$ in (11) for the j-th neuron. V and T are the amplitude and period of the sinusoidal external signal, A_j and τ_j correspond to the amplitude and activation moment of the information pulse applied to the j-th neuron. F is the inhibition potential, and λ is the inhibition strength coefficient.

The addition of the inhibitory feedback results in the appearance of new interesting dynamical modes of the system. Now it can store several data items in sequentially firing clusters of activity. Each of the items is represented by some subset of units. The inhibitory feedback provides time division of stored

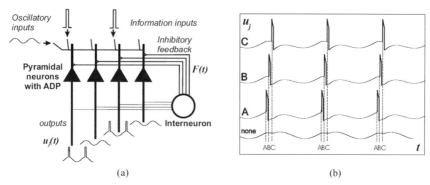

FIGURE 9.16 (a) The ADP-based working memory circuit described by system (13). (b) Dynamics of the circuit. Different curves correspond to different clusters. The curves are shifted vertically for convenience. The system stores *three* items A, B, C simultaneously in the form of three sequentially firing clusters.

items (this idea is similar to that from: Wang and Terman 1994; Campbell et al. 1999; Wang and Terman 1997). In Figure 19.16(b) one can see an example of such dynamics. Units of the network ($N=36$) are grouped into four clusters, three of them are excited periodically in different phases of the sinusoidal signal, and the fourth one oscillates under the subthreshold. Three periodically firing clusters correspond to three different items stored in the memory.

Sequential items loading. To explain this property of the system, let us consider the process of sequential loading of several items into the memory of the system. Let us load three items – A, B and C in a network of $N=6\times6=36$ units (Figure 19.17). For example, let A be a "line" of three units, B – a "square" of four units and C – a "triangle" of six units. Initially, all the units oscillate under the threshold. When we load the first item A, the situation is like the case of a network of independent units: the neurons which have received information pulses begin to fire periodically, and the cluster of periodic activity appears, corresponding to the first item. The second item B is loaded in a similar way but it is important to apply information pulses at the instant when the first cluster is not excited. Then, all the units corresponding to the second item are forced into the tonal spiking mode, like the units of the first item. But in the next cycle of the oscillatory signal, the first cluster fires a little earlier, when the second one is still under the threshold. The inhibitory feedback circuit activates and prevents excitation of the second cluster. Further behavior of the network depends on the inhibition strength. If it is sufficiently weak, the inhibition cannot stop the second cluster excitation. It will be excited in spite of the inhibition, and the inter-spike interval between the two clusters will be close to zero. This means that the two items will merge. But if the inhibition is

OSCILLATORY DYNAMICS OF SPIKING NEURONS 267

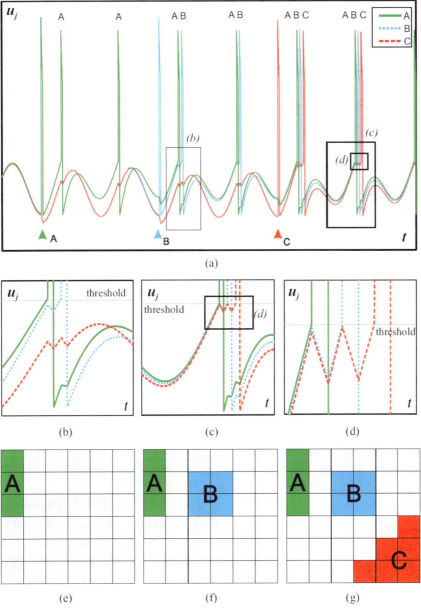

FIGURE 9.17 (a) The process of sequential item loading into the network. Different curves correspond to different clusters. The item A is loaded first, and the item B is loaded next. When the cluster A is excited, it prevents excitation of B, that's why B fires with some delay. When we later load the item C, the cluster C starts to fire after B. So three clusters start to fire sequentially, representing three items A, B, C. (b,c,d) Enlarged pieces of Figure 9.17 (a). (e,f,g) Clusters which are present in the network: (e) when the item A is loaded, (e) when the items A and B are loaded and (e) when all three items are loaded.

strong enough ($\lambda > \lambda_o$, where λ_o is a definite positive value), the second cluster cannot fire until the inhibition circuit is activated. So it will be excited only after excitation of the first cluster is terminated, and the clusters will fire with some sizeable delay. In this case the inter-spike interval equals some positive value τ_{is} which is larger than the spike duration τ_{sp}. And it will be so during further cycles. So, for $\lambda > \lambda_o$ two groups of units corresponding to different items fire periodically in different phases of the external signal. They will never merge or recombine with each other, and we will always be able to recognize each of them. Loading the next item C in the same way results in the appearance of three sequentially firing clusters representing all the items, and so on. This feature means that the modified network is able to store several items simultaneously.

13 Capacity of the Memory Model

The major property of the memory system is its capacity C (i.e., the maximal quantity of items that it can store). In our case it is the maximal quantity of clusters which can fire in one cycle of the sinusoidal signal. The most important parameters that influence the capacity are parameters that regulate time scales of the system. These parameters define how many clusters can go in one cycle of the sinusoidal signal. The major time scales of the system are:

(i)   The sinusoidal signal period T.
(ii) The ADP duration $\tau_{ADP} \sim \beta^{-1}$.
(iii) The inter-spike interval $\langle \tau_{is} \rangle$ which is the mean time delay between firing of the neighboring clusters.
(iv) The spike duration τ_{sp}.
(v)   The feedback delay τ_f.

In a further investigation, we set these scales so that the relationships are of the order of that in living systems (Lisman and Idiart 1995; Izhikevich 2005).

Let us try to estimate how the capacity varies in accordance with the system parameters. It is evident that the greater $\langle \tau_{is} \rangle$, the less C is, and the greater T, the greater C is: $C \sim \langle \tau_{is} \rangle$. The stronger the inhibition, the larger the inter-spike interval will be, so increasing λ results in decreasing capacity. But we know that if $\lambda < \lambda_o$ all the items merge, and $C=1$. This implies that the capacity is maximal for the values of λ which are somewhat more than λ_o and it falls with further increases to λ.

The capacity C is plotted in Figure 9.18(a) as the function of λ for different values of T. The function $C(\lambda)$ has the form that is described above. The capacity equals one for $\lambda < \lambda_o$, reaching the maximal value C_o for $\lambda = \lambda_o$ and

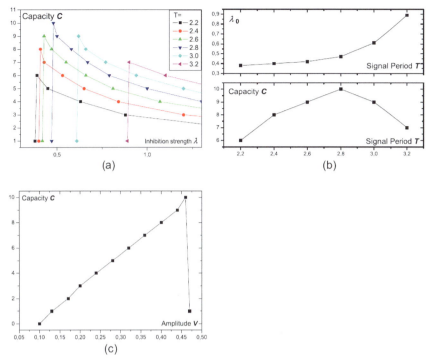

FIGURE 9.18 (a) Capacity C of the memory system versus inhibition strength λ for different values of T. (b) Functions $\delta_o(T)$ and $C_o(T)$. (c) Capacity C versus the sinusoidal signal amplitude V.

subsequently decreases. The values λ_o and C_o depend on T. The functions $\lambda_o(T)$ and $C_o(T)$ are plotted in Figure 9.18(b). Notice than λ_o monotonically grows with T, but the function $C_o(T)$ has a quite sharp maximum $C_o=10$ for $T=2.8$. This means that the optimal period of sinusoidal signal corresponds to the maximal capacity. In our case it equals 10.

Furthermore, we fixed $\lambda=0.48$ and $T=2.8$ and varied other parameters. First, we considered the capacity dependence on the ADP duration τ_{ADP} controlled by β. It appears that the capacity is semi-permanent in a wide interval of β values. But when λ becomes large enough ($\beta>0.07$), periodic firing of neurons becomes impossible, and information storage is impossible too (capacity equals zero). The function $C(V)$ is very interesting too (Figure 9.18C). If the sinusoidal signal is weak ($V<0.1$), periodic firing of neurons is impossible, and $C=0$. For larger amplitudes the capacity increases almost linearly with V. But for $V=0.47$, the value of $\beta_{\cdot o}$ becomes larger than $\beta_{\cdot}$, and capacity falls to one.

One can see that for realistic parameters, the model gives results that correlate well with known facts about working memory. The capacity of working memory of the human brain equals 7±2 (Lisman and Idiart 1995), and the maximal capacity of our systems equals ten and may vary for different parameters values. This fact is very interesting and it shows the model to be adequate.

14   Discussion

We have shown how higher level cognitive functions (e.g., pre-motor pattern formation and working memory) can be implemented using network mathematical models of underlying neuronal circuits. Starting from the cellular level we have constructed networks capable of qualitatively reproducing basic functional properties of corresponding brain circuits. The models are based on two basic concepts: (i) The single cell dynamics should robustly reproduce the key features of living cells at the cellular level in accordance with *in vitro* and *in vivo* experimental recordings from living cells; and (ii) The network's topology should reflect the morphological structure of the neuronal circuit responsible for the functions. Such models constructed as behavior-based caricatures have quite a wide "degree of freedom" to reproduce the required collective dynamics through appropriate parameter tuning. At this level, the model outcome can be qualitatively compared with experimental cognitive studies representing the final indicator of model validity.

Specifically, we have found that a spiking model of an ION neuron possesses the property of self-referential phase reset very much similar to that observed in *in vitro* imaging studies (Leznik et al. 2002). Since the phase of the subthreshold oscillation defines the time moments of spikes, the ION network model can effectively generate spiking patterns with controllable firing times (Lang et al. 1999). These patterns appear as certain distributions of phase clusters. The presence of internal inhibitory feedback blocking the gap junctions (Welsh and Llinas 1997) in the ION is necessary for the sustainability of the required cluster profile, which has been clearly shown by analysis of the model dynamics. The spiking patterns in the ION provide the internal representation of the pre-motor patterns. When the appropriate coherence is achieved the pattern is projected to the motor system implementing movement that is optimal given the current external (environmental)/internal (mind) brain functional state conditions.

We have proposed and investigated a model of working memory in the form of a network of neurons with after-depolarization and inhibitory feedback. It is a mathematical model describing the working memory circuit proposed by Lisman and collaborators. The most interesting property of the network is its ability to store several items ("memories") simultaneously. In this case several clusters of periodic activity coexist in the network, representing all the items. Each cluster corresponds to one item. The most valuable feature of the memory system is its capacity (i.e., the maxim number of items that can be stored in it simultaneously). We have studied its dependence on system parameters and found the optimal feedback strength value corresponding to maximal capacity. In this case the capacity equals 7 and this fact is in agreement with data of neurophysiologists and suppositions of Lisman et al. (Miller 1956; Lisman and Idiart 1995; Cowan 2000). Our results agree with the conception of Lisman et al. about working memory in the network of neurons with ADP (Lisman and Idiart 1995; Jensen and Lisman 1996; Jensen and Lisman, 2005) and with the experimental findings of gating of theta oscillations by a working memory task (Raghavachari et al. 2001) and correlation between firing of adjacent interneurons and pyramidal cells during working memory task (Rao et al. 1999).

Finally, we note that the presented models describe many interesting features of brain dynamics from the cellular to cognitive level. Relatively simple dynamical systems can be implemented using physical instruments based on electronic chip technologies (Kazantsev, et al. 2003). This opens unique possibilities to develop neuro-mimetic systems for novel technologies based on the principles of brain functioning.

Acknowledgments

This research was supported in part by the Russian Foundation for Basic Research (grants 08-02-97035, 09-02-00719, 08-02-00724), by the MCB Program of Russian Academy of Science and by the Russian Science Support Foundation.

References

Abeles, M. 1991. *Corticonics: Neural Circuits of the Cerebral Cortex.* Cambridge, UK: Cambridge University Press.

Atkinson, R. C., and R. M. Shiffrin. 1968. *The Psychology of Learning and Motivation: Advances in Research and Theory, Vol. 2,* ed. K. W. Spence. New York: Academic.

Baddeley, A. 1996. "The fractionation of working memory." *Proceedings of the National Academy of Sciences* 93, no. 24: 13468–13472.

Behrendt, R. P. 2003. "Hallucinations: synchronisation of thalamocortical gamma oscillations underconstrained by sensory input." *Consciousness and Cognition* 12, no. 3: 413–451.

Bisley, J. W., D. Zaksas, and T. Pasternak. 2001. "Microstimulation of cortical area MT affects performance on a visual working memory task." *Journal of Neurophysiology* 85, no. 1: 187–196.

Campbell, S. R., D. L. Wang, and C. Jayaprakash. 1999. "Synchrony and desynchrony in integrate-and-fire oscillators." *Neural Computation* 11, no. 7: 1595–1619.

Cowan, N. 2000. "The magical number 4 in short-term memory: A reconsideration of mental storage capacity." *Behavioral and Brain Sciences* 24, no. 1: 87–185.

D'Esposito, M, G. K. Aguirre, E. Zarahn, D. Ballard, R. K. Shin, and J. Lease. 1998. "Functional MRI studies of spatial and nonspatial working memory." *Cognitive Brain Research* 7, no. 1: 1–13.

FitzHugh, R. 1961. "Impulses and physiological states in models of nerve membrane." *Biophysical Journal* 1, no. 6: 445–466.

Fuster, J. M. 1989. *The Prefrontal Cortex*, 2nd ed. New York: Raven Press.

Fuster, J. M., and G. E. Alexander. 1971. "Neuron activity related to short-term memory." *Science* 173, no. 3997: 652–654.

Goldman-Rakic, P. S. 1995. "Cellular basis of working memory." *Neuron* 14, no. 3: 477–485.

Goldman-Rakic, P. S. 1987. "Circuitry of the prefrontal cortex and the regulation of behavior by representational memory." In *Handbook of Physiology, Section 1: The Nervous System, Vol. 5*, ed. F. Plum and V. Mountcastle, 373–417. Bethesda, Md.: American Physiological Society.

Haken, H. 2000. *Principles of Brain Functioning. A Synergetic Approach to Brain Activity, Behavior and Cognition*. Berlin: Springer-Verlag.

Hebb, D. O. 1949. *The Organization of Behavior: A Neuropsychological Theory*. New York: Wiley.

Henze, D. A., and G. Buzsaki. 2003. "Single cell contributions to network activity in the hippocampus." *International Congress Series* 1250: 161–181.

Izhikevich, E. M. 2005. *Dynamical Systems in Neuroscience: The Geometry of Excitability and Bursting*. Cambridge, Mass.: MIT Press.

Jensen, O., and J. E. Lisman. 1996. "Hippocampal CA3 region predicts memory sequences: accounting for the phase precession of place cells." *Learning & Memory* 3: 279–287.

Jensen, O., and J. E. Lisman. 2005. "Hippocampal sequence-encoding driven by a cortical multi-item working memory buffer." *Trends in Neurosciences* 28, no. 2: 67–72.

Kandel, E. R., J. H. Schwartz, and T. M. Jessell, eds. 1991. *Principles of Neural Science*, 3rd ed. New York: Prentice-Hall.

Kazantsev, V. B., V. I. Nekorkin, V. I. Makarenko, and R. Llinas. 2003. "Olivo-cerebellar cluster-based universal control system." *Proceedings of the National Academy of Sciences* 100, no. 22: 13064–13068.

Kazantsev, V. B., V. I. Nekorkin, V. I. Makarenko, and R. Llinas. 2004. "Self-referential phase reset based on inferior olive oscillator dynamics." *Proceedings of the National Academy of Sciences* 101, no. 52: 18183–18188.

Klinshov, V. V., and V. I. Nekorkin. 2008a. "Activity clusters in dynamical model of the working memory system." *Network* 19, no. 2: 119–135.

Klinshov, V. V., and V. I. Nekorkin. 2005. "Model of a neuron with afterdepolarization and short-term memory." *Radiophysics and Quantum Electronics* 48, no. 3 203–211.

Klinshov, V. V., and V. I. Nekorkin. 2008b. "Working memory in the network of neuron-like units with noise." *International Journal of Bifurcation and Chaos* 18, no. 9: 2743.

Koch, C. 1998. *Biophysics of Computation: Information Processing in Single Neurons*. Oxford: Oxford University Press.

Lang, E. J., I. Sugihara, J. P. Welsh, and R. Llinas. 1999. "Patterns of spontaneous purkinje cell complex spike activity in the awake rat." *Journal of Neuroscience* 19, no. 7: 2728–2739.

Leznik, E., V. I. Makarenko, and R. Llinas. 2002. "Electronically mediated oscillatory patterns in neuronal ensembles: an in vitro voltage-dependent dye-imaging study in the inferior olive." *Journal of Neuroscience* 22, no. 7: 2804–2815.

Lisman, J. E., and M. A. P. Idiart. 1995. "Storage of 7±2 short-term memories in oscillatory subcycles." *Science* 267, no. 5203: 1512–1515.

Llinas, R. 2003. "Consciousness and the thalamocortical loop." *International Congress Series*, 1250: 409–416.

Llinas, R. 2002. *I of the Vortex: From Neurons to Self*. Cambridge, Mass.: MIT Press.

Llinas, R., R. Baker, and C. Sotelo. 1974. "Electrotonic coupling between neurons in cat inferior olive." *Journal of Neurophysiology* 37, no. 3: 560–571.

Llinas, R., and Y. Yarom. 1986. "Oscillatory properties of guinea-pig inferior olivary neurons and their pharmacalogical modulation: An in vitro study." *Journal of Physiology* 376: 163–182.

Magee, J. C. 2003. "A prominent role for intrinsic neuronal properties in temporal coding." *Trends in Neuroscience* 26, no. 1: 14–16.

Miller, G. A. 1956. "The magical number seven, plus or minus two: Some limits on our capacity for processing information." *Psychological Review* 63, no. 2: 81–97.

Peterson, L. R., and M. J. Peterson. 1959. "Short-term retention of individual verbal terms." *Journal of Experimental Psychology* 58, no. 3: 193–199.

Rabinovich, M. I., P. Varona, A. I. Selverston, and H. D. I. Abarbanel. 2006. "Dynamical principles in neuroscience." *Reviews of Modern Physics* 78, no. 4: 1213–1265.

Raghavachari, S., M. J. Kahana, D. S. Rizzuto, J. B. Caplan, M. P. Kirschen, B. Bourgeois, J. R. Madsen, and J. E. Lisman. 2001. "Gating of human theta oscillations by a working memory task." *Journal of Neuroscience* 21, no. 9: 3175–3183.

Rao, S. G., G. V. Williams, and P. S. Goldman-Rakic. 1999. "Isodirectional tuning of adjacent interneurons and pyramidal cells during working memory: Evidence for microcolumnar organization in PFC." *Journal of Neurophysiology* 81, no. 4: 1903–1916.

Ruchkin, D. S., R. S. Berndt, R. J. Johnson, W. Ritter, J. Grafman, and H. L. Canoune. 1997. "Modality-specific processing streams in verbal working memory: evidence from spatio-temporal patterns of brain activity." *Cognitive Brain Research* 6, no. 2: 95–113.

Scott, A. 2002. *Neuroscience: A Mathematical Premier*. Berlin: Springer-Verlag.

Wang, D. L., and D. Terman. 1997. "Image segmentation based on oscillatory correlation." *Neural Computation* 9, no. 4: 805–836.

Wang, D. L., and D. Terman. 1994. "Synchrony and desynchrony in neural oscillator networks." Paper presented at Neural Information Processing Systems Foundation, Denver, Colorado, November 28–December 3.

Wang, X. J. 2001. "Synaptic reverberation underlying mnemonic persistent activity." *Trends in Neuroscience* 24, no. 8: 455–463.

Welsh, J. P., E. J. Lang, I. Suglhara, and R. Llinas. 1995. "Dynamic organization of motor control within the olivocerebellar system." *Nature* 374, no. 6521: 453–457.

Welsh, J. P., and R. Llinas. 1997. "Some organizing principles for the control of movement based on olivocerebellar physiology." *Progress in Brain Research* 114: 449–461.

CHAPTER 10

Frequency-Selective Generators of Oscillatory Brain Activity as Mapping Structure and Dynamics of Cognitive Processes

N. N. Danilova

In recent years, the methods of neuroscience have been extensively used in the studies of human cognitive processes. Researchers have focused greater attention on the study of brain mechanisms that serve as a biological foundation for the processes of attention, perception, memory, decision-making, and consciousness.

New methods of brain activity mapping, such as Positron Emission Tomography (PET), and especially functional Magnetic Resonance Imaging (fMRI) and spectroscopic imaging (MRS) that non-invasively image the brain activity foci, made a substantial contribution to the development of modern cognitive psychophysiology. The main achievement of the tomography methods is that they provide strong evidence of the systemic control of mental activity. It was demonstrated that any patterns of activity foci and their defaults distributed throughout the brain space are connected with performance of specific mental functions (Corbetta and Shulman 2002; Mantini et al. 2007; Corbetta et al. 2008).

However, a significant disadvantage of the tomography methods is their relatively low temporal resolution, which does not allow investigation into the process dynamics inside the activated locus, or the fast-paced interactions between the activated brain areas. To date, the minimal time required for tomography scanning of the brain and deriving a spatial map of the distribution of activation/inactivation foci is about two seconds. However, mental processes are characterized by a much higher speed. For example, the recognition of an object takes place within 100 ms. The high temporal resolution required for the study of the dynamics of mental processes is provided by EEG and MEG recording methods, but they also have their limitations. Specifically, MEG measures only cortical activity, while the EEG makes it difficult to differentiate between the processes that occur in the cortex and subcortical brain structures. Factor analysis applied to multichannel EEG recordings does not completely address this problem either. So, the current challenge is to develop an alternative technique comparable to the tomography method based on multichannel EEG recording that would allow determination of the localization of activated local neural networks in the entire brain volume and an investigation of their dynamics.

1   Localization of Local Neural Networks Using Gamma Rhythms

How can local neural network activity be found using multichannel EEG? One way to approach this challenge is by considering the high-frequency electrical activity of the brain, namely the gamma rhythm that covers a range from 30 to 200 Hz, up to 600 Hz (Sannita 2000) according to some reports. The high frequency of the gamma rhythm and high level of synchronization between gamma-oscillations of the local field and spike neuron discharges (Singer and Gray 1995; Logothetis et al. 2001) support this assumption.

Another important characteristic is the relationship between gamma oscillations and various cognitive processes. A positive correlation has been found between the gamma rhythm and the processes of attention (Spydel et al. 1979; Tiitinen et al. 1993), perception (Tallon-Baudry et al. 1995; Basar 1999; Basar et al. 2000; Danilova and Astafiev 2000; Danilova et al. 2002), memory (Tallonbaudry et al. 1999; Danilova and Hankevich 2001; Jensen and Lisman 2005), consciousness (Singer 1991; Singer and Gray 1995), and performance of semantic memory operations (Lutzenberger et al. 1994; Pulvermuller et al. 1995). The gamma rhythm is required for the performance of motor reactions. Bursts of gamma oscillations occur in the motor and pre-motor cortex, supplementary motor area, and parietal cortex prior to the beginning of motion recorded as an electromyogram (EMG). They continue during the execution of motion, and then come up again in order for the motion to stop. Gamma oscillations in the motor cortex have the same frequency and lead in phase, as to the rhythmic activity in EMG. That is a direct source of evidence for its control function. Amplified magnitude of the gamma rhythm has been described for the inhibition of motor reactions (Shibata et al. 1999; Mima et al. 1999; Popivanov et al. 1999). A relation between successful working memory and the gamma rhythm magnitude was also demonstrated for a delay interval during which previously obtained information had to be retained for subsequent use (Tallonbaudry et al. 1999).

The high correlation of the gamma rhythm with the psychological processes and its recording in various brain structures of humans and animals, including invertebrates, suggests its interpretation as a functional building block of sensory, cognitive, and executive functions (Basar 1999; Basar et al. 2000). The gamma rhythm improves recognition of stimuli playing the role of a special frequency-specific mechanism that selectively enhances efficiency of signal transmission in local neural networks. Accordingly, gamma oscillations can be used as a means for non-invasive electroencephalographic mapping of the local network activity. E. Basar comes to the same conclusion when he views gamma oscillations as a bridge from the activity of individual neurons to the activity of neuronal assemblies (Basar et al. 2001).

An important feature of oscillatory brain activity is its ability to perform spatial-temporal synchronization, as well as synchronization with a stimulus or event evoking a response. It should be noted that the discovery of the phenomenon of spatial-temporal synchronization of oscillatory activity is associated with the name of M. N. Livanov (1972). In his experiments on cats, he demonstrated that learning increases synchronization of a theta-rhythm recorded from the cortex and reticular formation. Later on, spatial-temporal synchronization was repeatedly observed at the frequency of gamma oscillations in human and animal brain activity.

The discovery of synchronization between gamma-oscillations in different brain regions laid the foundation for the concept of binding (Eckhorn et al. 1988). The principle of neurons binding into more complex structures based on correlation of their signals in time was proposed by K. von der Malsburg and W. Schneider (Von der Malsburg and Schneider 1995). Later on, synchronization of oscillatory activity of the different brain loci at the gamma-rhythm frequency began to be treated as a universal and primary mechanism of interaction between the neural networks underlying various psychological processes (Basar 1999).

2 Origin of the Gamma Rhythm

According to the concept of binding, the gamma-rhythm occurs due to feedback and horizontal links between neurons that temporarily form an ensemble, a system of interlinked cells. "Stimulus – specific synchronization" at high frequencies (35–90 Hz) has been demonstrated in the visual cortex neurons in cats. Spatially separate neurons with the same detector features were discharging by bursts of spikes repeated with a 40-Hz frequency in response to displacements of a visual strip in a certain direction. If the stimulus crossed the neuron receptive fields in the opposite direction, then there was no synchronization of the discharges at the gamma-rhythm frequency (Singer 1991).

Despite the attractiveness of the concept of spatial-temporal binding, not all of the experimental data support it. In investigations by Singer and Gray

(Singer and Gray 1995), neurons-detectors of the cat's visual cortex characterized by overall selectivity towards certain parameters of a stimulus and representing various columns of the visual cortex spatially separated from each other by a 7-mm distance demonstrate synchronization of gamma-oscillations at a zero-phase lag. This means that synchronization of gamma-oscillations is not always a sequential transmission of a signal from one neuron to the other. From the point of view of the binding concept, it is also difficult to explain some other properties: the closer are the characteristics of a stimulus to the selective properties of a neuron detector, the higher the amplitude of local rhythmic potentials at the 70–80 Hz frequency in the area of recorded neuron activity, which can only be explained by the fact that generation of gamma-oscillations is tied to a hypothetical resonance mechanism.

The alternative hypothesis is based on the concept of an intracellular gamma-rhythm origin and presumes that a neuron maintains its rhythmical activity even though it may be isolated from contact with other cells (Grechenko and Sokolov 1979; Sokolov 1981). Endogenous rhythmical activity of an isolated neuron is represented as a sequence of negative-positive pacemaker potentials that do not necessarily transition into spike discharges. Neurons that have endogenous rhythmical activity are usually referred to as pacemaker neurons. In such neurons, the pacemaker mechanism interacting with the chemiexitation and electroexitation membrane transforms the neuron into a device with a "built-in controlled generator" (Sokolov and Nezlina 2007). These intracellular generators are responsible for the generation of the gamma-rhythm (Sokolov 2003).

Intracellular microelectrode recording of the pacemaker neurons in the cat's thalamus demonstrated that the frequency of endogenous potentials depends on the neuron state as represented by the level of its membrane potential. Neuron depolarization increases the frequency of its endogenous potentials. Generation of gamma-oscillations in the pacemaker neuron is related to the activation of high-threshold calcium ion channels located on its dendrites. Low-threshold calcium conductance in the soma of the same neuron (Pedroarena and Linas 1997) is responsible for slow oscillations at the alpha-oscillation frequency. Another important property of the pacemaker neurons is their response to external stimuli. Postsynaptic potentials coming to the pacemaker neuron are able to induce a shift of the pacemaker wave phase, causing it to reset. As a result, the pacemaker wave of endogenous origin is synchronized with external stimuli. The input signal triggers the neuron hyperpolarization, an inhibitory pause in the endogenous rhythmic potentials, after which they reconstitute themselves at the same frequency (Kazantsev et al. 2004). The duration of the inhibitory pause that determines the phase shift magnitude is a function of the input signal parameters. The pacemaker neuron responds in this way to input signals and, therefore, may be controlled by them. The ability of the pacemaker neurons to reset was discovered in the snail Helix (Palikhova 1995; Sheviakova and Palikhova 2002). The pacemaker neuron has the characteristic of plasticity (Grechenko 2008) which allows this neuron to work at various frequencies and to become part of various neural networks. These properties make pacemaker neurons unique in the way that they are influenced by other neurons.

If the hypothesis based on the temporal binding of neurons assumes at least two activity foci separated in space, then the pacemaker hypothesis assumes parallel existence of isolated foci of gamma-oscillation activity. To date, it has been demonstrated that neurons with pacemaker properties are broadly represented in a variety of brain structures and involved in various psychological functions. They were found in the neocortex, thalamus, hippocampus, cerebellum, and inferior olive.

The hypothesis of the pacemaker origin of oscillatory brain activity has a number of important consequences. When the stimulus is repeated, the averaging of event-related potentials due to the reset of the pacemaker wave will not lead to the suppression of evoked gamma-oscillations phase-synchronized with the presented stimulus. Instead, a repeated stimulus will cause suppression of evoked gamma-oscillations tied to the stimulus only in time, but not in phase, as the induced rhythm is mediated by intermediate, internal factors such as recognition, evaluation, decision-making, and other cognitive processes (Galambos 1992; Basar et al. 2000).

3   Method of Microstructure Analysis of Oscillatory Brain Activity

Examination of the pacemaker origin hypothesis for rhythmic brain activity has enabled the formation of the following research paradigm that has become known as the method of microstructure analysis of oscillatory brain activity (Danilova 2005; Danilova et al. 2005; Danilova 2006). In the beginning, it was applied only to the gamma rhythm (30–75 Hz), but later it was extended to the beta-oscillations range (14–30 Hz). This method includes the following:

1.   A sensory stimulus is repeated multiple times to obtain the averaged event-related potential (ERP) for each channel of the brain activity recording.
2.   Frequency components in the 14–75 Hz range are separated from the ERP using the method of narrow-band frequency filtering with a 1-Hz step, the

so-called evoked oscillations, phase-synchronized with a stimulus which meets the characteristics of the pacemaker neurons.
3. An equivalent dipole is localized for each oscillation frequency based on the 15-channel ERP recording data.
4. The location of each equivalent dipole of narrow-band oscillations in the brain is superimposed onto the respective "slice" of the structural MRI scan obtained for each participant.
5. Time distribution of equivalent dipoles that differ in frequency and location is analyzed in a selected ERP time window and in an interval preceding the event.
6. The sum of localized equivalent dipoles is used as a measure of activity of narrow-band oscillations for a selected ERP time interval.

The results of two studies performed using the method of microstructure analysis of oscillatory brain activity are provided below. The first explored the contribution of "evoked" gamma-activity to the process of auditory signal perception during passive and active attention required for performance of a sensory-motor reaction. The second study investigated the function of evoked gamma- and beta-activity in working memory processes. Each series of audio stimuli included 120 stimuli presented at a constant interstimulus interval of 1.5 seconds with each stimulus being 130 ms in duration. Five people (3 women and 2 men) ages 18–24 participated. In the second study focused on working memory, the subject had to memorize four pairs of two-digit numbers (St1) and retain them in memory during a delay interval for subsequent comparison with stimuli (St2 or St3) containing a single two-digit number. A response to stimulus St2 was a motor reaction, if it matched one of the St1 numbers. St3 was a discriminative stimulus. The numbers to be memorized were never repeated. The study was performed on 10 subjects ages 20–23.

For each type of stimuli, the averaged event-related potential (ERP) was calculated and processed using the microstructure analysis method including narrow-band frequency filtration with a 1-Hz step in the beta (14–30 Hz) and gamma (31–75 Hz) rhythm band. The "Brainloc" software (model of a single moving dipole) for isolated oscillations was used to compute the coordinates of equivalent dipoles. At the EEG digitizing frequency of 400 Hz, the search for the presence of a dipole source was performed every 2.5 ms. The coordinates of the oscillation sources computed from the 15-channel EEG with a dipole coefficient of 0.95 were projected onto the individual structural MRI brain scans of subjects. These scans were made on the TOMIKON S50 (BRUKER) Magnetic Resonance Imaging machine at the Moscow State University Center of Magnetic Resonance.

4 Tomography and Spectroscopy (MGU CMRTS)

Multiple repetitions of the auditory stimulus confirmed the localization of the maximum ERP potential under electrodes positioned over the auditory cortex. Frequency filtration of ERP triggered by a sound reveals the presence of narrow-band gamma-oscillations in a frequency band of 30–75 Hz. It should be noted that different narrow-band gamma-oscillations appear in ERP with a varying probability which points to differences in their level of phase-synchronization with the stimulus. The discrete character of the narrow-band gamma-oscillatory activity appears on the ERP time-frequency histogram where oscillation activity is indicated by the number of dipoles for each frequency and each 100-ms time window for a period of 1.5 seconds after the stimulus (Figure 10.1). The Figure presents data for a subject (M.C.) performing a motor response in two experiments, with a one-year interval between each experiment. It is clear that the subject's activity in the first experiment (A) is characterized by a higher number of dipoles than in the second (B).

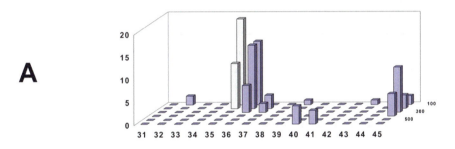

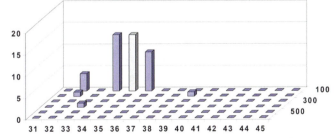

FIGURE 10.1 Time histograms of activated frequency-selected gamma-generators for ERP triggered by the auditory stimulus in two motor-reaction experiments. Data for one test subject C.M. The frequency scale in Hz is shown on the x axis; the sum of the localized dipoles is shown on the y axis; and the time scale is shown on the z axis.

In this case, the time-frequency selectivity of activated gamma-oscillations stays the same.

The time-frequency selectivity of gamma-oscillations in the ERP may be explained by the fact that the reset of oscillations, while remaining phase-locked to the stimuli, does not occur at all the frequencies. Thus, of the pacemaker neurons generating various frequencies of endogenous activity, only a handful of pacemakers respond to a presented stimulus by resetting their pacemaker. The high time-frequency selectivity of narrow-band gamma-oscillations during "evoked" phase-synchronization allow to distinguish the new EEG parameter: the frequency-selective generators imaging an activity of the pacemaker neurons. Activity level of a frequency-selective gamma generator is determined by its number of dipole sources. The more dipoles that are localized within a brain volume, the higher is the activity level of the frequency-selective gamma generator. Given the high activity of one frequency-selective gamma generator, the neighbors set differentiated by a 1-Hz frequency might not be activated. Over time, the activity of frequency-selective gamma generators has an intermittent character displayed by a change in the number of equivalent dipoles.

Analysis of the brain localization of equivalent dipole sources of activated gamma generators allows association of brain structures to the activation of different generators. This method can be used to obtain pictures of brain activity foci during various cognitive processes. It has been shown that during passive perception of auditory stimuli, at the interval of 100 ms after the stimulus, the predominantly activated component of the sensory response is the modality-specific area of the temporal lobe associated with auditory perception. During goal-oriented activity associated with performance of a sensorimotor reaction, another active area appears in the frontal and anterior cingulate cortex.

In conditions of active attention, the total number of localized dipoles increases. Dipoles localized in spatially separate areas represent gamma-generators that operate at a common frequency similarly phase-synchronized with a stimulus. Figure 10.2 shows localization of dipoles for the frequency-selective gamma generator operating at a frequency of 35 Hz. A high level of activity occurs for conditions of both passive (A) and active (B) attention to the stimulus.

Dipole localization is obtained for the initial ERP phase, at 100 ms after the stimulus, and projected onto the axial brain slices. In the indifferent series, the dipole sources appear locally in the modality-specific cortex of the temporal lobe. A response to the sound expressed in the form of a motor reaction changes the map of the frequency-selective gamma generator localization. An activity focus in the frontal cortex is now added to the activity focus in the

FREQUENCY-SELECTIVE GENERATORS OF OSCILLATORY BRAIN ACTIVITY   283

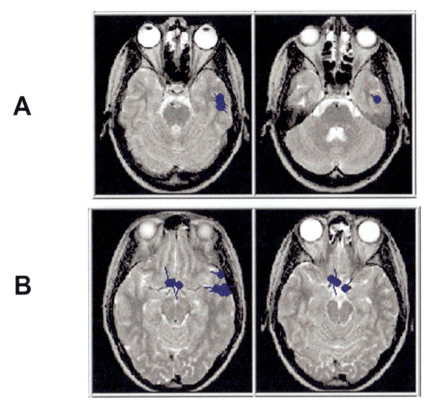

FIGURE 10.2   Localization of the 35-Hz frequency-selective gamma generator on the axial sections of the MRI brain scans performed for the M.C. test subject. A – for ERP triggered by the auditory stimulus in the placebo series, and B – for the motor reaction series.

temporal lobe. Joint activation of the frontal brain system and the modality-specific cortex that takes place in conditions of active attention occurs through simultaneous activation of the frequency-selective gamma generators working at a common frequency and are similarly phase-locked to the stimulus. Thus, frequency-selective gamma generators entrain spatially separated neural networks into joint activity by evoking coherent gamma-oscillations.

Activity in the frontal areas of the brain occurs earlier than in the modality-specific cortex, which underscores the leading role of the frontal cortex in the control of the modality-specific cortex. The phenomenon of activation of the frontal brain areas at the interval of 100 ms after the stimulus onset attests to the fact that the two information flows, "top-down" and "bottom-up," merge. The obtained results agree with the fMRI-derived pattern of foci of the brain hemodynamic activity. A number of authors (Corbetta et al. 2008; Mantini et al. 2007; Corbetta and Shulman 2002; Duncan 2004) describe it as a system of executive or goal-oriented attention that includes activity of the frontal lobe and anterior cingulate cortex. Its activation is required for the performance of an instruction, as well as processes of self-regulation and control.

Brain localization of equivalent dipoles of narrow-band gamma-generators revealed that they are point-bound to brain structures. Repeatedly occurring dipoles that reflect the activity of a specific frequency-selective generator retain their localization in a stable manner. This demonstrates that activity of frequency-selective generators is characterized not only by time-frequency but also by spatial discreteness.

5 Coding of Anticipation and Prediction

Another issue of great interests concerns the question of how anticipation and prediction are coded in the nervous system, and what is the mechanism for the selection and coordination of brain activity that predicts a stimulus onset? To solve this problem, localization of the activated frequency-selective gamma generators was investigated at an interval of 100 ms prior to stimulus presentation. The auditory stimulus was consistently presented at a fixed interstimulus interval inducing a formation of a conditioned reflex (Pavlov 1951). This conditioned reflex is a simple form of anticipation, where the subject memorizes the length of the interstimulus interval to help concentrate attention right before a stimulus is presented. However, anticipation becomes a more complex process with anticipatory activity related to precognition. The comparison between the dipole localizations for the frequency-selective gamma generators in the 100 ms time interval prior to the auditory stimulus and during the sensory response at 100 ms after the stimulus demonstrated a good match. Anticipation of the stimulus activates the same frequency-selective gamma generators and with the same localization in the brain as the stimulus itself. Figure 10.3 shows localization of the equivalent dipoles of the 35-Hz generator on the axial MRI slices of the subject's brain at the intervals of anticipation (A) and sensory response (B) for the conditions of active attention to the auditory stimulus. It can be seen that two activity foci characteristic of the sensory response (in the frontal parts of the brain and in the temporal cortex) emerge prior to the stimulus presentation and during its anticipation. During anticipation and sensory response, the dipoles appear to have a good proximity in terms of their coordinates.

Therefore, it can be stated that the anticipation reaction not only controls the conditioned-reflex type attention to the stimulus, but it also forms the

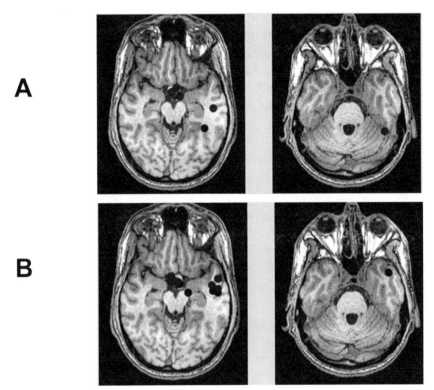

FIGURE 10.3   Projection of the dipole sources of the 35-Hz frequency-selective gamma-generator on the axial sections of the MRI brain scans of the M.C. test subject: at the interval of anticipation (A) – at 100 ms prior to the auditory stimulus, and during the sensory response (B) – the first 100 ms after the stimulus.

image of the stimulus, which facilitates and accelerates the process of stimulus recognition. Thus, electrical activity of the brain preceding the stimulus usually referred to as background or noise activity cannot be ignored. It contains information on the endogenous cognitive processes that are treated in general as a context. The formation in memory of a sensory image of the anticipated stimulus may be regarded as a particular case of the above. Active attention to the stimulus is accompanied by the merging of the two information flows: "bottom-up" and "top-down." Such an integration of sensory and memory processes becomes apparent both in the sensory response and during stimulus anticipation.

The results of a second study involving working memory confirmed the earlier conclusions obtained from the experiments with auditory stimulation pertaining to passive and active attention. In the experiments with working memory, the numbers for memorization were presented via the St1 stimulus that contained four 2-digit numbers. The St2 stimulus consisted of one 2-digit number that matched one of the four numbers retained in the memory, prompting the subject to make a motor response. The St3 stimulus contained a number not included in the set of four numbers, and did not require a motor response. The length of the delay interval was 5 seconds. The exposure time for each stimulus was 1 second.

For St2, at the 100 ms interval prior to the stimulus, the ERP appeared to contain an anticipatory reaction that to a large extent, reproduced the sensory response. Just as in the experiments with auditory stimuli, the activated generators during these reactions worked at the same frequency and were phase-synchronized with the stimulus. The similarity of the localization of the dipole sources was less obvious, which was apparently related to a larger uncertainty arising from the need to base the selection on a behavioral reaction that was absent in the auditory stimulation experiments. In the latter case, the same motor response was made in response to all auditory stimuli. In addition, the experiments with working memory demonstrated that the dipoles in the frontal cortex occurred more frequently during the anticipation interval than during the sensory response. In fact, the anticipation reaction coincided with the end of the delay interval and retained the properties characteristic of a memory trace retention process.

Increased activation of the frontal cortex is a distinctive feature of working memory tasks. Activation of the frontal cortex occurs both at the interval when numbers are presented for memorization and also during the delay interval. In addition to the frontal parts of the brain, activation also involves the association (temporal, parietal) cortex, sensory visual cortex, and cerebellum. Activity of the four above-mentioned structures dominates both during number presentation and during the delay interval. Only a small number of dipoles are localized in the thalamus and hippocampus areas.

Based on the number of localized equivalent dipoles of gamma- and beta-generators, the average level of total brain activity during the perception and memorization of numbers is two times higher than during the delay interval. Here, the activity in the frontal cortex, which continues to increase until the end of the stimulus presentation (Figure 10.4) plays the dominant role. It is evident that at the end of the number presentation, during the 400–1000 ms interval after the stimulus onset, the number of dipoles in the frontal cortex significantly exceeds the number of dipoles generated at the onset of perception 100–400 ms after the stimulus. Based on group data from the working memory experiments, during stimulus perception 32.9% of the overall number of dipoles was generated in the frontal lobe. Activity of the association

FREQUENCY-SELECTIVE GENERATORS OF OSCILLATORY BRAIN ACTIVITY   287

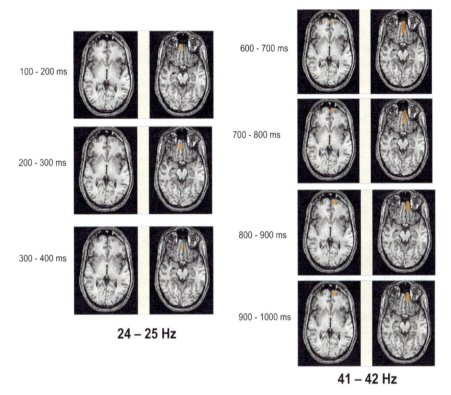

FIGURE 10.4   Growth of frequency-selective generator activity in the frontal system of the brain towards the end of the perception of numerical digits for memorization. It is shown as a growth in the number of localized dipoles and a rise in the frequency of the activated generator. Even though the generator frequency changes from the frequency band of beta-rhythm to gamma-rhythm, the dipole localization is preserved. Data for one test subject (C.Z).

and parietal cortex, and the cerebellum, measured by the number of localized dipoles and expressed as a percentage of their total sum, equals 28.3%, 20.5% and 18.2%, respectively. During the delay interval, the peak of activity moves from the frontal to the association cortex (34.1%) and the cerebellum (29.2%). The frontal areas and visual cortex are also involved but at a lower level, as represented by a smaller number of localized dipole sources (18.7% and 17.9%, respectively).

The shift of the activity from the frontal to the association cortex during the delay interval supports the hypothesis that there is a rewriting of information from the association areas of the brain into the prefrontal cortex. This suggests that this operation an important link for information retention in memory. The growth of cerebellum activity during the delay interval, as was discovered in these experiments, may be attributed to a motor readiness response and the ability to predict the moment of presentation of the eliciting stimulus. The same effect was observed during repetitive performance of the same motor task in response to auditory stimuli presented at fixed time intervals (Danilova and Bykova 2003a; Danilova and Bykova 2003b). Therefore, an assumption can be made that not only the sensory memory traces but also the motor memory traces are activated during the delay interval.

6   Microstructure Analysis Applied to Memory Retention

The method of microstructure analysis has also been applied to investigation of the dynamics of memory retention. It has been shown that there is increased brain activity associated with memory retention. In this case, the frequency-selective generators operating at different frequencies generate bursts of joint activity that appear and disappear over time. The frequency of their activity fluctuations is about 1 Hz. Figure 10.5 shows the time-distribution histograms for the sum of equivalent dipoles of gamma- and beta-generators within ERPs recorded for stimulus St1, visual presentation of four digits for memorization. The ERP duration is 6 seconds, including 1 second prior to the stimulus, 1 second during its presentation, and the 4-second delay interval. The time scale is subdivided into quanta of 100 ms each. Each quantum represents the sum of all localized equivalent dipoles that map the activity of frequency-selective generators in two frequency bands: beta (A) and gamma (B) regardless of their localization. The histograms demonstrate well-defined fluctuations of frequency-selective generator activity measured by the number of the localized dipoles.

Analysis of dipole localization during the delay interval showed that each wave of growth in the number of dipoles corresponds to a specific pattern of the brain activity foci. Figure 10.6 shows activity loci for all three generators activated during growth in the dipole number from 3300 to 3700 ms after the St1 stimulus onset. Thus, there is a strong binding that exists between each generator and its respective structure that can be maintained for 200–300 ms. Joint activity of generators localized in various brain structures can be regarded as formation of a system supporting interactions of spatially separated local networks. Their system integration is achieved through a special type of synchronization of frequency-selective generator oscillations that is based on low frequency modulation from another source. Fluctuations of this type were found in the hemodynamic signal in fMRI. In the studies of visual spatial attention in humans and monkeys, the authors identified a system for goal-directed

FREQUENCY-SELECTIVE GENERATORS OF OSCILLATORY BRAIN ACTIVITY   289

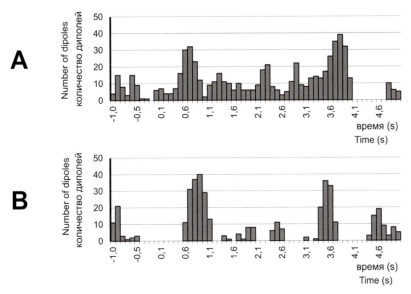

FIGURE 10.5   Time-distribution histogram for the number of dipoles of all activated beta-generators in the 14–30-Hz frequency band (A) and gamma-generators in the 30–75 Hz frequency band (B) found within ERP triggered by St1 containing numerical digits for memorization. Data for one test subject (C.Z.).

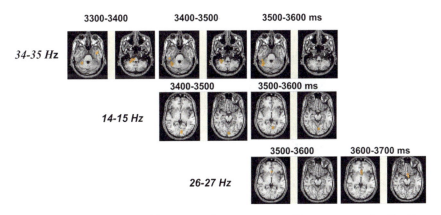

FIGURE 10.6   Joint activity of frequency-selective gamma- and beta-generators localized in the temporal cortex, cerebellum, visual cortex, and frontal area at the delay interval. Individual data (C.Z.).

attention and a default system (Corbetta et al. 2008). The systems have a reciprocal relationship: from time to time, the activity of one system is replaced by the activity of another. They view this process as a projection of behavioral competition between attention focused on a task and those processes servicing events, and thoughts irrelevant to the task. They tie fluctuations in the hemodynamic signal to the oscillatory activity of the neuronal assemblies, including ultra-slow fluctuations in the overall strength of the gamma-rhythm.

It should be noted that the joint activity of frontal brain areas with the visual and temporal cortices occurs during the delay interval and is absent during the perception of numbers. These facts agree with the hypothesis that interaction of local networks during a delay interval facilitates rewriting of the numerical information from the association brain areas into the prefrontal cortex, where it assumes an active form for subsequent use in behavior (Goldman-Rakic 1996). Our results suggest that the modality-specific visual cortex is also involved in the interaction between the prefrontal and association cortex.

In the investigation of the EEG mapping of activated memory traces, attention is usually given to oscillations of the theta-rhythm (4–7 Hz) that intensify during memory operations. Many researchers underscore either the absence of a correlation between gamma-oscillations and memory trace activation, or the lack of data on a relation between gamma-oscillations and working memory processes (Sarnthein et al. 1998; Jensen and Tesche 2002; Sauseng et al. 2007). Our results on the activation of frequency-selective generators operating in the delay interval at the gamma and beta rhythm frequencies point to the involvement of high-frequency oscillations in working memory processes, which agrees with the results obtained (Tallonbaudry et al. 1999) from wavelet analysis method. Traditionally, amplification of the gamma-rhythm is associated with increased attention. Another explanation is proposed here. Amplified activity of the frequency-selective gamma- and beta-generators is a manifestation of a local form of activation that may occur in neural networks performing various functions and containing pacemaker neurons. It is known that work with numerical data involves both short-term and long-term memory. Therefore, it can be assumed that joint activation of frequency-selective gamma- and beta-generators corresponds to the mechanism that transfers long-term memory traces associated with numbers into short-term working memory and retains the activated memory traces during the delay interval.

The activated engram has its own electrical equivalent. This equivalent involves activation of frequency-selective gamma- or beta-generator mapping operations by pacemaker neurons from the local neural network. Joint activity of the gamma- and beta-generators that occurs periodically points to the wave-like character of this process. Interaction between the local neural networks of the temporal, prefrontal, and visual cortex appears during joint activity. It is achieved through time-synchronization of oscillatory activity of the frequency-selective generators that are operating at different frequencies. The joint activity of the gamma- and beta-generators is modulated by low-frequency wave activity (Danilova 2005; Danilova and Bykova 2003a). Other researchers (Sauseng et al. 2007; Sauseng et al. 2008) have reached the same conclusions regarding the integration of different-frequency oscillations. However, their conclusion is based on the calculations of phase-synchronization between theta- and gamma-oscillations recorded for selected pairs of electrodes. We are analyzing the synchronization of activated frequency-selective gamma and beta generators.

7 Integration of Local Neural Networks

It is possible to talk about two mechanisms facilitating the system integration of local neural networks. One mechanism is joint activity of frequency-selective gamma- and beta-generators working at different frequencies that temporarily synchronize their wave activity. The other mechanism presumes arrangement of the local networks into a system by generating oscillations at a common frequency phase-synchronized with a stimulus. This type of mechanism was demonstrated during the sensory response in the experiments with auditory stimulation under active attention when activity loci in the frontal and modality-specific cortex generated oscillations at a single frequency (Danilova and Bykova 2003a; Danilova and Bykova 2003b).

Thus, the pacemaker hypothesis of the origin of high-frequency oscillatory brain activity is in agreement with the results of the experiments discussed here. The frequency-selective gamma- and beta-generators can be adequately explained with respect to the specific frequency of the pacemaker neurons. Retention of the frequency-specific reactions during the averaging of event-related potentials attests to the fact that pacemaker neuron resetting occurs independently in isolated pacemaker neurons with different frequencies of pacemaker activity. The point-binding that exists between individual frequency-selective generators and the local areas of the brain agrees with the concept of isolated pacemaker neurons, but not the ensemble- or network-type mechanism of gamma- and beta-rhythm generation. The fact that the frequency-selective generators occur in the frontal parts of the brain at the stimulus anticipation interval also agrees with mechanism of pacemaker reset.

8 Conclusion

A new experimental approach based on the pacemaker hypothesis of the origin of high-frequency EEG rhythms was proposed for the study of the structure and dynamics of cognitive processes. This approach has been used to develop the method for microstructure analysis of oscillatory brain activity, including narrow-band frequency filtering of event-related potentials (ERP), computation of equivalent current dipoles based on multichannel EEG data, and their superimposition onto structural Magnetic Resonance Imaging scans of an individual brain.

Frequency-selective gamma and beta generators were used in mapping activity of pacemaker neurons in local networks identified by this method illustrating a new electroencephalographic measure of local neural network activity. A frequency-selective generator is able to selectively adjust its frequency. Its activity is measured by a sum of localized equivalent dipoles and characterized by temporal and spatial discreteness (Danilova 2005; Danilova et al. 2005; Danilova 2006).

Two mechanisms of the local neural network integration into a system were identified: (a) joint activity of frequency-selective gamma- and beta-generators working at different frequencies that temporarily synchronize their wave activity; and (b) arrangement of local networks into a system by generating oscillations at a common frequency phase-synchronized with a stimulus.

This method allows for the mapping of the spatial localization of equivalent dipole sources of activated frequency-selective generators and the investigation of their fast transformations in time. Localized dipoles of frequency-selective generators was projected onto anatomical MRI images of the individual brain (Danilova et al. 2005; Danilova 2007) thereby improving the accuracy of the coordinates used in the mapping of the activated brain sections. The specific features of this method of microstructure analysis of brain oscillatory activity can compensate for the deficiencies found in individual tomography methods related to their low temporal resolution.

References

Basar, E. 1999. *Brain Function and Oscillations, Vol. II: Integrative Brain Function: Neurophysiology and Cognitive Processes*. Berlin: Springer.

Basar, E., C. Basar-Eroglu, S. Karakas, and M. Schurman. 2000. "Brain oscillation in perception and memory." *International Journal of Psychophysiology* 35, no. 2–3: 95–125.

Basar, E., C. Basar-Eroglu, S. Karakas and M. Schurman. 2001. "Gamma, alpha, delta, and theta oscillations govern cognitive processes." *International Journal of Psychophysiology* 39, no. 2–3: 241–248.

Corbetta, M., and G. L. Shulman. 2002. "Control of goal-directed and stimulus-driven attention in the brain." *Nature Reviews Neuroscience* 3, no. 3: 201–215.

Corbetta, M., G. Patel and G. L. Shulman. 2008. "The reorienting system of the human drain: from environment to theory of mind." *Neuron* 58 no. 3: 306–324.

Danilova, N. N. 2005. "Frequency specificity of the gamma rhythm oscillators." *The Russian Psychological Journal* 3, no. 2: 35–60.

Danilova, N. N. 2006. "A role of high-frequency rhythms of the brain electric activity in maintenance of mental processes." *Psychology: Journal of the Higher School of Economics* 3, no. 2: 62–72.

Danilova, N. N. 2007. "Oscillatory activity of the brain and cognitive processes." In *Conference Materials. Tendencies of Development of a Modern Psychological Science*. Moscow: Institute of Psychology of the Russian Academy of Sciences Press.

Danilova, N. N. and S. V. Astafiev. 2000. "Attention of the person as a specific link of EEG rhythms with wave modulators of heart rate." *Higher Nervous Activity* 50, no. 5: 791–804.

Danilova, N. N., and N. B. Bykova. 2003a. "A role of frequency-specific codes in attention processes." In *Reports of the second International Conference devoted to the 100 anniversary from the date of a birth of A. R. Luria*, ed. T. V. Ahutina and J. M. Glozman, 290–295. Moscow: Smisl.

Danilova, N. N. and N. B. Bykova. 2003b. "Oscillatory activity of the brain and informational processes." In *Psychology. Modern orientations of interdisciplinary researches*, ed. A. Zhuravlev and N. Tarablina, 271–283. Moscow: IPRAS Press.

Danilova, N. N., N. B. Bykova, N. V. Anisimov, Y. Pirogov, and E. N. Sokolov. 2002. "Gamma rhythm of electric activity of the person's brain in sensory coding." *Biomedical Technologies and Radio Electronics* 3: 34–42.

Danilova, N. N., N. B. Bykova, Y. Pirogov, and E. N. Sokolov. 2005. "Research of the frequency specificity of the gamma rhythm oscillators by methods of dipole analysis and anatomic magnetic resonance tomography." *Biomedical Technologies and Radio Electronics* 4–5: 89–97.

Danilova, N. N., and A. A. Hankevich. 2001. "Gamma rhythm in the conditions of time intervals distinction." *Herald of the Moscow State University* 14, no. 1: 51.

Duncan, J. 2004. "Selective attention in distributed brain system." In *Progress in Attention Research: Cognitive Neuroscience of Attention*, ed. M. Posner, 105–113. London: Guilford Press.

Eckhorn, R., R. Bauer, W. Jorden, M. Brosch, W. Kruse, M. H. J. Munk, and H. J. Reitboeck. 1988. "Coherent oscillations: a mechanism of feature linking in the visual cortex?

Multiple electrode and correlation analyses in the cat." *Biological Cybernetics* 60, no. 2: 121–130.

Galambos, R. A. 1992. "Comparison of certain gamma band (40-HZ) brain rhythms in cat and man." In *Induced Rhythms in the Brain*, ed. E. Basar and T. H. Bullak, 201–206. Boston: Brikhauser.

Goldman-Rakic, P. C. 1996. "Regional and cellular fractionation of working memory." *Proceedings of the National Academy of Sciences* 26, no. 9: 13473–13480.

Grechenko, T. N. 2008. "Pacemaker neuron activity: origin and functions." In *Neuron: Signals Processing, Plasticity, Modelling*, ed. E. N. Sokolov, V. A. Filippova, and A. M. Chernorizova, 324–432. Tyumen: Tyumen State University Press.

Grechenko, T. N. and E. N. Sokolov. 1979. "Endoneuranal plasticity of the isolated neurons of edible snail." *Higher Nervous Activity* 29, no. 5: 1093–1095.

Jensen, O., and J. E. Lisman. 2005. "Hippocampal sequence-encoding driven by a cortical multi-item working memory buffer." *Trends in Neuroscience* 28, no. 2: 67–72.

Jensen, O., and C. Tesche. 2002. "Frontal theta activity in humans increases with memory load in a working memory task." *European Journal of Neuroscience* 15, no. 8: 1395–1399.

Kazantsev, V. B., V. I. Nekorkin, V. I. Makarenko, and R. Llinas. 2004. "Self-referential phase reset based on inferior olive oscillator dynamics." *Proceedings of the National Academy of Sciences* 101, no. 52: 18183–18188.

Livanov, M. N. 1972. *The Spatial Organization of the Brain Processes*. New York: Wiley.

Logothetis, N. K., J. Pauls, M. Augath, T. Trinath, and A. Oeltermann. 2001. "Neurophysiological investigation of the basis the fMRI signal." *Nature* 412, no. 6843: 150–157.

Lutzenberger, W., F. Pulvermuller, and N. Birbaumer. 1994. "Words and pseudowords elicit distinct patterns of 30-Hz activity in humans." *Neuroscience Letters* 176, no. 1: 115–118.

Mantini, D., M. G. Perrucci, C. Del Gratta, G. L. Romani and M. Corbetta. 2007. "Electrophysiological signatures of resting state networks in the human brain." *Proceedings of the National Academy of Sciences* 104, no. 32: 13170–13175.

Mima, T., N. Simpkins, T. Oluwatimilehin, and M. Hallett. 1999. "Force level modulates human cortical oscillatory activities." *Neuroscience Letters* 275, no. 2: 77–80.

Palikhova, T. A. 1995. "Edible snails in psychophysiology." *Herald of the Moscow University* 14, no. 4: 54–62.

Pavlov, I. P. 1951. *Collected Works*. Moscow: AN USSR Press.

Pedroarena, C., and R. Llinas. 1997. "Dendritic calcium conductances generate high-frequency oscillation in thalamocortical neurons." *Proceedings of the National Academy of Sciences* 94, no. 2: 724–728.

Popivanov, D., A. Mineva and I. Krekule. 1999. "EEG patterns in theta-frequency-range and gamma-frequency-range and their probable relation to human voluntary movement organization." *Neuroscience Letters* 267, no. 1: 5–8.

Posner, M. I., ed. 2004. *Progress in attention research: Cognitive neuroscience of attention*. London: Guilford Press.

Pulvermuller, F., H. Preissl, W. Lutzenberger, and N. Birbaumer. 1995. "Spectral responses in the gamma-band: physiological signs of higher cognitive processes?" *NeuroReport* 6, no. 15: 2059–2064.

Sannita, W. G. 2000. "Stimulus-specific oscillatory responses of the brain: a time/frequency-related coding process." *Clinical Neurophysiology* 111, no. 4: 565–583.

Sarnthein, J., H. Petsche, P. Rappelsberger, G. L. Shaw, and A. Stein. 1998. "Synchronization between prefrontal and posterior association cortex during human working memory." *Proceedings of the National Academy of Sciences* 95, no. 12: 7092–7096.

Sauseng, P., J. Hoppe, W. Klimesch, C. Gerloff, and F. C. Hummel. 2007. "Dissociation of sustained attention from central executive functions: local activity and interregional connectivity in the theta range." *European Journal of Neuroscience* 25, no. 2: 1435–1444.

Sauseng, P., W. Klimesch, W. R. Gruber, and N. Birbaumer. 2008. "Cross-frequency phase synchronization: A brain mechanism of memory matching and attention." *NeuroImage* 40, no. 1: 308–317.

Sauseng, P., W. Klimesch, W. R. Gruber, S. Hanslmayr, R. Freunberger and M. Doppelmayr. 2007. "Are event-related potential components generated by phaseresetting of brain oscillations?" *Neuroscience* 146, no. 4: 1435–1444.

Sheviakova, A. and T. Palikhova 2002. "Pacemaker activity as a frequency filter." *International Journal of Psychophysiology* 45, no. 1–2: 14.

Shibata, T., I. Shimoyama, T. Ito, D. Abla, H. Iwasa, K. Koseki, N. Yamanouchi, T. Sato, and Y. Nakajima. 1999. "Event-related dynamics of the gamma-band oscillation in the human Brain – information-processing during a GO/NOGO hand movement task." *Neuroscience Research* 33, no. 3: 215–222.

Singer, W. 1991. "Response synchronization of cortical neurons: an epiphenomenon or a solution to the binding problem?" *Ibro News* 19, no. 1: 6–7.

Singer, W. and C. M. Gray. 1995. "Visual feature integration and the temporal correlation hypothesis." *Annual Review of Neuroscience* 18: 555–586.

Sokolov, E. N. 1981. *Neural Mechanisms of Memory and Learning*. Moscow: Nauka.

Sokolov, E. N. 2003. *Perception and a Conditioned Reflex: The New View*. Moscow. UMK.

Sokolov, E. N., and N. I. Nezlina. 2007. "The conditioned reflex and command neuron." *Higher Nervous Activity* 57, no. 1: 5–22.

Spydel, J. D., M. R. Ford, and D. E. Sheer. 1979. "Task dependent cerebral lateralization of the 40 Hz EEG rhythm." *Psychophysiology* 16, no. 4: 347–350.

Tallon-Baudry, C., O. Bertrand, P. Bouchet and J. Pernier. 1995. "Gamma-range activity evoked by coherent visual stimuli in humans." *European Journal of Neuroscience* 7, no. 6: 1285–1291.

Tallon-baudry, C., A. Kreiter, and O. Bertrand. 1999. "Sustained and Transient Oscillatory Responses in the Gamma-Band and Beta-Band in a Visual Short-Term-Memory Task in Humans." *Visual Neuroscience* 16, no. 3: 449–459.

Tiitinen, H., J. Sibkkonen, K. Reinkainen, K. Alho, J. Lavikainen, and R. Naatanen. 1993. "Selective attention enhances the auditory 40-Hz transient response in humans." *Nature* 364, no. 6432: 59–60.

Von der Malsburg, C., and W. Schneider. 1995. "Binding in models of perception and brain function." *Current Opinion in Neurobiology* 5, no. 4: 520–526.

CHAPTER 11

Oscillatory Self-organization of Cyclic Synthesis of Sensory Information and Memory Content for Object Recognition

Sergey A. Miroshnikov, Margarita G. Filippova, and Roman V. Chernov

1   **Introduction**

Within the curriculum and research of the faculty of psychology at the Saint-Petersburg State University, there are many deeply intertwined topics from general psychology, philosophy, and epistemology. That tradition is attributable to the fact that the chair of psychology was originally within the faculty of philosophy. And it is a common viewpoint there that psychology is more closely related to philosophy than to physiology.

On the other hand, there are strong physiological traditions in Russia, so students of psychology have opportunities to study physiology and to take part in physiological research with specialists from the Pavlov Institute of physiology, and the many laboratories in the University. Much historic research was done at the intersection of physiology and psychology, such as I. P. Pavlov's reflective theory of brain, P. K. Anokhin's theory of functional systems, and P. V. Simonov's informational theory of emotions. This interdisciplinary research has had a profound effect on the goals and objectives of many psychology researchers.

These features of the Russian psychological school are reflected in full measure within in the research described in this chapter, which synthesizes several different, and often opposed approaches, from different sciences: a philosophical understanding of information (as content of psychic reflection); an epistemological problem of identification of non-identical objects (both known and perceived objects); physical ideas about uniform fields and possible interactions of quantum biological structures; and, of course, neurophysiological and psychological research into perception and consciousness.

Both the main goal of the research – consciousness – and the particular approaches, including special attention to not only success, but distinctive errors of consciousness, are largely a product of the school of V. M. Allahverdov, with whom the author has communicated extensively, initially as a student and later as a research assistant.

2 Purpose of the Research

The purpose of our research is to develop a theoretical and computer model of the fundamental mechanisms of information processing underlying consciousness. The problem addressed in the current stage of experimentation concerns modeling the self-organization of the cyclic information synthesis by which sensory information and memory content produce a uniform conscious image that reflects a new object as a member of a known class.

The method emphasizes the computer modeling of systems of auto-oscillatory elements as they oscillate and cooperate through a uniform field. This research's theoretical hypothesis synthesizes the known "mutually exclusive" approaches and supplements them with the theory of oscillatory-field organization of the mechanisms that produce conscious phenomena. In brief, the theory says that besides the neural net impulse processing of information, there is another related, but rather independent, oscillatory-field mechanism of information processing, which likely plays a main role in consciousness phenomena. The central propositions of this theory are based on analysis of many neuronal, physical, and informational processes from an oscillating systems perspective, and on the known laws of diffusion and interaction of oscillations (universal for different types of fields and oscillators).

3 Prototypes and Models

Analogs of the theoretical and artificial computer "oscillators" (or auto-oscillatory modules – AOM) are found in real neuronal systems. They occur both with known systems of interconnected neurons and subcellular structures (such as membranes with fluctuations of superficial potentials), and with hypothetical quantum or other biophysical oscillators.

The analog of "field" here is the "excitable neural tissue" as a whole. Specifically, oscillatory modules may be most precisely described in terms of a field (just as in one aspect the photon is better described as a particle, and in others as a wave). The analog of "displacement" of an oscillator and field here is the deflection of a level of activity (amount of impulses, potential etc.) from some equilibrium state.

An artificial neural net may reproduce properties of a "threshold neuron" with selected properties of a biological neuron, and similarly, our artificial "field" instantiates a set of selected properties from larger scale excitable neuronal structures. These properties determine its ability to generate and diffuse oscillations. In this sense, our model of a "field" and system of oscillators is distinct from excitable tissue, much as a mathematical neuron is distinct from a biological one. In both cases, the common modeling approach is to identify specific informational properties of the real biosystem and to analyze their role in information processing. Subsequently, the main goal here is to investigate and reproduce facets of information processing accomplished through oscillating systems, irrespective of the physical realization of "oscillators" and "oscillatory fields" in biological systems. We believe this model presents a more unified whole than approaches based on systems of separate neurons, and its systemic features can result in new emergent phenomena, that correspond to the integrated organization of information processing in the brain as a whole. In other words, we believe that this particular organization, according to Chalmers' double aspect theory of information (Chalmers 1996), allows the phenomenal quality of wholly organized information to arise (by means of dynamical integration of isolated physical information units in the uniform field's oscillations).

The analogy between this theoretical "field" to global physical fields raises numerous research questions concerning the oscillatory field-information interaction in and between biological systems. But we do not analyze this perspective problem here. We base this research only on known properties of neuronal systems (or more widely, excitable tissue) and on universal laws of oscillatory motion in general.

This approach suggests:

> theoretically – a synthesis of basic theoretical positions, which are usually considered incompatible with empirical investigation;
> empirically – evidence for a new theory of oscillatory-field information processing;
> and experimentally – an approach to gain new experimental results that confirm the theory and open new perspective directions of research.

4 Basic Theoretical Positions of the Research

1. Synthesis of fundamental physical approaches. *Classical physics* is applicable to analysis of systems of a macro-world, including the domain

of neural-reflex based on impulse transfer and processing of information. Higher-level organization is based on diffusion and interaction of oscillations within a field and demands the approaches of classical and *quantum physics*. The development of the system as a whole, including its modeling, demands a *synergetic* approach to investigation, analysis and reproducing elements and their interactions.

2. Approach the problem of *mind, body and matter interrelation*: the contents of mind are information. When unorganized, it is a passive property or function of matter, but when mentally organized, it becomes a qualitatively new emergent whole and has a mutual influence on both body and external matter.

3. In the problem of *determinism and freedom of will*, any choice leads us to the logical impasse: is the mind an automatic device, or an unpredictable ruling force upon the organism that may be maladaptive and dangerous to the survival of the organism? However, we can synthesize these approaches, relating them to interconnected levels of organization, the macro- and micro-levels (quantum phenomena with characteristic spontaneity). We believe that determination in macro-objects reflects the systemic statistical quality of its indeterminate quantum substratum. The behavior of the subject is a result of interaction of the spontaneous and determined phenomena occurring at different levels of organization.

4. The *principal level of biosystem organization* discussed here cannot be precisely defined. Throughout our analysis of the psychophysical system, several levels must be addressed, from diffusion and interaction of oscillations of a uniform field to neurons, neural nets, and extending on to systems of conscious phenomena.

5. Our approach to the problem of localization, the neural-reflex level of an organism, is based on local representation of information in the nervous system. By contrast, consciousness occurs at a different level and is based on the distributed representation of information in the oscillations of modules and uniform field, therefore all the brain (equipotentially) participates in producing conscious phenomena (Miroshnikov 2000).

This proposed theory explains known neurophysiological and psychological data (including laws of the activity of consciousness). Nevertheless, without experimental confirmation, it remains just one hypothesis among many others. The basic experimental method employed for substantiation and development of the theory of oscillatory-field information processing in consciousness emphasizes parallel experimentation with a uniform set of stimuli presented to computer models and human test subjects.

5 Definition of the New Approach in Comparison with Known Artificial Neural Nets

5.1 Main Differences

(1) The unit of the system is not a neuron, but instead an auto-oscillatory module (AOM) cooperating with a uniform field. The equation that realizes this in a computer model in every i (a time unit) defines an acceleration of an oscillator (a) according to its own angular frequency (Wo) and its initial state – shift (A) from an equilibrium state.

$$a^i = W_o^2 A^{i-A}, \text{ where } W_o = \frac{2\pi}{T}$$

The characteristic behavior of such harmonious oscillators is shown on the next diagram for the interaction of two oscillators with different frequencies. This is synonymous with the synchronization of pendulums of average frequency (see Figure 11.1).

Within Figure 11.1, basic stages of the synchronization process are shown: from initial fluctuations of every pendulum in mutual anti-phase with its own period (50 and 54 time units) to synchronization on an average period (52 time units). The pendulum with a shorter period is "leading" and the second is "led,"

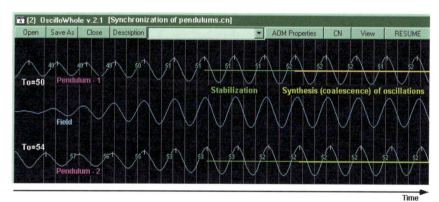

FIGURE 11.1 The simplest example of a spontaneous synchronization of oscillators and self-organization of the simplest oscillatory-field system

———— thin green line show stabilization of period of the oscillator
———— thick yellow-green line shows dependency of the oscillator in its coherent relation to other (with which it makes unified oscillatory system)
———— thick orange line shows influence, superiority of the oscillator in its coherent relation to other
To is own (ideal) period of oscillations for that oscillator
Numbers on diagrams of oscillations are working (real) periods of oscillations

which is shown by various colors of axial lines. The line F shows the shift of a field, which in known physical prototypes, can be realized by, for example, by the common horizontal strand (on which vertical strands of pendulums are attached) or an electromagnetic field (in an electromagnetic oscillatory contour).

We can see similar stages of interaction of oscillators in more complex systems, where self-organization of a recognition cycle is shown (see Figure 11.2 and 11.4). That is, we can treat the dynamics of pendulums here as an elementary model of information synthesis (given the assumption that oscillations carry some information, for example, about properties of a pendulum or about actions that evoked its fluctuations).

(2) The absence of discrete impulses (information is carried by continuous oscillations of modules and field).

(3) Absence of structural connections transmitting impulses. Connections between oscillators are only dynamic ones. They spontaneously arise on the basis of interactions with a field and synchronization of oscillators.

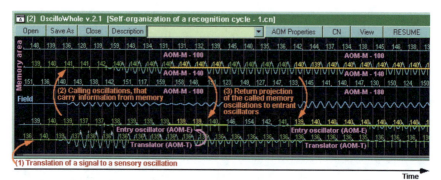

FIGURE 11.2   Self-organization of the "re-entering" cycle of object recognition. Here diagrams of oscillators and field are represented as follows (from bottom to up):

Stimuli.   The lowermost strip shows presence of a stimulus in sensory field corresponding to the AOM-Translator (here the stimulus of luminance 140 units is used).

AOM-T.   One inferior curve shows shift of the AOM-Translator (from equilibrium position).

AOM-E.   Entrant oscillators reflect actual contents of the corresponding sensory fields and related subjective experience (by acceptance initial "sensory" frequency from the related translator, and then – frequency called from AOM-Memory).

Field.   The blue curve shows a state of a field. It depends on shifts of all oscillators, and on the other hand, influences all oscillators.

AOM-M.   Three top curves show states of memory oscillators, "previously trained" for resonance activation by frequencies reflecting stimuli of luminance 100 (backgrounds), 140 and 180 units (AOM-M-100, AOM-M-140, AOM-M-180).

OSCILLATORY SELF-ORGANIZATION OF CYCLIC SYNTHESIS 303

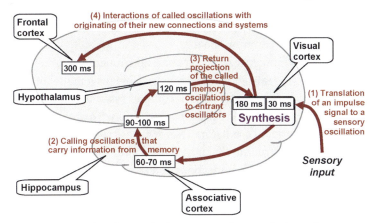

FIGURE 11.3 The scheme of information synthesis on the base of "re-entering" as it is described in papers of A. M. Ivanitsky. We show here the same main stages (1-2-3) as presented above on the diagram of the oscillatory processes in the model.

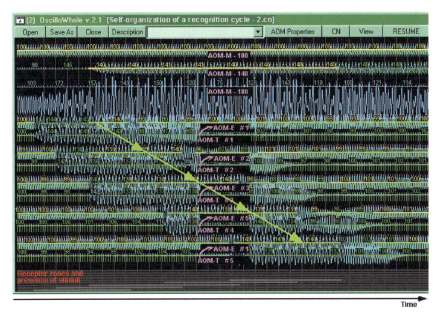

FIGURE 11.4 Oscillatory reflection of the moving stimulus. Thick horizontal green lines at AOM-E oscillators diagrams show periods of coherence with some memory oscillator AOM-E (that reflects experimental stimulus or background and marked by thick orange line when it is actively related with some entrant oscillator and projecting information to it). The thick diagonal multi-arrow green line shows movement of constant reflection (image) of the stimulus on oscillators according to movement of the reflected and recognized stimulus.

(4) Unity of three forms of representation of the information (which are characteristic of different "mutually exclusive" theories of consciousness): local (on one oscillator), distributed (on connected oscillators), and equipotential (on oscillations of the common "field").

(5) The greatest possible integrity of the system: all connections of all elements with one another are realized through one variable (as a model of one common field). Certainly, for a reconstruction of complex systems, a more complex model of a field may be required (e.g. extended field with areas that are more or less related with different oscillators). Nevertheless, the integrity of the system will be greatest – and structurally, energetically much more economic – than in any network organization of connections of all elements to one another.

5.2   Main Similarities

(1) With respect to the similarity between simulated types oscillators and known types of neurons – for example, in creating a whole regulating system, we must use three main types of oscillators:

AOM-T. Translators. They transform discrete signals from stimuli (physical agents or nervous impulses) into oscillations of the common field. Thus, they are "receptors," not of the neural systems, but the oscillatory system.

AOM-E. Entrant, or primary (initial) projective oscillators. They receive (by means of a resonance mechanism) both sensory information projections from translators and relevant information projections from memory and motivational zones.

AOM-M. Memory oscillators that carry information of sensory and motor experience of the subject, and related information (e.g. about subjective value of stimuli, related unperceived objects, necessary actions, etc.) As a whole, the informational content of these oscillators may be thought of as the subjective picture of the world, because the experience reflected in memory constitutes subjective ideas concerning the world and the subject itself, and what is generally consistent across situations.

(2) Similar properties of an oscillator and threshold neuron, in particular, threshold function, determine transition from a passive regiment of "expectation" and resonance "reception" to an active regiment of "radiation" (or "broadcast") of oscillations and the information corresponding to the field.

6   Experiment with Self-organization of a Cycle of Object Recognition

Our experiments with the model have shown that the described oscillatory system, despite simplicity and variations in stimuli, provides steady self-organization of a cycle of object recognition on the basis of "re-entering" of sensory information (after interaction with memory) to initial projections. This corresponds to experimental data of neuropsychology and to theories of recognition as a synthesis of actual sensory information and subjective memory content (Edelman and Mountcastle 1978; Edelman 1989; Sporns et al. 1989; Cauller and Kulics 1991; Sporns et al. 1991; Stoerig and Brandt 1993; Sergin 1994; Desmedt and Tomberg 1995; Gray 1995; Ivanitsky 2000).

When a stimulus of sufficiently similar luminance (to one stored earlier in memory) is present in the receptor area of a translator, we can observe the following stages of self-organization of a cycle of information synthesis (numbers correspond to stages at Figures 11.2 and 11.3):

(1) Translation of physical input from a stimulus (luminance) to oscillations of the field, and reflection of a stimulus in an initial sensory oscillation (that was not stored in memory earlier) of an AOM-Entrant oscillator by means of transferring sensory frequency to the AOM-E at its own frequency.

(2) "Projection" of a sensory oscillation to all AOM-Memory oscillators and activation of an oscillator, which frequency is both similar to the arriving sensory oscillation and reflects the specific class of stimuli; thus with its oscillations, information about similar objects from this class of objects is initialized within the field.

(3) Projection of the retrieved energetic memory oscillation (and its information) back onto an entrant oscillator, that is the "re-entering" of a sensory oscillation after its "interaction" with memory oscillators. This re-entering forms the synthetic oscillation, having these features:

Synthesis of properties (including propagated information) of an initial sensory oscillation (of the translator and the entrant oscillator) and the related oscillation retrieved from memory.

Reception of the frequency of the retrieved memory oscillation (reflecting the "known" class of stimulus) as the manifest frequency (i.e., transition from simple physical reflection of a stimulus from sensory oscillation, to reflecting a variant of the known class).

All these stages of information synthesis spontaneously arise (i.e., self-organize) in experiments with both the simplest and more complex models. In fact, these stages correspond to the stages giving rise to a conscious image that are observed in neurophysiological experiments and described in many papers (Edelman and Mountcastle 1978; Edelman 1989; Sporns et al. 1989; Cauller and Kulics 1991; Sporns et al. 1991; Stoerig and Brandt 1993; Sergin 1994; Desmedt and Tomberg 1995; Gray 1995; Ivanitsky 2000) as presented in Figure 11.3.

7 Experimentally Demonstrated Features of Oscillatory Information Synthesis Conforming to the Known Psychological Laws of Object Recognition and Its Manifestation in Consciousness

Simple experimental variations to initial conditions and pre-existing contents of the system elicit (during experiments with the oscillatory model) features of information synthesis conforming to the known psychological laws of object recognition and its manifestation in consciousness. In other words, the described approach results not only in steady and economic (of several elements) self-organization of cyclic synthesis of the actual information and memory content, but it also produces some secondary features of information processing. These features conform to basic psychological features and laws of the processes of consciousness. All these features and laws are well known and we have demonstrated them in parallel experiments with both computer models and human subjects studies:

(1) The greater the difference between a perceived stimulus and the prototype of the known class, there is a longer latency to attain object recognition (in experiments with humans). A similarly longer duration of self-organization for the information synthesis cycle (in models) has been observed.

(2) There are temporary "doubts" ("it is ..." / "it is not ...") in humans, similar to "fluctuations" of the object recognition cycle in models when perceiving stimuli that are sufficiently distinct from the characteristics of the prototype for an object class. These "subjective fluctuations" are based on:

> laws of process of synchronization (e.g., its dynamics in two dimensions: frequency and phase, and with "one preventing the other" – see Figures 11.2 and 11.4); and
>
> interference between conflicting memory oscillations elicited by different sensory oscillations; for example, recognizing a stimulus of luminance 145 or 155 as a known type (140 or 160) takes twice as long immediately after recognizing the stimulus of another type, in comparison with recognition of the same stimulus without previous recognition of alternative.

(3) There is a similar facilitation of object recognition by preliminary activation of knowledge about a corresponding class of stimuli (by direct presentation or through associations) in humans, and facilitation through the self-organization of the information synthesis cycle in models. This effect also appears with more frequent presentation of an intermediate

stimulus (e.g., the length of which is more than the first class and less than the second class) as a variant of the class, corresponding to an image recognized earlier. This effect is demonstrated in two situations:

when preliminary exposure to the stimuli was ether supraliminal or subliminal;
  when a stimulus of the same class is projected to the same or different receptor zones (see Figure 11.4 about presentation of a moving stimulus).

(4) Interference phenomena observed when perceiving similar stimuli – from constancy of perception to suppression and substitution of experience of one stimulus by the other stimulus. Figure 11.4 presents results demonstrating the *constancy of perception for a moving stimulus*. This effect is based on the constant activity of a memory oscillator (AOM-M-140) previously activated by sensory oscillation which continuously projects its oscillation (and information – the image of the typical object) onto different entrant oscillators according to movement of the stimulus from one receptor zone to another. This process corresponds to known neurophysiological experimental data and theoretical hypotheses about dynamic "locus of information interaction." This focus (presented also in Figure 11.3) reflects the dynamic integration of information received from entrant and memory oscillators. The progression of oscillatory activity corresponds to movement of the stimulus and its projection on entrant oscillators.

In these demonstrations, it is also evident that there is an effect of subjectively greater "visual speed" at the beginning of the movement trajectory and less "visual speed" at the subsequent portion of the trajectory.

The *constancy of perception for a changed stimulus* appears in the conservation of activity of one memory oscillator, projecting the information to the same sensory oscillator despite a change of stimulation, which approaches another known class of stimuli. For example, if the stimulus is identified as class "160" and the experienced stimulus AOM-M-160 is activated, consequently:

presentation of a stimulus of luminance from 159 to 147 results in the stimulus being experienced as *the same* '160' (in these cases, only short temporal fluctuations will occur if a new stimulus replaces the previous one).
  presentation of a stimulus of luminance from 146 to 143 results in long fluctuations that are a product of suppression of response to stimuli usually

recognized as class '140' by the concurrent image of '160'. For example, in the conditions mentioned, the stimulus '145' was not experienced at all in half of the cases (for a period ten times longer than the usual period of identification). This phenomenon may be interpreted as "replacement" of the image by the image of stimulus 160.

Only presentation of a stimulus of luminance from 142 to 140 that is very close to another standard (140) results in activation of AOM-M-140, causing stimulus 140 to be experienced, and the corresponding re-projection of the oscillation and recognition of the stimulus as different from the first.

There is an increased delay in choice behavior with an increase in the number of expected stimulation alternatives. The corresponding information is activated in memory, though is not localized on entrant oscillators.

There is a wavy (normal) allocation of results. With random variation in the relationship between stimulation time and phases of oscillators, the duration for recognition (from stimulation to re-entry in the circuit of information projection) changes more. This is an inevitable feature of the oscillatory-resonance mechanism: even a small difference in the ratio of stimulation time and phases of active oscillators (or with phases of the "states of the subject") results in larger differences in the time of information synthesis. And these differences are much greater than differences in time of arrival of a signal to the cortex (from receptors).

In Figure 11.5, we present a wave (normal) distribution for an oscillatory model in comparison to a logical model, a neural net, and a human (for the same simple stimulation, a light circle on a dark background). For analysis of the reaction time distribution, we used time units characterizing *different states of the models*, and thus characterized information processing at the level of the model's structure (logical blocks, neurons, connections or oscillator states) not a level deeper (of physical computer processes) than the model itself.

If the duration of one oscillation defines the time for stimulus recognition, the resulting curve will be similar to that oscillation. If the duration of multiple oscillations define the time for stimulus recognition, the resulting curve will be a superposition of many oscillations having a different period, magnitude, and importance for the information processing, etc. Therefore, the curve will be more widespread and similar to a normal distribution. This and other comparative results have been demonstrated with four types of experiments: a computer algorithmic model; a multilevel embodied artificial neural net with all-to-all connections; the above-described oscillatory model; and human subjects. Of course, results may be different if we use, for example, another type of

OSCILLATORY SELF-ORGANIZATION OF CYCLIC SYNTHESIS

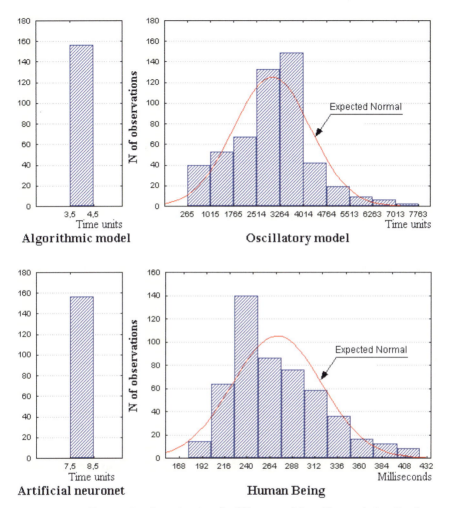

FIGURE 11.5 Frequencies of reaction time for different models and human being. Simplest stimulus on simplest background was presented to simplest models (in which only main ideas of the correspondent approach were realized without any additional mechanisms or stimulation for randomize reactions).

neural net. Moreover we can build algorithmic and neural net models that will have results more closely similar to the characteristics of human processing of the information. This is possible by means of special additional functions (for example, casual disorder of reaction time). However, here we compare models with respect to their basic functions. For an algorithmic model, it is "input–calculation–output." For a neural net, it is a network of the same elements with the transfer of results of processing through connections between elements.

For an oscillatory model, the functions are those attributable to the structure described above.

The difference between the oscillatory model and humans may depend on the number of active AOMs in the model. With more oscillating AOMs, the function is smoother and more similar to the human results. With fewer AOMs, the function is more angular and similar to that observed with the neural net and algorithmic models.

Similar to observations with humans, a smooth relationship is observed between the energy of stimulation (or time of stimulus exposure) and the probability of stimulus recognition by the subject (*S-function of thresholds*). This differs sharply from the ladder-shaped threshold function that is typical for algorithmic models and simple neural nets.

The *substitution of experience of a supraliminal stimulus by another previously presented subliminal stimulus* effect was found in experiments with oscillatory models, and then demonstrated in parallel experiments with human test subjects.

At the training stage of our experiment, subjects (N=52) were trained to distinguish three classes of simple figures. For the control condition, we first showed the subliminal figure (for 15 milliseconds with a subsequent masking stimulus, a brighter circle). Then (after 50–350 milliseconds), we showed the basic supraliminal figure (for 100 ms). Where the subliminal stimulus corresponded to the same class as the supraliminal one, the number of correct answers increased (as compared to the presentation only of supraliminal stimuli). Where the subliminal stimulus corresponded to another class (not the same class as the supraliminal one), the number of correct answers decreased (as compared to the presentation of only a supraliminal stimulus). The number of errors involving classification of the basic supraliminal stimulus as the same class as the previously presented subliminal stimulus underwent an increase. All of these tendencies are statistically reliable, and are consistent in experiments with both humans and oscillatory models.

8 New Theoretical Conclusions and Plans of Empirical and Modeling Research

From the point of view of cognitive science, the primary topic of the processes described above is information processing, in other words, the perception and identification of objects. But if we conduct more detailed and multilevel analyses of the essential processes integral to perception and identification in our model, and then analyze the possible additional roles of the structure and essential processes of the model described above, we can conclude that those additional processes and roles may have their own special significance for the psychic life of humans.

First, there is the informational content and the role of the relatively stable subjective picture of the world (including oneself, from abstract to concrete, from knowledge to skills, etc.), that determine all specific subjective aspects of information processing, which amounts to defining the informational processing system of a subject or person. Below we describe the processes that are integral components of perception and identification in our model, and then we suggest analog processes related to cognitive processes in animate systems.

An essential part of information synthesis are processes of confirmation. Accordingly, activation due to perceptive processes must overcome suppression of memory information due to antagonistic memory oscillators (and images represented by them), including suppression of previously activated oscillators (and the memory images represented by them). These processes of confirmation, or suppression of conflicting memory images that constitute the individual's world picture, are processes of objectively evaluating the adequacy of the world picture, with regard to its conformity to true (including truly possible) content of the real world. Consequently, such processes must have great significance for successful adaptation of an animate system to the world, a significance both for evaluation of the world picture's adequacy, and, more widely, for developing its adequacy (by means of correcting the world picture or the world). Therefore, these processes must be present as obligatory constituents in psychic life and are important more for evaluation of the adequacy of the subjects' own knowledge, expectations, etc., regarding reality, than for perception itself.

In living organisms, a hypothetical analog of the processes described in the proposed model occur with emotions (or affects), which may be subdivided into positive and negative affects (based on an evaluation of conformity to expectations and the situation). Later, emotions develop into more specific and differentiated experiences. For example, when one is confronted with an inadequate situation, the primary negative emotion may be experienced as grief (where correcting expectations) or indignation (with attempts to correct the actual state of affairs).

Second, processes involving activation of memory information are an essential part of information synthesis, as are activation of images from the world model and their effect on each other and on the behavior of the system in general. An active image may activate other relevant images, including images of operations that lead the subject to behavior that realizes the imagined object. In this way, the memory image determines the resulting behavior, and the experience of the actual object.

In living organisms, a hypothetical analog is found with impulses arising from an imagined object which result in activities to obtain the object. The intensity of such processes determines the subjective experience and personal attitude toward the image and corresponding object, from phlegmatic recollections of indifferent things, to an active need for the corresponding object. The strength of the activation of images depends on biologically determined relations, leading to more stable and stronger impulses and needs.

In accordance with these analogs, we can draw two conclusions about other essential roles and processes giving rise to the perception and identification of objects:

(1) every perceptive process has an affective (emotional) component, which becomes more pronounced when the experienced image is more vividly represented within memory, and when confirmation or suppression is more drastic.

(2) every experienced image (or experienced through memory) can have a wide range of effects, from relatively passive information to actively motivating activity. The effects realized depend on the strength of the experienced image and its ability to activate other images, and most of all on the presence of associated images of activity.

In this way, the information synthesis cycle, which is the basic dynamic structure in modeling perception and identification, provides the basis for understanding and modeling the broader content of psychic life as a whole, including spheres of motivation and emotions.

The proposed model represents a logical deduction from a theoretical model and its laws, and, on the other hand, the main hypothesis of the next stage of our research. That stage is directed towards validating the analogs discussed here by means of a series of experiments, confirmed both for computer models and humans. In particular, we plan to introduce specific emotions in accordance with the classification (of mechanisms of emotional experiences) based on the theoretical and computer model. We have plans for more complex experiments using associative relations and context to arouse incentives for certain choices, in accordance with theoretical mechanisms of perceptual images serving as incentives.

9 Conclusion

To date, we have only implemented several rather simple models and experiments. But our results give us a basis for a conclusion. The transition from logical blocks and network organization of a psychophysical model to a field-centered oscillatory whole has resulted in a working model illustrating information processing that corresponds to neurophysiological and psychological data, and also to the scientific and philosophical theories of consciousness, describing the conscious reflectance upon a new object as variant of a known class of objects. Our theoretical and experimental results show that the combination of impulsive and oscillatory information processing combines the advantages of both, resulting in more effective models that behave similarly to human information processing.

References

Cauller, L., and A. T. Kulics. 1991. "The neural basis of the behaviorally relevant N1 component of the somatosensory-evoked potential in S1 cortex of awake monkeys: evidence that backward cortical projections signal touch sensation." *Experimental Brain Research* 83, no. 3: 607–619.

Chalmers, D. 1996. *The Conscious Mind: In Search of a Fundamental Theory*. Oxford: Oxford University Press.

Desmedt, J., and C. Tomberg. 1995. "Neurophysiology of preconscious and conscious mechanisms of the human brain." *Electroencephalography and Clinical Neurophysiology/ Electromyography and Motor Control* 97, no. 4: S4.

Edelman, G. 1989. *The Remembered Present: A Biological Theory of Consciousness*. New York: Basic Books.

Edelman, G., and V. Mountcastle. 1978. *Mindful Brain: Cortical Organization and the Group Selection Theory of Human Brain Function*. Cambridge, Mass.: MIT Press.

Gray, J. A. 1995. "The contents of consciousness: A neuropsychological conjecture." *Behavioral and Brain Sciences* 18, no. 4: 659–676.

Ivanitsky, A. M. 2000. "Informational synthesis in crucial cortical area, as the brain basis of subjective experience." In *Complex Brain Functions: Conceptual Advances in Russian Neuroscience*, ed. R. Miller, A. M. Ivanitsky, and P. V. Balaban, 72–95. Amsterdam: Harwood Academic.

Miroshnikov, S. A. 2000. "Theoretical and computer modeling of the neuropsychological system: from reflex – to consciousness." *Cognitive Sciences eprints Archive* at http://cogprints.soton.ac.uk/documents/disk0/00/00/09/55.

Sergin, V. Y. 1994. "The consciousness as the system of inner vision." *Higher Nervous Activity* 44: 627–639.

Sporns, O., J. A. Gally, G. N. Reeke, and G. Edelman. 1989. "Reentrant signaling among simulated neuronal groups leads to coherency in their oscillatory activity." *Proceedings of the National Academy of Sciences* 86, no. 18: 7265–7269.

Sporns, O., G. Tonini, and G. Edelman. 1991. "Modeling perceptual grouping and figure-ground segregation by means of active reentrant connections." *Proceedings of the National Academy of Sciences* 88, no. 1: 129–133.

Stoerig, P. and S. Brandt. 1993. "The visual system and levels of perception: properties of neuromental organization." *Theoretical Medicine and Bioethics* 14, no. 2: 117–135.

SECTION 3 COMMENTARY

Models of Neural Dynamics Provide a Foundation for Neurocognitive Interventions

Chris Forsythe and Gabriel A. Radvansky

In this section, Danilova describes methods for studying the tomographic analysis of brain activity recorded using EEG and this activity's link to cognitive processes. Knyazev summarizes a program of research to understand brain correlates of personality, while placing conclusions within the context of human evolutionary development. Then, chapters by Nekorkin and Kazantsev, and Miroshnikov and colleagues, report progress toward computational modeling and simulation of the oscillatory dynamics of neural activity underlying cognitive processes.

    A common thread linking these chapters is a theoretical perspective that measurable behavior and cognitive performance arises from patterns of brain activity involved in the synchronous firing of neural units within certain frequency bands. Granted, this perspective is not new, and has become broadly accepted within modern psychophysiology (Klimesch, 1996). However, in these chapters, the authors develop this perspective towards a noteworthy level of detail, with accompanying elaboration concerning the associated mechanics. It should also be noted how there is an emphasis on, and advancement of, an oscillating systems model for neural processes. This emphasis is a hallmark of Russian cognitive neuroscience, and while not exclusive to Russian scientists, it is a centrally defining characteristic that serves well to distinguish their contributions.

    To better understand the broader implications of Russian cognitive neuroscience, we may begin with a consideration of the conceptual paradigm shaping the research interests, interpretations and theorizing of Russian scientists. The Russian approach has involved systems-oriented theorizing about brain processes, as clearly displayed by the oscillatory systems explanations for the associations observed between electrical recordings of brain activity, and behavioral and performance measures more generally. This method stands in contrast to approaches favoring the isolation and localization of functions. Instead, there is almost a Gestalt-like orientation and attention to larger-scale dynamics and subsystem interactions from the Russian standpoint. Furthermore, included within hypotheses concerning the processes of recruiting and entraining individual neural units to form oscillatory circuits, there is a tacit attempt to bridge different scales of representation and process, thereby explaining phenomena observed at more macro or molar levels on the basis of micro level events.

It should not be controversial to assert that the brain consists of a system of systems, and that events occurring at the interface between functional scales are critical to understanding its overall operation. Taking a step back, this represents an integrated paradigm for understanding brain function, from which certain research priorities emerge, as well as certain methodological approaches. Scientific theorizing is not exempt from inherent cognitive limitations. Our cognitive apparatus has the effect of delimiting what we can and cannot know to that which we can fit into our mental models, as well as arousing certain biases concerning the relative importance of different mechanisms, processes, and phenomena. In this respect, Russian cognitive neuroscience is no different from any other body of science. An oscillating systems model provides a conceptual paradigm for understanding brain processes, but one might ask about the things which this conceptual paradigm conceals, or de-emphasizes, in favor of conclusions consistent with the logic embodied within the paradigm. The chapters in this section were chosen based on the merits of the authors and to acknowledge their esteemed place within Russian, and international, scientific communities. The intent is not to diminish this work, but instead, to draw attention to the effect any conceptual paradigm may have in promoting certain ideas and experimental approaches, sometimes to the exclusion of alternatives.

For the sake of this discussion, we shall grant that this systems-oriented paradigm, and particularly, the oscillating systems perspective, offers a viable model for understanding and explaining the operations of the brain. One might next speculate on the potential applications and consequences of the knowledge that may result from further related scientific study, regardless of the researcher or their nationality. An oscillating systems model goes well beyond models within cognitive neuroscience that describe behavior and performance in terms of circuitry and linkages between different brain regions. This model points to the cyclical dynamics by which such circuitry functions.

A key product of an oscillatory systems paradigm is its implications for considering individual differences in cognitive processing. This paradigm suggests there would be specific brain activation measures that should correspond to behavioral and cognitive performance variables. From the resulting correlations, inferences may be drawn concerning how underlying brain mechanics may be manifested in a variety of observable measures. Related genetic and developmental studies offer further insight, and in combination, a general understanding may be developed in which there is a causal basis for the mechanics of brain activation, in turn giving rise to individual differences in behavior and cognitive performance.

A mechanistic understanding of individual differences in cognitive processes provides an explanatory basis for population distributions in performance, including the extremes of these distributions. In particular, where extreme behaviors are considered maladaptive, various mechanisms and approaches may be deduced for supplying the basis of interventions having the desired outcome of moving certain individuals closer to the desired norm or standard. With advances in biotechnology, potential likely interventions include pharmaceutical therapies, biofeedback training, stimulation using magnetic or direct current, or combinations of these and other techniques (e.g. pulsed light or sound therapy). However, certain dangers arise when applying a mechanistic understanding of individual differences in cognitive processing to supposedly remedy various maladaptive conditions.

First, there may be a temptation to overestimate how well the underlying neurophysiology is understood, risking the potential outcome that an overly simple model is unable to recognize key interactions. Implementing a narrow model may provide the unhelpful opportunity for creating unanticipated and unwanted consequences to therapeutic approaches. In other words, an intervention effectively altering brain dynamics to produce a desired pattern of activation, and perhaps an improvement in targeted outcome measures, may also disrupt or interfere with other systemic processes to produce unintended deficits. Another concern is that an intervention may have a deleterious effect, sufficing to alter the fundamental neural substrate, in a manner that may not be readily reversed. For example, an intervention intended to heighten activation in a given frequency band may cause the neural substrate to adapt by making adjustments in the opposite direction, creating a continued need for the intervention, perhaps in increasing dosages. This is a typical outcome that can occur in cases of drug addiction.

Regarding treatment options whereby brain functions, identified as negatively outside the norm, can be altered to more closely approximate normative patterns, there will be varying degrees of advocacy for providing these treatments. There will likely be cases in which treatments provide individuals with means to enhance their quality of life. However, there will also undoubtedly be other situations in which the deviations from normality are mild, and attempted treatments produce undesirable side effects or unwanted loss of aspects to the supposed affliction that under certain circumstances are beneficial. Moreover, there is the ever-present question of what is truly normative. Brain functioning beyond the statistical norm may be manifested through a differential set of competencies, both negative and positive, but they have only a minimal overall impact upon an individual's capacity to be happy and productive. However, the potential of therapeutic techniques may be unduly appealing to those people who feel uncomfortable about individuals with a different set of cognitive competencies, or feel frustrated by the need to make needed accommodations for those individuals.

Implicit to this discussion is the notion that various therapeutic interventions have undergone some sort of oversight review and approval, in addition to some empirical validation. However, inspired by only a hint that brain function may be altered for the better, some people will inevitably explore options that are readily available, including uncontrolled and unsupervised techniques for achieving the same supposed effects. One may imagine a range of options, including herbal remedies, sound and light exposure, application of electrical fields, etc. Advances in modeling the neural dynamics underlying cognitive function can encourage and enable these risky endeavors by providing the semblance of a scientific basis for crude enhancement techniques. Some approaches may actually be effective; others may prove benign (including results due to placebo effects), and the real potential exists that other techniques could be harmful.

Finally, the greatest risk arises from the potential for nefarious applications. This may occur either through state-sponsored programs or non-governmental clandestine efforts. A high likelihood exists that the scientific underpinnings and presumed utility of techniques will be grossly over-inflated. Scenarios may be envisioned in which technologies are deployed with hopes of heightening the cognitive capacities of military troops, without due consideration for the potential long-term effects of such approaches. Other possibilities involve the use of technologies meant to affect central nervous system functioning, directed at either adversarial forces or at unruly civilian populations.

This commentary has noted many of the risks arising with advances to our understanding of the neural dynamics underlying cognitive function, and in particular, some models providing insight into interventions that may be employed to enhance, or disrupt, cognitive function. This discussion is not intended to advocate any suspension or delay in pursuing these lines of scientific inquiry. Instead, attention is drawn to these risks as a basis for asserting the importance of understanding the negative technological outgrowths from scientific advances, and the need for continual vigilance as scientific and technological achievements pose potential threats to the well-being of individuals, groups, and populations. Furthermore, it should be emphasized that this discussion is directed toward scientific and technical communities, and policy makers at large, and the specific work of Russian researchers only serves to illustrate specific advances. There should be no conclusions drawn that the work of these Russian scientists is in any way more threatening than similar programs of research occurring within the U.S., Europe, and other regions.

Acknowledgement

Sandia National Laboratories is a multiprogram laboratory operated by Sandia Corporation, a Lockheed Martin Company, for the United States Department of Energy's National Nuclear Security Administration under contract DEAC04-94AL85000.

References

Klimesch, W. 1996. "Memory processes, brain oscillations and EEG synchronization." *International Journal of Psychophysiology* 24, no. 1–2: 61–100.

SECTION 4

Russian Translational Neuroscience Research

CHAPTER 12

Individual Alpha Activity Indices and Biofeedback

Olga Mikhailovna Bazanova

> A man is like a bit of Labrador spar, which has no lustre as you turn it in your hand until you come to a particular angle; then it shows deep and beautiful colors. There is no adaptation or universal applicability in men, but each has his special talent, and the mastery of successful men consists in adroitly keeping themselves where and when that turn shall be oftenest to be practiced.
>
> RALPH WALDO EMERSON (1883)

⋮

Individuality is one of most frequently investigated fields in cognition. Despite changes in research paradigms, it has not lost its relevance. Numerous results concerning the conceptualization of general personality traits (Teplov and Nebylitsyn 1963); (Sudakov 2005), their ontogenetic significance (Orekhova et al. 2003); (Voronin and Guselnikov 1964), and their manifestation have contributed to a better understanding of cognitive processes and intelligence (Ivanitsky, Nikolaev and Ivanitsky 2001); (Ivanitskiy and Lebedev 2007). The discovery of individual EEG predictors of cognitive and psychomotor activities allows brain-derived communication in paralyzed and locked-in patients to occur through Brain-Computer-Interface technologies (Birbaumer 2006), or to train healthy individuals for optimal performance using Biofeedback technology (Sokhadze and Shtark 1991).

From the time of the great Russian physiologist Ivan Michailovich Sechenov, it was pointed out that the body is an amazing system with many complexities and a special potential for improving itself (Bernstein 1966). Later it became clear that biofeedback provides a means for such improvement. Biofeedback involves measuring certain state(s) of the body and communicating them to a practitioner or patient. This information can then be used to reach a particular goal, such as alleviating dysfunctions and/or disorders. However, there does not need to be dysfunctions or disorders to improve the mind and body. This idea is to use biofeedback for improvement to achieve what is called "peak performance" (Lubar 2000), also known as "peak achievement" (Singer 2002), "optimal functioning" (Keefe 1978) or the "flow state" (Csikszentmihalyi 1992).

The recent identification of specific brain signatures involved in optimal cognitive and psychomotor functioning (peak performance) demonstrate an association with the so-called "alpha status" (Bazanova et al. 2003; Hummel et al. 2004); (Klimesch, Sauseng and Hanslmayr 2007). Despite different aspects of alpha activity, which have been known since Berger's time, it is not clear which quantities characterize "alpha status": an increasing or decreasing alpha amplitude and frequency, a synchronization or desynchronization.

Evidence from animal models suggests that alpha rhythmicity is a result of both the tuning of the local cortical network (Steriade et al. 1990; Lopes da Silva 1991; Steriade and Timofeev 2003), as well as the synchronous activation of thalamocortical projections via the thalamic reticular nucleus (Steriade and Timofeev 2003). Thus, alpha activity indices should reflect processes of generation (dominant frequency parameters), activation (desynchronization process) and autorhythmicity (phase resetting and spindle forming). Summarizing recent investigations, we proposed that the EEG alpha activity indices are: (1) the dominant posterior EEG rhythm frequency while the eyes are closed (Niedermeyer 1999; Nunez, Wingeier and Silberstein 2003), which is assessed as individual alpha peak frequency (IAPF) (Doppelmayr et al. 2005; Hooper 2005; Angelakis et al. 2007); (2) the amplitude suppression in response to eyes being open, which is assessed as the amount of alpha suppression (Nunez, Wingeier and Silberstein 2003; Kirschfeld 2005; Barry et al. 2007) and frequency range of amplitude suppression, or bandwidth (Bazanova and Aftanas 2006a); and (3) the spindle form of oscillations or autorhythmicity (Timofeev et al. 2002; Lebedev 2006; Thatcher, North and Biver 2008). (Figure 12.1)

1. The *IAPF* (Individual Alpha Peak Frequency), the dominant frequency within the alpha bandwidth for a given individual, is believed to reflect aggregate alpha generation (Lopes da Silva 1991; Hooper 2005). Investigations confirm the high heritability of the resting IAPF (Anokhin et al. 2006; Smit et al. 2006). It is evident now that IAPF reflects individual genetic influences on the underlying neural mechanisms of the generation of alpha activity (Steriade and Timofeev 2003). Overall, EEG power spectrum frequency Principal Component Analysis (fPCA) yields multiple alpha factors with similar or identical peak frequencies (Tenke and Kayser 2005). Furthermore, "test-retest" IAPF investigation of 96 male subjects aged 26–40 over 14–15 days showed that the intra-individual correlation coefficient (ICC) was strong for posterior IAPF in an eyes-closed condition, while it was weaker for anterior IAPF, with a non-significant anterior IAPF in the eyes-open condition (Figure 12.2).

It was established that the posterior IAPF in an eyes-closed condition was the only adequate indicator for individual differences (Doppelmayr et al. 2005;

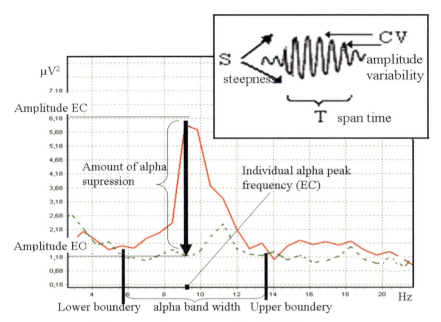

FIGURE 12.1   Alpha activity indices (EC – eyes closed – bold line spectra, EO – eyes open – dotted line spectra)

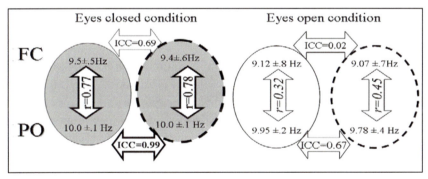

FIGURE 12.2   Individual alpha peak frequency (Means±SD) in test-retest investigation in eyes open and eyes closed conditions. FC – frontal-central area, PO – parietal-occipital area. ICC – intra-individual correlation coefficient; r – FC-PO correlation coefficient. Numbers in dotted ovals – IAPF value in the retest investigation.

Bazanova, Kondratenko et al. 2007). The IAPF intra-individual variability reflects changing corticothalamic interrelations and could provide a basis for the EEG frequency pattern (Gavrish and Malykh 1994; Klimesch, Sauseng and Hanslmayr 2007). The IAPF value varies as a function of age, as it increases in childhood and decreases after 40 years of age (Stroganova et al. 2000; Richard et al. 2004; Bazanova 2008), neurohumoral status (it increases with steroid concentration enhancement (Tops et al. 2006; Baker et al. 2007; Bazanova 2008), and cognitive involvement in a task (Hummel et al. 2004; Klimesch, Sauseng and Hanslmayr 2007). Neurofeedback training may be used for cognitive enhancement (Hanslmayr et al. 2007; Angelakis et al. 2007). However, a decrease in IAPF is always related to a drop in performance (Klimesch, Sauseng and Hanslmayr 2007).

Using the median posterior IAPF, healthy male subjects were divided into groups, low (LAF with IAPF<10 Hz) and high (HAF, with IAPF≥10 Hz.) alpha frequency subjects. It appeared that LAF and HAF subjects differed in psychometric strategies for achieving success in nonverbal creative tasks. LAF subjects emphasize originality while HAF emphasize fluency in reaching the same level of performance (Bazanova and Aftanas 2006a).

The subjects with highest and lowest IAPF level showed the highest originality in nonverbal creativity task performance (Figure 12.3). HAF subjects demonstrated higher fluency in cognitive task performance (Doppelmayr et al. 2005; Klimesch, Sauseng and Hanslmayr 2007). The different behavior strategies observed in LAF and HAF subjects could be due, in part, to different neurophysiological mechanisms of brain activation in low and high frequency ranges (Kirschfeld 2005; Tenke and Kayser 2005; Bazanova et al. 2008).

In general, individual alpha peak frequency is indicative of inter-individual differences in behavior strategy. One possible explanation of this could follow from understanding the LAF and HAF difference in brain activation mechanisms.

2. The *activation power* indicates the amount of alpha amplitude suppression in response to eyes-open conditions (Barry et al. 2007). In recent EEG-fMRI coupled investigations, Laufs and coauthors showed that spontaneous reductions in alpha amplitude is associated with increasing cognitive activity (2006). It is proposed that brain activation during alpha power suppression is connected to general brain activation in a wide (not just the standard 8–12 Hz) spectral frequency range (Laufs et al. 2006). Actually, until now, the alpha frequency range boundaries were defined on the basis of a general agreement – without a theoretical basis and without respect to functional features – about reactivity to visual stimulation (Kaiser 2001; Thatcher, North and Biver 2008; Arns et al. 2008). Meanwhile, the individual alpha bandwidth is dependent on age (increases from 3 until 20 years (Bazanova 2008)), neurohumoral status (in high estrogen and progesterone stages alpha band is wider than in lower hormonal phases during the female menstrual cycle (Bazanova 2008)), and gender (women have a higher low alpha band boundary frequency than men (Carrier et al. 2001; Bazanova 2008)). Moreover, individual alpha

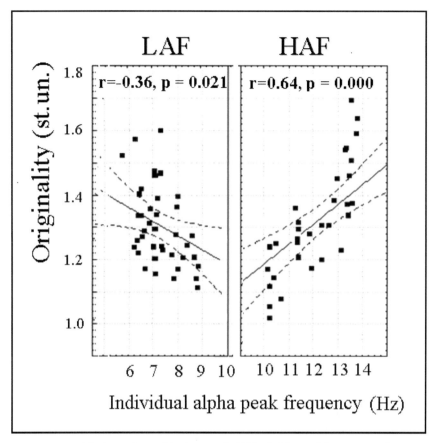

FIGURE 12.3   The interrelationships between individual alpha peak frequency and originality in nonverbal task performance in low (LAF) and high (HAF) alpha frequency male subjects

frequency range could vary in accordance with brain activation (Kaiser 2001; Bazanova and Aftanas 2006b). It is now quite clear that the alpha band has individual lower and upper frequency boundaries (Figure 12.4).

For example, IABW is wider in highly-skilled professional musicians than in non-musicians (Bazanova and Shtark 2007), and IABW is positively correlated with the overall Torrance creativity coefficient and flexibility in creative task performance, academic achievements (Bazanova and Aftanas 2006b) and biofeedback training efficiency (Bazanova, Kondratenko et al. 2007).

D. Kaiser (Kaiser 2001) and our laboratory have shown the importance of accounting for individual alpha ban range (Kaiser 2001) (Bazanova and Aftanas 2006b). Moreover, with the standard theta/beta decreasing neurofeedback

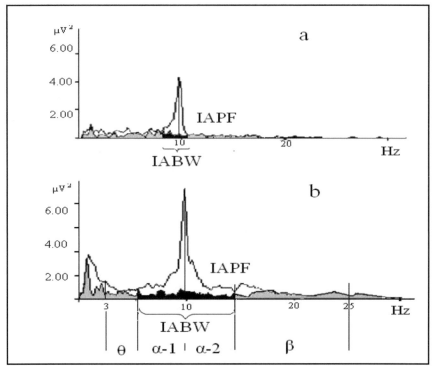

FIGURE 12.4   EEG spectral power in the parietal-occipital areas in the eyes-closed (white) and -open (gray) conditions. Spectral power decreases by more than 20% from baseline within individual alpha ranges (black); *a* and *b*) examples of different alpha-bandwidths. The abscissa shows frequency, Hz; the ordinate shows spectral power at the frequencies indicated, μV^2; IABW is individual alpha bandwidth; IAPF is individual alpha peak frequency.

training protocol, it was shown that neurofeedback training applied in individual EEG frequency ranges was much more efficient than neurofeedback training of standard EEG frequency ranges (Bazanova and Aftanas 2006b) (Figure 12.5).

The enhancement of the individual alpha bandwidth is one of the main indicators of success in both neurofeedback and other modalities of biofeedback training (Bazanova et al. 2008). It may be concluded that the ability for enhancing self-control could be associated with broadening the individual alpha band. Interestingly, despite the same amount of alpha suppression in HAF and LAF groups, HAF have a wider individual alpha bandwidth than LAF subjects (Bazanova et al. 2008). This means that the neurophysiological mechanisms by which this activation is generated are different in LAF and HAF subjects. More precisely, power activation in LAF is positively correlated with

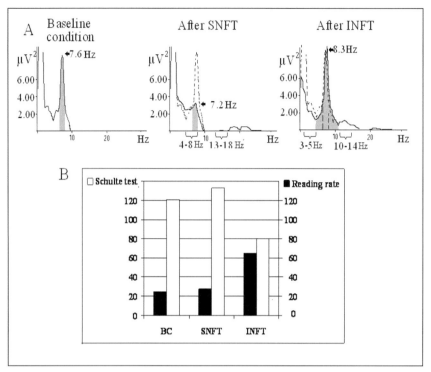

FIGURE 12.5   Spectra power (A) and psychometrical test performance (B) of boy with attention deficit disorder in baseline condition (BC), after 10 sessions theta/beta decreasing neurofeedback training in standard EEG ranges (SNFT – theta = 4–8 Hz and beta = 13–18 Hz) and in individual EEG ranges (INFT – theta = 3–5 Hz, beta = 10–14 Hz). Grey areas denote spectral power in individual alpha band. Spectra power in baseline condition – dotted line. Numbers with arrows – individual alpha peak frequency.

alpha spindle variability, while in HAF power activation is correlated with the alpha oscillation amplitude in the eyes-closed rest condition (Figure 12.6).

Demonstrated differences in correlations between alpha suppression and other alpha activity indices in low and high frequency ranges is consistent with the idea that alpha desynchronization serves an integrative role through a corticocortical "gating" (Kirschfeld 2005: Tenke and Kayser 2005). Mazaheri and Jensen found that 10 Hz oscillations after visual stimuli preserve their phase relationship with respect to before the stimuli, while 8 Hz phase-resetting oscillations are responsible for visually evoked responses (Mazaheri and Jensen 2006). The phase resetting process could not be assessed by regular spectral analysis. Hence, when examining the average brain electrical responses to stimuli, it is not clear whether the observed effect of stimuli is real

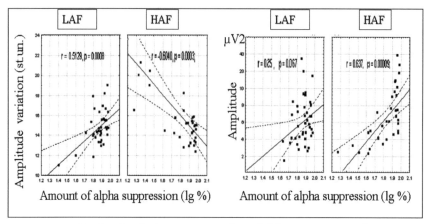

FIGURE 12.6 Results of multiple regression analysis of alpha suppression predictors. In low alpha frequency group (LAF), the best predictor is amplitude variability, in high alpha frequency group (HAF), the best predictor is alpha spindle amplitude.

(rather than a 'virtual' result of the averaging procedure), stable, and typical for the whole analyzed signal. For example, it is not clear (1) whether the change of total power of particular brain alpha oscillations results from a change in the number of occurrences per minute rather than the change of the average oscillations amplitude, and (2) whether change in the total power of alpha oscillations affects the whole analyzed signal or a small portion (Kaplan et al. 2002). Thus, regardless of how powerful or statistically significant the different estimations of averaged EEG effects may be, it is difficult to make meaningful interpretations if the estimations are not matched to the EEG piecewise stationary structure (Kaplan 1999).

To overcome the limitations of conventional spectral analysis based on averaging procedures and to reveal dynamic and temporal characteristics of alpha activity, an entire set of individual short-term stationary EEG segments may be obtained (Kaplan 1999; Towers and Allen 2009). Non-stationary phenomena are present in the EEG, usually in the form of transient events, such as alternation of relatively homogenous intervals (segments) with different statistical features (e.g., with different amplitude or variance) (Lopes da Silva 1991).

The idea that alpha oscillations have a spindle-like form only during sleep (Niedermeyer 1999) has been contradicted by Kellaway, who described the so-called lambda waves (8–13 Hz), which may be identified using simple procedures (Kellaway 2003). The lambda wave is believed to represent occipital lobe activity in a person actively reading or scanning a room. Often, the subjects have their eyes open and are looking carefully at the ceiling tiles. The technician will have the patient reproduce the activities that they felt caused the waves to appear in the first place (Kellaway 2003). It was proposed that the physiological basis of sleep spindles is probably quite similar to lambda and alpha waves. To determine if the brain activation state would modulate the composition of alpha spatial microstates (spindles), Cantero and colleagues used spatial segmentation methods to show that (a) the mean duration of alpha spindles is longer in relaxed wakefulness than in drowsy periods and REM sleep, and (b) the number of different amplitude values are more abundant in drowsiness than in other brain states (Cantero et al. 1999).

Overall, brain activation mechanisms could become clearer if we consider the third important EEG alpha activity feature, the spindle-ability of alpha oscillation.

3. The spindle-form or autorhythmicity of alpha oscillations is a product of the dynamics of neuronal assemblies in the underlying cortical activity (Livanov and Dumenko 1987; Singer et al. 1997; Lehmann et al. 1994; Dorokhov 2003). Starting from Livanov's studies, it has been shown that spindle oscillations are essential for memory formation (Lebedev 1994; Lebedev 2006; Gais et al. 2000), with short- and mid-term synaptic plasticity demonstrated (Steriade and Timofeev 2003). A probable molecular mechanism of this phenomenon was proposed by Destexhe and Sejnowski. They suggested that spindling may activate the protein kinase A molecular "gate," thus opening the door for gene expression (Destexhe and Sejnowski 2003) and allowing long-term changes to take place following subsequent inputs.

Average amplitude (A) within segment (μv) indicates the volume of the neuronal population. Indeed, the more neurons recruited into an assembly through local synchronization of their activity, the higher is the oscillation amplitude of the corresponding assembly (Livanov and Dumenko 1987; Lopes da Silva 1991; Kaplan 1999). The assumption that alpha amplitude reflects inhibition may, at first glance, appear contradictory to the idea that alpha plays an active role in information processing, but the idea is that inhibition is an important factor that controls the exact timing of an oscillation. Thus, inhibition helps to establish a highly selective activation pattern (Klimesch, Sauseng and Hanslmayr 2007).

Average spindle lifetime represents the functional lifespan of the neuronal population or the duration of operations produced by such a population (Maltseva and Masloboev 1997; Kaplan et al. 2002). It has been shown that longer spindles indicate a more relaxed state (Huupponen et al. 2008). The spindle lifetime is correlated with fluency in cognitive task performance (Bazanova and

Aftanas 2006b), and single biofeedback training session efficiency (Bazanova et al. 2007). Additionally, alpha-spindles are longer in highly-skilled musicians than in amateurs (Bazanova et al. 2007).

The shortest alpha segments belong to HAF subjects with the highest individual alpha peak frequencies and LAF subjects with the lowest individual alpha peak frequencies (Maltseva and Masloboev 1997; Bazanova et al. 2008). The longest spindles belong to persons with an average, or approximately average, 10 Hz individual alpha peak frequency. Multiple regression analysis showed that spindle lifespan is positively related to individual alpha peak frequency in LAF subjects, while related to spindle steepness in HAF subjects (Figure 12.7) (Bazanova et al. 2008). These data suggest the different neuronal mechanism of spindle formation in LAF and HAF subjects. Actually, as shown by Fuentealba and colleagues, the reticular neurons display membrane bistability, as indicated by two discrete electrical potential modes, with differential responsiveness to cortical inputs (Fuentealba et al. 2005). The membrane bistability might play

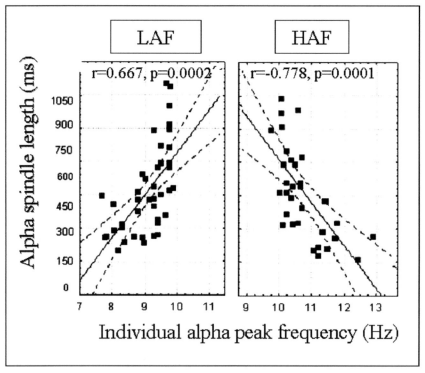

FIGURE 12.7 Results of regression analysis of the relationship between alpha spindle length and individual alpha peak frequency in low (LAF n = 48) and high (HAF n = 48) alpha frequency male subjects

an important role in different patterns of spindles displayed by thalamocortical neurons. In vivo (Steriade and Llinas 1988; Steriade and Timofeev 2003) and in vitro (Bal and McCormick 1996) intracellular studies have revealed at least two different patterns during spontaneously occurring spindles, which may be related to the actions exerted by non-bistable and bistable neurons, respectively. Indeed, non-bistable neurons fired stronger bursts with higher intra-burst frequencies, which are assumed to generate IPSPs, ~7–10 Hz. By contrast, IPSPs with lower amplitudes and higher frequency are likely to be mainly generated by single action potentials, as they occur during the depolarizing plateau in bistable cells (Fuentealba et al. 2005). These results suggest how two different frequency alpha-activity patterns could arise.

If we assume that longer spindles of stable brain activity imply less information to process (as reflected by a higher stability of the brain generator), whereas shorter segments imply a higher number of brain microstates caused by more different steps of information processing, then it is possible that the intra-segment alpha amplitude variability could be indexing a phasic event (Oprisan, Prinz and Canavier 2004). Probably, alpha-bursts are associated with a brain microstate change (such as sleep spindles), as demonstrated by its phasic intrusion in a desynchronized background of brain activity (Cantero et al. 1999). Intra-spindle amplitude variability decreases in coma or stupor (Brenner 2005), but increases during cognitive loading (Kaplan and Borisov 2003) and in relation to the ability for self-control in neurofeedback training (18–20 sessions) (Bazanova et al. 2008). Thus, amplitude variability, which is associated with phase resetting intensity (Oprisan, Prinz and Canavier 2004), reflects engagement of cognitive control mechanisms (Livanov and Dumenko 1987; Lebedev 1994; Hanslmayr et al. 2007; Hanslmayr, Pastötter et al. 2008). Moreover, in children the intensity of phase locking and spindle amplitude variability generally increases as a function of age (Bazanova et al. 2008; Thatcher, North and Biver 2008). Probably, this reflects the well-known fact that that the ability for self-control develops with age (Orekhova et al. 2003; Mischel 2004).

Therefore, alpha activity indices (individual alpha peak frequency, segmental parameters of alpha spindle individual alpha bandwidth, amount of alpha suppression and duration of this suppression in time) characterize the degree of cortical ability for activation, excitability, and neuronal plasticity, and in this way, self-regulation ability.

The impact of the biofeedback training (BFT) in increasing the ability for self-control in healthy subjects and patients with psychosomatic disorders (all male student musicians aged 18–25) was studied. We had compared two kinds of BFT: (1) simultaneous EEG alpha-2 increasing and EMG frontal muscle decreasing – alpha-EEG/EMG BFT and (2) simultaneous temperature increasing and EMG decreasing biofeedback training – T/EMG BFT. Pairwise comparisons of alpha activity indices showed that individual amount of alpha suppression (IAAS), individual alpha bandwidth (IABW) and alpha spindle lifespan (T) were not different (p>0.05) in male patients with headache (n = 9) and focal dystonia (n = 12), but were lower (t ≤ -8.67, p ≤ 0.001) in patients than in healthy subjects (n = 32). The frontal muscle EMG power was higher in patients than in healthy subjects (t ≥ 5.17, p ≤ 0.001). Moreover, the motivational competence or self-actualization, as measured by the Rheinberg test (Rheinberg, Vollmeyer and Engeser 2003), was higher in HAF healthy, than LAF healthy (t = 4.78, p = 0.002) and in healthy than patients alpha frequency corresponding groups (t > 3.42, p<0.03).

The results of the first biofeedback training session showed that the impact of BFT on the individual alpha activity indices did not depend on training modalities (p>0.05). The individual alpha EEG indices, IAPF, IAAS, IABW, alpha spindle lifespan and amplitude, increased (p<0.004) and EMG decreased (p<0.05) in healthy and patient musicians after the first alpha/EMG BFT session. This change was greater in HAF- than in LAF-healthy subjects (p<0.02), and in healthy than in patient subjects (Figure 12.8). The efficiency of single BFT sessions of both modalities was higher in HAF than LAF subjects and positively correlated with IAPF in the baseline rest condition in LAF-healthy and patient subjects (r>0.67, p<0.003) and with IABW, IAAS, T and CV in all healthy and patient subjects (r>0.54, p<0.033).

After 18–20 sessions of both alpha/EMG and T/EMG BFT, the means of IAPF, IAAS, IABW, A, T, S and CV increased simultaneously with decreased EMG in LAF-healthy subjects (F>5.51 p<0.05) and in all patient subjects (F>9.03 p<0.001) (Figure 12.9) The impact of alpha/EMG BFT could not be distinguished from the impact of T/EMG BFT on psychometric traits, motivational competence, musical execution skills and alpha activity level. The self-actualization and musical performance scores, which were higher in HAF than LAF subjects, grew only in LAF healthy musicians and in all patient subjects. So it looked like biofeedback training was not necessary for HAF healthy student musicians. Increasing the individual alpha indices was greater in LAF- than HAF-healthy (p<0.003), and greater in patient than in healthy (p<0.001) subjects (Figure 12.9).

It may be concluded that alpha activity enhancement as a result of biofeedback training leads to increased ability for self-control. In the first biofeedback session, efficiency is greater in subjects with better self-regulation ability (HAF musicians) than in healthy LAF and patient musicians, the BFT course efficiency is less for healthy musicians with low alpha frequency or with

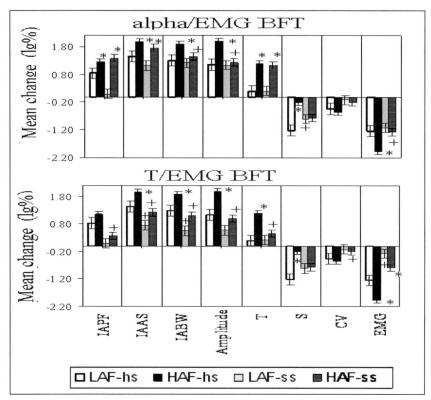

FIGURE 12.8 The mean change (lg%) of the individual alpha indices level and EMG power after first session of alpha-EEG/EMG-BFT and T/EMG-BFT. Abbreviations IAPF – individual alpha peak frequency, IAAS – individual amount of alpha suppression, IABW – individual alpha band width, Amplitude, T, S and CV – correspondently amplitude, lifespan, steepness and intrasegment amplitude variability of alpha spindle; LAF and HAF – low and high alpha frequency, hs – healthy ss – sick subjects. Differences are significant (p<0.05): * – HAFs vs LAFs, + – healthy vs sick subjects.

psychosomatic disorders. Therefore, alpha activity indices studied correspond to the level of neurophysiologic adaptive ability and play a key role in training cognitive self-regulation. Successful strategies in self-control training depend on the individual alpha frequency EEG pattern.

Conclusion

The general line of our argumentation is that alpha activity indices reflect a certain type of self-control (top-down) process. The active role of alpha is seen

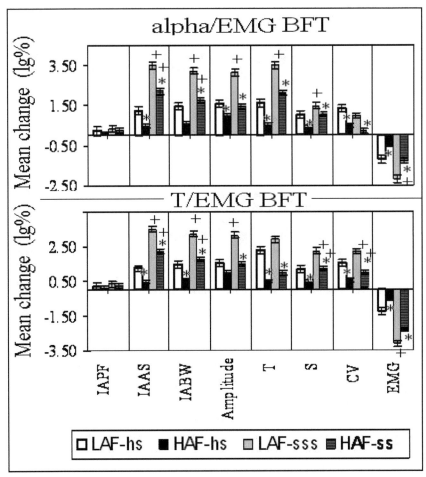

FIGURE 12.9 The mean change (lg%) of the individual alpha indices and EMG power after 18–20 sessions of alpha-EEG/EMG-BFT and T/EMG-BFT. Abbreviations is the same as in fig. 12.8. Differences are significant ($p<0.05$): * – HAFs vs LAFs, + – healthy vs patient subjects.

in a mechanism that may also underlie the functional role of other oscillations (Klimesch, Sauseng and Hanslmayr 2007). Synchronization in the alpha frequency range helps neurons in distributed networks to effectively activate common target cells (Klimesch, Sauseng and Hanslmayr 2007). This alpha-frequency dependent mechanism plays an important role in the top-down control of cortical activation. Mechanisms giving rise to alpha amplitude desynchronization also reflect the dependence of brain activation on the alpha frequency range. Klimesh has proposed that upper-frequency alpha oscillations are related to top-down processes in a complex sensory-motor system that controls the access to and manipulation of stored information (Klimesch, Sauseng and Hanslmayr 2007). As with overall brain activity, top-down control is not a unitary phenomenon (Klimesch, Sauseng and Hanslmayr 2007). For example, when a task requires that certain types of processes be performed with stored information (e.g., stored information must be kept in mind, must not be retrieved, or must be manipulated such as with highly-skilled musicians during musical performance), individual alpha-activity increases ("alpha status" develops). The neuronal activation strategies for achieving the "alpha status" as a result of BFB are different according to the individual alpha frequency. Several factors may be common in the generation of different types of oscillations. Nonetheless, the exact mechanisms for generating an oscillation may differ widely between different frequency waves such as low and high frequency alpha, depending on network properties, cell types, cell physiology and other factors. Thus, for a better understanding of the functional role of alpha activity indices in Biofeedback or DCI technologies, the investigation of their neurophysiologic interplay may be of crucial importance.

References

Angelakis, E., S. Stathopoulou, J. L. Frymiare, D. L. Green, J. F. Lubar, and J. Kounios. 2007. "EEG neurofeedback: A brief overview and an example of peak alpha frequency training for cognitive enhancement in the elderly." *Clinical Neuropsychology* 21, no. 1: 110–129.

Anokhin, A. P., V. Muller, U. Heath, A. C. Lindenberger, and E. Myers. 2006. "Genetic influences on dynamic complexity of brain oscillations." *Neuroscience Letters* 397, no. 1–2: 93–98.

Arns, M., J. Gunkelman, M. Breteler, and D. Spronk. 2008. "EEG phenotypes predict treatment outcome to stimulants in children with ADHD." *Journal of Integrative Neuroscience* 7, no. 3: 421–438.

Baker, F. C., T. L. Kahan, J. Trinder, and I. M. Colrain. 2007. "Free in PMC Sleep quality and the sleep electroencephalogram in women with severe premenstrual syndrome." *Sleep* 30, no. 10: 1283–1291.

Bal, T., and McCormick D. A. 1996. "What stops synchronized thalamocortical oscillations?" *Neuron* 17: 297–308.

Barry, R. J., A. R. Clarke, S. J. Johnstone, C. A. Magee, and J. A. Rushby. 2007. "EEG differences between eyes-closed and eyes-open resting conditions." *Clinical Neurophysiology* 18, no. 12: 2765–2773.

Bazanova, O. M. 2008. "Age related alpha activity change differs for males and females and for low and high alpha frequency EEG pattern." *Revista Espanola de Neuropsicologia* 10, no. 1: 82–83.

Bazanova, O. M., A. Kondratenko, O. Kondratenko, E. Mernaya, and E. Zhimulev. 2007. "New computer-based technology to teach peak performance in musicians." *Information Technology Interfaces* 7: 39–44.

Bazanova, O. M., A. V. Gvozdev, F. A. Mursin, E. G. Verevkin, and M. B. Shtark. 2003. "EEG-EMG Dimensionality of the musical performance." *Cognitive Processing* 4, no. 3: 33–47.

Bazanova, O. M., and L. I. Aftanas. 2006a. "Learnability and individual frequency characteristics of EEG alpha activity." *Vestnik Rossiiskoi Akademii Meditsinskikh Nauk.* no. 6: 30–33.

Bazanova, O. M., and L. I. Aftanas. 2006b. "Relationships between learnability and individual indices of EEG alpha activity." *Annals of General Psychiatry* 5, no. Suppl 1: 74–75.

Bazanova, O. M., and M. B. Shtark. 2007. "Biofeedback in optimizing psychomotor reactivity: I. Comparison of biofeedback and common performance practice." *Human Physiology* 33, no. 4: 400–408.

Bazanova, O. M., and E. M. Mernaya. 2008. "Alpha-activity fluctuations in various hormonal states and associated with them musical performance proved differently in the opposite individual alpha peak frequency groups." *Revista Espanola de Neuropsicologia* 10, no. 1: 100–101.

Bazanova, O. M., O. A. Jafarova, E. M. Mernaya, K. B. Mazhirina, and M. B. Shtark. 2008. "Optimal functioning psychophysiological bases and neurofeedback training." *International J. of Psychophysiology* 69, no. 3: 164.

Bernstein, N. A. 1966. *Notes on Movement Physiology and Physiology of Activity*. Moscow: Meditsina.

Birbaumer, N. 2006. "Breaking the silence: brain-computer interfaces (BCI) for communication and motor control." *Psychophysiology* 43, no. 6: 517–532.

Brenner, R. P. 2005. "The interpretation of the EEG in stupor and coma." *Neurologist* 11, no. 5: 271–284.

Cantero, J. L., M. Atienza, R. M. Salas, and C. M. Gomez. 1999. "Brain spatial microstates of human spontaneous alpha activity in relaxed wakefulness, drowsiness period, and REM sleep." *Brain Topography* 11, no. 4: 257–263.

Carrier, J., S. Land, D. J. Buysse, D. J. Kupfer, and T. H. Monk. 2001. "The effects of age and gender on sleep EEG power spectral density in the middle years of life (ages 20–60 years old)." *Psychophysiology* 38, no. 2: 232–242.

Csikszentmihalyi, M. 1992. *Optimal Experience: Psychological Studies of Flow in Consciousness*. Cambridge, UK: Cambridge University Press.

Destexhe, A., and T. J. Sejnowski. 2003. "Interactions between membrane conductances underlying thalamocortical slow-wave oscillations." *Physiological Reviews* 83, no. 4: 1401–1453.

Doppelmayr, M., W. Klimesch, K. Hödlmoser, P. Sauseng, and W. Gruber. 2005. "Intelligence related upper alpha desynchronization in a semantic memory task." *Brain Research Bulletin* 66, no. 2: 171–177.

Dorokhov, V. B. 2003. "Alpha-bursts and K-complex: phasic activation pattern during spontaneous recovery of correct psychomotor performance at difference stages of drowsiness." *Zhurnal Vysshei Nervnoi Deiatelnosti Imeni I P Pavlova* 53, no. 4: 503–512.

Emerson, R. M. 1883. "Experience." In *Emerson's Works, Vol. III: Essays, Second Series*, 52. Cambridge, Mass.: Houghton Mifflin.

Fuentealba, P., V. I. Timofee, M. Bazhenov, T. J. Sejnowski, and M. Steriade. 2005. "Membrane bistability in thalamic reticular neurons during spindle oscillations." *Journal of Neurophysiology* 93, no. 1: 294–304.

Gais, S., W. Plihal, U. Wagner, and J. Born. 2000. "Early sleep triggers memory for early visual discrimination skills." *Nature Neuroscience* 3, no. 12: 1335–1339.

Gavrish, N. V., and S. B. Malykh. 1994. "The nature of the variability in the individual differences of the frequency characteristics of the alpha-rhythm EEG in 6- to 8-year-old children." *Zhurnal Vysshei Nervnoi Deiatelnosti Imeni I P Pavlova* 44, no. 1: 8–17.

Hanslmayr, S., B. Pastötter, K. H. Bäuml, S. Gruber, M. Wimber, and W. Klimesch. 2008. "The electrophysiological dynamics of interference during the Stroop task." *Journal of Cognitive Neuroscience* 20, no. 2: 215–225.

Hanslmayr, S., et al. 2007. "Alpha phase reset contributes to the generation of ERPs." *Cerebral Cortex* 17, no. 1: 1–8.

Hooper, G. S. 2005. "Comparison of the distributions of classical and adaptively aligned EEG power spectra." *International Journal of Psychophysiology* 55, no. 2: 179–189.

Hummel, F., et al. 2004. "To act or not to act: neural correlates of executive control of learned motor behavior." *NeuroImage* 23, no. 4: 1391–1401.

Huupponen, E., et al. 2008. "Electroencephalogram spindle activity during dexmedetomidine sedation and physiological sleep." *Acta Anaesthesiology Scandinavica* 52, no. 2: 289–294.

Ivanitskiy, A. M., and A. N. Lebedev. 2007. "Solving the riddle of the brain rhythms." *Zhurnal Vysshei Nervnoi Deiatelnosti Imeni I P Pavlova* 57, no. 5: 636–640.

Ivanitsky, A. M., A. R. Nikolaev, and G. A. Ivanitsky. "Cortical connectivity during word association search." *International Journal of Psychophysiology* 42, no. 1 (2001): 35–53.

Kaiser, D. A. 2001. "Rethinking standard bands." *Journal of Neurotherapy* 5: 96–101.

Kaplan, A. I. 1999. "The problem of the segmental description of the human electroencephalogram." *Fiziol Cheloveka* 25, no. 1: 125–133.

Kaplan, A. I., S. V. Borisov, S. L. Shishkin, and V. A. Ermolaev. 2002. "Analysis of the segmental structure of EEG alpha-activity in humans." *Rossiĭskii fiziologicheskiĭ zhurnal imeni I M Sechenova* 88, no. 4: 432–442.

Kaplan, A. I., and S. V. Borisov. 2003. "Dynamic properties of segmental characteristics of EEG alpha activity in rest conditions and during cognitive tasks." *Zhurnal Vysshei Nervnoi Deiatelnosti Imeni I P Pavlova* 53, no. 1: 22–32.

Keefe, T. 1978. "Optimal functioning: The eastern ideal in psychotherapy." *Journal of Contemporary Psychotherapy* 10, no. 1: 16–24.

Kellaway, P. 2003. "Orderly approach to visual analysis: elements of the normal EEG and their characteristics in children and adults." In *Current Practice of Clinical Electroencephalography*, ed. J. S. Pedley and T. A. Ebersole, 100–159. Philadelphia: Lippincott Williams and Wilkins.

Kirschfeld, K. 2005. "The physical basis of alpha waves in the electroencephalogram and the origin of the 'Berger effect'." *Biological Cybernetics* 10, no. 1: 177–185.

Klimesch, W., P. Sauseng, and S. Hanslmayr. 2007. "EEG alpha oscillations: The inhibition–timing hypothesis." *Brain Research Reviews* 53, no. 1: 63–88.

Laufs, H., et al. 2006. "Where the BOLD signal goes when alpha EEG leaves." *Neuroimage* 31, no. 4: 1408–1418.

Lebedev, A. N. 2006. "Mikhail Nikolaevich Livanov (on his 100th anniversary of his scientific, scientific-organizational, pedagogical and public activities)." *Uspekhi Fiziologicheskikh Nauk* 37, no. 3: 87–94.

Lebedev, A. N. 1994. "The neurophysiological parameters of human memory." *Neuroscience and behavioral physiology* 24, no. 3: 254–259.

Lehmann, D., W. K. Strik, B. Henggeller, and M. Koukkou. 1994. "Microstates in spontaneous momentary EEG potential maps during visual imagery and abstract thought." *Brain Topography* 6: 251.

Livanov, M. N., and V. N. Dumenko. 1987. "The neurophysiological aspect of research on the systems organization of brain activities." *Uspekhi Fiziologicheskikh Nauk* 18, no. 3: 6–16.

Lopes da Silva, F. H. 1991. "Neural mechanisms underlying brain waves: from neural membranes to networks." *Electroencephalography and Clinical Neurophysiology* 79, no. 2: 81–93.

Lubar, J. 2000. "Determining optimal EEG patterns for enhancing performance in specific tasks." *Optimal Functioning 2000 Third Annual Meeting*. Palm Springs, Cal.: Optimal Functioning.

Maltseva, I. V., and Y. P. Masloboev. 1997. "Alpha rhythm parameters and short-term memory span." *International Journal of Psychophysiology* 27, no. 2: 369–380.

Mazaheri, A., and O. Jensen. 2006. "Posterior activity is not phase-reset by visual stimuli." *Proceedings of the National Academy of Sciences* 103, no. 8: 2948–2952.

Mischel, W. 2004. "Toward an integrative science of the person." *Annual Review of Psychology* 55: 1–22.

Niedermeyer, E. 1999. "The normal EEG of the waking adult." In *Electroencephalography: Basic principles, Clinical Applications and Related Fields*, ed. F. Lopes da Silva and E. Niedermeyer, 149–173. Philadelphia: Williams and Wilkins.

Nunez, P., B. Wingeier, and R. Silberstein. 2003. "Spatial-temporal structures of human alpha rhythms: theory, microcurrent sources, multiscale measurements, and global binding of networks." *Human Brain Mapping* 13, no. 3: 125–164.

Oprisan, S. A., A. A. Prinz, and C. C. Canavier. 2004. "Phase resetting and phase locking in hybrid circuits of one model and one biological neuron." *Biophysical Journal* 87, no. 4: 2283–2298.

Orekhova, E. V., T. A. Stroganova, I. N. Posikera, and S. B. Malykh. 2003. "Heritability and 'environmentability' of electroencephalogram in infants: the twin study." *Psychophysiology* 40, no. 5: 727–741.

Rheinberg, F., R. Vollmeyer, and S. Engeser. 2003. "Die Erfassung des Flow-Erlebens. Diagnostik von Motivation und Selbstkonzept." In *Tests und Trends N.F. Bd. 2*, ed. J. Stiensmeier-Pelster and F. Rheinberg, 261–279. Göttingen, Germany: Hogrefe.

Richard, C. C., et al. 2004. "Spontaneous alpha peak frequency predicts working memory performance across the age spa." *International Journal of Psychophysiology* 53: 1–8.

Singer, R. N. 2002. "Preperformance state, routines, and automaticity: What does it take to realize expertise in self-paced events?" *Journal of Sport and Exercise Psychology* 24, no. 4: 359–375.

Singer, W., A. K. Engel, A. K. Kreiter, M. H. J. Munk, S. Neuenschwander, and P. R. Roelfsema. 1997. "Neuronal assemblies: necessity, signature and detectability." *Trends in Cognitive Sciences* 1, no. 7: 252–261.

Smit, C. M., M. J. Wright, N. K. Hansell, G. M. Geffen, and N. G. Martin. 2006. "Genetic variation of individual alpha frequency (IAF) and alpha power in a large adolescent twin sample." *International Journal of Psychophysiology* 61, no. 2: 235–243.

Sokhadze, E. M., and M. B. Shtark. 1991. "Scientific and clinical biofeedback in the USSR." *Biofeedback and Self-regulation* 16, no. 3: 253–260.

Steriade, M, and I. Timofeev. 2003. "Neuronal plasticity in thalamocortical networks during sleep and waking oscillations." *Neuron* 37, no. 4: 563–576.

Steriade, M., and R. R. Llinas. 1988. "The functional states of the thalamus and the associated neuronal interplay." *Physiological Reviews* 68, no. 3: 649–742.

Steriade, M., P. Gloor, R. R. Llinas, F. H. Lopes da Silva, and M.-M. Mesulam. 1990. "Basic mechanisms of cerebral rhythmic activities." *Electroencephalography and Clinical Neurophysiology* 76, no. 6: 481–508.

Stroganova, T. A., M. M. Tsetlin, S. B. Malykh, and E. V. Malakhovskaia. 2000. "The biological bases for individual differences in infants in the 2nd half-year of life. II. The nature of the individual differences in temperament traits." *Fiziol Cheloveka* 26, no. 3: 38–47.

Sudakov, K. V. 2005. "Individuality of emotional stress." *Zhurnal Nevrologii i Psikhiatrii Imeni S S Korsakova* 105, no. 2: 4–12.

Tenke, C. E., and J. Kayser. 2005. "Reference-free quantification of EEG spectra: Combining current source density (CSD) and frequency principal components analysis (fPCA)." *Clinical Neurophysiology* 116, no. 12: 2826–2846.

Teplov, B. M., and V. D. Nebylitsyn. 1963. "Experimental study of the properties of the human nervous system." *Zhurnal Vysshei Nervnoi Deiatelnosti Imeni I P Pavlova* 13: 789–797.

Thatcher, R. W., D. M. North, and C. J. Biver. 2008. "Intelligence and EEG phase reset: a two compartmental model of phase shift and lock." *Neuroimage* 42, no. 4: 1639–1653.

Timofeev, I., F. Grenier, M. Bazhenov, A. R. Houweling, T. J. Sejnowski, and M. Steriade. 2002. "Short- and medium-term plasticity associated with augmenting responses in cortical slabs and spindles in intact cortex of cats in vivo." *Journal of Physiology* 542, no. Pt 2: 583–598.

Tops, M., J. M. van Peer, A. E. Wester, A. A. Wijers, and J. Korf. 2006. "State-dependent regulation of cortical activity by cortisol: An EEG study." *Neuroscience Letters* 404, no. 2: 39–43.

Towers, D. N., and J. J. Allen. 2009. "A better estimate of the internal consistency reliability of frontal EEG asymmetry scores." *Psychophysiology* 46, no. 1: 132–142.

Voronin, L. G., and V. I. Guselnikov. 1964. "Phylogenesis of internal mechanisms of analysis and integration in the brain." *Federation Proceedings. Translation Supplement: Selected Translations from Medical-related Science* 23: 105–112.

CHAPTER 13

The Psychophysiology of Combat Activity

A. A. Bochenkov

As illustrated by data from a comprehensive socio-psychological study and psychophysiological assessment of young conscripts, in modern-day sociodemographic conditions, those drafted into the army do not possess sufficient prerequisites to achieve a high level of professional performance. Among the conscripts, 40% of individuals are characterized by low tolerance to stress, 28% by inadequate mental development, 40% display low moral qualities, 53% are smokers, 39% are alcohol drinkers, 40% do not have adequate physical fitness, and 17% display erratic cardiovascular control and respiratory problems which lead to degraded physical performance and resistance to stressors (Pogodin et al. 1998). 45% of conscripts demonstrate distinct signs of emotional deviations (enhanced emotional sensitivity, mood lability, high anxiety, rapid fatigue, immature intellect, etc.) (Baranov 1988, 123–141). There has been a gradual decline in measures of the young conscripts' ability to serve in military occupational areas (Table 13.1).

An assessment of military personnel in the first year of service identified three classifications of adaptation to military service conditions: 25% constitute the easily adaptable group, 55% the adaptable group, and 20% belong to the risk group. Concurrently, the psychosomatic condition of army conscripts continues to deteriorate. Thus, in 1989–1992, the general intelligence level of military students at regional training centers dropped by 38.9% and tolerance to stress by 33.2% (Pogodin et al. 1998).

TABLE 13.1 Fraction of the population that can be drafted versus the numbers registered with the military authorities, (Rossiyskaya Gazeta dated 03/25/2004, #60)

	1988	1994	1998	2003
Have the right to deferred service	54	51	66	64
Can be drafted	33	28	18	10
Draft-exempt	12	22	16	25

Factors related to the specifics of combat activity make a significant impact on the functional state of the body and performance of military personnel. For example, during a two-day combat mission, physical endurance declined by 28%, static endurance of body muscles by 51%, hearing sensitivity by 32%, time of sensomotor reactions by 40%, maximum oxygen intake by 15–25%, and contractile heart function by 25%. At the same time, professional military performance was also impaired: speed of driving fell by 14%, time of fire mission performance by 35%, and effective target destruction by 40% (b).

After 20–30 days of conducting high-intensity combat operations in Chechnya (the city of Grozny, in January 1995), 80% of officers and 100% of military conscripts displayed apparent signs of asthenia and dysadaptation disorders. On average, within 3–6 months after withdrawal from the battlefield, 50% of the soldiers develop post-traumatic stress disorders primarily characterized by psychopathic personality development (Pogodin and Bochenkov 2007).

Fear in combat is a common phenomenon. It is experienced by 80–90% of military personnel. In addition, there are a number of autonomic symptoms, such as sickness, feelings of fatigue, heartache, stomach and muscle ache, dizziness, sweating, and insomnia. According to U.S. data, 25% of soldiers develop vomiting and 10–20% involuntary urination and defecation during combat action. Only 25% of the U.S. soldiers participating in the landing operations during the opening of the Second Front used their weapons in combat; furthermore, the same 25% of soldiers remained active in combat during the subsequent military actions (Agrel 1970, 248–254).

The deterioration of health among draftees, as well as changes in the functional state of the body during professional activity, drive the need to develop a system of psychophysiological support of military combat activity to improve combat performance of large and small units.

In the area of electric power engineering, payoffs from implementation of a psychophysiological system supporting professional activity of respective specialists are achieved in about 0.3–0.5 years (Abramova et al. 1988). Psychophysiological support of military combat activity is a system of psychophysiological measures designed to maintain high levels of combat performance of large and small units, and consists of occupational psychophysiological selection and psychophysiological support of combat military personnel.

Military psychophysiology is an applied-science discipline that studies the principles underlying successful professional activity of the military. This discipline addresses means of activating functional systems of the body in accordance with the needs of military activity, and based on the interaction of social-psychological, psychic, and physiological mechanisms. Psychophysiological support of military combat activity is implemented at three levels that assure successful professional performance: social-psychological, psychic, and physiological.

1 Occupational Psychophysiological Selection

Occupational psychophysiological selection in the armed forces is an integrated set of measures directed at achieving quality recruitment of citizens who join the army. This is accomplished by matching important occupation-related qualities at three levels of successful professional performance of requirements of military professional activity.

The procedure of occupational psychophysiological selection consists of a social-psychological assessment, psychological and physiological testing. It includes the following: (1) Social-Psychological Level – the social-psychological evaluation of personality, such as military professional orientation, motivational attitudes, etc.; (2) Psychological Level – the evaluation of the level of development of cognitive psychic processes, mental condition, and personality characteristics; and (3) Physiological Level – the study of the functional reserves of the body and some additional characteristics related to the specifics of military professional activity.

The objectives of occupational psychophysiological selection are as follows:

> Through the use of psychophysiological measures, determine the vocational aptitude of citizens who join the army to do military service under contract and conscription;
> Consistent with psychophysiological characteristics, provide a rational distribution of military personnel by training tracks and military positions;
> Perform psychophysiological selection of candidates to train small unit leaders;
> Participate in the designation of flying crews, manning details, teams, and small units based on psychological compatibility; and
> Perform psychophysiological selection of candidates to study at the military training schools.

It should be emphasized that the selection must be occupational psychophysiological, not occupational psychological. Experience shows that occupational psychophysiological selection and psychophysiological support of professional activity are better developed and performed by physicians-psychophysiologists with participation of psychologists, psychiatrists, and other specialists. The truth is that, by the nature of their professional training, psychologists, unlike physicians-psychophysiologists, are not able to assess the level of functional reserves of the body, or identify borderline states of the human psyche and evaluate their influence on successful professional performance, which results in ineffective occupational psychological screening.

The above approach was implemented to predict successful performance of pilots in combat conditions. In particular, in the process of mathematical-statistical modeling of the "decision function" (mathematical model), parameters were selected in order to satisfy the following requirements:

a. good discriminating ability;
b. weak correlation relationships (independent characteristics);
c. high factor loadings to factors that have a correlation with "external criterion."

Based on research by A. A. Bochenkov et al. (1989), the above requirements are met by two psychophysiological parameters, the Starr index characterizing the heart stroke volume, and G and I factors of the 16-FLO technique. These parameters were used to implement a procedure for automatic classification of tested pilots followed by discriminative analysis to build a mathematical model (of the "decision function") predicting successful professional performance (Y) of combat helicopter pilots:

$$Y = -0.04 X_1 + 1.1 X_2 - 0.1 X_3 - 5.0,$$

where,

X_1 is a Starr index value (heart stroke volume),
X_2 is a G factor value associated with the 16-FLO technique,
X_3 is an I factor value associated with the 16-FLO technique.

When $Y > 0$, test subjects are able to successfully perform combat activity in conditions of desert and mountainous terrain, and should be used for the most challenging combat missions. When $Y < (=) 0$, test subjects are less successful in performing combat activity in conditions of desert and mountainous terrain, and should be used for less challenging combat missions. The accuracy of the decision function was 88.2% in total for both categories (Pogodin and Bochenkov 2007).

Thus, the accuracy of predicting successful performance is significantly higher when physiological data is used together with psychological parameters.

It is also important because, in combat (Dovgusha et al. 1995, 182–191), a change in physiological parameters can be more reliably identified than a change in psychological parameters (Table 13.2), and is a function of the intensity of activity (Table 13.3).

TABLE 13.2   Psychophysiological assessment data for helicopter MI-8 and MI-24 aircrews (M±δ)

Parameters	In USSR	In Afghanistan (at the end of month 5)
Heart rate, bpm	68.72 ± 3.5	73.7±7.99*
Robinson index, conv. units	74.36±6.19	78.96±8.59*
Vital lung capacity, ml	4756.1±470.2	4468.3±540.5*
Timed inspiratory capacity (Stange test), s	62.4± 3.06	51.8±6.61*
Number of neurological symptoms and syndromes	0.21±0.41	1.62.± 1.19**
Reactive anxiety, Spilberger test, points	36.0±4.24	41.0±6.64
Scale of neuroticism, Ayzenk test, points	6.54±2.21	8.47±3.76
Scale of health, "SAN" test, points	47.89±0.78	43.18±5.08
Scale of mood states, "SAN" test, points	13.9±0.92	11.73±1.36

Note: Significant difference of * P<0.05 and ** P<0.01 "SAN": Health, Vigor, Mood.

TABLE 13.3   Heart Rate (HR) and Breathing Rate (BR) dynamics in MI-8 commanders at various flight stages in Afghanistan (M±δ)

Parameters	HR, bpm	BR, cycles/min
Non-flying days	74.7±6.08	15.26±1.2
Immediately before mission sorties	86.8±9.12	17.1±1.1
After launching unguided missiles and air-to-ground fire from bow guns	144.02±10.7***	22.8±2.25**
After landing on unprepared field	115.2±10.52***	21.1±1.95**
Night-time en-route flight	99.4±11.32*	19.3±1.64
Post-flight	81.6±10.52	19.1±2.43

Note: Significant difference of * P<0.05; ** P<0.01; *** P<0.001 as compared to data for non-flying days.

Based on the above premise, the last phase of the mathematical-statistical analysis and modeling, which involved assessment of more than 500 pilots, established the key psychophysiological parameters underlying successful adaptation of pilots to the combat environment and effective performance in the conditions of desert and mountainous terrain of Afghanistan (Novikov et al. 1997, 77–90). These parameters were psychological characteristics of the 16-FLO technique indicating the socially driven nature of individual's abilities: (1) level of communicative ability (A factor), (2) level of mental tolerance to stress and moral norm (C and Q3 factors), (3) conscientiousness (G factor), and (4) level of functional reserves of the pilots' cardio-respiratory system (CRS) (physiological Starr index: heart stroke volume).

Based on the most prevalent psychophysiological parameters, all of the tested pilots were arranged to fit one of the 4 conventional groups based on a combat effectiveness level (Figure 13.1). The data shown in Figure 13.1 was validated by the results of an investigation into the specifics of functional states

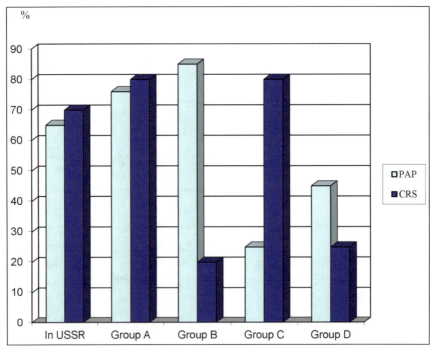

FIGURE 13.1 Distribution of helicopter aviation aircrews participating in combat missions in the desert and mountainous terrain conditions in Afghanistan versus data obtained in the USSR (time of peace) for groups representing combat performance (groups A, B, C, and D) and based on Personal Adaptive Potential (PAP) and Cardio-Respiratory System (CRS) measures that were equal to 6 or more increments on a 10-point scale of a normal distribution.

TABLE 13.4 Psychophysiological parameters of helicopter pilots in relation to combat performance groups (M±δ)

Parameters	Group A	Group B	Group C	Group D
Starr index, stens	6.8±0.08	4.64±0.17***	6.93±0.11	4.56±0.09***
Level of situational anxiety, points	35.9±2.48	43.2±3.78**	41.2±6.14*	48.57±4.75***
A factor, stens	6.76±0.33	7.8±0.43	5.93±0.19*	6.46±0.83
C factor, stens	7.68±0.12	7.0±0.39	6.0±0.38**	5.92±0.12**
G factor, stens	8.32±0.22	8.53±0.3	6.46±0.47***	7.84±0.15
Q3 factor, stens	6.16±0.17	7.03±0.25	5.6±0.36*	5.88±0.31*
Personal Adaptive Potential (PAP from MLO[a] technique), stens	6.1±0.13	6.33±0.24	4.2±0.33**	5.01±0.1*

a Translator's note: MLO stands for Multilevel Personality Questionnaire developed by A. G. Maklakov and S. V. Chermyanin.

Note:
- Significant difference in parameters for pilots in groups B, C, and D is shown in comparison to pilots from Group A;
- Significant difference of * – P < 0.05, ** – P < 0.01, *** – P < 0.005;
- Factors A, C, G, and Q3 of the 16-FLO technique.

of a pilot's body in the process of combat operations in relation to combat performance groups (Table 13.4). The data presented in Table 13.4 attests to the fact that there are significant differences between the pilots in the identified groups (Novikov et al. 1997, 53–55).

Group A. Pilots from this group are characterized by high combat performance ("external criterion:" 6 or more increments on a 10-point scale). These pilots were able to quickly adapt to a combat environment, successfully performed flight assignments, and demonstrated good flight-load tolerance. In nonstandard combat situations, they acted bravely and decisively. They had a high sociometric status in the units, and were characterized by a clear-cut military professional orientation. During 12 months of combat operations, they never avoided flying for reasons of health. As shown by the psychophysiological assessment data, 76% of pilots from this group had an integrated value of Personal Adaptive Potential (sum of values for factors A, C, G, and Q3) of 6 or more increments. 80% of pilots from the group demonstrated good cardiovascular system functional reserves (6 or more increments). Group-A pilots made up 30% of the tested sample population. Finally, longitudinal research indicates that, after their return from Afghanistan, 75% of Group-A pilots were able to successfully continue their professional activities for as long as 10 years.

Group B. Pilots from this group are characterized by a sufficient level of combat performance ("external criterion": 5.5 increments). They did well on their flight assignments. Some had chronic cardiovascular and nervous system diseases in their past medical history. Their process of adaptation to adverse climate conditions of the desert and mountainous terrain was somewhat complicated. Pilots from this group had insufficient cardiovascular system functional reserves, therefore, would be repeatedly grounded and taken out of combat due to excessive fatigue symptoms. They would generally turn down offers to be sent on a special short leave, arguing that the other crews of the unit would have to be charged with additional duties. Based on the psychophysiological assessment data, individuals from Group B had the highest valid parameters of the moral norm, communicative abilities, and interest group orientation. Their sociometric status in the unit was very high. The military professional orientation was sustaining. Group-B pilots composed 21% of the overall tested population. In 10 years after Afghanistan, 43% of the Group-B pilots were successfully serving in aviation units.

Group C. Pilots from this group (18% of the overall tested population) were characterized by suboptimal combat performance ("external criterion": 4 or increments on a 10-point scale). During service in Afghanistan, they were never grounded for reasons of health, but would often demonstrate inferior performance on their flight assignments. During flight assignments, Group-C pilots did not fully utilize combat capabilities of the helicopters. Sometimes, they acted indecisively in complex combat situations. It was difficult for them to adapt to an adverse combat environment. Pilots from this group had a high level of cardiovascular system functional reserves, but scored the lowest in the tested sample parameters of mental tolerance to stress, inferior moral qualities, and were less focused on group task performance. Their sociometric status in the units was low. In general, their military professional orientation was dubious or even negative. Within 10 years after their return from Afghanistan, 78% of the Group-C pilots were retired from flying and dismissed from service in the armed forces.

Group D. Pilots from this group (31% of the overall tested population) were characterized by low combat performance. It was extremely difficult for them to adapt to combat activity. The overwhelming number of these pilots had chronic diseases in their past medical history. At the initial phase of service in Afghanistan, they would demonstrate satisfactory flight assignment performance. After extreme situations encountered during combat missions, these individuals experienced neurotic reactions and reactive states as a result of which most of them were subjected to in-patient examination. Subsequently, the overwhelming majority of these pilots were retired from flying. The level of functional reserves of the body was low, and tolerance to flight loads unsatisfactory. These pilots had high situational anxiety and low Personal Adaptive Potential. As a whole, such pilots had a low sociometric status. Flight work orientation in most of the subjects was negative. Within 10 years after their return from Afghanistan, only 5% of the Group-D pilots were able to continue to fly.

Overall, the presented data is another confirmation of a need to account for the functional resource level of the body during occupational psychophysiological selection.

2 Psychophysiological Support of Combat Activity

Psychophysiological support of combat activity is a system of psychophysiological measures designed to maintain and enhance combat performance of large and small units through optimization of the functional state of the body of military personnel. Psychophysiological support of combat activity of military personnel includes a rational distribution of military personnel by training tracks and military positions consistent with their psychophysiological characteristics; evaluation of combat effectiveness of large and small units based on the functional state of the body of personnel; psychophysiological correction; and psychophysiological rehabilitation.

Psychophysiological support of combat activity is provided at three levels that assure successful professional performance. The goal is to enhance the effectiveness of combat activity, individual training and education, and maintaining occupational health based on psychophysiological and personality specifics of the military personnel.

The objectives of the psychophysiological support of military combat activity are:

1. In-depth psychophysiological assessment conducted in the process of dynamic observation in order to facilitate early detection of individuals with dysadaptation disorders;
2. Evaluation of combat effectiveness of large and small units through the use of measures related to functional states of the body;
3. Division of military personnel into groups based on the level of their combat proficiency;
4. Rational re-distribution of personnel by units and military positions consistent with their psychophysiological characteristics;

5. Application of psychophysiological correction measures for military personnel experiencing difficulties with military professional adaptation;
6. Application of psychophysiological rehabilitation measures;
7. Prediction of long-term effects of combat stress on military personnel.

With respect to military personnel, psychophysiological correction of the functional state of the body is defined as a combination of interventions applied to a virtually healthy individual with a purpose of normalizing or stimulating functional reactions of the body in order to restore professional working capacity, rapidly increase it, or maintain it at a pre-set level for an extended period of time. In combat conditions, psychophysiological correction measures are applied by specially formed medical-psychological groups with participation of psychologists and unit mentors.

Depending on the military professional occupation, 30% to 90% of military personnel require psychophysiological correction of the functional state of the body (Bochenkov et al. 1996, 35–40). Given specifics of military professional activity in combat conditions, the main focus of psychophysiological correction should be active diagnostics of individuals with dysadaptation disorders. Psychophysiological correction measures should follow the principle of professionalism, i.e. be applied by physicians-psychophysiologists and other specialists knowledgeable in the use of psycho-diagnostics, psycho-correction, and psycho-therapy techniques in the field.

The principles on which psychophysiological correction measures are chosen emphasize reliability, availability, optimality, and field-proven techniques. Therefore, in selecting the techniques, preference should be given to those that are short in duration and effective in terms of impact.

Psycho-corrective work should be done on a case-by-case basis depending on somatic state and personality traits. Factors that should not be overlooked include: reduction in performance of critical professional abilities, intensity of psychical dysadaptation, and sensitivity and tolerance to psycho-correction techniques. Based on the research data, the most effective psychophysiological correction techniques for helicopter pilots in a combat environment (Table 13.5) are: group and individual rational psychotherapy, and active and passive muscle relaxation per Jacobson (Novikov et al. 1997).

Practical experience shows that the most effective way to administer the techniques is by creating special mobile psychophysiological teams consisting of 5 experts (two psychophysiologists, psychiatrist, psychopharmacologist, and psychologist) who are able to evaluate within 24 hours the combat effectiveness level through psychophysiological parameters and perform psychophysiological correction for 250–300 warriors.

Psychophysiological rehabilitation of military personnel is a combination of psychophysiological measures to restore the functional state of the body and

TABLE 13.5 Heart rate and subjective health (ACC questionnaire) in helicopter pilots before and after application of psycho-correction measures in combat conditions

Parameters	Before psycho-correction	After rational psychotherapy	After active and passive muscle relaxation per Jacobson with elements of suggestion
Heart rate, bpm	76.8	72.1	68.3
Subjective health (ACC questionnaire), conv. units	33.6	38.1	43.4

fitness for military service in individuals who suffered traumas, diseases, and wounds. The measures of psychophysiological rehabilitation are administered by the psychophysiological service experts in district (Navy) hospitals during the course of treatment. The results obtained from the socio-psychological study, psychological and physiological assessment of the military personnel during occupational psychophysiological selection, and psychophysiological support of combat activity allow one of the following conclusions:

Category 1 of occupational psychophysiological fitness fully corresponds to the requirements of a given profession or position;

Category 2 of occupational psychophysiological fitness more or less corresponds to the requirements of a given profession or position;

Category 3 of occupational psychophysiological fitness has the least correspondence to the requirements of a given profession or position (nominally fit);

Category 4 occupational psychophysiological fitness does not correspond to the requirements of a given profession or position (unfit).

3   System of Psychophysiological Support of Combat Activity

Teachings concerning key professional qualities and abilities serve as a methodological and theoretical foundation for the physiological support of combat activity. Key professional qualities in reference to a specific activity are determined by means of job (cognitive task) analysis. Based on a job specification, a prioritized list of key professional qualities is formed, for example, in the form of a psychogram. Then, each key professional quality is lined up with a technique that measures the individual's abilities consistent with a key professional quality, or such techniques are developed from scratch.

The typical definition of abilities is that of a combination of natural inclinations and qualities developed through upbringing, education, and labor activity (Maklakov et al. 2005). The concept of individual anatomic and physiological features and differences in mental capacity existing from birth and affecting development explains distinctive abilities exhibited by different people.

Once the occupational psychological selection and rational distribution of military professions is complete, adaptation of personnel to military service begins. Adaptation is defined as a "... system response of the body to prolonged or multiple exposures to the external environment which facilitates performance of the main activity tasks with the goal of achieving adequate primary response while minimizing the payback response. This response is related to a change in the structure of homeostatic regulation" (Medvedev 1983).

The process of adaptation contributes to optimizing body system functions and a balanced state of the "man – machine – environment" system (Berezin 1988). Excessive fatigue in the adaptation processes leads to a failure of the adaptation mechanisms and development of dysadaptation and later deadaptation disorders in the somatic and mental areas.

Success in military professional activity should be considered from the point of view of the functional system theory (Anokhin 1975). In this case, we are dealing with a functional system that provides activation of the body functions consistent with the needs of activity directed at achieving an objective, with the effectiveness of military professional activity playing the role of a system-forming factor. Once occupational selection, training, manning, and equipment issues are taken care of, 65% of the effectiveness of military professional activity is predicated by the functional state of the body of military personnel (Pogodin et al. 1998). There is a direct link between the functional state of the body and working capacity. Therefore, the optimal functional state of the body is imperative for maintaining high performance of the military.

Psychophysiological support of the military is provided at all phases of combat activity. Psychophysiological support of *daily combat training* serves to maintain occupational health and enhance military professional performance of personnel. The objectives of the psychophysiological support of daily combat training are as follows:

1. Identify specific phases and components of training that raise the bar for physical fitness, health, and mental tolerance to stress of the servicemen (tank "rollover", parachute jumps, record firing, exercises, etc.);

2. Evaluate the functional state of the body of servicemen, and identify risk-group individuals;
3. Provide rational re-distribution of personnel by military jobs and units;
4. Predict combat performance of personnel based on parameters of the functional state of the body;
5. Apply psychophysiological correction measures to servicemen from the risk-group;
6. Implement measures to enhance (rapidly restore) military professional working capacity.

The results of the dynamic psychophysiological assessment and evaluation of effectiveness of the psychophysiological correction measures are used to predict the mental readiness of servicemen for combat missions.

The goal of psychophysiological support at the stage of *preparations for deployment to a combat area* is to enhance combat performance of large and small units. Additional socio-psychological and psychophysiological assessments are conducted to more precisely identify combat performance groups based on parameters of the functional state of the body and provide recommendations on the rational distribution (re-distribution) of personnel by units, predict the level of their operational effectiveness, and apply psychophysiological correction measures. The level of retention of mental self-regulation techniques is also tested.

The main focus of psychophysiological correction at this stage of preparations for combat is:

a. Identification of risk-groups based on parameters of the functional state of the body;
b. Acceleration of adaptation to combat environment;
c. Correction of dysadaptation disorders in the functional state of the body of military personnel.

In combat, psychophysiological support is mostly focused on optimization of the functional state of the body of combatants. The following objectives are addressed:

d. Express-diagnostics of body functional state and identification of individuals who need correction of their state;
e. Development of recommendations for unit leaders on the rational use of personnel in combat consistent with the functional reserves of the body and mental abilities;
f. Application of psychophysiological correction measures.

The main thrusts of psychophysiological correction at the stage of direct combat engagement include:

g. Reduction of intensity of combat manifestations of stress;
h. Sleep normalization;
i. Rapid boost in physical performance of select categories of military personnel (reconnaissance units, special forces, etc.);
j. Maintaining a high level of mental capacity in tactical control operators and officers.

To provide psychophysiological support in combat conditions, it is important to know in advance the intensity of changes in the functional state of the body of personnel to fine-tune techniques for diagnostic assessments and psychophysiological correction measures. In this regard, the most informative types of research were assessments conducted during combat actions in Afghanistan and Chechnya, which had a different intensity of operational load/stress (Novikov 1996, 37–40).

The data obtained demonstrate that the highest load/stress during combat actions in Chechnya occurred with assault troopers (Table 13.6). A total of 1312 servicemen were assessed in Chechnya, from which 28% were essentially healthy (did not have any health complaints) and 72% were found to have asthenodepressive (46%) or psychotic (26%) reactions. Asthenodepresive states were manifested through the disturbance of sleep, feelings of fatigue, lack of motivation for professional activity, high anxiety levels, nervous emotional tension, and hypochondrical fixation. Psychotic reactions were characterized by aggression, alteration of normal moral orientation, deterioration of interpersonal contacts, affective arousal, or inhibition. Mental tolerance to stress in servicemen during combat action in Chechnya was demonstrated by about 40% of the military personnel (Table 13.7).

In 32% of the cases, reactive anxiety level exceeded the nominal value. These servicemen were subjected to psychophysiological correction in the form of rational psychotherapy, and active and passive muscle relaxation. Practically all of the servicemen tested in combat conditions in Chechnya had symptoms of asthenization with various neuropsychic disorders (Tables 13.8 & 13.9).

TABLE 13.6 Psychophysiological characteristics of servicemen during combat action in Chechnya (%)

Servicemen diagnoses	Motorized riflemen	Scouts	Assault troopers
Virtually healthy	18	70	13
Asthenodepressive reactions	45	30	18
Psychotic reactions	35	1	68

The above-mentioned specifics were also supported by the fact that combat effectiveness in Chechnya was much lower than effectiveness of combat operations in Afghanistan (Table 13.10). The same trend was observed in the analysis of personality traits of aircrews, both pilots and navigators (Table 13.11).

TABLE 13.7 Mental tolerance to stress level in servicemen during combat action in Chechnya (conv. units)

	Outside of combat	After 9–20 days of combat	After 21–49 days of combat
Level of mental-to-stress tolerance	34	37	47

TABLE 13.8 Structure of neuropsychic disorders in soldiers during combat action in Chechnya (%)

Neuropsychic disorders	%
Asthenization	98
Intense anxiety	71
Disturbance of sleep	65
Intense physical fatigue	39
Neurotic reactions	40
Acute affective reactions	1
Pathological characterological reactions	5

TABLE 13.9 Structure and number of health complaints (%) and Situational Anxiety (SA) in servicemen in Chechnya

Complaints and SA	Combat operations in the city of Grozny (January, 1995)	Combat operations in the suburbs of Grozny (December, 1999)
Situational anxiety, conv. units	49	40.4
Headache	12	13
Dizziness	28	6
Rapid pulse	18	7

TABLE 13.9   Structure and number of health complaints (%) and Situational Anxiety (*cont.*)

Complaints and SA	Combat operations in the city of Grozny (January, 1995)	Combat operations in the suburbs of Grozny (December, 1999)
Abdominal discomfort	40	10
Chest pains	19	8
Muscle weakness	50	30
Other complaints	50	30

Note: In a number of cases, the servicemen would present several complaints; therefore, the sum is not equal to 100%.

TABLE 13.10   Combat performance of servicemen (%)

Combat Performance	Afghanistan	Chechnya
Satisfactory	63	52
Unsatisfactory	37	48

TABLE 13.11   Comparative analysis of aircrew personality traits using 16-FLO technique during combat operations in Afghanistan and Northern Caucasus (24)

Parameters (M±δ)	Afghanistan (n = 50)	Northern Caucasus (n = 25)
Factor A	9,42 ± 2,07	6,80 ± 0,67
Factor B	3,63 ± 2,23	3,32 ± 0,62*
Factor C	8,14 ±1,69	7,90 ±0,51
Factor E	5,14 ± 1,68	6,50 ±0,58
Factor F	5,60 ± 1,89	5,60 ± 0,22
Factor G	8,95 ± 2,28	7,50 ±0,68
Factor H	6,33 ± 1,58	7,00 ±0,16
Factor I	5,37 ± 1,91	4,20 ± 0,43
Factor L	5,02 ± 1,98	5,20 ± 1,61
Factor M	5,37 ± 1,60	4,50 ± 1,48
Factor N	5,49 ± 2,06	5,90 ± 0,46
Factor O	6,61 ± 1,71	5,70 ± 0,62

TABLE 13.11   Comparative analysis of aircrew personality traits using 16-FLO (cont.)

Parameters (M±δ)	Afghanistan (n = 50)	Northern Caucasus (n = 25)
Factor Q1	6,60 ±2,19	6,30 ± 1,66
Factor Q2	5,25 ± 1,78	5,20 ±0,59
Factor Q3	8.09 ± 1.68	6.30 ± 0.58*
Factor Q4	5.12 ± 1.56	4.30 ± 0.64

Note: significant difference of P < 0.05

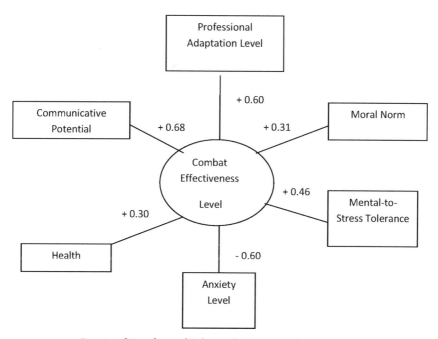

FIGURE 13.2   Density of Correlational Relations between Combat Performance and Psychophysiological Characteristics of Servicemen

In the process of combat operations in Afghanistan, a decrease in the amount of hemoglobulin, erythrocytes, leucocytes, and eosinophiles in the peripheral blood of aircrew members proved to be a statistically valid observation (Chermyanin and Bochenkov 1985, 89). A review of correlational relations between combat performance and psychophysiological parameters (Figure 13.2) shows that the strongest relationships are with the professional adaptation level (+0.60), anxiety level (−0.60), and communicative potential (+0.68).

Sociopathic accentuation of personally traits begins to occur in servicemen after an extended presence in the area of armed conflict. In particular, such individuals had higher values on the Hy, Pa, and Pd scales of the MLO technique two to four times more often than in the control sample, which attests to heightened impulsiveness, and affective rigidity, as well as emotional tension channeled through behavior that conflicts with social attitudes and ethic norms (Novikov 1996, 37–40).

4 Evaluation of Combat Performance of Large and Small Units Based on Measures of Functional State of Body

Evaluation of combat performance of large and small units based on measures of the functional state of the body must be performed during the assignment of young recruits to units, updated during preparation of the units for combat action, and carried out periodically in the process of combat operations. Combat performance of large and small units is evaluated by means of socio-psychological screening and psychophysiological assessment of servicemen at three levels that assure successful professional activity (socio-psychological, psychological, and physiological) in order to identify individuals with a varying ability to perform combat missions.

Evaluation of combat performance of large and small units includes:
1. Socio-psychological screening and psychophysiological assessment of servicemen;
2. Assessment of functional reserves of the body and personality traits of servicemen;
3. Determination of combat performance groups based on measures of the functional state of the body;
4. Development of recommendations for the senior command concerning the rational distribution of personnel by units and military positions during combat operations.

The results of the psychophysiological assessment during combat operations provide an objective characteristic of the functional state of the body as well as recommendations on the rational use of military personnel and their redistribution by units on the battlefield.

As shown by the psychophysiological assessment data, there are 3 combat performance groups that may be singled out in the process of operations:

> The first group (about 25% of servicemen) is characterized by the optimal functional state of the body, adequate anxiety level, and high adaptive

potential. It seems practical to form storm troop units from personnel belonging to this group provided they have appropriate professional training. High performance of the units formed from such servicemen as well as minimal temporary casualties and mortality in these units exert a positive influence on moral psychological preparedness of other servicemen to do battle;

The second group (about 50–60% of servicemen) is characterized by a satisfactory functional state of the body. High combat effectiveness may be achieved after application of psychophysiological correction measures. Servicemen from this group should be used in support units;

The third group (about 15–25% of servicemen) is characterized by an unsatisfactory functional state of the body with the development of somatic and mental disorders and rapid deterioration of combat effectiveness. In the process of operations, this group has the largest number of temporary and irrevocable losses. It seems practical to use them in sustaining units in non-combatant areas.

Psychophysiological support is provided at the stage of preparations for combat operations, during combat, and after withdrawal from the combat zone in order to predict post-traumatic stress syndrome.

Psychophysiological support of combat activity is implemented to enhance combat performance of large and small units. This goal is achieved through implementation of the following tasks:

a. Socio-psychological screening exam and psychophysiological assessment of military personnel;
b. Rational distribution of military personnel by units and military positions consistent with their psychophysiological characteristics;
c. Identification of individuals with functional and pathological disorders;
d. Evaluation of combat performance of large and small units based on measures of the functional state of the body;
e. Application of psychophysiological correction and rehabilitation measures;
f. Prediction of development of the post-traumatic stress syndrome (PTSS) with recommendations on special medical-psychological treatment.

Evaluation of combat performance of large and small units consists of the following phases:

1. Investigation of relations in the military collective;
2. Psychological and psychophysiological assessments of military personnel and analysis of results;

3. In-depth assessment of individuals who show signs of deteriorating psychophysiological state or are unable to cope with official duties;
4. Determination of combat performance groups based on measures of the functional state of the body;
5. Development of recommendations for the command on rational distribution of servicemen by units and military positions.

Psychological and psychophysiological assessments of military personnel are performed using psychological questionnaires, psychological tests (usually, paper tests), observation, interviews, and examination by a psychiatrist. Psychological characteristics of personality are studied using the Multi-Level Personality Questionnaire "Adaptiveness" (MLO), Spilberger's scale of situational anxiety, and ACC technique (Subjective Health Questionnaire). Standard physiological tests evaluating physiological reserves of the body (Stange-Gench's tests) are used as additional methods of assessment.

Based on the assessment results, subjects may be subdivided into three groups. The first group includes military personnel with satisfactory parameters for the functional state of the body; the second group has borderline parameters; and the third group has unsatisfactory parameters. The criteria used include the level of personal adaptive potential (MLO test), situational anxiety (Spilberger test), subjective and objective characteristics of the functional state of the body (integrated value of ACC technique, physiological parameters). The final assessments are shown in Table 13.12.

TABLE 13.12 Final personnel performance assessment based on evaluation of psychological status and functional state of body

Parameters of Techniques (stens)

Personal Adaptive Potential (MLO)	Situational Anxiety	Integrated Value (ACC)	Bogomazov Index	Combat Performance Group
6 and higher	6 and higher	6 and higher	6 and higher	1
3–5	3–5	3–5	3–5	2
1–2	1–2	1–2	1–2	3

Note: The final performance assessment takes into account the minimal parameters for each of the techniques. The combat performance group cannot be higher than the minimal group in each of the techniques.

THE PSYCHOPHYSIOLOGY OF COMBAT ACTIVITY

While working with the MLO test, the scales of the 4th (integrated scale) and 3rd (behavioral regulation, communicative potential, moral norm) levels are used. The servicemen whose integrated scale parameter is equal to 6 or more increments have psychological characteristics that correspond to the established norm. Parameters in the range of 3–5 increments are indicative of diminished functional reserves of the body and borderline mental state. The integrated scale parameter of 2 or less increments is an indicator of low adaptive reserves and unsatisfactory mental state (Table 13.19).

TABLE 13.13 Conversion of Personal Adaptive Potential (PAP) from MLO test to standard points (stens), determination of Combat Performance Group (CPG)

Stens	1	2	3	4	5	6	7	8	9	10
PAP, points	103 and >	81–102	73–80	60–72	51–59	45–50	36–44	31–35	23–30	22 and <
CPG	3		2			1				

TABLE 13.14 Conversion of Mental-to-Stress Tolerance (MST), Communicative Potential (CP), and Moral Norm (MN) from MLO test to standard points (stens), and determination of Combat Performance Group (CPG)

Stens	1	2	3	4	5	6	7	8	9	10
MST	46–>	38–45	30–37	22–29	16–21	13–15	9–12	6–8	4–5	0–3
CP	27–31	22–26	17–21	13–16	10–12	7–9	5–6	3–4	1–2	0
MN	18–>	15–17	12–14	10–11	7–9	5–6	3–4	2	1	0
CPG	3		2			1				

TABLE 13.15 Interpretation of Combat Performance Groups (CPG) based on MLO test ("Adaptiveness")

CPG	Interpretation
1	Groups with high and normal adaptation. Individuals from these groups easily adapt to new activity conditions, quickly "fit in" with a new collective, easily and adequately orientate themselves in a situation, and quickly develop a strategy of behavior and socialization. They are not prone to

TABLE 13.15 Interpretation of Combat Performance Groups (CPG) (cont.)

CPG	Interpretation
	conflict and have high mental tolerance to stress. The functional state of the body is good, and working capacity is high.
2	The group with satisfactory adaptation. Most of the individuals from this group demonstrate signs of negative tendencies which are partially compensated in familiar conditions and become apparent during stress. Therefore, success of adaptation largely depends on the external environment. Generally, these individuals have low mental stability in response to stress. The process of socialization is complicated; asocial reactions, aggression, and proneness to conflict are also possible. The functional state of the body may be degraded. Individuals from this group need to be continuously monitored and subjected to psychophysiological correction measures.
3	The group with low adaptation. Individuals from this group have negative tendencies with respect to personality traits and certain psychopathic symptoms; their mental state may be characterized as borderline. The adaptation process is very difficult. Neuropsychic breakdowns and long-lasting disorders in the functional state of the body are possible. Mental tolerance to stress is low; proneness to conflict, deviant and delinquent behavior is possible.

TABLE 13.16 Brief interpretation of MLO test scales

Scale name	Interpretation of low values (stens)	Interpretation of high values (stens)
Mental Tolerance to Stress	Low level of mental tolerance to stress, proneness to neuropsychic breakdowns, lack of adequate self-assessment or adequate perception of reality	High level of mental tolerance to stress, adequate self-assessment, adequate perception of reality
Communicative Potential	Low level of communicative abilities, difficulty in making contact with others, aggression, proneness to conflict	High level of communicative abilities, ease of making contact with others, not prone to conflict

TABLE 13.16 Brief interpretation of MLO test scales (cont.)

Scale name	Interpretation of low values (stens)	Interpretation of high values (stens)
Moral Norm	Low level of socialization, inability to adequately evaluate own place and role in the collective, no desire to observe conventional norms of behavior	High level of socialization, ability to adequately evaluate own role in the collective, guided by conventional norms of behavior.

TABLE 13.17 Conversion of Situational Anxiety (SA) parameters to sten scale and determination of Combat Performance Group (CPG)

Stens	1	2	3	4	5	6	7	8	9	10
Points	69 and more	68–64	63–57	56–51	50–46	45–40	39–36	35–31	30–26	25 and less
CPG	3		2			1				

TABLE 13.18 Conversion of subjective health values to sten scale and determination of Combat Performance Group (CPG)

Stens	1	2	3	4	5	6	7	8	9	10
Points	11 and <	12–14	15–22	23–28	29–33	34–38	39–42	43–45	46–47	48–49
CPG	3		2			1				

TABLE 13.19 Conversion of Bogomazov index values to sten scale and determination of Combat Performance Group (CPG)

Stens	1	2	3	4	5	6	7	8	9	10
Points	49 and <	50–56	57–69	70–87	88–95	96–101	102–110	11–113	114–120	121 and >
CPG	3		2			1				

A scale of situational anxiety is used in the Spilberger test. A situational anxiety parameter equal to 6 increments or higher corresponds to the generally accepted norm. A parameter of three to five increments indicates a heightened anxiety level. A parameter of one to two increments indicates an excessively high level of situational anxiety (Table 13.17).

The ACC technique serves to evaluate subjective health and potential somatic complaints of servicemen. An ACC parameter of 6 increments or more in the absence of (or presence of isolated complaints) is an indication of a satisfactory functional state of the body. Reduction of the ACC parameter to three to five increments in combination with health complaints attests to the presence of borderline functional states of the body. An ACC parameter of one to two increments in combination with a large number of health complaints reflects an unsatisfactory functional state of the body.

Evaluation of the physiological reserves of the body is performed using the standard stress tests of Stange and Gench. The Stange test involves the maximum holding of breath at the intake and after three breathing cycles, at ¾ of the full inspiratory capacity. The test is performed in the upright position. The Gench test involves the maximum holding of breath at the exhale. After three breathing cycles, the subject takes a maximum deep breath, then breathes out deeply, pinches his nose with the right-hand fingers and remains in this position for as long as he is able to continue the test. The time between the two tests should be not less than 3 minutes. A statement on the condition of the cardiorespiratory system is made using the Bogomazov index calculated as follows:

$$\frac{\text{Stange test (s)} + \text{Gench test (s)} \cdot 100}{90}$$

The values of parameters of the cardiorespiratory system reserves calculated using the above equation for the Bogomazov index are converted to a 10-point scale of normal distribution (stens) in the Table. Servicemen whose level of cardiorespiratory system reserves lies in the range of one to two increments should be given a short break followed by corrective pharmacological measures.

A Bogomazov index of 6 increments or more is an indication of a satisfactory functional state of the body. When this parameter is reduced to three to five increments, it indicates a borderline level of the physiological reserves of the body. A Bogomazov index of one to two increments is an indication of an unsatisfactory state of the physiological reserves of the body.

5   Conclusion

The results of the psychophysiological assessment of military personnel serve as a basis for the development of recommendations for the unit leaders regarding the rational use of personnel and application of psycho-correction measures. Servicemen from the 1st Combat Performance Group (overall state: good) demonstrate high performance and can be recommended for various combat task duties that require maximum efficiency of professional activity. It is advisable to form combat teams that must first engage the enemy from servicemen who have both good occupational training and good functional state of the body (high personal adaptive potential, adequate level of anxiety and subjective health, and sufficient physiological reserves of the body). Highly effective performance of such combat teams exerts a positive influence on the moral and psychological state of the other servicemen, which contributes to enhanced performance of the entire unit while avoiding unjustifiable losses. They do not require psychophysiological correction.

Servicemen from the Second Combat Performance Group (overall state: satisfactory) are able to effectively perform job duties. But, to reach high efficiency of professional activity, they need more time to adapt to combat conditions as well as measures for psychophysiological correction. Servicemen from the 3rd Combat Performance Group (overall state: unsatisfactory) constitute the risk-group and need to be more closely monitored by unit leaders, medical service, and psychologists. It is advisable to evacuate them from the combat zone as their functional state of the body will progressively deteriorate and somatic pathology will become more apparent in the combat zone.

Psychological correction measures are administered upon approval by the unit leader during off-duty hours. It is advisable to conduct at least 3 sessions. The maximum effect is achieved after 5–6 sessions. The psychological correction measures can be performed in any room or even outdoors when the air temperature is 15°C and higher. The primary methods of the psychophysiological assessment of military personnel are observation, interview, and psychophysiological examination.

During the psychophysiological assessment, factors analyzed include the information content of the interview and behavioral reactions: presence of explosive or stuporous reactions. Special attention during the assessment should be paid to peculiarities of facial expressions and speech (extremely fast or extremely slow), symptoms of vegetative dysregulation (excessive sweating, reddening or blanching of skin tissues, etc.), neurotic symptoms and signs (tics, loss of coordination, hand tremor, etc.).

During the interview, the focus is on the appropriateness of judgments (on the time and place, and understanding of the events), type of self-assessments, realness of claims and motivations, general health, availability of complaints, etc. Based on the analysis, a conclusion is made on the degree of manifestation of neurotic or psychotic symptoms and signs. The presence of apparent neurotic symptoms and signs (heightened anxiety level, feeling of fear, vegetative dysfunction, disturbance of sleep, lowered thresholds of tolerance to occupational hazards, asthenodepressive, senestho-hypochondriacal, and psychosomatic symptoms, etc.) serves as an indication of declining performance and of the need to perform psychophysiological examination.

In combat conditions, neurotic disorders that are recorded include asthenic and asthenodepressive states characterized by increased fatigability, exhaustion, weakness, loss of ability to handle long-lasting physical and mental strain, affective lability with predominantly low mood and tearfulness, irritable weakness, frequent headaches, sleep disorders, depressive and desperate anguish, bleak view of the present environment and own future, absence of motivation for professional activity, and suicidal thoughts. Servicemen who have psychotic reactions are subject to a psychiatrist's examination during which emergency psychiatric support is provided followed by evacuation to the rear. The symptoms of psychotic reactions include explosive or stuporous manifestations, autism, excessive aggression, signs of general psychopathization and social dysadaptation, depersonalization, hallucinations, etc.

Implementation of the system of psychophysiological support of combat activity will assure enhanced performance of large and small military units through optimization of the functional state of the body and, as shown by the experience of its application, reduced temporary and irrevocable losses in the process of combat.

References

Abramova, V. N., V. V. Belekhov, E. G. Belskaya et al. 1988. *Psychological Methods of Personnel Management at NPPs*. Moscow: Energoatomizdat.

Agrel, Y. 1970. *Stress: Military Consequences – Psychological Aspects of Problem/ Emotional Stress*. Leningrad: Medicina.

Anokhin, P. K. 1975. *Essays on Physiology of Functional Systems*. Moscow: Medicina.

Baranov, Y. 1988. *Neuropsychic Instability and Methods of Its Diagnostics in Draftees. Relevant Issues of Occupational Psychological Selection and Rational Distribution of Draftees in Military Enlistment Offices*. Moscow: MO USSR.

Berezin, F. B. 1988. *Human Psychological and Psychophysiological Adaptation.* Leningrad: Nauka.

Bochenkov, A. A. 2009. "Concept of psychophysiological support of combat activity of military." Paper presented at the All-Russia Science Conference "Military Medicine in Local Wars and Armed Conflicts," Saint Petersburg, February 12–13.

Bochenkov, A. A., S. V. Chermyanin and A. V. Otochkin. 1989. "Predicting successful professional performance for pilots. Issues of occupational training at the phase of accelerated progress in science and technology." Abstract presented at the Interagency Science Conference, Kirovograd.

Bochenkov, A. A., A. N. Glushko, E. B. Naumenko, V. I. Bulyko, and S. V. Chermyanin. 1994. "Methodology and principles of integrated psychophysiological testing of military specialists' aptitude." *Military Medical Journal* 11.

Bochenkov, A. A., V. I. Shostak, and A. N. Glushko. 1996. "Relevant Issues of Military Psychophysiology." *Military Medical Journal* 12.

Chermyanin, S. V. and A. A. Bochenkov. 1985. "Hemogram dynamics in helicopter pilots during intense flight missions. Safety and efficiency of aircraft operations." Abstract presented at the IY All-Russia Flight Safety Conference, Leningrad.

Chermyanin, S. V., V. A. Korzunin, N. V. Kunitsyn, and V. I. Levshakova. 2009. "Specifics of professional activity and psychophysiological state of Army Aviation aircrews at initial phase of warfare in northern." Paper presented at the All-Russia Science Conference "Military Medicine in Local Wars and Armed Conflicts," Saint Petersburg, February 12–13.

Chizh, I. M., and E. G. Zhilyaev. 1998. "Relevant issues of psychophysiological support of military professional activity." *Military Medical Journal* 3.

Dovgusha, V. V., I. D. Kudrin, and M. N. Tikhonov. 1995. *Environmental and Hygienic Aspects of Combat Actions of Helicopter Aviation in Afghanistan. Introduction to Military Ecology.* Leningrad: VMedA.

Glushko, A. N., B. V. Ovchinnikov, L. A. Yanshin, S. V. Chermyanin, and V. I. Bulyko. 1994. "On Issue of Psychophysiological Recovery and Adjustment." *Military Medical Journal* 3.

Maklakov, A. G. et al. 2005. *Military Psychology.* Saint Petersburg: Piter.

Medvedev, V. I. 1983. *Theory of Adaption and Its Value for Military Medicine: Commencement Address.* Leningrad: VMedA.

Novikov, V. S. 1996. "Psychophysiological support of combat activity of military personnel." *Military Medical Journal* 4.

Novikov, V. S. and A. A. Bochenkov. 1997. *Theoretical and Applied Foundations of Occupational Psychological Screening of Military Personnel.* Saint Petersburg: VMedA.

Novikov, V. S., A. A. Bochenkov, and S. V. Chermyanin. 1997. "Methodological basis for psychophysiological correction of helicopter pilots in combat conditions. Relevant issues of aviation and space medicine: correction of functional states." In *Works of the Military Medical Academy*, 245. Saint Petersburg: VMedA.

Novikov, V. S., A. A. Bochenkov, and S. V. Chermyanin. 1997. "Psychophysiological justification of correction and adjustment challenges for military personnel involved in combat actions." *Military Medical Journal* 3.

Novikov, V. S., A. A. Bochenkov, A. G. Maklakov, and S. V. Chermyanin. 1997. *Psychological Support of Academic Activities in Higher Education Institutions*. Saint Petersburg: VMedA.

Pogodin, Y., and A. A. Bochenkov. 2007. *Psychophysiology of Professional Activity*. Moscow: Paradis.

Pogodin, Y., V. S. Novikov, and A. A. Bochenkov. 1998. "Psychophysiological support of military professional activity." *Military Medical Journal* 11: 27–36.

Shabalin, V. A., S. N. Rusanov, A. A. Bochenkov, A. Kondratyev, and A. D. Fesyun. 2009. "Evaluation and prediction of military personnel tolerance to stress in conditions of local wars." Paper presented at the All-Russia Science Conference on Military Medicine in Local Wars and Armed Conflicts, Saint Petersburg, February 12–13.

Shostak, V. I., ed. 1991. *Theoretical Foundations of Military Psychophysiology*. Saint Petersburg: VMedA.

CHAPTER 14

The Use of Fuzzy Logic and Artificial Neural Networks to Predict the Professional Fitness of Operators of Technical Systems

A. P. Bulka

At present, diagnostic procedures for the selection of professional operators of complex technical systems are increasingly being computerized. Scientific studies of the use of computer technology are primarily geared toward new ways of gathering primary data and adapting existing psychophysiological methods to automation. Much less attention is being paid to research exploring new ways of processing test results. Up to now, researchers have preferred to use manual data processing in mathematical modeling, and not to entrust it to complex software algorithms. Therefore, the simplest mathematical models, such as regression, discriminant, cluster, or factor analysis, are most frequently used. This approach for mathematical modeling of data from psychophysiological studies has seemingly reached the outer limit of effectiveness, since the predictive ability of such algorithms does not exceed 60–65%, and the correlation coefficients for psychophysiological methods for determining success of operators' work do not exceed 0.2–.03. Meanwhile, mathematical algorithms are good only insofar as they reflect the real processes of the phenomenon under study. And if the object of research is so complex a bio-social system as that of a person conducting professional work, then the mathematical model must reflect the characteristics of that system.

As a whole, this approach to the construction and study of mathematical models of complex subjects, provisionally termed biologization, has increasingly become the basic trend in cybernetics development. This occurred because of the dissatisfaction of researchers with the "classical" methods of information processing. The classical methods presuppose the systematic study of individual cases, with their later integration into a unified whole. Dialectically contrary to this trend (although not in opposition) is the school of research using the philosophical systems principle. In short, this principle may be formulated as follows: one cannot understand the part without having some knowledge of the whole and of the interrelationship of the parts.

The philosophical systems principle and the cybernetic systems approach that is based on it, have gained recognition in diverse areas of scientific research.

They have a particularly well-established position in modern medicine and other sciences that study biological subjects. Unfortunately, until recently, the empirically established patterns of the systems approach have not found adequate objective verification or mathematical realization. The depiction of complex systemic objects was carried out by non-systemic analytical methods. With the appearance and development, in the second half of the 20th century, of the theory of artificial neural networks and the development of the theory of fuzzy sets, this contradiction could be effectively eliminated. The mathematical algorithms of fuzzy neural networks considered in this chapter can hypothetically serve as a model for actual cognitive processes occurring in the human brain. The formulas introduced express, in a very crude approximation, the nerve impulse generating mechanisms discovered by physiologists and an approximation of the decision-making processes inherent to human thinking. One mathematical implementation of the systems approach is put forward here.

The research participants were students at centers for training young military specialists–operators of military technical systems. These were young people healthy enough for military service, aged 18–20 years. The work made use of material from several research studies conducted in 1995 (n = 456), 1997 (n = 1588), and 2002 (n = 164). The results of these studies were used for analysis of existing scientific methodological models for predicting professional fitness.

The Department of Military Psychophysiology of the S. M. Kirov Academy of Military Medicine had developed a "fuzzy neural network" computerized system for professional diagnostics, (Bulka 2005) which is an automated expert system for assessing professional fitness. Also in 2003, there was supplementary observation of 440 cadet operators.

The sample surveyed was divided into two groups:

> The first group of 320 people was used for additional study of statistical patterns of correlation between professionally important psychophysiological indices and success in professional military activity. The same sample was used to validate the proposed diagnostic methods. Then it was used to construct a mathematical model of a fuzzy neural network, and to develop and train an automated system;
>
> The second group of 120 people was used as a control, for testing the automated computer system. One out of four soldiers was chosen from each subunit of the survey to create a controlled sample.

For each survey group, methods were used to evaluate the following:
a. Condition of the cardiovascular system;
b. Condition of neural processes;
c. Condition of cognitive processes;
d. Individual psychological characteristics;
e. Distinctive social-psychological features.

After completing their training, the operators' professional fitness was then evaluated by expert officers, drawn from the faculty and commanding officers.

The research showed a low and unstable relationship between the indices derived from the psychophysiological tests and the expert evaluation. The correlation coefficients between individual psychophysiological characteristics and external criteria rarely reached 0.3. The overall character of these relationships is expressed in the example shown in Figure 14.1. The most general pattern observed in Figure 14.1, exemplifies each activity, there is a minimum threshold of abilities necessary to successfully complete the task. Nevertheless, a high score does not guarantee a high degree of success.

Analysis of the effectiveness of scientific methodological models of predicting operators' professional fitness that are based on multivariate regression analysis and multidimensional scaling showed that they can reliably distinguish the level of professional military fitness in the polar groups. The coefficients of determination from the 1995 research are $R^2_{1995}=0.139$; from the 1997 research, $R^2_{1997}=0.119$; from the 2003 research, $R^2_{2003}=0.113$, which accounts for 12–14% of the variation in observed relationships. This makes it possible to identify accurately those individuals who are not professionally fit for an operator's work, but does not predict the differences among cadets who perform their work at "excellent," "good," and "satisfactory" levels (Figure 14.2).

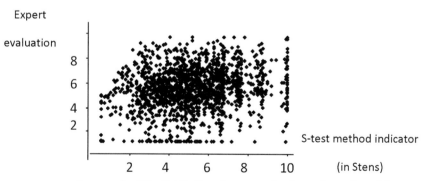

FIGURE 14.1 An example of the distribution of expert evaluation and sampling of those surveyed (research from 1997, n = 1588)

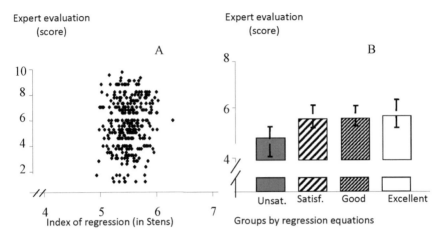

FIGURE 14.2   Distribution (A), mean values and confidence intervals (B), of scores by expert evaluation as a function of the calculated regression estimator (with p<0.05, 2003 research, n = 320)

The concept of "fuzzy sets" as an extension of the usual (classical) sets was introduced by L. Zadeh in 1965 (Zadeh 1965). With respect to the professional selection of military technical systems operators, we can define the following fuzzy sets:

1. "Category I professional fitness" – cadets who were evaluated as "excellent" by the training results at the learning center;
2. "Category II professional fitness" – cadets who were evaluated as "good" by the training results at the learning center;
3. "Category III professional fitness" – cadets who were evaluated as "satisfactory" by the training results at the learning center;
4. "Category IV professional fitness" – cadets who were unable to master the training program and were evaluated as "unsatisfactory."

In fuzzy logic, these sets are characterized by the membership functions $\mu_1(x)$, $\mu_2(x)$, $\mu_3(x)$, $\mu_4(x)$. Figure 14.3 provides a graphic illustration of the membership functions of the variable x (in Stens) for the above four sets of values.

In fuzzy systems, an element can partly belong to any set. The degree of membership in the set A, which is an extension of the characteristic function, is called the membership function $\mu A(x)$. The values of membership functions are rational numbers from the interval [0, 1], where 0 means no affiliation to the set, and 1 means full membership. The concrete value for the membership function is called the degree, or the coefficient of membership.

THE USE OF FUZZY LOGIC AND ARTIFICIAL NEURAL NETWORKS

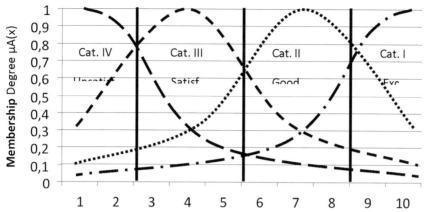

FIGURE 14.3   Illustration of the concept of a membership indicator for professional fitness in categories I, II, III or IV of professional fitness (the dashed or dotted lines are a fuzzy system, the solid lines are a precise system).

The degree of membership can be given by a standard Gaussian function, represented in rational form (Osovsky 2002):

$$\mu_A(x) = \frac{1}{1 + \left(\dfrac{x-c}{\sigma}\right)^{2b}} \qquad (1)$$

where:

- x – the value of a concrete psychophysiological indicator;
- c – the formal center of the fuzzy set;
- σ – the index of function variation;
- b – the index of breadth of function.

The model of fuzzy sets presented here can be linked to the mathematical theory of neural networks with an output decision rule for vocational selection, as follows:

$$y = \frac{\sum_{i=1}^{M} c_i \left[\prod_{j=1}^{N} \mu_{A_i}(x_j)\right]}{\sum_{i=1}^{M} \left[\prod_{j=1}^{N} \mu_{A_i}(x_j)\right]} \qquad (2)$$

The defining characteristic of the fuzzy neural network as a methodological model is the incorporation into its algorithm of errors made in training, as defined by Euclidean norms as:

$$E = \frac{1}{2}\sum_{i=1}^{p}\left(y(x^1) - d^1\right)^2 \qquad (3)$$

where:

- d – expert evaluation;
- p – number of training pairs (y, d).

The training error E serves as a feedback model, which is input into the system at the end of the training cycle and corrects the input weights of indicators $c_j^{(i)}$, $\sigma^{(i)}$, $b_j^{(i)}$. Training of neural networks is based on the minimization of errors. The initial parameters $c_j^{(i)}$, $\sigma^{(i)}$, $b_j^{(i)}$ depend upon the established quantity of neurons in the network and the distance between their sensitivity thresholds. The output signals Y for each subject and error E are calculated. The magnitude of the error is input into the mathematical model. The sizes of parameters $c_j^{(i)}$, $\sigma^{(i)}$, $b_j^{(i)}$ are corrected using the magnitude of the training error and the vector, so that from one training cycle to the next, the error is minimized. Thus, the system adaptively converges on the actual data available and, as new surveys are added, incorporates their properties into the general algorithm.

Because of the features that have been enumerated, mathematical algorithms of fuzzy neural networks make it possible to simulate the basic features inherent to a systems approach methodology:

A. Approximation and fluctuation of indicators assembled during biomedical research (this possibility is ensured by introducing the membership function $\mu_A(x)$).

B. Individual strategies for developing the systems object (individual styles developed by different people in their work) and the dynamics of those strategies.

C. Forward and backward linkages which structure the system object into a coherent whole (by the integration of membership functions of indicators x_i, with one another through forward links, and the introduction of training error as a model of feedback).

Mention should be made of another, purely technical advantage of the use of fuzzy neural networks. A fuzzy logic mathematical model does not operate with the size of indicator x_i, but rather with its function of membership in a particular fuzzy set $\mu_A(x)$. In the mathematical theory of fuzzy logic, this

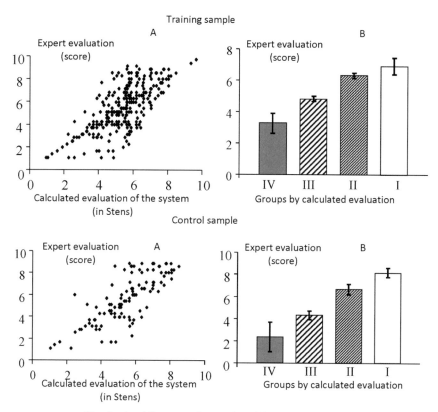

FIGURE 14.4 Distribution (A), mean values and confidence intervals (B) of expert evaluation, as a function of the calculated evaluation of the automated system

function is called a "linguistic variable." In essence, this means that the most diverse indicators, belonging to any measurement scales, can be used as such variables in one study. Application of rank and interval based numerical measures, in conjunction with qualitative variables in a nominative scale, in no way hampers the work of a fuzzy neural network mathematical model.

Testing the automated expert system showed that it authentically and reliably classifies the differences among all categories of professional fitness, both in the training sample and in the control sample (2003 research, Figure 14.4.). The effectiveness of the model that was developed, has, for the control sample, a precision indicator of 71%, and a confidence coefficient of 87.5%. The coefficient of determination (R^2) is 0.614, which is 4–5 times greater than that of traditional mathematical algorithms.

In 2005, tests of the automated expert system were done, which generally corroborated the high degree of effectiveness of the proposed method of predicting success of professional activity. The program's effectiveness for vocational selection in the research sample (n = 112) was 67.53% according to the precision indicator, and 83.12% according to the confidence coefficient. The correlation coefficient between the data predicting success in professional military work and the expert evaluation (r) was 0.76. The coefficient of determination (R^2) was 0.56. The reliability of differences in the effectiveness of successful professional activity prediction was confirmed for all research groups.

The fuzzy neural network model described above is not, of course, the only one. To date, dozens of effective algorithms have been developed to solve a great variety of tasks. The range of application of fuzzy neural networks is very broad – from household appliances to the management of complex industrial processes. Many modern management problems simply cannot be solved by classical methods, because of the very high degree of complexity of the mathematical models that describe them.

Fig. 14.5 shows areas of the most effective use of modern technologies for mathematical data processing. It is clear from the diagram that classical methods of mathematical modeling work with a fully specified research subject, in a specified environment; for systems with incomplete information and highly complex subjects, the optimal choices are fuzzy control methods, artificial neural networks, and combinations of the two.

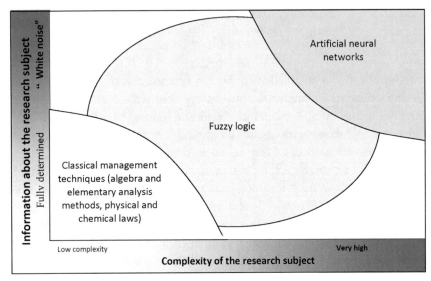

FIGURE 14.5   Areas of application for various mathematical models

The following are the most general scientific problems for which neural networks in general, and fuzzy neural networks in particular, are used:
1. *Classification of images.* The task consists of indicating the affiliation of the input image (e.g., symptoms), having a vector of attributes, with one or more predefined classes (e.g., diagnoses of diseases).
2. *Clusterization/categorization.* For the task of clustering, which is also known as classification of images "without a teacher," there is no training sample that is labeled as to class. The clustering algorithm is based on the similarity of images, and places similar images in one cluster.
3. *Function approximation.* In a training sample which has pairs of input-output data $((x_1,y_1), (x_2,y_2), \ldots (x_n,y_n))$, a certain function $F(x)$ is defined as a result of the operations of the network; this function approximates the relationship of x to y. Function approximation is necessary for solving most scientific modeling problems. In particular, the algorithm discussed above performs a function approximation.
4. *Prediction/prognosis.* Future change in the indicators over specified time intervals is predicted based on specified changes in system indicators, over certain time intervals (according to certain system dynamics). Such a task can be used, for example, to predict disease outcome or the success of future professional activity.
5. *Optimization.* Many problems in medicine (e.g., evaluation of the effectiveness of treatments) can be treated as optimization problems. The task of an optimization algorithm is to find a solution that satisfies the system constraints and maximizes or minimizes the objective function.

Beyond these common problems, other scientific and applied tasks involving complex, dynamically changing systems may be addressed using mathematical models of fuzzy neural networks.

References

Bulka, A. P. 2005. "Prediction of soldiers' success in professional activity on the basis of mathematical models of a fuzzy neural network." Dissertation in Medical Sciences. Saint Petersburg, Russia.

Osovsky, S. 2002. *Neural Networks for Processing Information.* Moscow: Finances and Statistics.

Zadeh, L. 1976. *The Concept of the Linguistic Variable and its Application to Making Approximate Decisions.* Moscow: Mir.

SECTION 4 COMMENTARY

Neuroscience Applications Extending from the Clinical to the Professional to Everyday Domains

Chris Forsythe and Gabriel A. Radvansky

The chapters in this section present two themes in general. First, Bazanova discusses the scientific inquiry into the neural patterns of activation corresponding to differing aptitudes, and the use of neurofeedback techniques for performance enhancement. Second, Bochenkov and Bulka each discuss the application of psychophysiology-based techniques for improving performance of military personnel. In both cases, principles, understandings, and techniques from cognitive neuroscience are applied to achieve increased levels of performance in tasks typical of experimental research studies, and of professional activities.

To a large extent, the study of neuroscience, including cognitive neuroscience, has been motivated by the desire to understand and mitigate various brain maladies that lessen the quality of life and productive potential of the afflicted. Most readers of this commentary have had some experience, whether with family, friends, neighbors or co-workers, with brain-based maladies and they appreciate the desire to find effective treatments. However, that said, beyond clinical applications to date, neuroscience has done little to touch the lives of many outside of scientific and medical communities.

Currently, various neurological technologies are advancing that could forever change the impact of neuroscience on the general population. A large part of this change results from advances in sensor technologies. This involves improvements in materials and signal processing, but perhaps most importantly, in innovations that minimize and eliminate preparation and calibration of biometric measurement devices. Sensors may be embedded within apparel, and recording brain activity becomes as easy as donning headwear and turning on the affixed wireless transmitter. These innovations can already be seen within commercial gaming products which use biometric signals to direct the activity of game characters and devices. It has been suggested that we are on the cusp of a "neurotechnology revolution" that will have as great an impact on human culture as the ongoing digital revolution (McBride 2007). It has been proposed that a day will soon arrive in which neuroscience impacts almost everyone through widely used products, as well as a wide range of technologies that sense and adapt to signals reflecting neurophysiological states and processes.

The chapters in this section share a common theme in that each addresses the practical application of neuroscience, and particularly, applications that may impact large numbers of people beyond clinical settings. Such application may occur through biofeedback technologies used to enable individuals to maximize their intellectual and physical performance. Whether in an educational setting or on the sports field, most would welcome a technological innovation that, with no apparent harm, allows an individual to improve his or her performance, even if the gain is on the order of 5% or less. The impact of neuroscience may also occur through techniques used more in industrial/organizational settings, where they are used to screen individuals for jobs or assignments based on their neurophysiological aptitude for the associated cognitive and physical demands. For example, firefighter and police candidates may be assessed with respect to their capacity to withstand and retain good judgment when faced with intense levels of stress. Finally, in situations such as combat or disaster relief where there is a cumulative toil from sustained physical and psychological demands, neuroscience-based measurement and techniques may offer the means for monitoring and remediation to improve ongoing effectiveness and minimize the long-term negative effects upon personnel.

In considering the promise of neurotechnology, it is worthwhile to also be mindful of the risks. Perhaps most evident among these risks is the potential for neurophysiological profiling. Scenarios may be imagined in which individuals exhibiting certain patterns of brain activation are deemed ideal for certain occupations or tasks, excluding all others. Similarly, certain patterns of brain activation may be linked to cognitive and physical deficiencies that preclude groups from pursuing certain opportunities. While many measures may be quite appropriate (e.g. for occupations having responsibilities for public safety), there is great potential for their inappropriate application, unfairly disqualifying individuals who are quite capable of performing in an acceptable manner. Likewise, there exist the accompanying risks of stereotyping, where individuals once categorized on the basis of their neurophysiological profile, are permanently attributed with various negative characteristics, perhaps falsely, associated with that profile.

With these warnings in mind, it is important to note the positive aspects of the association of brain activation profiles with aptitudes for cognitive and physical performance. Specifically, it is acknowledged that there is an organic basis for cognitive and behavioral performance. The widespread acceptance and availability of neurophysiological screening permits a consideration of each individual's capacities, placing personal performance in perspective. Thus, it becomes less likely that disappointing levels of performance will be falsely attributed to a lack of motivation or unwillingness to exert the requisite level of effort. Furthermore, the potential exists for more effective administration of training and education, if it can be recognized when tasks exceed what an individual can realistically accomplish, and training materials can be designed according to the developing capacities and progress of each individual. In essence, the insights provided by such neurological assessments open the door for more effective and efficient "designer" training regimens. An objective link may be established between observed performance and the corresponding neurophysiological processes, allowing interventions to be tailored to the specific competencies and capacities of each individual.

Along with the promise of neurotechnologies, there will likely come degrees of undue hope. Unrealistic expectations are likely to emerge, especially when hyped by the media and businesses standing to profit. Biofeedback seems particularly prone to this risk. Given a few success stories, the popular conception may develop that biofeedback can be broadly utilized to achieve changes in brain states or capacities that far exceed what is truly achievable. This situation may be worsened by a failure to appreciate individual differences in personal capacity to employ feedback to achieve desired effects. As a result, individuals may be criticized for their inability to achieve improvements attained by others, and their failures will be ignorantly attributed to a lack of motivation or effort.

Chapters by Bochenkov and Bulka both address the use of screening procedures that treat an individual's neurophysiological make-up as a basis to select personnel that are best equipped to endure the stresses of combat. Such approaches offer the hope that individuals may be screened to identify those who are most susceptible to stress-related maladies (such as Post-Traumatic Stress Disorder), and as a result, the incidence and severity of stress-related maladies may be reduced. However, a word of caution must be made to avoid certain conclusions, or taking other conclusions for granted. Specifically, it should not be concluded that individuals judged to have a greater capacity for resilience do not experience any stress. Likewise, there should not be any disregard for, or smaller consideration of, the stressors individuals are asked to endure. Additionally, individuals placed under the expectation to show greater resilience to stress may be less likely to acknowledge the effects of stress on their well-being, and hence they may refrain from taking advantage of techniques intended to help them manage and cope with ongoing stressors, or the longer-term effects of stress.

While noting the link between concepts discussed by the authors in this section to the broader emergence of neurotechnologies, and the associated socio-cultural impact of this revolution in technology, this commentary has not attempted to address the implications of neurotechnologies in general, but only those implications relevant to the research reported in this section. Attention has been drawn to the need for careful forethought, and a useful framework for identifying and managing the ethical, legal, and social implications of neurotechnology (Forsythe and Giordano 2011). Furthermore, there is some degree of urgency here. Currently, within the clinical domain, there is rapid growth in the availability and application of neurotechnologies, whether they be pharmaceuticals, neuroimaging and other diagnostic techniques, therapeutic approaches, or medical devices (e.g. drug administration). Within the home video gaming industry, one sees an initial introduction of neurotechnologies to the consumer products sector. There is increasing interest in purported mechanism for achieving cognitive enhancement through various methods, including pharmaceutical, nutriceutical, cognitive training, and neurofeedback methods. As constituent technologies become increasingly available and easy to use, a wave of innovation is anticipated with a resulting plethora of products targeting all facets of life, including entertainment, education, sports, transportation, work, and so on. Finally, the emergence of neurotechnologies has been appreciated within the national security sector. Numerous programs have been undertaken and are under way to develop neurotechnology applications to enhance performance, improve training effectiveness, provide better personnel selection, and treat combat related maladies.

Overall, neurotechnology is still in its nascent stages. We assert that it is urgent to establish a framework for addressing the ethical, legal, and social implications of neurotechnology while there remains an opportunity to be proactive. Otherwise, it is inevitable that the consideration of these implications will be called for in a reactive manner later in the future, once the eventual harms become unavoidable, and there will be fewer possibilities for shifting course.

Acknowledgement

Sandia National Laboratories is a multiprogram laboratory operated by Sandia Corporation, a Lockheed Martin Company, for the United States Department of Energy's National Nuclear Security Administration under contract DEAC04-94AL85000.

References

McBride, D. 2007. *Neurotechnology Futures Study*. Arlington, Virginia: Potomac Institute for Policy Studies.

Forsythe, C. and J. Giordano. 2011. "On the need for neurotechnology in the national intelligence and defense agenda: Scope and trajectory." *Synesis* 2, no. 1: T5–T8.

Index

Alpha waves   141–149, 180–189, 199, 203–204, 230–237, 323–337
Animal psychology   4–5, 41, 44, 48, 106, 111, 227–228
Anokhin, Pyotr Kuzmich   56

Behavior   58–61, 64–67, 73–77, 94–95, 157, 223–228, 316–317
  as adaptive   4–5, 17, 42–44
  as purposive   6–10, 13, 17–22, 120, 125–130
  and personality   231–232
Behaviorism   5, 156
Bekhterev, Vladimir Mikhailovich   27
Beritashvili, Ivane S.   5–7, 119, 125, 127
Bernard, Claude   26, 29, 39,
Beta waves   180, 184, 192–198, 203, 222–223, 280, 288–292,
Botkin, Sergey Petrovich   26, 39, 73
Brain   18, 28–29, 35, 66, 87–88, 107
  and thought   100, 114, 178–187, 242–243, 276–279, 290–291
Brain structure   43, 59, 66, 95, 101–103, 109, 126–130, 139–141, 155, 194, 202–203, 223–225, 315–317
Brainwave oscillation   140, 184, 188, 222–230, 242–245, 255–271, 291, 316, 330
  in men and women   216
  and personality   231–235
  and synchronization   277–282, 298–309
Brain stimulation   225

Consciousness   6–7, 31, 73, 76, 228, 297–298, 300, 306
  and unconscious   13, 19–23, 35, 43, 73, 128–133, 138, 230–231
  and emotion   72–75, 115
Conditioned reflex   4–5, 9–10, 15, 40–52, 126–130, 284–285

Dennett, Daniel C.   73
Descartes, René   3, 29, 59–60, 118
Determinism   29, 60, 91, 99, 104, 180, 312, 317
du Bois-Reymond, Emil   27

Emotion   31, 98–102, 120, 170–173, 206, 229, 311–312
  and behavior   17–21, 130–148
  and consciousness   72–76, 114–115, 228–236
Environment   91–102, 105–110, 231–236
  and behavior   3–5, 8–13, 35–37, 42–44, 74–75, 126–130
  and mind   14–13

Facial expression   20, 101, 130–146, 216
Fuzzy logic   372–379

Gamma waves   276–292
Gestalt   5, 88, 118–120, 315

Hegel, G. W. F.   58
Helmholtz, Hermann   27
Hippocampus   108, 111, 140–141, 147–149, 229, 243, 260–261, 279, 286

Inhibition   30, 45–47, 182–183, 188, 230–232, 244, 255–257, 265–267
  and behavior   12, 29, 222–225, 236–237

James, William   73

Language   21, 68–72, 99, 169–170
Lenin, Vladimir   52
Livanov, Mikhail Nikolaevich   140, 146, 277, 331
Lorenz, Karl   111

Memory   12–17, 92, 99, 101, 131, 138–140, 156–157, 204, 263–264, 288–291, 304–308, 311–312
  and emotion   229
  short-term   243, 260–266, 270–271, 280, 286, 290
Military psychology   343–349, 351–353, 361–364
Motor activity   28, 30, 101, 243–244, 276, 286
  and sensory   65, 76, 280, 282, 287, 337, 344

Nebylitsyn, Vladimir Dmitrievich 50, 323
Neuron 103–104, 158–167, 277–283, 304–307
　as organic 62, 66
　connectivity 58, 62, 107–115, 179, 226–227, 243–246
　pyramidal 6, 261
　as specialized 64–65
　as networked 154–158, 162–171, 186–187, 243, 260–267, 291–292, 334–337
Neuroscience 56, 64–68, 118–120, 215–216, 242–243, 315–316, 380–381

Pavlov, Ivan Petrovich 4, 26, 39–42, 44–48, 50–53, 119–120, 297
Perception 10–15, 104, 111, 115, 128–131, 165–172
　and cognition 156–158, 198, 281–282, 310–313
　and value 16–23, 131–132, 148–149
　See also Sensation, Stimulus
Personality 37, 179–183, 196–207, 222–237, 345–364
Peter the Great 26
Prochaska, Georg 3
Psychology 18, 27, 35–37, 58, 157
　as objective 35–36
Psychological testing 345–349, 360–362, 373
Psychophysiology 57–73
　origins of 5–8, 12–18, 20–24, 27–35, 120–122, 129, 140

Reflex arc 59, 62, 66, 82, 92, 118, 155, 215
Reflexes 3–8, 29–37, 59–62, 111, 119–120, 126–127, 244, 300
　See also Conditioned reflex

Reinforcement, of behavior 108–114
　of reflex 43–49

Sechenov, Ivan Michailovich 4, 5, 7, 26–34, 36, 42, 118, 125, 323
Sensation 6, 20, 30, 49, 147, 163–164, 286–288, 304–308
　and motor function 65–66, 76, 108, 244, 282
　See also Perception
Simonov, Pavel Vasilevich 96, 119, 297
Stimulus 5–7, 61–62, 75–76, 132–133, 156–161, 164–170, 245–248, 254–261, 282–288, 302–310, 320
　and reflex 29–30, 91–92, 104, 1 230–231, 26–129
　and thought 98–99, 183–185
　and emotion 132–141, 170–173, 231–234
　and learning 145–146, 155–158
　as associated 15–16, 36–37, 45–48, 109–111, 277–282

Teplov, Boris Mikhailovich 50
Theta waves 139–149, 227–236, 261, 271, 277, 290–291, 327
Thorndike, Edward 40
Truth 18, 71

Ukhtomsky, Alexei Alexeyevich 7–10, 13–24, 26, 88, 119–120, 130

Vvedenksy, Nikolay Evgenievich 7, 26, 47